T0372455

Professional Development for In-Service Teachers

A volume in
Research, Innovation & Methods in Educational Technology
Chrystalla Mouza and Nancy C. Lavigne, *Series Editors*

Research, Innovation & Methods in Educational Technology

Chrystalla Mouza and Nancy C. Lavigne, *Series Editors*

Professional Development for In-Service Teachers

Research and Practices in Computing Education

edited by

Chrystalla Mouza
University of Delaware

Anne Ottenbreit-Leftwich
Indiana University

Aman Yadav
Michigan State University

INFORMATION AGE PUBLISHING, INC.
Charlotte, NC • www.infoagepub.com

Library of Congress Cataloging-in-Publication Data

A CIP record for this book is available from the Library of Congress
http://www.loc.gov

ISBN: 978-1-64802-906-6 (Paperback)
   978-1-64802-907-3 (Hardcover)
   978-1-64802-908-0 (E-Book)

Printed in the United States of America

*To our families for their support and patience while preparing this book
in the midst of the COVID-19 pandemic*

CONTENTS

PART I

PROFESSIONAL DEVELOPMENT APPROACHES FOR ELEMENTARY AND MIDDLE SCHOOL CONTENT AREA TEACHERS

PART II

PROFESSIONAL DEVELOPMENT APPROACHES FOR HIGH SCHOOL TEACHERS

PART III

ONGOING AND SCALING-UP PROFESSIONAL DEVELOPMENT APPROACHES

PART IV

ALTERNATIVE PROFESSIONAL DEVELOPMENT APPROACHES: UNIVERSITY COURSES AND MICRO-CREDENTIALS

INTRODUCTION

EXAMINING PROFESSIONAL DEVELOPMENT MODELS FOR COMPUTING EDUCATION

BACKGROUND AND NEED FOR THE BOOK

Rapid technological advances in our society have established computer science (CS) as a fundamental component of 21st century education. As a result, initiatives have been implemented worldwide that seek to promote the teaching of CS as well as its integration into existing content area curricula (e.g., mathematics, science). In the United States, increased attention to CS education has been promoted through initiatives by the White House (i.e., CSforAll) aimed at supporting the continuous growth and development of K–12 students (Smith, 2016). In addition, such initiatives have been widely supported by nonprofit, corporate, and other funding agencies including Code.org, Google for Education, and the National Science Foundation to name a few. As CS initiatives are growing, however, there is a pressing need for qualified teachers who are well prepared to deliver both stand-alone CS courses as well as integrate CS principles into existing content area curricula.

The need to prepare highly qualified teachers in computing and the inability of higher education institutions to prepare adequate numbers of CS teachers has given rise to a number of professional development (PD)

Professional Development for In-Service Teachers, pages xi–xxii
Copyright © 2022 by Information Age Publishing
www.infoagepub.com

initiatives both in the United States and abroad. These efforts are typically motivated by the need to help existing teachers learn new and unfamiliar CS content as well as equity-focused pedagogical practices needed to achieve the goal of CS for all students (Codding et al., 2020, Madkins et al., 2020). While there is a proliferation of standalone workshops and other short-term PD approaches (Menekse, 2015), research suggests that ongoing and continuous PD is more likely to foster changes in teacher learning and subsequent practice (Desimone, 2009). Yet research focusing on effective approaches to supporting teachers with the implementation of CS instruction has been severely limited. As a result, we continue to know little about the CS concepts that teachers succeed or struggle with, the computational pedagogies they engage with, and their self-efficacy and confidence in teaching CS (Rich et al., 2021). The chapters in this book begin to address some of these issues, providing important findings and lessons learned that could guide efforts to support CS education for ALL students in a digital world.

DESCRIPTION OF THE BOOK

This book has been in preparation for more than 2 years. When we issued the call for proposals, we were overwhelmed by the response but simultaneously delighted by the number of scholars looking to support CS education through teacher PD. Our work was somewhat delayed by the COVID-19 pandemic which imposed increased demands on academics around the world as we transitioned online and turned attention to supporting our university students. At the same time, the COVID-19 pandemic has demonstrated our increased reliance on computing and its power to adapt and innovate, while simultaneously highlighting existing disparities for student learning associated with computing (Code.org, 2020). This realization has made the content of this book even more important, pointing to specific ways of supporting computing education while also addressing issues of equity through the use of well-studied culturally responsive frameworks (e.g., Gay, 2002).

The chapters in this volume represent authors from different backgrounds, regions, and countries as well as different approaches, including theoretical and empirical. Each chapter was first reviewed by the editors and subsequently by authors of this volume through blind peer reviews. Revised chapters were subsequently reviewed by the editors and went through a second round of revisions. The resulting book is divided into four parts. The specific parts and the corresponding chapters are described below.

Part I: Professional Development Approaches for Elementary and Middle School Content Area Teachers

In recent years, interest in computational thinking (CT) and CS education for elementary and middle school students has been growing steadily (Code.org, 2020; Google, Inc., & Gallup, Inc., 2016). Accompanied by new K–8 curricula (e.g., Code.org, Google's CS First, Project Lead the Way, etc.), efforts have been underway to infuse CT/CS into content area instruction in ways that support the development of computing knowledge and skills among *all* students. To be clear, efforts to bring CT to younger audiences has had a long history in education. In the 1960s, for instance, Seymour Papert pioneered the development of the Logo programming language which focused explicitly on helping young students become creators of computing innovations (Papert, 1980). Contemporary efforts to introduce CS and CT into K–8 contexts, however, face some of the same challenges that surfaced in Papert's early efforts, namely teacher preparation and support.

Research indicates that elementary and middle school teachers are particularly under-prepared and under-supported as they work to infuse CS into existing curricula and demanding schedules (Rich & Hu, 2019). Importantly, we continue to know little about the knowledge or support strategies needed to effectively support elementary and middle school teachers (Howard, 2019). While workshops and industry supported PD have proliferated in efforts to support the development of teacher knowledge, skills, self-efficacy and interest towards CS, research in this area remains underdeveloped. More research is needed identifying effective approaches to PD for K–8 teachers that helps delineate the CS/CT skills needed to succeed as they become more comfortable and confident in delivering computing education. The chapters this section discuss specific PD approaches for elementary and middle school teachers that seek to improve knowledge and practice, particularly content driven CT-integrated practice.

Chapter 1, "Computational Thinking in Elementary Classrooms: A Toolkit to Scaffold Teacher Learning" presents a toolkit developed to support elementary teachers as they integrate CT practices into their classrooms using unplugged mathematics and science activities. Specific examples of how the toolkit was used in teacher PD to support CT practices of abstraction, decomposition, patterns, and debugging are presented. Further, examples related to the role of unplugged activities in bringing computationally rich practices in elementary school contexts are also discussed.

Chapter 2, "Teacher Co-Design in a CSforAll Research–Practice Partnership: Curriculum Development and Teacher Learning" presents work from the first year of a 4-year research- practice partnership focused on integrating CT into elementary curriculum in a mid-size school district in the

Northeast. This approach to curricular integration engages participating teachers in PD related to CS and CT with emphasis on supporting teachers in the activity of co-design. Working in pairs, teachers developed modules that integrated CT into elementary level science lessons. Through case study design and analysis, results indicated that the practice of co-design highlighted the need to create curricula with the potential to be adapted for different classroom contexts and allow for differentiation. Results also revealed productive tensions related to differences in pedagogical practices among the teachers involved in the co-design.

Chapter 3, "Professional Development Supporting Middle School Teachers to Integrate Computational Thinking Into Their Science Classes" describes a PD model that supports teachers in efforts to integrate CT into middle school science and STEM classes. The model includes collaborative co-design of storylines or curricular units aligned with the Next Generation Science Standards that use programmable sensors. Throughout the process, teachers develop or modify CT-integrated science curricular materials that use sensor technology, implement the storylines and meet to collaboratively reflect on their instructional practices as well as their students' learning. Throughout this cyclical, multi-year process, teachers develop expertise in CT-integrated science instruction. The chapter presents the experience of two teachers as they went through the PD process over a 2-year period.

Chapter 4, "Teachers' Knowledge and Skills in Computational Thinking and Their Enactment of a Computationally Rich Curriculum" presents a PD approach that supports the integration of CT-rich computer modeling and simulation activities into middle school science classrooms. Using a mixed methods approach, the authors first describe correlations between teachers' participation in PD (i.e., number of hours), their knowledge and skills in CT, and the number of CT-integrated science activities they implemented. Two case studies that illustrate how teachers of varying levels of CT knowledge and skills enacted the curriculum to meet their instructional goals are presented. Finally, the authors discuss implications of their findings for teacher PD programs aimed to prepare in-service science teachers to infuse CT and CS into middle school science classrooms.

Chapter 5, "Looming Code: A Model, Learning Activity, and Professional Development Approach for Computer Science Educators" describes a conceptual model, instructional activity, and PD approach, called Expansively-framed Unplugged (EfU), designed to prepare school librarians or educators with limited CS background learn to lead coding activities in elementary and middle school settings. The authors demonstrate how an EfU PD approach can be used to design activities such as looming code, a coding activity where students use block-based programming to model weaving patterns. The authors discuss the PD experience of one elementary school librarian and present lessons learned and next steps for supporting teachers with limited coding knowledge.

Part II: Professional Development Approaches for High School Teachers

Most research focusing on CS-focused PD to date has concentrated on high school teachers delivering specific stand-alone CS curricula. Margolis et al. (2017), for instance, examined the role of coaching which accompanies the PD program associated with the Exploring Computer Science (ECS) curriculum. The ECS PD program centers on three key areas that include inquiry-based learning, equity, and content. Similarly, Price et al. (2016) examined a PD program associated with the Beauty and Joy of Computing (BJC) curriculum. The BJC PD centers on computing principles, collaborative labs, and equitable pedagogies. Other efforts focusing on high school teachers include work associated with CS4Alabama, a PD program which utilizes a statewide Teacher Leader (TL) model.

While the above efforts are noteworthy, we continue to know little about specific design principles and models that best support high-school teachers as they learn to teach CS or integrate CS into disciplinary content (Menekse, 2015). Such work is important because high school CS teachers typically have little or no prior experience in CS and are recruited from other subject areas, notably mathematics (Century et al., 2013). Importantly, to realize the promise of CS for All, it is essential to understand PD features that help teachers learn how to utilize equitable pedagogies that help connect CS to students' lives. Prioritizing equitable CS access can help address racial and economic disparities prevalent in computing, drive innovation, prepare a diverse workforce, and ensure students develop the knowledge and skills needed to understand the social, cultural, and political impacts of computing (Kapor Center, 2021). The chapters in this section directly address these critical challenges focusing on culturally responsive methods and pedagogical practices which are inviting to students underrepresented in computing. They also discuss resources available to teachers and provide examples of nationwide efforts to support high school teachers' PD (i.e., Ireland)

Chapter 6, "Re-Making Education in STEM Classrooms With Computational Making" examines ways of incorporating computational making in STEM classrooms through the iterative exploration of phenomena using different tools and materials. The authors present a model for Re-Making STEM through professional learning by asking teachers to (re)negotiate relationships to tools and materials, to disciplinary thinking, and to students through computational making. The Re-Making STEM model includes four phases—computational play, co-learning with students, reflection, and curricular design and enactment. Examples of the ways in which high-school teachers negotiated their relationships between disciplinary activity and making are presented to demonstrate the potential of the model to support teachers' as they try to re-make STEM learning in their classrooms, making it inviting for students underrepresented in CS.

Chapter 7, "Culturally Responsive Methods for Engaging All Students in Computer Science Principles," presents the design and implementation of a week-long PD experience for prospective CS teachers, which was explicitly framed by a culturally responsive pedagogical perspective. Subsequently, the authors present findings related to the ways prospective CS teachers perceived culturally responsive pedagogy and their implementation of culturally responsive CS during the following academic year. Findings from 17 teacher participants indicated that teachers' perceptions and implementations of culturally responsive computing included three facets: belief in students' academic potential, affirming student realities, and critical self-reflexivity.

Chapter 8, "E-Books for High School Computer Science Teachers" describes a model for online CS teacher development using eBooks. As the authors point out, online PD offers multiple advantages in terms of time, space, and cost but only if it incorporates engaging opportunities for teachers to practice without overloading learners. The design of the eBook presented in this chapter, "examples+practice" is guided by principles from the learning sciences and it provides an emphasis on *worked examples* and *practice* at different levels of challenge. The authors present results from this work which suggest that eBooks are efficient and effective for CS teacher learning.

Chapter 9, "Implementing a Professional Development Framework to Assist the Rollout of Computer Science in Second-Level Schools in Ireland" describes the rollout of CS in secondary schools in the Republic of Ireland and details the PD framework which supported the rollout. A key component of the framework was the teachers' communities of practice. The authors draw on social identity theory (SIT) to examine whether such communities of practice can be readily established. They also provide insights related to assumptions around the homogeneity of CS teachers, who are primarily coming from different fields, and their motivation for adopting the subject. Finally, the authors present implications related to the identity development of CS teachers.

Part III: Ongoing and Scaling Up Professional Development Approaches

As the need to build teacher capacity for CS has grown, PD programs have also proliferated. Yet as the authors in the following chapters point out, many of the existing programs have focused on introductory PD experiences that lack continuity and plans for scaling-up outside of specific contexts. These PD features are important for supporting teacher ongoing development and fostering changes in classroom practice. Research indicates that PD programs sustained over time are more likely to foster changes in teaching practice and student outcomes (Desimone, 2009). This may be particularly true in CS where most teachers start as novices, both in terms of content and pedagogy, thus requiring time to build the knowledge and skills needed to deliver effective CS instruction.

Similarly, scaling up PD programs is a complex endeavor as there are different dimensions at play (Coburn, 2003). Yet we continue to know little about the mechanisms that support scale-up or how to extend programs that have worked well in certain contexts to other settings (Adler et al., 2005). While some research on the scaling of educational innovations broadly exists (e.g., Cobb & Smith, 2008), such research is only beginning to emerge in the context of CS PD. The chapters in this section present different approaches to PD that aim to support teachers' ongoing learning or scale to various statewide (e.g., Minnesota, North Carolina, Texas) or nationwide (i.e., Ireland) contexts.

Chapter 10, "Supporting Ongoing Teacher Capacity and Development: Moving Beyond Orientation Professional Development to Support Advanced Teacher Learning," discusses the ways in which school systems support teachers in the development of their CS pedagogical content knowledge, outside of specific curricula or courses. The authors present a conceptual framework focusing on ongoing teacher development beyond introductory experiences. Using data from 150 school districts, the authors discuss the current state of ongoing support for teacher development and the strategic goals set by districts in relation to ongoing PD pathways for CS teachers. Examples of best practices are also presented.

Chapter 11, "Leveraging Collective Impact to Scale Computer Science Teacher Professional Development and Certification," explores the use of a collective impact approach called WeTeach_CS to address the challenge of scaling-up educator preparation for teaching CS in the state of Texas. The authors discuss how WeTeach_CS elevated elements of collective impact to create collaborative networks of partners focused on supporting in-service teachers as they build the CS knowledge and skills necessary to achieve a high school CS certification. Further, the authors present a quasi-experimental study illustrating the success of the model in increasing the rate of CS teacher certification. Finally, the authors discuss implications for other states considering collective impact models with the potential to scale up teacher development.

Chapter 12, "Expanding Computer Science Opportunities: A Personalizable, Flexible Model for Professional Learning" presents a PD model implemented in North Carolina that is flexible and personalizable with the goal of supporting CS teachers at scale beyond initial introductory workshops. The professional learning activities include online courses, web-based learning resources, and communities of practice aimed at providing support beyond face-to-face workshops. The authors discuss barriers and opportunities for teacher development as well as implications for research, practice, and policy that may help other states scale-up teacher PD.

Chapter 13, "Code Savvy Educators: A Professional Development Model for In-Service Educators" presents the MNCodes Educator Training Program which was Minnesota's first statewide PD experience for K–12 in-service teachers in CS. The authors describe the program, including its history, guiding framework, and specific learning components. Further, the authors present lessons learned and opportunities for strengthening the model to support teacher development in CS.

Part IV: Alternative Professional Development Approaches: University Courses and Micro-Credentials

In addition to traditional in-service PD programs, university courses have always provided a reliable mechanism for supporting teacher learning. Although institutions of higher education do not currently have the capacity to respond to the growing need for CS teachers, well-designed courses that provide multiple entry points for content area teachers, such as the one described in this section, present a viable mechanism for engaging teachers with no background knowledge in CS. Importantly, as a field it is essential that we consider other approaches to teacher PD that are job-embedded and performance-based, allowing teachers to expand and demonstrate their professional learning. Towards this goal, micro-credentials offer an important opportunity to support teacher learning at scale.

Micro-credentials leverage online platforms to provide teachers with a more personalized, flexible, and cost-efficient approach to PD (Brown, 2019; Hunt et al., 2020). Recently the Code.org Advocacy Coalition recommended that state and local education agencies support the use of micro-credentials as an approach for teachers seeking CS endorsements (Code. org, 2019). Despite their promise, research is still emerging on the design, implementation, and outcomes of micro-credentials in CS education. Two chapters in this section describe micro-credentials designed by leaders in the field and present findings from participating districts and teachers. They also illuminate several lessons and next steps that could help advance teacher learning through the use of micro-credentials.

Chapter 14, "Supporting In-Service Teachers in Understanding the Potential of Data and Artificial Intelligence to Influence and Impact Learning" discusses the role of university coursework in developing teacher understanding of CS principles. The focus is CS concepts related to artificial intelligence (AI) and data in educational contexts. The authors describe the specific course and present findings from five teacher participants over a period of time. They also discuss lessons learned and implications for the design of university courses that can support different entry points for content-area teachers interested in incorporating CS in their practice.

Chapter 15, "Empowering Teachers in Computational Thinking Through Educator Microcredentials" presents the development and implementation of educator micro-credentials in computational thinking. Motivated by efforts to support competency-based education, these credentials include three components: student-generated projects, instructor lesson plans, and evidence of teachers' reflective practice. The authors present examples and highlight select submissions and survey results from the implementation of micro-credentials with K–8 educators. Finally, the authors discuss the potential of micro-credentials as alternative models for teacher preparation in computing.

Chapter 16, "From Clock-Based to Competency-Based: How Micro-Credentials can Transform Professional Development" also discusses the use of micro-credentials as one option for shifting from clock-based to competency-based PD. The authors present a micro-credential approach focusing on the integration of CT in mathematics and science. Utilizing several data sources, they subsequently examine district and state leaders' perspectives on the purpose of CS micro-credentials, and their understanding of the similarities and differences between traditional PD and micro-credential PD. Further, the authors present findings from the implementation of the CS micro-credential and discuss perspectives related to initial expectations compared to the actual implementation process. Lessons learned and next steps are also discussed.

NEXT STEPS

To realize the promise of CS, PD should be a key mechanism for preparing in-service teachers who have little formal background in CS content and pedagogy. Yet compared to other disciplines there are fewer opportunities as well as research documenting the design, implementation, and outcomes of PD programs in computing (Menekse, 2015; Vegas & Fowler, 2020). In this book, we presented different approaches to PD that helped teachers across K–12 settings improve their knowledge of CS content and pedagogy as well as application of CS in practice. As such, this book provides important insights for those planning, conducting, and studying innovative PD programs aimed at computing teachers at the K–12 level.

Nonetheless, more work still remains to be done in this area. In particular, we identify four important lines of future work. First, literature indicates that teachers rarely implement pedagogical strategies introduced during PD in uniform ways. In fact, Qian et al. (2018) demonstrated differences in the manner in which teachers implemented PD content back in their classrooms based on their prior CS content knowledge. Therefore, more work is needed to identify how teachers' background, both in terms of content and pedagogy, influence PD uptake. Second, we need more studies such as the ones presented in this book that document teacher practice using direct observations and other rich data sources beyond self-reported data. Third, we agree that the long-term success of CS initiatives must move beyond fundamental understandings towards ongoing support for learning and mastery (see Chapter 10, this volume). Such PD efforts will ensure that computing teachers have opportunities to engage in continuous professional growth for them and their students. Finally, there is additional need to move beyond boutique PD approaches to consider scale-up efforts that reach teachers at the state and national levels.

—**Chrystalla Mouza**
Anne Ottenbreit-Leftwich
Aman Yadav

REFERENCES

Adler, J., Ball, D., Krainer, K., Lin, F.-L., & Novotná, J. (2005). Reflections on an emerging field: Researching mathematics teacher education. *Educational Studies in Mathematics, 58*(3), 359–381.

Brown, D. (2019). *Research and educator micro-credentials.* Digital Promise. https://digitalpromise.dspacedirect.org/bitstream/handle/20.500.12265/46/Researcher-And-Educator-Microcredentials-2019.pdf?sequence=1

Century, J., Lach, M., King, H., Rand, S., Heppner, C., Franke, B., & Westrick, J. (2013). *Building an operating system for computer science.* CEMSE, University of Chicago with UEI, University of Chicago. http://outlier.uchicago.edu/computerscience/OS4CS/

Cobb, P., & Smith, T. (2008). The challenge of scale: Designing schools and districts as learning organizations for instructional improvement in mathematics. In K. Krainer & T. Wood (Eds.), *International handbook of mathematics teacher education* (Vol. 3; pp. 231–254). Sense Publishers.

Coburn, C. E. (2003). Rethinking scale: Moving beyond numbers to deep and lasting change. *Educational Researcher, 32*(6), 3–12.

Code.org. (2019). *2019 State of computer science education.* https://advocacy.code.org/2019_state_of_cs.pdf

Code.org. (2020). *2020 State of computer science education: Illuminating disparities.* https://advocacy.code.org/2020_state_of_cs.pdf

Codding, D., Alkhateeb, B., Mouza, C., & Pollock, L. (2020). Building equitable computing classrooms through culturally responsive professional development. In D. Schmidt-Crawford (Ed.), *Proceedings of society for information technology & teacher education international conference* (pp. 1736–1745). Association for the Advancement of Computing in Education.

Desimone, L. M. (2009). Improving impact studies of teachers' professional development: Toward better conceptualizations and measures. *Educational Researcher, 38*(3), 181–199.

Gay, G. (2002). Preparing for culturally responsive teaching. *Journal of Teacher Education, 53*(2), 106–116.

Google Inc., & Gallup Inc. (2016). *Trends in the state of computer science in U. S. K–12 schools.* http://goo.gl/j291E0

Howard, N. R. (2019). EdTech leaders' beliefs: How are K–5 teachers supported with the integration of computer science in K–5 classrooms? *Technology, Knowledge and Learning, 24*(2), 203–217. https://doi.org/10.1007/s10758-018-9371-2

Hunt, T., Carter, R., Zhang, L., & Yang, S. (2020). Micro-credentials: The potential of personalized professional development. *Development and Learning in Organizations, 34*(2), 33–35. https://doi.org/10.1108/DLO-09-2019-0215

Kapor Center. (2021). *Culturally responsive-sustaining computer science education: A framework.* https://mk0kaporcenter5ld71a.kinstacdn.com/wp-content/uploads/2021/07/KC21004_ECS-Framework-Report_v9.pdf

Madkins, T. C., Howard, N. R., & Freed, N. (2020). Engaging equity pedagogies in computer science learning environments. *Journal of Computer Science Integration, 3*(2), 1–27.

Menekse, M. (2015). Computer science teacher professional development in the United States: A review of studies published between 2004 and 2014. *Computer Science Education, 25*(4), 325–350. https://doi.org/10.1080/08993408.2015.1111645

Margolis, J., Estrella, R., Goode, J., Holme, J. J., & Nao, K. (2017). *Stuck in the shallow end: Education, race, and computing.* MIT Press.

Papert, S. (1980). *Mindstorms: Children, computers, and powerful ideas.* Basic Books, Inc.

Price, T. W., Cateté, V., Albert, J., Barnes, T., & Garcia, D. D. (2016). Lessons learned from "BJC" CS Principles professional development. In *Proceedings of SIGCSE'16*, March 2–5, 2016, Memphis, TN.

Qian, Y., Hambrusch, S., Yadav, A., & Gretter, S. (2018). Who needs what: Recommendations for designing effective online professional development for computer science teachers. *Journal of Research on Technology in Education, 50*(2), 164–181.

Rich, P. J., & Hu, H. (2019). *Surveying the landscape: Statewide data on K–12 CS education implementation* [Paper presentation]. Annual meeting for Research on Equity and Sustained Participation in Engineering, Computing, & Technology (RESPECT).

Rich, P. J., Mason, S. L., & O'Leary, J. (2021). Measuring the effect of continuous professional development on elementary teachers' self-efficacy to teach coding and computational thinking. *Computers & Education, 168,* (2021), 104196.

Smith, M. (2016, January 30). *Computer science for all.* The White House: President Barack Obama. https://obamawhitehouse.archives.gov/blog/2016/01/30/computer-science-all

Vegas, E., & Fowler, B. (2020, August 4). *What do we know about the expansion of K–12 computer science education? A review of the evidence.* Brookings Institute. https://www.brookings.edu/research/what-do-we-know-about-the-expansion-of-k-12-computer-science-education/

ACKNOWLEDGMENTS

We greatly acknowledge the chapter authors for their contributions, patience, and hard work while navigating the challenges of the COVID-19 pandemic.

Finally, we acknowledge the support of our colleagues at our respective institutions and the staff at Information Age Publishing.

Professional Development for In-Service Teachers, page xxiii
Copyright © 2022 by Information Age Publishing
www.infoagepub.com
xxiii

PART I

PROFESSIONAL DEVELOPMENT APPROACHES
FOR ELEMENTARY AND MIDDLE SCHOOL
CONTENT AREA TEACHERS

CHAPTER 1

COMPUTATIONAL THINKING IN ELEMENTARY CLASSROOMS

A Toolkit to Scaffold Teacher Learning

Aman Yadav
Michigan State University

Kathryn M. Rich
Michigan State University

Christina V. Schwarz
Michigan State University

Rachel A. Larimore
Michigan State University

Professional Development for In-Service Teachers, pages 3–25
Copyright © 2022 by Information Age Publishing
www.infoagepub.com

3

ABSTRACT

In this chapter, we present a toolkit developed to support elementary teachers as they integrate computational thinking (CT) practices into their classrooms through unplugged mathematics and science activities. We describe the elements of the toolkit, which include a reference guide, lesson screener, and lesson planner, and describe how we used them in professional development. We also discuss specific examples of how we related each of our four focal CT practices (abstraction, decomposition, patterns, and debugging) to elementary classroom activities. To conclude the chapter, we provide an example of how we used these unplugged experiences to support elementary teachers transition from thinking about CT in unplugged contexts to thinking about how to use CT to bring computationally rich activities to their classrooms.

Recent educational reforms in K–12 education, such as the Next Generation Science Standards (NGSS) and Common Core State Standards (CCSS), either explicitly or implicitly call out the need for students to engage in computational thinking (CT). CT has been defined as

> breaking down complex problems into more familiar/manageable sub-problems (problem decomposition), using a sequence of steps (algorithms) to solve problems, reviewing how the solution transfers to similar problems (abstraction), and finally determining if a computer can help more efficiently solve those problems (automation). (Yadav et al., 2016, pp. 565–566)

These efforts to bring CT to K–12 classrooms have been driven by the fact that the world students are growing up in, and will eventually be working in, is driven more and more by computation. A recent report argued that with computing technologies transforming many dimensions of our personal and work life, CT is a critical part of "what is important to know and know how to do in a computational world" (Digital Promise, 2017, p. 4). This has led a number of organizations, such as the International Society for Technology in Education (ISTE) and the Computer Science Teachers Association (CSTA), to develop standards for educators and students in CT. And as Denning (2017) suggested, these standards do not consistently define CT and associated concepts in similar ways. As educators participate in different professional development workshops, this inconsistency could lead to confusion on what CT is and how to bring CT ideas to their classrooms.

Research on how in-service teachers conceptualize CT has suggested they often believe CT involves doing mathematics, logical thinking, problem solving, using computers, coding, or simply using technology in the classroom (Sands et al., 2018). While some of these ideas overlap with CT, teachers still lack an understanding of how to bring CT ideas to their classrooms. For example, relating CT to coding is accurate, but it limits the power of CT ideas and how they could be applied to other disciplines. While CT is central to computer science (Denning, 2017; Wing, 2006), we also see it as an important set of practices for students to learn within the context of other disciplines (Yadav et al., 2016). We need to engage students in CT ideas and practices in multiple contexts, starting at the elementary level.

In order for CT to permeate K–12 education, we need to educate teachers in what these ideas are and how they relate to what happens in their classroom on a day-to-day basis. While there is emerging work on teacher education at the high school level, there has been less attention on how to bring CT to elementary classrooms. Furthermore, elementary schools face additional pressures of accountability as a result of federal mandates; thus, more resources are being devoted to the standardized test subject areas of language arts and mathematics (Marx & Harris, 2006). This means there is limited time during the school year to add new initiatives like computer science even as other core subjects like science are being pushed out (Marx & Harris, 2006).

One approach to integrating CT in elementary classrooms has been to work within the constraints of K–12 systems and integrate it within core subject areas, such as mathematics, science, and language arts. We believe that unplugged approaches—without the use of computers or other technology—provide an easy on-ramp for elementary teachers to embed CT into their curricula. As teachers get more comfortable with CT concepts and recognize CT connections within their lessons, we can scaffold teacher learning from unplugged activities to plugged CT activities using computational tools and environments. Starting with unplugged activities lessens the cognitive load that comes with learning computational tools as well as understanding how CT ideas connect to core subject areas. After teachers become comfortable with CT practices through unplugged activities, we can highlight the same practices in the context of plugged examples to allow teachers to bring computationally rich activities into their classrooms.

The focus on CT ideas first using unplugged approaches has been shown to develop elementary teachers' understanding of how these ideas connect and fit within their classrooms (Yadav et al., 2018). Specifically, Yadav and colleagues examined how unplugged approaches to CT could provide elementary teachers with opportunities to embed CT within science. Using teaching vignettes, the authors examined how teachers' understanding of CT shifted over the course of a year. Results suggested that teachers began with ideas of CT as generalized and broad, but their views of CT shifted to be more sophisticated and nuanced versions of those ideas.

While some work is beginning to emerge on how to engage K–12 teachers in CT ideas, there is much debate on how to do so. For example, Denning (2017) argued that engaging in computational modeling is at the heart of CT and that we engage in CT ideas, such as abstraction and decomposition, to get a model to accomplish certain work. Similarly, a recent blog post summarized a Twitter discussion on whether CT exists and how it could be brought to K–12 classrooms (Guzdial, 2018). Largely, this debate centers around whether we can truly expose students to CT ideas without coding, which is how computer science is primarily introduced in elementary and secondary schools.

We don't disagree with these views on the need for computational models and coding as vehicles to introduce CT. Rather, we argue that coding may not be the best starting place for elementary teachers. As noted above, we think this approach places a significant cognitive load on teachers that could be alleviated by introducing CT ideas through unplugged contexts. What do these CT ideas mean, and how can elementary teachers bring them into their classrooms? In prior work with elementary teachers, we used in-depth interviews to study how elementary teachers conceptualize CT within the context of their mathematics and science instruction (Rich et al., 2019). We found teachers focused on the problem-solving aspects of CT and made stronger connections between CT and mathematics than between CT and science. We also found that teachers were able to make some connections between their classroom practices and each of the six CT practices presented to them: abstraction, algorithmic thinking, automation, decomposition, debugging, and generalization. Given that teachers see natural connections between CT and their classroom activities, how can we support them to bring these practices into their lessons? In this chapter, we discuss how we have supported elementary teachers to bring CT into their mathematics and science lessons as a part of a National Science Foundation funded project, CT4EDU.

THE CT4EDU PROJECT

CT4EDU is a National Science Foundation funded Researcher Practitioner Partnership project with Oakland Intermediate School District (Michigan) where the goal is to design CT into their classrooms (CT4EDU, n.d.). Specifically, the partnership uses a networked improvement community (Bryk et al., 2010) approach where the work is carried out by educators and researchers together by identifying problems of practice, factors that contribute to those problems, and solutions to the problems. Within the context of the CT4EDU project, school district leadership, curriculum consultants (math, science, & technology), partner teachers, and researchers worked together to identify opportunities to embed CT in elementary math and science.

Our cyclical approach first identified problems of practice within our partner teachers' classrooms and how CT could be integrated to address those problems. This process led us to focus on four CT practices that elementary teachers could use to bring CT into their mathematics and science lessons: abstraction, decomposition, patterns, and debugging. Other CT concepts, such as algorithms, are present within these four ideas and not explicitly called out given the context of our work—math and science in elementary schools. We have used these four practices primarily as an on-ramp for teachers to first see connections between CT and their classroom activities and then incorporate automation through coding/simulations to engage students in learning math and science concepts. In order to facilitate teacher learning and integration of CT into disciplinary subjects, we created a toolkit for teachers that described the four focal CT practices. The toolkit included a *lesson screener tool* and a *lesson planner tool*. Below we describe each of the CT practices and how we used and adapted the lesson screener and planner tools to facilitate teacher learning and implementation.

A TEACHER TOOLKIT: SCAFFOLDING CT INTEGRATION

As discussed previously, based on our interviews with elementary teachers and the focus of CT integration in elementary math and science, we focused on four CT practices (i.e., abstraction, decomposition, patterns, & debugging). In order to scaffold CT integration, we developed a CT teacher reference guide with three tools. The first tool was a quick *CT reference guide*, which included a description and essential features for each CT concept as well as a list of questions teachers could use to engage students in the computational ideas (Yadav et al., 2019). In addition, we developed a *lesson screener* tool that teachers could use to identify where CT concepts were already present in their lessons and could be more explicit through lesson enhancements. Lastly, we developed a *lesson planner* tool designed to support the detailed planning of lessons that include CT practices.

In addition to facilitating teacher learning of each of the four CT practices by engaging them as learners, we also worked with the teachers to co-design lesson plans that integrated CT in math and science lessons of their choice. The teacher learning of CT practices happened over two Saturday meetings (Spring 2018) and a 3-day summer institute (June 2018). During August 2018, the teachers came back for a 3-day summer institute where the focus was on designing CT integrated lessons. After the June meeting, teachers were asked to pick math and CT thinking and bring those lessons to the August meeting. The co-design sessions were based on disciplinary and/or grade level groups and included the teachers, university researchers with expertise in computer science education, mathematics education, and science education, and district level curriculum staff. The first part of the co-design session asked teachers to identify the existing CT practices in a math or science lesson they already taught. In order to scaffold teachers' integration of CT within their math/science lessons, we used a CT lesson screener tool that asked the teachers to first consider the heart of the learning in the lesson and key math/science ideas they wanted their students to learn as well as what standards the lesson addressed.

After thinking about the key lesson ideas, the co-design session focused on ways the CT practice(s) were already embedded in the lesson and ways those CT practices could be made explicit. Table 1.1 shows the template lesson screener teachers used to identify CT opportunities within an existing lesson. After the teachers completed the lesson screener for an existing lesson, the co-design session engaged teachers in thinking about developing a detailed plan for bringing CT into the lesson. Table 1.2 shows the lesson planner tool that teachers used to create a lesson plan.

TABLE 1.1 Lesson Screener Tool		
Math or Science Focus		
What is the heart of the learning in this lesson? What are the key ideas and tasks? What mathematics or science standards does the lesson address?		
CT Concept	**Ways CT Is Already Embedded**	**Ways CT Ideas Could Be Made Explicit**
Abstraction:		
Do students identify key information in the task?		
Do they use representations or other tools to reduce complexity?		
Decomposition:		
Is there a complex task or situation that students could break down?		
Can the task or situation be broken down in multiple ways?		
Patterns:		
What patterns do students see within a problem?		
What patterns do students see across similar problems?		
How do students connect the work of the lesson to things they have done in the past?		
Debugging:		
Do students have opportunities to reflect upon their work?		
Do they have opportunities to revise their thinking or make improvements?		

TABLE 1.2 Lesson Planner Tools			
Math or Science Focus			
What is the heart of the learning in this lesson? What are the key ideas and tasks? What CT language do you plan to highlight in this lesson?			
Activity & Time [Add number of minutes] [Add function/ purpose of activity]	Procedures: • What the Teacher and Students will DO & SAY • What you plan to do and say for each activity • What you expect the students to say and do • Ways you might encourage, monitor, & respond to equitable student sense-making		Considerations for Diverse Learners Specific strategies to meet specific, individual students' learning needs
	Teachers Say & Do	Students Say & Do	
Activity 1			
Activity 2			

COMPUTATIONAL THINKING EXAMPLES IN ELEMENTARY CONTEXTS

Before teachers thought about whether and how the four CT practices could be integrated into their classroom, we introduced each of the CT practices using a generic activity and then made connections to math and science. Below we discuss each of these practices in detail and give an example of activities that allowed teachers to explore them.

Abstraction

Abstraction has been suggested as one of the main computer science practices and is at the heart of computation and CT (Denning, 2017; Kramer, 2007). Abstraction is a central problem-solving technique in computer science that reduces complexity by focusing on the most relevant and essential details relevant to the problem/phenomena at hand. In Computer Science (CS), "Good abstractions hide the details of the machinery implementing them, allowing programmers to debug them without having to dig into the details of the underlying machines" (Denning & Tedre, 2019, p. 99). For example, when coding in a programming language, a programmer does not have to think about whether and how the machine is implementing their program at different levels: programming language → compiler → machine language → logic gates. Programmers also develop abstractions when they write functions that generalize aspects that can be reused in a program. When they write a function definition, programmers have to think about the details of how the function works.

However, when they use a function call for a function that has already been defined, they do not have to think about how the function works—only what it does. These different levels of detail are sometimes called *levels of abstraction* (Hillis, 1998), and computer scientists often have to move among levels of abstraction as they solve problems (Wing, 2006).

In our work with elementary teachers, we focused on abstraction as reducing complexity or identifying general principles that can be applied across situations or problems. In particular, we suggested that abstraction could be integrated within elementary classrooms by encouraging students to focus on the most important information and hide unnecessary detail as they are working on math or science tasks as well as providing opportunities for students to represent problems/phenomena in ways that simplify them. Another aspect of abstraction focused on encouraging students to identify principles that can be applied across situations/problems. In the teacher CT reference guide, we also provided our teacher partners with the following list of suggested questions to promote abstraction as a part of students' vocabulary and thinking:

1. How can we simplify this problem/task?
2. What information is most important for solving this problem/task?
3. What information can we ignore in solving this problem/task?
4. How can we clearly represent the important information?
5. What lessons can you take away from this problem and apply to other problems?

But what does this look like in the context of elementary mathematics and science instruction?

Abstraction: A Generic Activity

In order to explore the idea of abstraction, we adapted the Tour Guide activity from Computing at Schools London and CS4FN (CS4FN, n.d.). We asked the teachers to visit different landmarks around Detroit by starting at their hotel and returning to the hotel without visiting any location twice. We first used a map that includes the landmarks overlaid on a satellite map (see Figure 1.1) and showed a lot of information about Detroit, which was not necessarily useful in solving the problem. We then introduced the idea of abstraction and how we can ignore a lot of the information present in the original map and create a representation that removes unnecessary detail to make the problem easier to solve (see Figure 1.2). We also discussed how we simplified the map by representing the information as a graph.

Figure 1.1   Map of Detroit with landmarks.

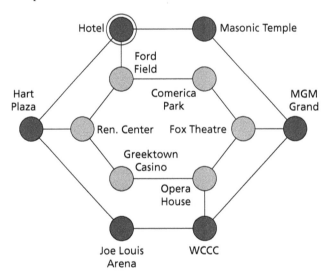

Figure 1.2   Graph representation of the map.

Abstraction and Mathematics

One of the standards for mathematical practice in the CCSS for mathematics (CCSS-M) is to model with mathematics (Common Core State Standards Initiative [CCSSI], 2010). The standard states, "Mathematically proficient students who can apply what they know are comfortable making assumptions and approximations to simplify a complicated situation, realizing that these may need revision later" (CCSSI, 2010, p. 7). At the elementary grades, we can use abstraction as an instructional approach by explicitly encouraging students to focus on relevant information when solving mathematics word problems. This is different from encouraging students to look for keywords—it focuses instead on making sense of the overall problem before doing any arithmetic (Rich & Yadav, 2020). In addition, abstraction could also be leveraged when students translate "real world" situations into mathematical representations (including graphs, numbers, and operations). This process is akin to moving amongst levels of abstraction discussed previously. When students are initially looking at a situation, they attend to all the details as they decide what is relevant. As they create mathematical representations that highlight the relevant details, they are able to move to a higher level of abstraction and ignore less relevant information in the situation. In our recent work, we analyzed how an elementary mathematics task asked students to move between levels of abstraction and found that students tend to make errors when making those implicit shifts (Rich et al., 2019). As such, we believe that preparing teachers to explicitly call out abstraction and teach elementary kids to move amongst levels of abstraction might be a productive approach within mathematics instruction. These experiences with abstraction might also be leveraged when students learn computer science (Rich et al., 2019).

Abstraction and Science

Abstraction in science is about being purposeful to abstract particular aspects that are helpful for predicting and explaining phenomena. First, similar to computer science, abstraction in science involves the process of removing detail to simplify a complex phenomena/object. Second, much of the abstraction involves abstracting from phenomena to representations and applying those to other phenomena rather than traversing from one form of representation to another. This second aspect of abstraction within science is about generalization that involves developing a general concept that can be applied across different situations.

One way to engage in abstraction within science is through the practice of developing and using models (NRC 2012; Schwarz et al., 2009). The entire purpose of this practice is to abstract by embodying ideas about systems into representations that can be used to predict and explain phenomena. We, therefore, argue engaging students in developing and using models involves students abstracting. That is, modeling encourages students to focus on parts that help them figure out how/why the world works rather than the details that don't impact how/why things work.

To clarify, there are many different types of models or representations that are used to predict and explain (e.g., physical models, diagrammatic models, mathematical models, computational models for solar system dynamics, ecosystems, climate, etc.). Models are important in science because they abstract phenomena that we have difficulty thinking about because they are too small (e.g., particles of matter), too big (e.g., distribution of planets in our solar system), too fast (e.g., most moving objects), too slow (erosion), or otherwise not visible (e.g., energy) with respect to our everyday experiences.

In science, abstraction involves asking students to develop and use models that embody what the system is, what parts of the system to abstract and how to represent it, what each important part of the system does, and how to use that system to design/predict/explain something. For example, to meet the NGSS performance expectation 5-PS1-1 ("Develop a model to describe that matter is made of particles too small to be seen"), a teacher can ask students to draw and continually revise models of what makes a basketball expand, what happens to sugar when it dissolves in water and can no longer be seen, and so on. This means deciding what parts of the phenomenon might not be relevant to understanding why the basketball expands (e.g., details of the pictures in the room in which the basketball is located). Further, NGSS performance expectation 5-LS2-1 entitled, "Develop a model to describe the movement of matter among plants, animals, decomposers and the environment," is a good example of a context for model development. For example, a teacher can ask students to develop and refine a model (e.g., flow chart) that connects matter with living things. This model can be revised over time with respect to bringing in additional information and then it can be applied to future contexts to decide what happens when part of that environment is changed (e.g., decomposers are eliminated for some reason). An important part of the process of developing and using models over time is talking about and comparing/contrasting models in class to generate consensus and disagreements about those representations.

Decomposition

One way to simplify complex tasks is by decomposing them into smaller parts that may be more easily solved. As Wing (2006) argued, decomposition is an essential CT skill. Within computer science, large complex systems are designed by putting together a collection of smaller parts and focusing on the design of those individual parts. For example, Brennan and Resnick (2012) provided an example of how programming in Scratch involves focusing on individual sprites and stacks of code, which helps a programmer not only debug different parts, but also makes the code easier for others to read. As such, decomposition is about managing complex tasks or situations by breaking them down into smaller, more manageable parts. Using the CT practice of decomposition can allow students to approach problems that, at first, may seem intimidating. In our work with teachers, we focused on how teachers could provide opportunities for students to break down a phenomenon or object into parts as well as choose tasks where students can break down the problem in multiple ways. The following question prompts were included in the CT reference guide for teachers to engage their students in decomposition:

1. What details do you notice in this problem, phenomenon, or object?
2. How can you use the details to identify parts of this problem, phenomenon, or object?
3. What parts are familiar to you? What parts are unfamiliar?
4. What are the different ways you could break down this problem, phenomenon, or object?
5. Can you break down the parts further into smaller parts?
6. How might breaking down this problem or phenomenon be helpful for solving or understanding it?

Given our focus on CT integration within mathematics and science, below we highlight three examples of how teachers could bring decomposition to their classrooms.

Decomposition: A Generic Activity

In order to introduce decomposition, we used an activity that paired teachers and asked each one to write down directions for their partner to draw a design they were given at the beginning of the activity. Each partner was given a different design and one could not show their design to their partner. Each participant wrote down step-by-step directions for their partner to follow and try to re-create the design by only following the directions. We then discussed how participants came up with the directions and how well the directions worked. The discussion brought up the CT practice of decomposition as participants mentioned how they broke down their designs into smaller parts and wrote down the directions for each of the subparts. In addition, this process also brought up the CT practice of *debugging* as participants troubleshooted and fixed their directions.

Decomposition and Mathematics

The content standards in the CCSS-M for Grades K–5 contain multiple references to decomposition. For example, one standard for third grade says, "Find areas of rectilinear figures by decomposing them into non-overlapping rectangles and adding the areas of the non-overlapping

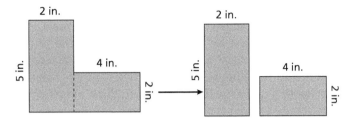

Figure 1.3 Decomposing to find the area of a rectangle in elementary mathematics.

parts, applying this technique to solve real world problems" (CCSSI, 2010, p. 25). Because they typically know the area formula for only rectangles, third graders may initially try to find the area of the shape shown at the left of Figure 1.3 by resorting to covering the shape with squares and counting. However, this standard encourages students to instead decompose the problem of finding the area of the whole shape into two smaller problems, each involving finding the area of a rectangle, and then adding the areas (see right side of Figure 1.3).

Problems like these provide a nice entry point into the idea of decomposition, as students can see the decomposition visually. As students become more comfortable with decomposition, they can also decompose more complex problems that do not visually suggest how they might be decomposed. For example, when we asked our partner teachers to order a large collection of mixed numbers on a number line, we encouraged them to think about breaking the task into parts. Some teachers separated the whole numbers and halves from the rest of the mixed numbers, placed those on the number line first, and then worked on placing the remaining mixed numbers. Others focused just on the fractions between 0 and 1 first, and then moved on to placing the numbers between 1 and 2, and so on. Still others started by putting the cards in order, and only after that thought about arranging the correct spacing between numbers on the number line. Our partner teachers agreed that decomposition might help many of their students gain entry into problems that would otherwise overwhelm them. Using the CT idea of decomposition can help students realize that there is always a *part* of a problem they can work on, even if they do not immediately know how to finish the whole problem.

Decomposition and Science

One of the science and engineering practices in the NGSS is planning and carrying out investigations. This practice involves using previous knowledge to ask questions (another science and engineering practice) about a phenomenon and then test smaller parts of this bigger question. We contend this process is a form of decomposition—breaking the problem down into simpler, more discrete components. For example, one third grade performance expectation focuses on the similarities within the unique and diverse life cycles of different organisms (i.e., 3-LS1-1). A teacher might first expose students to the phenomenon of a bean sprout, baby bird, and a chrysalis and pose a question about how these three organisms are similar in their life cycles. As students begin to investigate and answer this question it will be necessary to break the problem down into birth, growth, reproduction, and death. This might mean conducting an investigation around planting beans while also hatching and raising chicks to compare organism birth. Yet as these organisms grow, students may have additional questions about what each organism needs to survive. For example, they may conduct an investigation to break down the problem of whether a plant needs light, water, or soil. In other words, as they gain new knowledge about a phenomenon students will have new questions to investigate and each will require students to decompose and break down the problem. This decomposition process not only breaks the problem into smaller, more manageable investigations, but also narrows in on a particular aspect of the phenomenon.

Patterns

Knuth (1981) argued that recognizing patterns is one of the essential practices that computer scientists use as a part of generalization to quickly solve "new problems based on previous solutions to other problems and building on prior experience" (Csizmadia et al., 2015, p. 8). Csizmadia and colleagues suggested that recognizing patterns of process/strategies being used to solve a problem is important, as it allows computer scientists to translate a general solution across a class of problems. Patterning also comes into play when scientists use computational tools to explore, analyze, interpret, and synthesize massive amounts of data (NRC, 2011). Wing (2008) highlighted the importance of patterns within CT and its relationship to other disciplines stating, "In the humanities and the arts, digital libraries of books, collections and artifacts create opportunities through computational methods such as data mining and data federation to discover new trends, patterns and links in our understanding and appreciation of humankind" (p. 3719). In our work with elementary teachers, we highlighted that given the ubiquitous nature of patterns—present everywhere and used every day—it is important to engage students in patterning by having them look for and discuss patterns during activities. In addition, they could also provide opportunities for students to generate and meaningfully use patterns using the following question prompts:

1. What similarities or patterns do you notice between the problems, phenomena, or objects? For example, how many objects are there? What colors do you see?
2. How can you describe the patterns?
3. How could you use the pattern to make predictions or draw conclusions?

Below are three examples of what attention to patterns might look like in elementary mathematics and science lessons.

Patterns: A Generic Activity

To introduce teachers to the concept of recognizing patterns, we used an activity where they had to work together as a group to identify patterns in the *Zoom* picture book (Banyai, 1995), which zooms out from a farm to a ship to a city street to a deserted island, and so on. In particular, we distributed laminated pages of the *Zoom* book randomly to teachers, who had to figure out how the pages relate to each other and determine what it meant to put them in order. As teachers worked to solve the problem, they observed that pages showed objects zoomed in or out (e.g., one page only had a zoomed in image of a rooster comb, which only became clear once you saw another page that showed the whole rooster). Once the pattern became clear to the teachers after looking at a few pictures, they started applying it to other parts of the book and then eventually to all the pages.

Patterns and Mathematics

A focus on patterns in mathematics can help students develop efficient strategies for solving problems, while still ensuring they understand why the efficient method works. For example, while using visual models to compare fractions, students may begin to notice that when the numerators of two fractions are the same, the greater fraction is the one with the smaller denominator, as smaller denominators mean bigger pieces of the whole. When students derive this rule by looking for patterns in visual models, rather than just being told the rule and asked to memorize and practice it, the rule is meaningful.

Patterns can also be used in combination with the decomposition strategies described above. For example, if students decompose the task of placing a set of mixed numbers on a number line by focusing on the numbers between 0 and 1 first, they can look for patterns in that section of the number line and apply them to work on other parts of the task. For example, if they notice that ⅓ is closer to ½ than to 1, they can reason that 1⅓ will be closer to 1½ than to 1 and that 2⅓ will be closer to 2½ than to 2.

Patterns and Science

Patterns are another core aspect of science and are listed as the first crosscutting concept in *A Framework for K–12 Science Education* (National Research Council, 2012). The framework describes the importance of patterns because "observed patterns of forms and events guide organization and classification, and they prompt questions about relationships and the factors that influence them" (National Research Council, 2012, p. 84). Patterns play an important role in making sense of data and phenomena. For example, when addressing the performance expectation 3-ESS2-1 of "representing data in tables and graphical display to describe typical weather conditions expected during a particular season" students need to be able to see a regular occurrence of a weather phenomenon that can predict future occurrences. For example, one weather pattern is that winter in the upper Midwestern United States is typically quite cold and along with other weather conditions can sometimes give rise to snow. Patterns in science depend on observing systems to determine what is similar or different in the information, data or phenomena.

Debugging

Within computer science, debugging is an essential practice that allows programmers to find and fix errors when a given computational tool or program does not provide a desired outcome. When defining CT for mathematics and science classrooms, Weintrop and colleagues (2016) also argued that

> the ability to troubleshoot a problem is important, as unexpected outcomes and incorrect behavior are frequently encountered, especially when working with computational tools. Students who have mastered this practice will be able to identify, isolate, reproduce, and ultimately correct unexpected problems encountered when working on a problem, and do so in a systematic, efficient manner. (p. 140)

Elementary teachers could use debugging as a CT practice by encouraging their students to debug when something doesn't work as they had expected or planned. In particular, teachers should avoid the urge to fix problems for students. Instead they should allow the students to reason through courses of action for themselves. The following questions could prompt students to use debugging as a strategy:

1. Does the result match what you expected?
2. How can you tell whether or not your plan, model, or solution worked?

3. How can you modify your approach to address the problem?
4. How do you know you have fixed the error?

Debugging and Mathematics

Developing habits of checking the accuracy and reasonableness of solutions to problems is important in elementary mathematics. Our partner teachers readily embraced debugging as a way to encourage students to thoughtfully look back at their work and think about how it could be fixed or improved. For example, when considering their answers to word problems, teachers encouraged students to consider whether their answers made sense in context. If the answers did not make sense, students debugged by considering what might have gone wrong: Was it the arithmetic, the interpretation of the problem, or something else? Some of our partner teachers also emphasized debugging through considering *why* certain problem-solving steps were not productive. For example, when students added fractions by adding the numerators and denominators, one teacher encouraged students to think about why it did not make sense to add the denominators (because the denominator is not a count, but rather identifying the size of the piece of the whole).

Debugging and Science

Debugging can occur throughout scientific inquiry. Planning and carrying out investigations is a clear context in which to engage students in debugging. This is particularly true when students are able to make decisions regarding the design of the investigation—either as a whole class or individually. For example, in attending to the NGSS performance expectation 4-PS3-3 which states, "Ask questions and predict outcomes about the changes in energy that occur when objects collide," fourth grade students can design an investigation that might involve using different marbles rolling down ramps that collide with cups or blocks at the bottom of the ramp. Students need to debug both the design and the data collection involved so that it actually provides useful information about the phenomenon. For example, how can students get the marbles going to hit the cups? If they use a ramp, does it have to be at the same height for each marble? What if the cup at the bottom falls over? Do they have enough different marbles of different mass to see any difference in the outcomes? Also, what might students measure regarding the collision—how far the cup moves? Whether it gets dented? How might students represent the information? All of these aspects involved in the design and implementation involve debugging to find a solution to planning and carrying out the investigation that actually works and generates usable information.

Other strong contexts/practices for debugging in science include analyzing and interpreting data, revising conceptual models over time, and constructing explanations and designing solutions. Each of these involves a product (e.g., model, data, explanation) that can be revised over time using debugging to compare the product with expectations, theory, and evidence.

One thing that is different about debugging in science compared to computer science is there may not be an obvious end goal to indicate when an investigation "works" or "doesn't work." In science debugging may be a process of continually working to improve the outcome. For example, while students may debug an investigation to get it to actually generate the phenomenon, there is a question as to the quality of that investigation. Improving that investigation (e.g., better data, easier to conduct) involves other qualities that then fold back into the problem that students can use debugging to address.

Computational Thinking: A Plugged Activity

We have used the unplugged approaches discussed above as a way for teachers to see connections between CT practices and their mathematics/ science instruction and as an on-ramp to more computationally rich activities. For example, at a spring workshop for the first cohort of CT4EDU partner teachers, we used a mathematics activity to help teachers see how the CT ideas they had been using in their classrooms could be applied when programming Dash robots. To begin, we ask teachers to write directions for how to get from a *start* number on a number grid to an *end* number. They could only use directions to add 1s, add 10s, subtract 1s, or subtract 10s. These directions correspond to moving right, up, left, and down on the number grid. The teachers exchanged directions with a partner without revealing their *end* number, and partners attempted to follow the directions and see if they ended up at the correct number. Teachers *debugged* their directions as needed, discussed how they had *decomposed* their directions into individual steps, and discussed how the *patterns* in the number grid allowed them to *abstract* four simple kinds of directions that allowed them to direct their partner to go anywhere on the number grid.

Next, we introduced a floor-mat style number grid large enough for teachers to walk on. We challenged teachers to translate their addition and subtraction directions into directions involving moving forward and turning. An example of corresponding addition/subtraction and move/turn directions are shown in Figure 1.4.

Finally, teachers were invited to translate their move-and-turn directions into scripts directing Dash robots to follow the same path on the floor grid. The similarities between the processes of writing directions and programming the script helped teachers to see how the CT ideas they had been

Start Number: 45
End Number: 28

Add & Subtract Directions	Move & Turn Directions	Path
Subtract 20	Face toward the top of the number grid.	
Add 4	Move 2 steps forward	
	Turn right	
Subtract 1	Move 4 steps forward	
	Turn left twice	
	Move 1 step forward	

Path grid:

									10
11	12	13	14	15	16	17	18	19	20
21	22	23	24	25	26	27	28	29	30
31	32	33	34	35	36	37	38	39	40
41	42	43	44	45	46	47	48	49	50
51	52	53	54	55	56	57	58	59	60
61	62	63	64	65	66	67	68	69	70
71	72	73	74	75	76	77	78	79	80
81	82	83	84	85	86	87	88	89	90
91	92	93	94	95	96	97	98	99	100

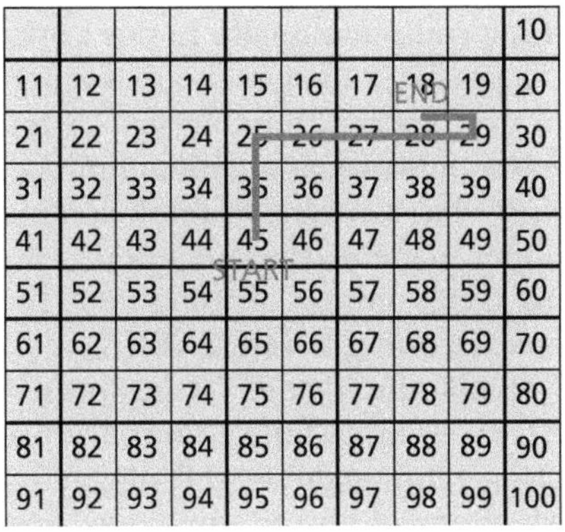

Figure 1.4 Translating addition/subtraction directions into move-and-turn directions.

embedding in mathematics and science activities also applied in programming activities.

DISCUSSION

With a number of current educational frameworks (e.g., NGSS and CCSS) highlighting the need for students to experience CT in the K–12 curriculum, this toolkit provides a mechanism for researchers and teachers as they integrate CT into elementary classrooms. For example, as discussed previously, teachers could bring the CT concept of abstraction into their science instruction when students develop and use models (data models as well as theoretical models), by having students represent phenomena in ways that simplify them. Our work with CT4EDU teacher partners has shown that the toolkit can scaffold their use and integration of CT practices within their classrooms. In one study, we found that the toolkit helped our partner teachers to frame their lessons around CT practices, prompt students to use the practices during the lessons, and invite students to reflect on how they used CT as they worked through the lesson (Rich & Yadav, 2019; Rich et al., 2020).

We see the use of these practices as a starting place for elementary teachers to integrate CT into their curriculum and as an on-ramp from unplugged CT integration to plugged CT integration that brings computationally rich tools and activities into classrooms. At the elementary level, unplugged approaches to CT integration could be valuable for young learners as they hone and sharpen ways of thinking computationally and practicing skills associated with CT (Denning & Tedre, 2019). As Denning and Tedre (2019) suggested, CT is a learned skill as our brains do not naturally think computationally. In our work, we see value in highlighting individual CT practices so elementary teachers can first deliberately engage students in this "special thinking skill" (Denning & Tedre, 2019, p. 6) before they move on to using computation. As teachers and students become familiar with what it means to think computationally and with students moving to upper grade levels, computers can play a bigger role with students designing computations or using them for explaining and interpreting phenomena (Denning & Tedre, 2019).

While the idea of CT has been around since the 1980s (Grover & Pea, 2013), we know little about what teachers' enactment of CT looks like both using unplugged as well plugged approaches. We also know little about whether and how an unplugged approach can serve as an on-ramp to more computational rich activities. In our CT4EDU work with partner teachers, we are beginning to understand how teachers take up CT practices and what they look like in the classroom. Rich and Yadav (2019) found that teachers use CT in three ways: (a) to guide their own lesson planning, but without making CT explicit to students; (b) to guide lesson planning, and also structure their implementation of the lesson around the CT practice and make it explicit to their students; and (c) to make CT explicit to students as a general problem solving strategy. We also know that as teachers get exposed to CT, their conceptions about CT and its role in their classrooms becomes more sophisticated (Yadav et al., 2018; Yadav et al., 2014).

As the work on CT integration is starting to emerge, there are some important questions that still need to be investigated, both focused on teachers and students. Specifically, future work on CT integration needs to examine whether and how the unplugged approach can serve as an on-ramp to increase teacher self-efficacy and knowledge to bring more computationally rich activities to teach disciplinary ideas. Computer science education researchers should investigate how factors, such as teachers' background and comfort with technology might influence integration of plugged computational approaches. In addition, what scaffolds might be needed to support teachers as they move from unplugged to plugged contexts? Relatedly, we need to study how students transfer their learning from unplugged to plugged contexts. In particular, research should study whether and how students leverage CT practices, such as decomposition, in traditional computer science learning (i.e., coding).

ACKNOWLEDGMENTS

This work is supported by the National Science Foundation under grant number 1738677. Any opinions, findings, and conclusions or recommendations expressed in this material are those of the author(s) and do not necessarily reflect the views of the National Science Foundation.

REFERENCES

Banyai, I. (1995). *Zoom*. Puffin Books.

Brennan, K., & Resnick, M. (2012). *New frameworks for studying and assessing the development of computational thinking*. Paper presented at annual American Educational Research Association meeting, Vancouver, BC, Canada.

Bryk, A. S., Gomez, L. M., & Grunow, A. (2010). Getting ideas into action: Building networked improvement communities in education. *Carnegie Foundation for the Advancement of Teaching.* http://www.carnegiefoundation.org/spotlight/webinar-bryk-gomez-building-networked-improvement-communities-in-education

Csizmadia, A., Curzon, P., Dorling, M., Humphreys, S., Ng, T., Selby, C., & Woollard, J. (2015). Computational thinking: A guide for teachers. *Computing at School.* https://eprints.soton.ac.uk/424545/

CS4FN. (n.d.). *The tour guide activity.* https://teachinglondoncomputing.org/the-tour-guide-activity/

CT4EDU. (n.d.). *Welcome.* http://ct4edu.org/home/

Denning, P. J. (2017). Remaining trouble spots with computational thinking. *Communications of the ACM, 60*(6), 33–39. https://doi.org/10.1145/2998438

Denning, P. J., & Tedre, M. (2019). *Computational thinking*. MIT Press.

Digital Promise. (2017). *Computational thinking for a computational world.* https://digitalpromise.org/initiative/computational-thinking/

Gilbert, J. K., & Justi, R. (2016). *Modelling-based teaching in science education* (Vol. 9). Springer International Publishing.

Grover, S., & Pea, R. (2013). Computational thinking in K–12: A review of the state of the field. *Educational Researcher, 42*(1), 38–43. https://doi.org/10.3102/0013189X12463051

Guzdial, M. (2018). Computational thinking, education for the poor and rich, and dealing with schools and teachers as they are: A Twitter convo. https://cacm.acm.org/blogs/blog-cacm/231422-computational-thinking-education-for-the-poor-and-rich-and-dealing-with-schools-and-teachers-as-they-are-a-twitter-convo/fulltext

Hillis, W. D. (1998). *The pattern on the stone*. Basic Books.

Knuth, D. E. (1981). *Algorithms in modern mathematics and computer science*. Springer. https://doi.org/10.1007/3-540-11157-3_26

Kramer, J. (2007). Is abstraction the key to computing? *Communications of the ACM, 50*(4), 36–42. https://doi.org/10.1145/1232743.1232745

Marx, R., & Harris, C. (2006). No child left behind and science education: Opportunities, challenges, and risks. *The Elementary School Journal, 106*(5), 467–478. https://doi.org/10.1086/505441

National Research Council. (2012). *A framework for K–12 science education: Practices, crosscutting concepts, and core ideas.* The National Academies Press.

Rich, K. M., & Yadav, A. (2020). Applying levels of abstraction to mathematics word problems. *TechTrends, 64*(3), 395–403. https://doi.org/10.1007/s11528-020-00479-3

Rich, K. M., Yadav, A., & Larimore, R. A. (2020). Teacher implementation profiles for integrating computational thinking into elementary mathematics and science instruction. *Education and Information Technologies, 25*(4), 3161–3188. https://doi.org/10.1007/s10639-020-10115-5

Rich, K., & Yadav, A. (2019). Infusing computational thinking instruction into elementary mathematics and science: Patterns of teacher implementation. *Proceedings of Society for Information Technology & Teacher Education International Conference 2019.* AACE.

Rich, K. M., Yadav, A., & Schwarz, C. V. (2019). Computational thinking, mathematics, and science: Elementary teachers' perspectives on integration. *Journal of Technology and Teacher Education, 27*(2), 165–205.

Rich, K. M., Yadav, A., & Zhu, M. (2019). Levels of abstraction in students' mathematics strategies: What can applying computer science ideas about abstraction bring to elementary mathematics? *Journal of Computer in Mathematics and Science Teaching, 38*(3), 267–298.

Sands, P., Yadav, A., & Good, J. (2018). Computational thinking in K–12: In-service teacher perceptions of computational thinking. In M. S Khine (Ed.), *Computational thinking in the STEM disciplines* (pp. 151–164). Springer.

Schwarz, C. V., Reiser, B. J., Davis, E. A., Kenyon, L., Achér, A., Fortus, D., Shwartz, Y., Hug, B., & Krajcik, J. (2009). Developing a learning progression for scientific modeling: Making scientific modeling accessible and meaningful for learners. *Journal of Research in Science Teaching: The Official Journal of the National Association for Research in Science Teaching, 46*(6), 632–654.

Weintrop, D., Beheshti, E., Horn, M., Orton, K., Jona, K., Trouille, L., & Wilensky, U. (2016). Defining computational thinking for mathematics and science classrooms. *Journal of Science Education and Technology, 25*(1), 127–147. https://doi.org/10.1007/s10956-015-9581-5

Wing, J. M. (2006). Computational thinking. *Communications of the ACM, 49*(3), 33–35.

Wing, J. M. (2008). Computational thinking and thinking about computing. *Philosophical Transactions of the Royal Society A: Mathematical, Physical and Engineering Sciences, 366*(1881). https://doi.org/10.1098/rsta.2008.0118

Yadav, A., Hong, H., & Stephenson, C. (2016). Computational thinking for all: Pedagogical approaches to embedding a 21st century problem solving in K-12 classrooms. *TechTrends 60,* 565–568. https://doi.org/10.1007/s11528-016-0087-7

Yadav A., Krist, C., Good. J., & Caeli. E. (2018). Computational thinking in elementary classrooms: Measuring teacher understanding of computational ideas for teaching science. *Computer Science Education, 28*(4), 371–400. https://doi.org/10.1080/08993408.2018.1560550

Yadav, A., Larimore, R., Rich, K. M., & Schwarz, C. (2019, March 18). Integrating computational thinking in elementary classrooms: Introducing a toolkit to support teachers. In K. Graziano (Eds.), *Proceedings of the Society for Information Technology & Teacher Education International Conference* (pp. 347–350). Association for the Advancement of Computing in Education.

Yadav, A., Mayfield, C., Zhou, N., Hambrusch, S., & Korb, J. T. (2014). Computational thinking in elementary and secondary teacher education. *ACM Transactions on Computing Education, 14*(1), 1–16.

CHAPTER 2

TEACHER CO-DESIGN IN A CS FOR ALL RESEARCH– PRACTICE PARTNERSHIP

Curriculum Development and Teacher Learning

Florence R. Sullivan
University of Massachusetts

W. Richards Adrion
University of Massachusetts

Catherine Tulungen
University of Massachusetts

Emrah Pektas
University of Massachusetts

Professional Development for In-Service Teachers, pages 27–58
Copyright © 2022 by Information Age Publishing
www.infoagepub.com
All rights of reproduction in any form reserved.

ABSTRACT

In this chapter, we present work from the first year of a 4-year research practice partnership devoted to integrating computational thinking (CT) into
elementary curriculum in a mid-size school district in the Northeast. Our approach to curricular integration is to engage participating teachers in professional development (PD) related to computer science (CS) and CT and to
support them in the activity of co-design. Working in pairs, teachers developed modules that integrated CT into elementary level science lessons. We
conducted case study analysis of this process as it related to curriculum design
and teacher learning. Results indicate that the practice of co-design highlighted the need to create curricula that is flexible enough to be adapted to
specific classroom contexts and allow for differentiation. Results also revealed
productive tensions related to differences in pedagogical practices among
the teachers involved in the co-design. At the conclusion of the chapter, we
discuss next steps, especially concerning PD and research.

Recent research on CS education at the elementary level has emphasized
the need to investigate how teachers might learn to embed CS concepts in
the elementary curriculum (Yadav et al., 2018). Moreover, researchers have
called for an examination of the role of unplugged CS activities for younger
children (Caeli & Yadav, 2019) and of the use of means other than the popular coding program, Scratch (Resnick, 2009), for engaging K–8 students
in CS learning (Zhang & Nouri, 2019). Zhang and Nouri (2019) have also
noted the paucity of research on CS learning in kindergarten. These calls
spring from the rapid expansion of the CSforAll movement over the last
decade, which, while originally focused on creating high school curricula
and training high school teachers (Cuny, 2012) has now shifted to include
CS education at the elementary level (Cuny, 2016).

In this chapter, we respond to these calls for research. Here we present two
case studies of in-service elementary teachers (kindergarten and third grade)
engaged in co-design of modules that integrate computational thinking (CT)
concepts into science lessons, including plugged and unplugged activities.
Our work is poised to support the field's developing understanding of how
to support in-service elementary teachers to learn about, integrate, and teach
CS/CT concepts. This, in turn, will support the national effort to improve CS
learning at all levels of K–12 education (Cuny, 2016).

These case studies were collected in the first year of a large-scale research
project situated in a university-public school district research practice
partnership (RPP) in Springfield, Massachusetts. Our RPP is supporting
teacher-led design teams to engage in collaborative design-based implementation research (DBIR; Penuel et al., 2011). Our work focuses on the
interpretation and incorporation of CT concepts and practices as defined
in the digital literacy and computer science (DLCS) frameworks created

by the Massachusetts Department of Elementary and Secondary Education (MDESE; 2016). CT is conceptualized in the DLCS frameworks as consisting of five topic areas including: (a) abstraction, (b) algorithms, (c) data, (d) programming and development, and (e) modeling and simulation.

In line with the DBIR approach, we assembled an interdisciplinary team of researchers, comprised of computer scientists, learning scientists, sociologists, and educational administration experts, to work with both district personnel and classroom teachers throughout the project. In the case studies presented here, the focus was on the role of teachers as co-designers of the CT curriculum. After engaging in professional development (PD), teachers collaborated in grade level groups to iteratively design and test integrated CT modules in their classrooms. The larger RPP team supported the design process by helping to outline the activities, frame questions, provide feedback and input on the lessons, and facilitate access to relevant informational and structural artifacts. Key actors in the design process were the coordinating teachers, including school-based technology and math specialists, who were serving as instructional leaders in the district. In this chapter, we focus on the iterative design process of a group of four teachers at the kindergarten level and four at the third-grade level, as it unfolded in the first year of this 4-year project. The groups worked in pairs, with an authoring team, and a piloting team at each grade level.

The case studies presented here provide insight into the process of teacher co-design as a means of developing teacher knowledge of CS/CT and creating integrated curriculum that is specific to the context of elementary school. Following the DBIR approach, we were broadly interested in "what works for whom, when, and under what conditions" (Fishman et al., 2013, p. 149). Specifically, the guiding questions for the research study were: (a) "How did authoring teams work together to develop and implement the initial iteration of the module?"; (b) "What issues arose for the piloting teachers who implemented the module?"; and (c) "To what extent were design ideas taken up by the authoring teams based on the piloting teachers feedback?"

BACKGROUND

CS for All is a relatively new movement in the United States. The movement gained momentum in 2016 when then President Barack Obama suggested that CS for All should become a top priority at all educational levels nationwide (Smith, 2016). At the high school level, the movement was well underway, with the National Science Foundation's (NSF) funding the development of CS curriculum at the high school level, resulting in two curricula—Computer Science Principles (Astrachan & Briggs, 2012) and Exploring Computer Science (Goode & Margolis, 2011)—and further funding the training of thousands of high school teachers to teach these curricula (Cuny, 2012). This movement is now expanding into elementary level education. In this project, the participating elementary teachers were working to integrate CT into the elementary subject area curriculum.

The construct of CT has been defined by various researchers over the last several years. Inspired by Wing's (2006) initial essay on the significance of CT, these definitions tend to focus on the practices and concepts associated with solving problems with computers. Similarly, the Massachusetts DLCS frameworks (Massachusetts Department of Elementary and Secondary Education, 2016) provide the following definition:

> Computational thinking is a problem solving process that requires people to think in new ways to enable effective use of computing to solve problems and create solutions. The capacity of computers to rapidly and precisely execute programs makes new ways of designing, creating, and problem solving possible. Computational thinking is characterized by
>
> - analyzing, modeling, and abstracting ideas and problems so people and computers can work with them;
> - designing solutions and algorithms to manipulate these abstract representations (including data structures); and
> - identifying and executing solutions (e.g., via programming). (p. 9)

Prior research related to elementary teachers' integration of CS/CT concepts into subject area curriculum indicates that teachers tend to see CT as strongly related to math (Rich et al., 2019), and that integrating CT into math instruction in 3rd and 4th grade provided a new level of student agency in the classroom, including instances in which the students had more knowledge of the technology-based activity than the teacher (Gadanidis, 2017). Elementary teachers were less readily able to see the connection between CT and science (Rich et al., 2019). However, the Next Generation Science Standards (NGSS, 2012) create an entry point for considering CT in relation to applied science. Indeed, Hestness et al. (2018) found that in their PD work with in-service elementary teachers, the NGSS framing helped teachers to see both a theoretical connection between the CT and science, as well as begin to reflect on pedagogical approaches to teaching integrated lessons. Despite such breakthroughs, teachers were concerned, generally, with the lack of time for teaching science (and by extension CT-integrated science) in their classrooms, particularly given the heavy focus in elementary school on math and English language arts (Hestness et al., 2018).

Importantly, while researchers have begun to do research with in-service elementary teachers on integrating CS/CT in their classrooms, only Gadanidis (2017) has engaged teachers in co-design of lessons. However, the report of this work focuses on student learning not on teacher's experiences. Therefore, we draw on co-design research as it has developed in the learning sciences to help us further ground our study.

Co-Design and Expansive Learning

Our definition of co-design is derived from the work of Roschelle and Penuel (2006) who write,

> Co-design [is] a highly-facilitated, team-based process in which teachers, researchers, and developers work together in defined roles to design an educational innovation, realize the design in one or more prototypes, and evaluate each prototype's significance for addressing a concrete educational need. (p. 606)

Co-design is at the heart of our RPP. Our work is rooted in and builds on studies that view the practitioner as a key participant in classroom change and innovation initiatives (Kali et al., 2015). A primary goal of DBIR in RPPs is to investigate means for bringing about "systemic change," particularly as it regards the roles and relationships of practitioners and researchers in developing, implementing, and sustaining educational innovations (Fishman et al., 2013, p. 137). Prior DBIR-based RPP studies have taken a cultural-historical activity theory (CHAT) approach to investigating educational change (O'Neill, 2016; Severance et al., 2016). CHAT is a comprehensive approach to investigating the complexity of system change initiatives, such as the one undertaken here. Penuel et al. (2016) describe CHAT as an approach that

> assume(s) the situatedness of human action, the centrality of cultural mediation, the need to take seriously the study of the history of the process under study, and a focus on social dynamics within changing institutions and communities. (p. 490)

Our 4-year RPP seeks to enable system-wide curricular change at the elementary level.

Engeström (2015), through the theory of expansive learning, is well known for having substantially furthered our understanding of how to use CHAT to engage in educational research focused on institutional change. This theory proceeds from two principles, one related to methodology, and one related to outcome. These two principles are double stimulation and ascending from the abstract to the concrete (Sannino et al., 2016). Double stimulation refers to the Vygotskyan research methodology of using mediational means (the second stimulus) to assist the research participant in a re-interpretation of the activity in which they are participating (the first stimulus). Re-interpretation assists in the development of higher order thinking processes (Sannino et al., 2016). Ascending from the abstract to the concrete refers to the developmental process that unfolds when an "initial simple idea is transformed into a complex form of practice" (Engeström et al., 2012). These twin principals are concerned with origination, development and transformation of ideas into practices, aided by mediational means, or tools of some sort.

This theory of expansive learning is useful for analyzing the work of the teachers in this first year of our study. Here the abstract idea of CS education for all is being transformed into new curricula and new teaching practices. This activity is being supported with conceptual tools (Sannino et al., 2016), which serve as mediating means for the teachers to engage in this work. Several conceptual tools have been used, the most notable include (a) DLCS frameworks developed and promoted by the DESE, (b) the Launch CS online course (for more information see https://launchcs .thinkific.com/courses/computational-thinking-integration-BYOD), (c) the co-design process the teachers engaged in over the course of the year, (d) the technologies to be used, and (e) a template for organizing and recording the lesson into a format that can be used by other teachers. This last conceptual tool is provided below (see Appendix) as an exemplar of the work that has come out of this project in support of CS/CT curriculum development.

Recent teacher co-design research results attest to its efficacy as a mediational means for expansive learning. Co-design supported teacher learning includes changes to pedagogical practice regarding the use and integration of technology in classrooms (Cober et al., 2015; Voogt et al., 2015), teachers' improved ability to work with classroom assessment data to enhance instruction (Glasswell et al., 2016; Matuk et al., 2015), improvement in teachers' ability to reflect on their own practice (Matuk et al., 2016), and empowerment resulting in changes in teacher's professional identities as designers (Svilha et al., 2015). Our work contributes to the field's understanding of how a scaffolded, iterative, co-design approach can facilitate the realization of new CS/CT curriculum at the elementary level and result in teacher learning and changes in pedagogical practices.

METHODS

Our research method is case study (Dyson & Genishi, 2005), in which we elucidate and analyze in detail the specific experiences of representative teams as they worked to co-design curricula. We draw on data collected from activities the teachers participated in as follows:

- all module drafts and revisions, including—initial development →
  revision before handing off to piloting teachers → revisions after
  piloting;
- reports from and activities in design team meetings—in initial development, through feedback from project members → in later meetings, through reports on implementation, feedback and discussion;
- first implementation by authoring teams and second implementation by piloting teams; and
- interviews with authoring teams and piloting teachers.

We provide detailed information on these activities below. Informed consent was obtained from all participants and pseudonyms are used for all
participants and individual schools.

Setting and Participants

Our study took place in the Springfield Public School district, a mid-size
urban district serving 11,590 students in Grades K–5. The student population is primarily Latinx (66.6% of students), with the next largest group
being Black students (18.9%), and the remainder of the students White
(10.2%), and Asian, Native American, non-Hispanic, and multi-race students (4.3%). Eighty-three percent of district students are considered high
needs, and 76.7% are economically disadvantaged. The four schools that
were part of the case studies in this chapter had student populations representative of the larger district student population. The teachers who participated in this study were recruited by our district partner, the chief information officer (CIO), through direct emails to all kindergarten and third
grade teachers. After the initial email was sent, the district CIO reached
out to teachers known to him as early adopters and frequent participants
in district technology initiatives. In Year 1, all of the participating teachers
self-identified as White teachers.

Participating teachers included five teachers who were serving as primary
coordinators of the work of the 16 design team teachers. The coordinating
teachers included an overall project manager, a technology specialist, and
three teachers who were respectively coordinating the grade level curricula design (Year 1—kindergarten and third grade, Year 2—first and fourth
grade, Year 3—second and fifth grade). Three of the coordinating teachers
worked as instructional specialists in their schools (two focusing on math,
one focusing on English language arts). Each of these five teachers were
located at a different elementary school within the district. Three of these
teachers (the project manager, the technology specialist, and one of the

grade level coordinators) had prior knowledge and experience with teaching CT concepts in their respective classrooms. The coordinating teachers were the linchpin of the project as they worked to develop the timeline for design, implementation, and re-design of the curricula, provided feedback and tools for creation (the lesson template) and learning (web sites, short PD sessions) for the participating teachers. The coordinators worked closely with the research team to convene design team meetings and overall planning meetings. In Year 1, the 16 design team teachers included eight kindergarten teachers and eight third grade teachers. Finally, special education and English language learning specialist teachers were also recruited to participate in the project, specifically to provide feedback to teachers on the design of their units from the special education and English language learning perspectives. These teachers did not participate in PD. Their focus was on issues of accessibility for students which does not require specialized content knowledge.

Participants and researchers met throughout the year in several configurations (see Table 2.1 for the project personnel). The teacher coordinators met weekly, the research team and design teams each met on a bi-monthly basis, and the three groups combined to form a larger professional learning community, which met six times over the academic year. A Microsoft TEAMS site devoted to the RPP served as a main conduit of organization, communication and collaboration on the project. For example, design team teachers were able to ask for and receive help from the coordinating teachers via this site and the research team was able to view teacher created artifacts and organize research visits to classrooms via this site. One of the teachers in the kindergarten piloting team was not able to implement the lesson due to a scheduling conflict, so she was not included in the study. The seven remaining teachers in the case studies presented here include six White females and one White male. We provide detailed information about these teachers in the results section.

TABLE 2.1 Project Personnel

Coordinating Teachers	Design Team Teachers		Research Team
	Kindergarten	3rd Grade	
Project Manager	Kindergarten	3rd Grade	PI–Computer Science Faculty
Technology Specialist	Dyad Team 1	Dyad Team 1	Co-PI–Learning Scientist
Grades K & 3 Coordinator	Dyad Team 2	Dyad Team 2	RA #1 Learning Sciences
Grades 1 & 4 Coordinator	Dyad Team 3	Dyad Team 3	RA #2 Teacher Education
Grades 2 & 5 Coordinator	Dyad Team 4	Dyad Team 4	

Professional Development and Stages of Lesson Development

In the first year of this project, elementary school teachers at the kindergarten and third grade level were recruited to participate. These teachers spent the first month of participation working closely with the coordinating teachers in design team meetings. During these meetings, the coordinating teachers introduced the concept of CT as outlined in the DLCS (discussed above), and they showcased curriculum that had already been created for a third-grade math class. This work was developed in a smaller scale grant that served as a proof of concept for the larger grant. After this first month of learning, teachers then engaged in a 40-hour PD curriculum called *Launch CS*, created by Project Lead the Way (Launch Computer Science, n.d.).

Launch CS is a collaborative online program in which teachers work together to learn the content. In this curriculum, there are eight modules covering the following topics: (a) algorithms, sequence, and programming; (b) programming and debugging; (c) decomposition and events; (d) events; (e) loops; (f) conditionals; (g) data; and (h) abstraction. In each of the modules, the program presents examples of both unplugged and computer-based activities appropriate for young children to learn the topics. For example, one unplugged activity called "Rosie's Runtime" uses a grid on the floor and specific instructions to teach children about algorithms through physical activity. Several of the kindergarten teachers in our project developed modified versions of Rosie's Runtime for their students. Launch CS was selected as the first-year PD program due to the project's need to quickly bring teacher's up to speed. The online program was a clearly defined package and teachers could work through the curriculum online after school and on weekends. The teachers collaborated in the online learning platform and in after school design team meetings.

After engaging in this PD, teachers co-designed lessons to integrate CT into the subject area curriculum. Pairs of teachers in the design team created CT integrated modules for each of the four quarters of the school year, with attention paid to creating a progressive curriculum, such that the skills learned in one quarter would be built on in subsequent quarters. Each design team was in charge of one quarter. The first iteration of the modules was developed in a narrative form in order to provide flexibility to the authoring teams to experiment in the classroom with the modules. These first CT unit iterations were then presented to the larger RPP team in a design team meeting. During this meeting, RPP members asked clarifying questions and provided critical feedback to each of the authoring teams, who then revised their units based on this feedback. The revised units were implemented in the respective design teachers' classrooms. As part of the implementation, teachers kept track of what worked and what could be improved through personal note-taking and reflection. In a second large group design team meeting, teachers reported on the success of their implementations and discussed plans for revision. Teachers then took a few weeks to revise their lessons at which point they handed them off to another design team for further piloting.

The next phase of the lesson development incorporated the piloting teachers' experience. After this second implementation, a third large group design team meeting was held, where teachers met and provided feedback to one another on the implementations. The researchers, coordinating teachers, and specialist teachers also provided feedback on enacted and written curriculum. The research team attended all of the second implementations in all classrooms. Their feedback was based both on classroom observations and review of the written version of the unit. The design teams revised their units based on this feedback, and a third round of implementation was completed. The fourth and last design team meeting occurred at the end of the school year—and final revisions to the unit were completed over the summer. Table 2.2 provides the timeline as described.

Data Sources

The data sources for the case studies reported here were derived from two sets of teachers at each grade level, the authoring teams and the piloting teachers. For the purposes of this chapter, we elected to focus on two illustrative cases. We selected these cases through research team discussions that sought to balance representativeness across grade levels. At the kindergarten level, we elected to analyze the design and development of the fourth quarter lesson; from the third grade level, we chose the second quarter lesson. As noted above, due to scheduling issues, only one member of the kindergarten piloting team implemented the lesson in the second implementation.

We observed the piloting of the modules in the second implementation, wrote field notes, gathered video and audio data of classroom instruction and interviews of both the authoring and the piloting teams. The authoring teams were responsible for all revisions to the modules, and the modules went through various drafts. Along with the various draft versions of the module, including the original narrative abstract and the drafts of the completed module template, we collected accompanying materials, such as graphic organizers and worksheets, teacher reflections recorded after module implementation, classroom photographs, and video and audio recordings of design team meetings.

To process these data, video logs of classroom teaching observations were created, and all audio files (design team meetings and teacher interviews) were professionally transcribed and further reviewed for accuracy by

TABLE 2.2 Timeline of Project Activities

Oct/Nov/Dec	January	February	March	April	May/June
Participant Recruitment, Design Team Formation and Planning, Computational Thinking (CT) Computational Thinking (CT) Initial Co-Design	1st Feedback Oriented Design Team Meeting (World Café), Minor Revisions 1st Classroom Implementation Data Collection (field notes)	2nd Feedback Oriented Design Team Meeting First Full Revisions Completed, Data Collection (modules, field notes)	2nd Classroom Implementation (Pilot, new teachers, new classroom) Data Collection (video/audio of classroom enactments, field notes, interviews, modules)	3rd Feedback Oriented Design Team Meeting Second Full Revisions Completed Data Collection (field notes)	3rd Classroom Implementation (pilot, new teachers, new classroom) 4th Feedback Oriented Design Team Meeting Second Full Revisions Completed, Data Collection (video/audio of classroom enactments, field notes, interviews, modules)

our team. For the purposes of this study, the primary sources of data were the various iterations of the modules and the interviews with the teachers. The video files were used as reference and for triangulation purposes (to see how it happened in the class). Photographs are presented as figures to illustrate enacted lessons.

Data Analysis

The data were analyzed using content and narrative analysis (Riessman, 1993). The content analysis focused on describing the content of the modules created by the teachers as well as analysis of the design team meeting discussions. Content analysis helped us to build a picture of how the modules changed over time. We used narrative analysis to help us make sense of the design team teachers' processes and integrate the piloting teachers' experiences to reveal how they worked to iteratively design the curriculum. After independent review of the various data sources, the researchers met on a weekly basis to present and discuss observations in order to develop a deeper understanding of the teachers' experiences.

All of the authors of this chapter were active participants in the data collection process (classroom visits, writing of field notes, attendance at design team meetings, and interviewing of teachers). In this way, the team had intimate knowledge of the design team experience in developing the modules since project inception. These working relationships strongly supported the analysis phase of the project. The researchers sought to build an understanding of the various challenges teachers faced and the solutions they developed in creating the modules.

RESULTS AND DISCUSSION

Here we present our content and narrative analysis of each of the case studies. For each of the integrated-CT modules, we begin by introducing the teachers and presenting basic information about the module, and then we present analysis of the teachers' modes of working together, including revision suggestions, in order to co-design the lessons.

Case Study #1—Kindergarten Quarter Four Lesson— The Plant Life Cycle

The kindergarten authoring team consisted of Ms. Sadler and Ms. Ellis of Braddock Elementary School. Ms. Sadler was a second-year teacher with a master's degree. She started her current job after working in the private pre-school sector for approximately 10 years. Ms. Ellis was a third-year teacher with a master's degree. The pilot was conducted by Ms. Hatch at Baines Elementary School. Ms. Hatch had been teaching kindergarten for 4 years. She had been a paraprofessional teacher for 7 years and she had taught in a private pre-school for 8 years prior to that. Baines Elementary has similar demographics to the district as a whole (described above).

The authoring team chose to integrate the CT concepts of creating an algorithm and debugging into a science lesson that they regularly enacted with their respective students. This science lesson was "The Plant Life Cycle." Typically, this lesson was taught using a book, such as *Pumpkin, Pumpkin* (Titherington, 1986), which depicts the life cycle of a plant from seedling to fully formed pumpkin. Table 2.3 presents the third iteration of the objectives/goals, knowledge, skills, and essential questions the authoring team developed to guide student inquiry in this module. These elements serve as a representation of the full module, as space does not allow us to present the full module. See Table 2.3 for the lesson template to see which elements are not represented.

When the authors, Ms. Sadler and Ms. Ellis, were asked how they developed the module, they discussed some criteria they used while creating it, as well as how they incorporated feedback from the piloting teacher. The original criteria involved the integration of the CT concepts of algorithms and debugging into an existing, already familiar science module. Revisions after receiving feedback involved keeping the module concise and making the module more flexible in order to address issues of context and differentiation.

Integrating CT Into an Existing Module

The authors chose to integrate aspects of CT into a science module called "The Plant Life Cycle," which was taught every year at the kindergarten level in the fourth quarter of the year. The sequential nature of the plant life cycle leant itself to a computational approach. That is to say, students could conceptualize the plant life cycle algorithmically. In the lesson developed, students used Bee-Bots, programmable floor robots, to sequence a pumpkin plant life cycle, elements of which were drawn on a poster laid on the floor (see Figure 2.1). If the program directed the Bee-Bot in the wrong sequence, the students had the opportunity to debug the program. The teachers selected this science unit because they were familiar with it, as Ms. Sadler noted, "We already had that foundation there [how to teach the plant life cycle] so we could really hone in on the stuff that we were still learning about, too." In this way, the selection of a regularly taught science unit for CT integration supported both teacher and student learning.

TABLE 2.3 Kindergarten Quarter 4 Lesson—The Plant Lifecycle

Lesson 1

Objectives/Goals	Knowledge (students should know)	Skills (students should be able to do)	Essential Questions
• Students will be able to discuss the basic lifecycle of a plant.	• Students should know different parts of a plant. • Students will have a basic understanding of the stages of a plant's lifecycle. • Students will know the stages of a plant's lifecycle and the order they go in. • Students will have a basic understanding of a sequence.	• Students should be able to sequence the steps of the plant life cycle.	• What are the steps of the life cycle of a plant? • What is the correct order of the steps in the plant life cycle?

Lesson 2

Objectives/Goals	Knowledge	Skills	Essential Questions
• Students will be able to sequence the events in a plant life cycle • Students will be able to sequence a Bee-Bot	• The sequence of plant life cycle	• Identify plant life cycle • Identify plant needs	• What is the sequence of the plant life cycle? • How do we sequence a Bee-Bot?

(continued)

TABLE 2.3   Kindergarten Quarter 4 Lesson – The Plant Lifecycle (continued)

Lesson 1		
Objectives/Goals	Knowledge (students should know)	Skills (students should be able to do)
		Essential Questions
Lesson 3		
Objectives/Goals	Knowledge	Skills
• Use Bee-Bot to sequence plant life cycle correctly.	• The sequence of the plant life cycle • How to program the Bee-Bot	• Sequence the events of a plant life cycle • Make the Bee-Bot go from one place to another
		Essential Questions
		• What is the correct order of plant life cycle? • How do I get the Bee-Bot to go from box to box?
Lesson 4		
Objectives/Goals	Knowledge	Skills
• Student will be able to identify bugs in Bee-Bot sequence. • Student will be able to discuss and predict how "bugs" would affect plant.	• The correct sequence of the plant lifecycle. • The importance of checking their work in order to find errors in the sequence.	• How to sequence Bee-Bot. • How to adjust the program Bee-Bot to fix the bug. • How to check their work in order to identify an error in the sequence.
		Essential Questions
		• How do bugs affect the sequence of a program? • How do "bugs" affect the lifecycle, or sequence, of a plant?

Figure 2.1 A kindergarten student programs the Bee-Bot to follow a sequence.

Keeping the Module Concise

As a result of interactions with the piloting teacher, Ms. Hatch, the authoring team realized that their module could be more concise. Specifically, the team reflected more on the timing of their module during the school year. The authoring team created a lesson for the fourth quarter of the year. Therefore, assuming that Bee-Bot programming would have been introduced in previous quarters, there would be no need to teach students how to use the Bee-Bot. As Ms. Sadler noted in our interview with her, "So that was the big piece of the feedback that we don't need to spend so much time explicitly teaching the technology. They'll already know it." Based on this feedback, the authoring team reduced their module from six lessons to four.

Making the Module More Flexible: Context and Differentiation

Ms. Hatch provided further feedback to the authoring team regarding designing the module to take into consideration different contexts and the need for instructional differentiation. For example, she suggested that the decision on which picture book to use (originally *Pumpkin, Pumpkin,*

Titherington, 1986) could be left to the implementing teacher. This would allow the teacher to consider their own context and which book might work best for their students or for the season.

The issue of differentiation arose for Ms. Hatch when she realized that her students would have difficulty drawing directional arrows as required in Lesson 2. The authoring team planned to have students draw arrows on a worksheet to show forward, backward, right and left and program the Bee-Bot to follow the sequence on the worksheet. However, the drawing of arrows proved difficult for some of the kindergarten students and so Ms. Hatch did not have her students draw arrows. Instead, she created worksheets and premade arrows for her students. After coming up with the idea of providing students with these supports, the authoring team took up her suggestion/feedback. Indeed, Ms. Ellis also noted that her students had found it challenging to draw arrows:

> One of the groups that we got feedback from, they had taken what we wrote and they changed the worksheets that we made, and they made their own version, and the version that they made was much better than the one I made...my kids couldn't really draw arrows. So, the second group [piloting team] that did our lesson, they had premade cut-out arrows so all the kids had to do was place them. It was a very simple tweak and it just made all the difference.

Likewise, Ms. Hatch developed a way of differentiating the main activity in Lesson 3. The authoring teachers originally had all the students work with a poster board of the plant life cycle, laid out as a grid, with the first element (picture of a seed) in the lower left square, and an image of the final flowering plant in the upper right square. Students were meant to create an algorithm that would move the Bee-Bot along this poster board, moving from image to image in the correct sequence. However, Ms. Hatch found that this activity did not meet the varying ability levels of her students, so she created two additional flower/plant life cycle poster board grids: one that included a few unnecessary steps the students would have to navigate the Bee-Bot around, and a third with many unnecessary steps and a more challenging path. Figure 2.2 presents the images of each poster board grid, side-by-side. After creating and using three different poster boards for her students, Ms. Hatch suggested this differentiation to the authoring team and they took up her suggestion. As Ms. Ellis noted:

> At the end of our lesson we have the kids using the technology to show their knowledge of the plant life cycle. So, one of the other groups suggested we do a[n] above grade level board that they can use, and an on grade level board, and a below grade level board. We did not think of that, but it was a great idea. So that was just something that we took from them to differentiate. And that was a great idea.

Figure 2.2   Three poster boards of the plant life cycle at varying levels of difficulty.

In the teachers' design experience of the kindergarten Quarter 4 module, teacher learning was supported through co-design activities that included integration of CT concepts into well-known lessons, classroom implementation, critical analysis, feedback, and revision. The authoring teams' original work emanated from their knowledge of their own students. However, by sharing the lesson with the piloting teacher, who had a different classroom, and a different view of learning, the module was amended and made more appropriate for other teachers and classroom situations. Teacher learning, in this instance, included not only learning about CT, how to integrate it in a unit, and how to teach it, but also learning to carefully consider the range of students and potential learning environments. If teachers involved in designing curriculum consider only their own contexts, the usefulness of their work may be limited. In this study, once the lessons moved to the piloting phase in other schools, the problems of context and differentiation were exposed and could be directly addressed. Indeed, the design process was set up in such a way that it facilitated the provision of feedback and encouraged discussion of classroom differences, leading to an improved module.

Case Study #2—Third Grade Quarter 2 Lessons—Writing Precise Instructions

The third-grade authoring team included Ms. Murray and Mr. Nielson of Pinckney Elementary School. Ms. Murray had been teaching for 10 years with 6 years at the third-grade level. The first year of the project was her first year of teaching only math and science. In Pinckney Elementary School, the third-grade teachers rotate so Ms. Murray taught all of the third grade students. Because she met the students more frequently, within the authoring team, she was the one who piloted the unit. Her partner, Mr. Nielson was in his second year of teaching after switching careers. Prior to his move into teaching, he had worked for 13 years for a large firm as a hydrologist and wetland scientist. The module was then piloted in Thomas Elementary School by Ms. Miel and Ms. Cooper. Ms. Miel, a second-year teacher with training in special education, was the primary teacher in the third-grade special education inclusion classroom. Ms. Cooper, a special education teacher with 11 years of experience, was a co-teacher of the class consisting of 24 students and following a push-in-pull-out model. The two women worked closely as a team, and in recent years both have been awarded teacher of excellence awards.

The third-grade, Quarter 2, module consisted of an engineering design challenge focused on writing precise instructions for building a two-story structure able to bear weight. The lessons embedded algorithm development and debugging concepts. In the course of the module, one group of students wrote instructions for building the structure, then the instructions were given to another group and that group had to build the structure and find the bugs in the instructions. The original group then made final revisions on the instructions, built the structure and tested it. Table 2.4 presents the objectives/goals, knowledge, skills, and essential questions that guided student inquiry in this module.

Open-Ended Design Approach

In developing the module, Ms. Murray and Mr. Nielson took from CS the importance of precise instructions in coding, programming and writing of algorithms and integrated it into an engineering design task in a science context. Ms. Murray explained that the module was about

> using accurate and precise language so that anyone that doesn't know what they're doing could complete that... it also included debugging, because when they [the students] got someone else's directions and their structure failed, they then had to look at it and say, "Okay, now what part of this direction isn't specific enough? What do we have to edit? What do we have to revise?"

In discussing their initial criteria for creating the lesson, the authoring team specified an open-ended approach in which they were able to try things out and revise, before handing off to another team. Once they handed the lesson off and received feedback from the piloting team, they made a number of changes including revising an activity meant to activate student prior knowledge (an activator), differentiating the lessons, and adding a

TABLE 2.4 Third Grade Quarter 2 Lesson—Writing Precise Instructions

Lesson 1

Objectives/Goals	Knowledge (students should know)	Skills (students should be able to do)	Essential Questions
• Students Will Be Able To (SWBAT) write directions to successfully draw a house using specific directions.	• Objects will not move when equal forces are applied to both sides showing that each force cancels the other out. • How an object will move when an unbalanced force act on it.	• Define a simple design problem that reflects a need or want. • Using assorted models to distinguish why some objects move and some objects stay in place. • Explaining how friction affects an object's motion. • Identifying an object's motion by examining models of different forces. • Illustrating how forces acting on an object can affect its motion.	• How can unbalanced forces change an object's motion? • How do you evaluate a solution to a design problem?

Lesson 2

Objectives/Goals	Knowledge	Skills	Essential Questions
• SWBAT plan and draw a design for a structure that can hold a certain weight for 15 seconds. *Note:* In these lessons we are attempting to implement the 5E constructivist learning cycle; helping students build their own understanding from experiences and new ideas. Considering this, students' buildings may not hold the requisite weight and fail. This is okay. Students should be	• Objects will not move when equal forces are applied to both sides showing that each force cancels the other out. • How an object will move when an unbalanced force act on it.	• Define a simple design problem that reflects a need or want. • Using assorted models to distinguish why some objects move and some objects stay in place. • Explaining how friction affects an object's motion. • Identifying an object's motion by examining models of different forces. • Illustrating how forces acting on an object can affect its motion.	• How can unbalanced forces change an object's motion? • How do you evaluate a solution to a design problem?

(continued)

TABLE 2.4 Third Grade Quarter 2 Lesson—Writing Precise Instructions (continued)

Objectives/Goals	Knowledge	Skills	Essential Questions
allowed to struggle through the process. Should their structure fail to hold the weight, they should improve it based upon their experience (Iterate step—Engineering Design Process). The teacher should facilitate the process. Students who are used to this model understand that failure is part of the learning process. Students who are not accustomed to this may feel badly. The teacher should be aware of this possibility and be prepared to explain the process to the student. The student should never feel badly about failing in this context.			

Lesson 3 & Lesson 4

Objectives/Goals	Knowledge	Skills	Essential Questions
• SWBAT follow written instructions to complete a 3D model. • SWBAT revise and edit written instructions for clarity and precision.	• Objects will not move when equal forces are applied to both sides showing that each force cancels the other out. • How an object will move when an unbalanced force act on it. • Recognize the importance of precise language when giving direction.	• Define a simple design problem that reflects a need or want. • Using assorted models to distinguish why some objects move and some objects stay in place. • Explaining how friction affects an object's motion. • Identifying an object's motion by examining models of different forces. • Illustrating how forces acting on an object can affect its motion.	• How can unbalanced forces change an object's motion? • How do you evaluate a solution to a design problem?

lesson specific to writing instructions. Key to the iterative co-design was the authoring team's openness and willingness to change the lesson based on feedback, resulting in a substantially changed lesson.

The authoring team started by working with a basic concept and an attitude of seeing where the idea would take them. Mr. Nielson explained,

> With the first lesson, we had an idea of what we wanted to do, and we came up with a general idea, and were just going to run with it. We didn't get very specific at first with lots of different supports, throwing all kinds of supports at it, because we wanted to see where we actually needed supports and where the kids would actually struggle.

After this initial piloting by Ms. Murray the authoring team made revisions using the template and then passed the module on to Ms. Miel and Ms. Cooper at Thomas Elementary School. Because Ms. Miel and Ms. Cooper were co-teachers in the same classroom, both of them experienced the instruction, observed the student responses, and discussed the feedback they would later provide.

New Activator Activity

After Ms. Murray piloted the module, the authoring team realized they needed an activator to begin to focus the students on the importance of writing precise instructions. Without first piloting it, the authors added an activator that they drew from Launch CS. The activator involved the teacher giving two sets of directions to the students to draw a smiley face. The first set of directions was intentionally unclear, so it would be expected that the students' smiley faces would all look very different. It was then expected that with the second set of directions, which was more detailed and more precise, the students would produce smiley faces that looked more alike. This activator didn't work. The researcher observed that the students were having trouble following the more precise set of instructions. They were not used to this kind of activity and many struggled with drawing.

Ms. Miel, the lead teacher who piloted the module in the third grade classroom at Thomas Elementary School, said,

> When I looked and I saw nobody was understanding based on the smiley face activity, that activity did not help them see the difference between my instructions. One of my higher students recognized "Okay, her directions were very precise the second time." He said, "Well the first ones were not detailed, the second ones were," but he was probably one of the only ones who understood that.

In the moment, then, Ms. Miel improvised a different activity, in which the students had to give her precise directions to make it to the door of the classroom, open it and leave the room. Ms. Miel added, "On the fly I did that so that they could understand the importance of precise instructions a little bit more." So, when Ms. Cooper and Ms. Miel provided the feedback on the activator, the authoring team took it up and made it the activator in the next draft of the module.

Differentiation, Adding Visuals, and a Hands-On Component

In the module, there were a number of revisions made in the lessons to help address the need to differentiate. In the revision process, the authoring team added what they called "supporting" materials to provide access to concepts and ideas. Following feedback from Ms. Miel and Ms. Cooper, the authors created a PowerPoint presentation. The slides presented key terms with definitions and visuals, including photographs of an engineer, an architect, and a blueprint, an example anchor chart with a mathematical algorithm, an illustration of a simple structure with floors holding weight, a target with arrows in the bullseye to signify precision, a cartoon bug in a "not-allowed" symbol and a computer code with a section highlighted as a "bug" in the program.

Also in response to a request made by Ms. Miel and Ms. Cooper, the authors added a hands-on component to give the students the option to work with the building materials as they wrote the instructions for building the structure. Mr. Nielson explained that in the original plan, "We had them planning the building ahead of time and looking at the equipment or the stuff they were going to use to build it. And that didn't work . . . the other teachers found that [the students] were unable to kind of project what it was going to look like before they built it." Ms. Cooper, as the Special Education teacher, felt strongly that some students would benefit from working with the materials first–to handle them first–in order to imagine how they might build their structure. As they were teaching the module, Ms. Miel and Ms. Cooper also thought about the materials themselves and suggested that students could use Strawbuilders in building the structure. Mr. Nielson later explained,

> They [the piloting team] had some children who had some other challenges and they had a hard time building it as well. She recommended something called Strawbuilders. You could definitely build a successful structure fairly easily [with Strawbuilders], and so we actually included that in our last round as something that, maybe a way to differentiate this. So, I included that in the last one. That would actually help children who have a hard time manipulating things. It'd be really easy for them to build it together, they wouldn't have to worry about breaking off clay or anything like that.

In the revised module, then, the authors differentiated through providing an option to handle the materials while writing instructions, through potential group and peer collaboration, and by adding the option of using other materials, like Strawbuilders.

Adding a Lesson About Writing Instructions

In response to the difficulties the students had in the writing of instructions, the authors added a lesson that scaffolded how to write precise instructions. Mr. Nielson explained, "Originally all the children floundered with the writing, because it was almost directionless." The authors had assumed that the students would not have as much trouble with writing directions, so when the students struggled, they said they knew they needed more "supports." In the initial expanded version of the module, the authors had thought a graphic organizer and a word bank would help, but Ms. Miel and Ms. Cooper suggested that they needed to scaffold how to write. In the revised module, the authors then added a lesson in which the students would work together with the teacher to jointly construct a set of precise instructions for drawing (not building) a house. The authors created an example of a drawing and a set of directions, but the directions for the teacher allowed a great deal of flexibility and room to respond to the various needs and ideas of their students in the joint construction.

Openness and Willingness to Revise

Key to making the revisions in the module was the openness and willingness of the authoring team to learn from experience and listen to feedback and suggestions. Ms. Murray explained,

> After we got feedback from the other teachers that taught it, we almost did a complete overhaul. We deleted the activator. We took an activator that they had used. We added additional resources that they had suggested that we use. We changed some of the materials around also. So, we made a pretty big change when it...after their feedback to us. It took us quite a bit of time.

Mr. Nielson described it in this way:

> We changed everything based upon what they said...We've tried to incorporate as much as we possibly could...Whatever didn't work, we broke it and put something new in or we reordered things so it made more sense. From the start, we didn't assume anything would work and we were willing to throw everything out at any minute. When something did work, we kept it. When something didn't work, we changed it, we threw it out the window, and we adjusted everything we possibly could to a point.

Ms. Murray noted, "Their feedback had a big impact on us. There were some things they suggested that we just felt like, you know what, it really needs to be in there." This was particularly true with some of the scaffolding of how to write instructions. Ms. Murray stressed, "We definitely added more supports that we didn't even think the students would need."

There was even an openness and eager willingness to make radical changes in the module. At the heart of the module was the engineering challenge to build a two-story structure with floors that would bear a certain amount of weight. Mr. Nielson explained,

> The big recipe of this thing was to have an engineering challenge accompany a direction writing portion. That was the big thing. So, the engineering challenge we selected was like a popular one that the kids like to do. They like to build these little buildings. In my class they did, so that's why I selected it. However, when we started thinking about how many different ways you can build a building, especially if you're letting the kids be as creative as possible, then the algorithm can be equally challenging. Therefore, the language that has to support that algorithm has to be massive. So now your word bank is through the roof, which is kind of unrealistic. So, we almost scrapped it...And we talked to the coordinators about this at our meeting with them, "Should we just completely scrap the building part of it and bring in another engineering challenge that's simpler?" But, the coordinators thought the building of the building was really engaging, which it is. The kids really like doing that.

Such a willingness to make changes led to significant changes in the module in both the first and second iterations. The author's openness to, even desire for, feedback and suggestions motivated the authors to reconsider all aspects of the module. Changes were made in the module to more clearly communicate the intended focus/objective of the module, to simplify some parts, to make the organization of the module more logical, to provide terms and definitions, to clarify roles, to provide possible answers to questions, and to scaffold the writing of the instructions. Ms. Murray and Mr. Nielson modified almost every section of every lesson plan template, and even added a lesson focused solely on writing instructions.

Teaching, Learning, and Classroom Culture

Teachers have different views of what it means to teach and how students learn. Such views or beliefs influence the decisions teachers make and the ways they develop and establish classroom practices (or their classroom culture). In some cases, larger institutional demands might also dictate the classroom practices. In order to implement the modules, the teachers interpret the lessons through (the institutional lens and) their own personal lens. Classrooms have shapes and forms; they have pedagogical approaches, participation structures, use of certain materials, and expectations as to how students should behave in the classroom. There are different ideas about what students should be allowed to be/do in the classroom and about the value of individual or group work. There may be some philosophical approach at the school level or at the district level, and these might even be heavy-handed, in that they are imposed on teachers. But, ultimately, the teacher develops the culture and establishes the routines and classroom practices. Classroom culture is very specific to the teacher. So, it's about what the teacher does.

Ms. Murray and Mr. Nielson shared certain aspects of classroom culture and, therefore, designed the modules in that space together. To the degree that the piloting team shared similar notions of teaching and learning with the authoring team, the ensuing piloting, feedback, and revision worked to reinforce or strengthen those aspects of the module. On the other hand, when certain aspects of the module came into conflict with the ideas or practices of the piloting teachers, this created a potentially productive tension, motivating dialogue and discussion, and leading potentially to revisions in the module.

In Ms. Miel and Ms. Cooper's class, tensions arose in response to the way the students were expected to work together in groups, participating in the iterative design engineering process, to write instructions and build the structure. The students in Ms. Miel and Ms. Cooper's class were accustomed to asking the teachers for help and were not accustomed to relying on other group members for assistance. Ms. Cooper explained, "Our class has trouble being independent [like] when we weren't providing them help and they had to go into their groups and seek that help." Mr. Nielson discussed the tension this way: "It sounded like the people who piloted the second round were a little more hands on than we would have been." An underlying idea in the piloting classroom was that the teachers provide assistance, and the established classroom practice was that the students turned to the teachers and not their peers for assistance. Ms. Murray explained, "But in their classrooms, they said that, they made reference to the fact that they always run to help their students. When their students are failing, they go there to give them the answer." Because the students were not accustomed to the kind of group work that was part of this module, the students struggled and the teachers felt frustrated.

More tension arose out of what was at the heart of the module. The authoring team shared established classroom practices concerning students working together, through trial and error, to create something. The students in Mr. Nielson and Ms. Murray's classes were accustomed to being given engineering challenges in which failure was expected and their participation in the iterative design process was more important than successfully completing the design challenge. However, this type of pedagogical practice was not typically enacted by the piloting teachers; hence, their students became frustrated with the activity. To address differences in pedagogical practice, and to support teachers in developing a new engineering practice that values failure, the authoring teams revised the module for the third iteration by adding a note about it. So, along with the additional lesson that would help teachers and students focus on the writing of precise instructions, the authors added a clarifying comment for teachers in the second lesson as part of the objective (see Table 2.3, "Lesson 2: Objectives/Goals"), this comment on the importance of failure to learning in engineering design activities reflects the challenges and possibilities of co-design as a means of developing integrated-CT lessons for elementary school.

Co-design activities force teachers to grapple with other views of teaching and learning and to come into contact with other classroom cultures. As a result of co-design, teachers have the chance to reflect on their own approaches to teaching and learning, towards the goal of expanding their own understanding and their own practice. These possibilities hold great promise for supporting the integration of CS/CT curricula in elementary school. In this chapter, we have presented evidence for the efficacy of co-design to not only result in improved lessons, but also to support teachers' professional growth.

Teaching is a dynamic and adaptive activity; it requires deep consideration of the context, including the policies of the district, the needs of the students, and integration of innovations in practice (Darling-Hammond & Bransford, 2005). In this project, we have sought not only to engage teachers in the development of lessons that integrate CS/CT, but also to build lessons that can be adapted to their particular context. This outcome is seen most plainly in the results concerning design revisions that called for flexibility in materials to be used and in differentiation, which occurred in both the kindergarten and the 3rd grade design teams. We view teachers as professionals who are able to flexibly adapt curriculum to the teaching context (Lin et al., 2005); the goal with this co-design work was to create modules that are flexible such that they can be differentiated for various contexts.

NEXT STEPS

Co-design has promise as an expansive learning practice for in-service teacher professional learning of CS & CT concepts. The mediational means provided to the teachers, the Launch CS course, the DLCS frameworks, the technology, the lesson plan template along with the process of iterative design, provided teachers with strong supports for developing concrete curricular materials and pedagogical practices to support student learning. A logical next step of this work is deeper analysis of student learning with the modules. Our group is working on two approaches to understanding student learning with these modules: the first is the creation of clinical interview materials to understand students' incidental learning, prior to formal instruction. Additionally, we are conducting artifact interviews with children to examine what they have learned through engagement with the curriculum. Both of these approaches are robust (Kuhn, 2002), yet time consuming methods of assessment. Therefore, work on teacher noticing as a form of assessment is also warranted (Francisco & Maher, 2011). Teacher noticing of student CT will allow them to make supportive and/or corrective comments to students in-situ, to further support children's understanding of and engagement with CS/CT concepts.

The results of our study suggest two other important next steps. First, with regard to teacher learning and the process of co-design, our results indicated that teachers' ideas about pedagogical practice vary and an iterative design activity can help to surface these differences. In our second case study, the authoring team was more willing to allow students to struggle and fail with the engineering task than the piloting team. This created a tension for the authoring team as to how to proceed with the module design. An important next step for us is to work with teachers in PD to deepen discussions of various pedagogical practices, including the rationale for selecting certain practices at certain times. Such conversations allow for important inter-design team professional learning. One of the third-grade authoring team teachers worked for years as an engineer, so his knowledge of professional practice informs his pedagogical practice and supports student learning in engineering. These pedagogical ideas and rationales are important to share.

A second important result from our study regards the need to design flexibly, such that adopting teachers are able to adapt and differentiate the lessons for their own classroom contexts. This need for flexibility was identified in the co-design experience in both case studies, in which teachers initially designed with their own students in mind. We argue that an important next step regarding flexibility in design revolves around addressing issues of equity in design. While differentiating instruction is, in and of itself, an equitable approach to curriculum design, it is not the end of designing for equity. An important next step in this work with teachers is to support not only to design with differentiation in mind, but also to design with gender and culture differences in mind.

Toward that end, in our own work we have created specific PD activities to help teachers think more about culture in the CS/CT classroom. These activities include reflecting on and discussing various learning situations that are more or less supportive of various groups of students (e.g., the use of gendered language in referring to inorganic robotic devices; Sullivan et al., 2019). The goal of these activities is to help our subsequent cohorts of teachers broaden their view of equitable practices in teaching and learning, such that we truly create CS curriculum for all.

APPENDIX
Lesson Template for CT-Integrated Modules

Module Authors: Grade: ____ Content Area: _____ Lesson # ____ of ____

DLCS Standards:	*Pacing:* (Include content areas, units, and specific times of year) Which content and what unit?
Content Standards:	What month would you see this in?

Objectives/Goals:

Knowledge: (Students should know . . .)	*Skills:* (Students should be able to . . .)
Can be pulled from the UPGs, should connect the objectives and standards of the lesson.	Can be pulled from the UPGs, should connect the objectives and standards of the lesson.

Essential Questions: (Can be specific to the lesson or overarching the entire module (can be found in the content area UPGS.)

Vocabulary	**Resources Needed**	
Content Vocabulary (definition)	Content Resources (books, articles, websites, handouts, etc.)	Web Resources (URLs, scratch, code.org, etc.)
Computer Science Vocabulary (vocabulary definition)	Hardware (computer, webcam, microphone, speakers, micro:bit, etc.)	Robotics and other manipulatives: (markers, snapcubes, etc.)

Plan for Instruction		

Crafting: (Teacher Lead Instruction) Presentation of new material—Include script for lesson.

Teacher Role	**Student Role**	**Checks for Understanding**
What is the teacher doing?	What are the students doing? (How will you monitor student understanding throughout the entire lesson?)	
Composing Meaning: (Independent) Students working by themselves, with partners, or in groups—Include script for lesson.		Checks for Understanding
What is the teacher doing?	What are the students doing?	(how will you monitor student understanding throughout the entire lesson?)
Processing: (How will students reflect on today's lesson and make connections to the objectives/goals and essential questions?)—Include script for lesson.		Checks for Understanding
What is the teacher doing?	What is the teacher doing?	(how will you monitor student understanding throughout the entire lesson?)

Assessment: (how will you know students reached lesson goals? How will students be involved in ongoing assessment? How will students assess themselves?)

ACKNOWLEDGMENTS

The work reported in this chapter is supported by a grant from the National Science Foundation DRL-1837086 and a grant from the Google CS-ER program. Any opinions, findings, and conclusions or recommendations expressed in this material are those of the authors and do not necessarily reflect the views of the National Science Foundation or Google.

REFERENCES

Astrachan, O., & Briggs, A. (2012). The CS principles project. *ACM Inroads, 3*(2), 38–42.

Caeli, E. N., & Yadav, A. (2019). Unplugged approaches to computational thinking: A historical perspective. *Tech Trends, 64*, 29–36. https://doi.org/10.1007/s11528-019-00410-5

Cober, R., Tan, E., Slotta, J., & So, H. J. (2015). Teachers as participatory designers: Two case studies with technology-enhanced learning environments. *Instructional Science, 43*, 203–228. https://doi.org/10.1007/s11251-014-9339-0

Cuny, J. (2012). Transforming high school computing: A call to action. *ACM Inroads, 3*(2), 32–36.

Cuny, J. (2016, March 2–5). *Catching the wave.* Proceedings of the 47th ACM Technical Symposium on Computing Science Education.

Darling-Hammond, L., & Bransford, J. D., (2005). *Preparing teachers for a changing world: What teachers should learn and be able to do.* Jossey-Bass.

Dyson, A. H., & Genishi, C. (2005). *On the case: Approaches to language and literacy research.* Teachers College Press.

Engeström, Y. (2015). *Learning by expanding: An activity theoretical approach to developmental research* (2nd ed.). Cambridge University Publishing.

Engeström, Y., Nummijoki, J., & Sannino, A. (2012). Embodied germ cell at work: Building an expansive concept of physical mobility in home care. *Mind, Culture and Activity, 19*(3), 287–309. https://doi.org/10.1080/10749039.2012.688177

Fishman, B. J., Penuel, W. R., Allen, A. R., Cheng, B. H., & Sabelli, N. (2013). Design-based implementation research: An emerging model for transforming the relationship of research and practice. *National Society for the Study of Education, 112*(2), 136–156.

Francisco, J. M., & Maher, C. A. (2011). Teachers attending to students' mathematical reasoning: Lessons from and after-school research program. *Journal of Mathematics Teacher Education, 14*, 49–66. https://doi.org/10.1007/s10857-010-9144-x

Gadanidis, G. (2017). Five affordances of computational thinking to support elementary mathematics education. *The Journal of Computers in Mathematics and Science Teaching, 36*(2), 143–151. http://silk.library.umass.edu/login?url=https://search.proquest.com/docview/1947584319?accountid=14572

Glasswell, K., Singh, P., & McNaughton, S. (2016). Partners in design: Co-inquiry for quality teaching in disadvantaged schools. *Australian Journal of Language and Literacy, 39*(1), 20–29.

Goode, J., & Margolis, J. (2011). Exploring computer science: A case study of school reform. *ACM Transactions on Computing Education, 11*(2), 1–12.

Hestness, E., Ketelhut, D. J., McGinnis, J. R., & Plane, J. (2018). Professional knowledge building within an elementary teacher professional development experience on computational thinking in science education. *Journal of Technology and Teacher Education, 26*(3), 411–435. http://silk.library.umass.edu/login?url=https://search.proquest.com/docview/2111121749?account id=14572

Kali, Y., McKenney, S., & Sagy, O. (2015). Teachers as designers of technology enhanced learning. *Instructional Science, 43*, 173–179. https://doi.org/10.1007/s11251-014-9343-4

Kuhn, D. (2002). A multi-component system that constructs knowledge: Insights from microgenetic study. In N. Granott & J. Parziale (Eds.), *Microdevelopment: Transition processes in development and learning* (pp. 109–130). Cambridge University Press.

Launch Computer Science. (n.d.). *Launch CS.* http://launchcs.thinkific.com

Lin, X. D., Schwartz, D. L., & Hatano, G. (2005). Toward teachers' adaptive metacognition. *Educational Psychologist, 40*(4), 245–255. https://doi.org/10.1207/s15326985ep4004_6

Massachusetts Department of Elementary and Secondary Education. (2016). *Digital learning and computer science frameworks.* http://www.doe.mass.edu/stem/dlcs/?section=planningtools

Matuk, C. F., Gerard, L., Lim-Breitbart, J., & Linn, M. C. (2016). Gathering requirements for teacher tools: Strategies for empowering teachers through co-design. *Journal of Science Teachers Education, 27*, 79–110. https://doi.org/10.1007/s10972-016-9459-2

Matuk, C. F., Linn, M. C., & Eylon, B. S. (2015). Technology to support teachers using evidence from student work to customize technology enhanced inquiry units. *Instructional Science, 43*, 229–257. https://doi.org/10.1007/s11251-014-9338-1

Next Generation Science Standards. (2012). *Next generation science standards.* https://www.nextgenscience.org/search-standards

O'Neill, D. K. (2016). Understanding design research–practice partnerships in context and time: Why learning sciences scholars should learn from cultural-historical activity theory approaches to design-based research. *Journal of the Learning Sciences, 25*, 497–502. https://doi.org/10.1080/10508406.2016.1226835

Penuel, W. R., Cole, M., & O'Neill, K. D. (2016). Introduction to the special issue. *Journal of the Learning Sciences, 25*(4), 487–496. https://doi.org/10.1080/10508406.2016.1215753

Penuel, W. R., Fishman, B. J., Cheng, B. H., & Sabelli, N. (2011). Organizing research and development at the intersection of learning, implementation and design. *Educational Researcher, 40*(7), 331–337. https://doi.org/10.3102/0013189X11421826

Resnick, M. (2009). Scratch: Programming for all. *Communications of the ACM, 52*(11), 60–67. https://doi.org/10.1145/1592761.1592779.

Rich, K. M., Yadav, A., & Schwarz, C. V. (2019). Computational thinking, mathematics, and science: Elementary teachers' perspectives on integration. *Journal of Technology and Teacher Education, 27*(2), 165–205. http://silk.library.umass.edu/login?url=https://searchproquest.com/docview/2283398869?accountid=14572

Riessman, C. K. (1993). *Narrative analysis*. SAGE Publications.

Roschelle, J., & Penuel, W. R. (2006). *Co-design of innovations with teachers: Definitions and dynamics*. Proceedings of the 7th International Conference on Learning Sciences.

Sannino, A., Engeström, Y., & Lemos, M. (2016). Formative interventions for expansive learning transformative agency. *Journal of the Learning Sciences, 25*(4), 599–633. https://doi.org/10.1080/10508406.2016.1204547

Severance, S., Penuel, W. R., Sumner, T., & Leary, H. (2016). Organizing for teacher agency in curricular co-design. *Journal of the Learning Sciences, 25*(4), 531–564. https://doi.org/10.1080/10508406.2016.1207541

Smith, M. (2016). *Computer science for all*. White House Blog. https://obamawhitehouse.archives.gov/blog/2016/01/30/computer-science-all

Sullivan, F. R., Veeragoudar, S., Tulungen, C., & Pektas, E. (2019, August 12–14). *Supporting elementary teacher's reflections on equity in cs education*. Proceedings of the International Computer Education Research Annual Conference.

Svilha, V., Reeve, R., Sagy, O., & Kali, Y. (2015). A fingerprint pattern of supports for teachers' designing of technology-enhanced learning. *Instructional Science, 43*, 283–307. https://doi.org/10.1007/s11251-014-9342-5

Titherington, J. (1986). *Pumpkin, pumpkin*. Greenwillow Books.

Voogt, J., Laferriere, T., Breuleux, A., Itow, R. C., Hickey, D. T., & McKenney, S. (2015). Collaborative design as a form of professional development. *Instructional Science, 43*, 259–282. https://doi.org/10.1007/s11251-014-9340-7

Wing, J. M. (2006). Computational thinking. *Communications of the ACM, 49*(3), 33–35.

Yadav, A., Krist, C., Good, J., & Caeli, E. N. (2018). Computational thinking in elementary classrooms: Measuring teacher understanding of computational ideas for teaching science. *Computer Science Education, 28*(4), 371–400. https://doi.org/http://dx.doi.org/10.1080/08993408.2018.1560550

Zhang, L., & Nouri, J. (2019). A systematic review of learning computational thinking through Scratch in K–9. *Computers & Education, 141*, 1–25. https://doi.org/10.1016/j.compedu.2019.103607

CHAPTER 3

PROFESSIONAL DEVELOPMENT SUPPORTING MIDDLE SCHOOL TEACHERS TO INTEGRATE COMPUTATIONAL THINKING INTO THEIR SCIENCE CLASSES

Quentin Biddy
University of Colorado

Alexandra Gendreau Chakarov
University of Colorado

Jennifer Jacobs
University of Colorado

William Penuel
University of Colorado

Mimi Recker
Utah State University

Tamara Sumner
University of Colorado

Professional Development for In-Service Teachers, pages 59–83
Copyright © 2022 by Information Age Publishing
www.infoagepub.com

ABSTRACT

We describe a professional development (PD) model that supports teachers to integrate computational thinking (CT) into middle school science and STEM classes. The model includes the collaborative design (co-design; Voogt et al., 2015) of storylines or curricular units aligned with the Next Generation Science Standards (NGSS Lead States, 2013) that use programmable sensors such as those contained on the micro:bit. Teachers spend several workshops co-designing CT-integrated storylines and preparing to implement them with their own students. As part of this process, teachers develop or modify curricular materials to ensure a focus on coherent, student driven instruction through the investigation of scientific phenomena that are relevant to the students and use sensor technology. Teachers implement the storylines and meet to collaboratively reflect on their instructional practices as well as their students' learning. Throughout this cyclical, multi-year process, teachers develop expertise in CT-integrated science instruction as they plan for and use instructional practices that align with three dimensional science teaching and foreground CT. Teachers alternate between wearing their "student hats" and their "teacher hats," in order to maintain both a student and teacher perspective as they co-design and reflect on their implementation of CT-integrated units. This chapter illustrates two teachers' experiences of the PD process over a 2-year period, including their planning, implementation, and reflection on two co-designed units.

Modern scientific inquiry increasingly depends on computation in all aspects of its enterprise. Yet in many K–12 schools computing has often been isolated in separate, elective classes, leading to inequities in opportunities to learn (Margolis et al., 2008). There is a growing push by districts in the United States to integrate computer science and computational thinking (CT) into mainstream science classes that are taken by all students. Such an approach has several advantages: it ensures that diverse students have opportunities to learn CT, it reflects the changing practices of contemporary data-driven science, and it builds on the *Framework for K–12 Science Education* and the Next Generation Science Standards (NGSS) which explicitly identify CT as one of the eight core science and engineering practices ("Using Mathematics and Computational Thinking"; NRC, 2012; NGSS Lead States, 2013).

In order to integrate CT into the K–12 curriculum, the definition of CT must be detailed enough so teachers and curriculum developers understand how to create and implement lessons and assess student understanding (Grover & Pea, 2013). Based on a synthesis of research, Weintrop and colleagues (2016) distilled four categories of CT practices in science: data practices, modeling and simulation practices, computational problem solving practices, and systems thinking practices. These categories of practices can help the education community develop a common language of this relatively elusive construct, move towards the focused development of

CT-integrated curriculum, and ultimately lead to science instruction that deeply and purposely incorporates CT.

Integrating CT into mainstream science classes that align with the NGSS is a highly demanding endeavor, which enters new conceptual and pedagogical territory for most teachers. An effective and sustainable model of professional development (PD) is needed that brings teachers together to form a professional learning community, with the goals of supporting their lesson planning, CT learning, classroom teaching, and ultimately improving student engagement and learning outcomes. Our approach is to develop and study a new PD model, called the CT-integration cycle, intended to build science and STEM teachers' capacity to create engaging and equitable student CT-integrated science learning experiences.

BACKGROUND

Our research team generated a set of focal issues that guided both our PD model and the CT-integrated units that the participating teachers helped to design and implement. Focusing on these issues ensured our work was situated within the current literature on both science and CT, as well as best practices for classroom instruction to support the learning of diverse students. The focal issues were to (a) deeply integrate multiple CT practices into mainstream science lessons; (b) incorporate performance expectations (PEs), science and engineering practices, and cross-cutting concepts as defined in the NGSS; (c) ensure that lessons are engaging, interesting, and relevant to students; (d) include place-based or locally relevant scientific investigations and activities; and (e) use a sensor platform to conduct data driven explorations of scientific phenomenon.

The goal of the NGSS is to infuse science content with practices in which students are "doing science," thus leading to instruction that is more student-driven where students can "feel like scientists." One strategy that has proven successful for ensuring that the NGSS are implemented in the intended manner is to develop storylines (Reiser, 2014) based around scientific phenomena. A scientific phenomenon is something that exists in the real world, is observable, and that accumulated scientific knowledge can help explain (NGSS Lead States, 2013), such as how the moon affects tides. Storylines serve as unit guides and are generated before writing individual lessons to ensure coherence and incremental knowledge building (Penuel & Reiser, 2018; Reiser, 2014; Shwartz et al., 2008). Of critical importance is selecting a scientific phenomenon that "anchors" the storyline to issues that are locally relevant and interesting for students, much as a driving question in project-based learning ensures student motivation and promotes deeper levels of thinking (Blumenfeld et al., 1991).

One novel way to conduct scientific investigations is through a low cost, mobile sensor platform that provides an entry point for teachers to go beyond traditional data analysis of either small, curated data sets or large, pre-existing data sets that students simply download from the Web. Sensor platforms have the potential to support several of the CT practices defined by Weintrop and colleagues (2016). For example, sensors can collect real-time environmental streams of data, such as heat, temperature, light, sound, and so forth. Also a sensor platform can be programmed to collect, filter, analyze, and display students' data. Much of the previous work on integrating CT into science classes has focused on computational modeling using simulated data sets (Sengupta et al., 2013; Tisue & Wilensky, 2004). Using these sensor platforms present an alternative pathway for the integration of CT into science classes.

Finally, research suggests that place-based investigations can offer a powerful tool for engaging learners from underrepresented groups in STEM (Anastopoulou et al., 2012). Place-based investigations focus on personally or locally relevant phenomena or activities that address issues meaningful to the local community. Students consider questions such as, "Why here?" and "So what?" that provide a context for the phenomenon they are learning about (Buxton, 2010).

CT-INTEGRATION CYCLE

The CT-integration cycle (see Figure 3.1) is a PD approach to help build teacher capacity to implement CT-integrated instructional storylines activities. The CT-integration cycle provides a structure and process for teachers to learn about CT, new computing technologies, and their integration into NGSS-aligned science classrooms (Gendreau Chakarov et al., 2019). Teachers participate in a connected series of PD workshops that involve learning, planning, implementation, and reflective activities with peers (Kazemi & Hubbard, 2008). The CT-integration cycle combines aspects of the problem-solving cycle model of mathematics PD (Borko et al., 2015) with elements of science curriculum co-design workshops (Severance et al., 2016). Importantly, the CT-integration cycle is meant to be an iterative process, whereby teachers take part in multiple cycles each academic year, and ideally participate across multiple years.

Each iteration of the CT-integration cycle consists of three phases: co-design, implementation, reflection. During the first phase, teachers participate in collaborative lesson planning based on a selected storyline. Next they implement the lessons from the storyline in their classroom, and at least some of the lessons are video recorded. Recorded lessons generally include the beginning of the unit, students' use of the sensor platform, and

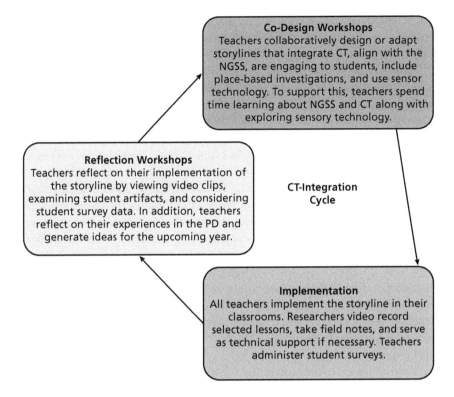

Figure 3.1 The CT-integration cycle.

the conclusion of the unit. Lastly the teachers meet and engage in targeted reflection of the storyline and their implementation. To focus the reflection process, researchers select video clips that contain particularly interesting teacher moves and potentially include productive student interactions.

The storyline that teachers help to plan for, implement, and reflect on is generally different for each CT-integration cycle, although if teachers participate over multiple years they might implement the same storylines with new groups of students. During the co-design workshops, teachers and researchers work together to create and/or modify lessons from a given storyline. Building on the storylining approach (Reiser, 2014), the group develops or adapts NGSS-aligned units in which students employ CT as they make sense of scientific phenomena using a sensor platform. Teachers play a central role in planning their upcoming instruction in an effort to increase their own learning, ensure students' engagement and interest in the curriculum, and consider the feasibility and appropriateness of the units for their local classroom context (Severance et al., 2016). In addition, the design phase includes opportunities for the teachers to engage in

CT activities by taking part in rehearsals, including assuming the roles of both teachers and students in order to feel adequately prepared, gain new knowledge, and better appreciate the student perspective.

Another important part of the co-design process involves determining and "unpacking" the science content that will be included in the unit. Unpacking includes identifying the PEs from the NGSS that students will engage with, and deconstructing the language of the PEs to determine how they should look in the classroom. Additionally, teachers ensure there is a match between the PEs, the scientific phenomenon they plan to investigate, the targeted CT practices, and the capabilities of the sensor platform.

After implementation, the set of focal issues that guided both our PD model and the CT-integrated units serve as guidelines for reflection activities. In other words, teachers consider how well their storyline implementation went with respect to each focal issue (CT practices, NGSS alignment, student engagement, place-based, and use of a sensor platform). Teachers view selected video clips that highlight interesting or unique aspects of their implementation. Teachers also share and discuss student artifacts, such as written models or explanations constructed by their students. Additionally, teachers consider aggregated student survey data collected throughout the storyline implementation, as a vehicle to reflect on their students' interest and engagement in the storyline.

To wrap up each iteration of the CT-integration cycle, teachers reflect on their professional learning experiences and discuss what they would like to improve on during the next iteration. Typically, teachers help to plan for upcoming iterations by considering candidate phenomena for new storylines, whether and how to incorporate additional sensors, and ways to attend more carefully to the integration of CT practices. Teachers also reflect on how their views and understanding of CT have evolved over the course of the CT-integration cycle, how the sensor platform has influenced their science instruction, and how they can better foster their students' learning and engagement in CT-integrated science classes.

METHOD

This study builds on an existing research-practice partnership between the research team and a large, diverse urban school district. The partnership is centered on co-design and testing of new materials and tools to support equitable STEM learning and instruction. The district serves over 90,000 students, is racially diverse (>86% from nondominant backgrounds), largely low income (69% qualify for free or reduced lunch), and includes a large number of English language learners (37%).

During the 2017–2018 school year, three middle school science teachers and one integrated STEM teacher participated in the study. In the partner district, integrated STEM is a required elective course that meets less frequently than regular classes. It includes topics such as civil engineering, introductory programming, and electronics. All four teachers took part in the first iteration of the CT-integration cycle beginning in Fall 2017 (due to the timing of the project's funding, there were no prior summer workshops). The teachers attended four full-day PD workshops (two in Fall 2017 and two in Spring 2018). Additionally, all of the teachers implemented a weeklong CT-integrated unit between the fall and spring workshops.

The second iteration of the CT-integration cycle began in Summer 2018 and included five teachers: two returning teachers (one science and one integrated STEM), plus four additional teachers (three science teachers and one integrated STEM). The teachers attended three full-day workshops in the summer and four full-day workshops during the school year. They implemented a 3-week CT-integrated unit between the second and third workshops.

Researchers recorded and took field notes on selected lessons from each teacher's implementation of the storylines during each iteration. Researchers also conducted interviews with each teacher after their storyline implementation and after completing a full CT-integration cycle. Further, teachers completed written reflections in response to specific prompts during most of the PD workshops. Research points to the importance of interest and identity for promoting learning, particularly for students from nondominant communities (National Academies of Sciences Engineering and Medicine, 2018; National Research Council, 2012). As part of the storyline, teachers had the option to collect student survey data at the conclusion of several lessons. The key goals of this survey go beyond gauging mastery of standards, with a strong focus on eliciting information about the extent to which students make meaningful connections between the curriculum and their own lives (Penuel & Watkins, 2019). The survey asked students to provide mostly closed-ended responses to prompts emphasizing their experience of the lessons, including their perceptions of the sensor platform, lesson and unit coherence, their contributions during the lessons, and how engaging and relevant they found the lesson activities. The survey is intended to be practical to administer and use and takes the form of an "exit ticket."

THE CT-INTEGRATION CYCLE IN ACTION: TWO ITERATIONS

This section describes two iterations of the CT-integration cycle as they were enacted by our research team and the participating teachers. The first cycle centers around the development and implementation of a storyline about detecting the potential for mold growth in schools. The second cycle focuses on the development and implementation of a storyline about maglev trains and how they work. For each cycle, we consider how the PD workshops supported teachers to co-design, implement, and then reflect on the focal storyline. We also discuss the experiences of two teachers using case study descriptions woven into the narrative of each iteration of the CT-integration cycle. These teachers represent different academic disciplines: Trent[1] is a science teacher, and Carolyn is an integrated STEM teacher. They both took part in the study for 2 years, enabling us to compare their first and second iterations of the CT-integration cycle. After describing each iteration, we highlight lessons learned and revisions to the CT-integration cycle.

Iteration One: Mold Growth Storyline

For logistical purposes, the first iteration of the CT-integration cycle began in Fall 2017. Because the concepts of CT were relatively new to the teachers, the research team placed less of an emphasis on co-design and generated a one-week storyline for the teachers to review and revise during the first two workshops. This storyline centers around investigating school buildings to determine whether they have the conditions necessary for mold growth (see Figure 3.2). It was designed to integrate certain CT practices, so that teachers could gain insight through enactment of what it might look like to engage students in these practices and how they overlapped and differed from teachers' current practices.

The "anchoring phenomena" of mold growth was chosen for a variety of reasons. The sensor platform used during this cycle (see Figure 3.3) was equipped with an environmental combo sensor and could serve as a data collection mechanism to repeatedly sample temperature, humidity, pressure, altitude, carbon dioxide, and total volatile organic compounds. There is an ideal temperature and humidity range that supports mold growth and investigating a building's potential for mold allowed students to get outside of the traditional "science lab" and gather data from their entire school. In this way, classes engaged in a place-based investigation in a familiar and meaningful location.

Although the mold growth storyline was quite short, it targeted the scientific idea of how environmental factors can affect organisms' growth. The storyline also engaged students in science and engineering practices such as asking questions and planning and carrying out investigations while incorporating the cross cutting concept of cause and effect. Furthermore, the unit targeted CT through its focus on data practices. For example, the students collected data using the sensor platform, manipulated the data on their computers to display the relevant information, and created visualizations to communicate their findings. However, because the sensor was

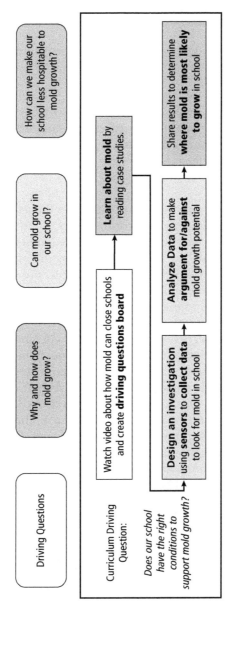

Figure 3.2 The mold growth storyline: The bold text refers to the science content and science and CT Practices.

Figure 3.3 The sensor platform used in the first CT-integration cycle includes an ESP-32 wroom board equipped with an environmental combo sensor and an SD card that records measurements from the sensor.

pre-programmed to collect all sensor readings once every second, there was not an opportunity for students to engage in programming and the small scale of the storyline limited the possibility of other CT practices such as modeling and computational problem-solving.

Co-Design Workshops

The goal of the first workshop was to introduce the teachers to the project and to get them excited about incorporating CT and a sensor platform in their classrooms. A primary emphasis of the co-design workshops was for the teachers to experience the storyline by playing the role of students and then reflecting on those experiences. For example, the teachers included generated questions about mold and used the sensor platform to collect data on the conditions for mold growth in the PD building. After completing the activities wearing their "student hats," the teachers reflected on their experiences and suggested modifications to the storyline and sensor platform to make them more suitable for classroom implementation.

In addition, the teachers created a set of questions about CT and what it might look like in middle school science classes. As part of this activity, the teachers posed, shared, and organized questions about CT in an effort to highlight the nature of their understanding, areas of confusion, and main topics of interest regarding this broad conceptual area. The questions were saved and revised throughout the CT-integration cycle as teachers answered some of their questions and posed new ones in order to build knowledge and gain a better understanding of how to help their students develop CT abilities.

Teachers varied in their prior knowledge and experience with CT. Many of the science teachers (including Trent) had little to no programming background and lacked confidence in their ability to implement sensor and CT activities in the classroom. Although Trent stated that he did not really understand what CT was, he was excited to learn more about it and begin to incorporate the sensor platform into his disciplinary instruction. As an integrated STEM teacher, Carolyn typically taught lessons that focused heavily on technology and engineering, including programming activities in Scratch. She expressed an interest in deepening her CT knowledge to be able to better assess the development of her students in this area.

The second workshop focused on preparing teachers to implement all of the components of the mold growth storyline. One topic they discussed in depth was how students' analysis of the sensor data could be used in their concluding explanations related to mold growth in different locations. Working in small groups, the teachers developed detailed plans for how they would implement the storyline in their own classrooms, including how they would use the existing resources and what additional supports their students might need.

The teachers also continued their exploration of CT by unpacking a subset of data practices (Weintrop et al., 2016). The mold growth unit emphasized data practices in particular, as this aspect of CT represents a familiar entry point for science teachers who often engage in various kinds of data collection and analysis in their classrooms. Unpacking the data practices required the teachers to closely examine given text and envision how each practice might unfold in the classroom (Krajcik et al., 2014). As teachers went through the data practices, they discussed how those practices could manifest in the mold growth storyline and highlighted specific areas throughout the storyline that illustrated various practices.

Implementation

Each of the four teachers implemented the five-lesson unit in their classrooms in Spring 2018. In all classes, groups of approximately four students each received a sensor platform. The three science teachers completed the unit over a 1-week period, whereas the integrated STEM teacher implemented it over a 3-week period (because she saw her students only once or twice per week). A researcher was present for the first and last lesson recording video and taking field notes. During each teachers' first use of the sensor platform, a researcher was present in the classroom if the teacher requested it (three of the four teachers did) to provide support. Students ranged from fifth grade to eighth grade, were evenly split between girls and boys, and over 50% self-identified as Hispanic. Below we detail the implementation and student experience of Trent and Carolyn. Trent taught seventh grade life science and Carolyn implemented the unit in her fifth grade integrated STEM class.

Trent case study: The mold growth storyline in a science class. Throughout his implementation of the mold growth unit, Trent highlighted the fact that finding mold could lead to shutting down their school. Students collected data using the sensor platform, analyzed that data, and wrote a letter to their principal about the potential for mold growth.

Trent encouraged his students to write a convincing argument about whether their school should close if mold was discovered, and to use the results from their data analyses in the letters. Although none of the students actually found mold growing in their school, Trent suggested they predict what could happen to create an environment favorable for mold growth, such as a pipe bursting or a leaky air conditioner. Trent personally found the question of when a school should be closed intriguing and was confident it would resonate with his students. Trent explained, "That's to me how you can be a good teacher. You have to be a storyteller and have some sort of story that is attractive to kids."

Trent also felt that it was important for his students to construct graphs from their sensor data in order to interpret and make sense of the data they collected. Trent argued that his students were engaging in CT when they compared the humidity and temperature data they collected and graphed with the ideal conditions for mold growth that they learned about earlier in the unit. Trent reported, "I guess that, to me, is the computational thinking side of it. They're comparing their data to those [ideal] ranges, so I think that's what was leading them to those conclusions."

Trent reflected that his students appeared more engaged than usual, perhaps because they were able to get out of the classroom and investigate their school. Trent also noted that his students took away from the unit an appreciation for quickly and easily collecting, analyzing, and interpreting a large data set. Trent's impressions were supported by student survey data. The majority of Trent's students expressed that using the sensor platform was both easy and fun. In addition, 82% of students reported that they wanted to use the sensor platform more often to conduct investigations. Most students (88%) reported that they understood why they undertook the activities in class that day. More than 60% of students said the investigation was relevant to them personally, to their class, and to their community.

In Trent's implementation of the storyline, the content focus, the use of the sensor platform, and the inclusion of CT practices were all in the service of supporting a personally-relevant argument. Trent's follow-up interview and written reflections suggest he associated CT with data collection and analysis using computational tools, albeit on a larger scale than his students had previously experienced. Trent explained that he viewed the primary goal of the PD as getting "kids used to using different tools to allow them to see themselves as scientists."

Carolyn case study: The mold growth storyline in an integrated STEM class. To begin the unit, Carolyn showed the class her daughter's water bottle that often sits near the radiator in another classroom in their school. The water bottle had mold visibly growing on the mouth piece, which led to an animated conversation about mold. Carolyn reflected in an interview: "I think the questions that they were generating demonstrated that they were hooked and interested . . . I was pleasantly surprised by their intrigue." Carolyn referred back to her daughter's moldy water bottle throughout the unit, which inspired some of her students to inspect and collect sensor data near their own classroom's radiator.

Carolyn allowed her students to use the sensor platform somewhat more independently compared to Trent. However, anticipating that they might struggle with analyzing the large amount of data collected by the sensor platform, Carolyn decided to create a series of short instructional videos that supported data analysis for her students, a successful strategy she had employed for other investigations. After students viewed the videos independently or in small groups, most were able to then use a spreadsheet to organize, analyze, and visualize their data with minimal guidance.

Like Trent, Carolyn felt her students were empowered by looking at the data they collected about mold growth in their school and by being asked to make decisions about what to do next. As they considered their data, Carolyn's students actively engaged in small group discussions about the pros and cons of different types of graphs, thought carefully about which data was most useful for their purposes, and inspected the labels automatically generated by the spreadsheet for accuracy. In the post implementation interview, Carolyn spoke about the fact that her students had spent an entire class period engaging in the data analysis through "looking for patterns, graphing and filtering data that did not pertain to their driving questions." Carolyn noted, "We had discussions about how scale can make things look more dramatic. The data was fairly consistent [but] they could make it look like it was climbing by making the scale (range) small enough."

In contrast to Trent's students, Carolyn's students did indeed find mold growing in some places in their school. Discovering mold, along with learning computational practices for interpreting big data sets they personally collected, appeared to help Carolyn's students feel a sense of ownership throughout the unit. The vast majority (86%) reported that they knew why they conducted the activities in their class on a given day and over 80% reported that the investigations mattered to themselves and their class. Almost 70% of the students expressed that during the unit they were excited about the material and felt like scientists.

Carolyn explained, "I think they were empowered because they were looking at data that they had collected and making some decisions and then thinking about what's next." Carolyn's students generated recommendations for preventing mold growth, such as "we should get ventilators for the boiler room to circulate moisture." Some of Carolyn's students later spoke with local stakeholders (including the principal, facilities manager, and food services manager) about where the mold was in their school and how to prevent mold growth. They even offered to continue to monitor those locations in the future.

Reflection Workshops
Teachers attended two workshops after their implementation of the mold growth storyline in order to share and reflect on their enactments and plan

for the second cycle. During the workshop immediately after teachers used the storyline, they watched and analyzed video clips, wrote and shared reflections, and looked at aggregated data collected on their students' experiences. Videos were selected that exhibited various ways teachers launched the unit and their approaches to supporting students' data analysis. Additionally, teachers shared and reflected on student models of how mold grows, their experiences using the sensor platform, the written arguments students created about the potential for mold growth in their schools, and suggestions for modifying the storyline in the future.

During the last workshop in the cycle, teachers reflected on the process for developing effective storylines and discussed what the next CT-integrated storyline might entail. Trent mentioned that one of his goals was to "get kids used to using different tools to allow them to see themselves as scientists." Carolyn shared that she wanted to make "computational thinking engaging and transparent for kids." The teachers generated a set of candidate phenomena to include on a student survey so they could gauge their students' interest and decide which phenomenon should anchor the storyline to be used in the next iteration of the CT-integration cycle. Other researchers have found that allowing students to play a key role in deciding the phenomena to investigate in a storyline can lead to curricular units deemed engaging, relevant, and meaningful (e.g., Tzou & Bell, 2010).

As they concluded the first iteration of the CT-integration cycle, the teachers took some time to look back on how the entire process had played out. Two major takeaways teachers noted were the value of engaging in activities from a student perspective and the importance of gaining expertise in both CT and storylining. Carolyn verbalized a central tension of the PD,

> [We need to find] that grand balance of what we want students to take away from this. Do we want them to take away CT or some programming knowledge? Do we want them to take away knowledge of [the scientific concept] . . . Like what is the big picture?

Lessons Learned From Iteration 1

Our research team learned several lessons from the first implementation of the CT- integration cycle, including lessons about how to organize and focus the PD activities and adequately supporting the co-design process. In terms of the PD activities, teachers appear to need more opportunities to learn about CT (a subject most of them were initially unfamiliar with). They also appear likely to benefit from greater clarity about how to deeply integrate the CT practices into science instruction in order to resolve the tension about how much time to spend on science versus CT.

For example, although both Trent and Carolyn declared their implementation of the mold growth unit successful, our research team agreed we need to be more explicit with the participating teachers about what counts as CT and how CT data practices differ from the traditional data analysis practices that science teachers are familiar with. Trent's instruction around data analysis retained more traditional methods outside of including significantly larger datasets for the students to analyze and interpret. On the other hand, Carolyn probed her students to experiment with a variety of data analyses and discussed with them how different ways of visualizing information can lead to different interpretations of the results. Although Trent was satisfied with how he included the CT data practices in his lessons, his classes generally lacked rich discussions around appropriate data analyses and visualizations, thereby hindering his students' opportunity to engage in CT data practices relative to Carolyn's lessons.

Thus, the next iteration of the CT-integration cycle included activities that more explicitly highlighted CT in action, especially through the analysis of video excerpts from teachers' lessons and detailed examples in the teacher guide accompanying the storyline. It also included a summer design workshop where teachers and researchers began working on a new storyline. By playing a larger role in shaping the storyline, teachers had the opportunity to more intentionally incorporate CT practices, generate the necessary resources to support their students' learning, and ensure the storyline fit with their current curricular goals.

Iteration 2: Maglev Train Storyline

The second iteration of the CT-integration cycle took place during the 2018–2019 school year and focused on supporting the participating teachers to develop a stronger understanding of CT practices, testing the usability of a more robust sensor platform, and building capacity to co-design CT-integrated NGSS-aligned storylines. Five middle school teachers participated; two had participated in the first iteration and three were new to the project.

A more collaborative approach was used to create the storyline, which largely drew on two NGSS PEs about understanding invisible fields between objects, such as magnetic and gravitational fields. Trains powered by magnetic levitation, called maglev trains, served as the anchoring phenomenon to drive students' questions and investigations (see Figure 3.4). The maglev train storyline was designed to be implemented over 3 full weeks of classroom instruction. The increased length of this storyline relative to the mold growth storyline enabled the investigation of a larger number of science concepts at a deeper level. The focus on place, or a location relevant to students, was not as foregrounded, but the unit did include connections to traffic problems experienced by the local community that might be

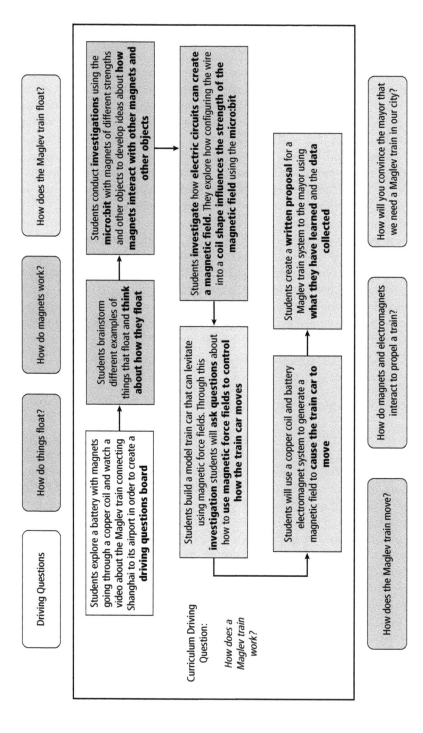

Figure 3.4 The Maglev train storyline: The bold text refers to the science content and science and CT practices.

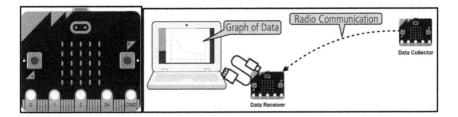

Figure 3.5 The sensor platform used in the second CT-integration cycle, including two micro:bits that enable radio communication and can be connected to a computer for real-time data visualization.

mitigated by high speed maglev and concluded with students writing a proposal to the mayor about the ideal location for a maglev train in their city.

The micro:bit was selected to replace the sensor kit used in the mold growth storyline (see Figure 3.5). The micro:bit, which has onboard light, temperature, accelerometer, and magnetometer sensors, was deemed preferable for several reasons. First, the micro:bit is much more affordable (a consideration that many schools take into account when deciding to integrate CT) and it is built specifically for educational environments to be used by students. Second, the micro:bit gives students additional control over the data collection process, thereby supporting the integration of computational problem solving practices. Third, it allows students to engage in programming to collect specific data through simple block coding. In our case, we selected MakeCode[2] which enables students to customize their data collection and visualizations to answer questions about the scientific phenomenon under investigation. Fourth, the micro:bit has an LED display and the capability to broadcast data streams to a paired micro:bit connected to a computer, thus allowing students to see and analyze their data in real time. Together these features support students to engage in multiple CT practices simultaneously, providing opportunities for more authentic CT integration.

Co-Design Workshops

Towards the end of the first CT-integration cycle, the teachers developed a student interest survey containing a small set of phenomena that related to specific disciplinary core ideas in the NGSS and that could be used to anchor a storyline that incorporated CT-integrated investigations. Several teachers administered this survey to their students and the results were used to select a phenomenon on which to base the next co-designed storyline. Two phenomena were identified as the most promising anchoring phenomena: maglev trains and playground paint that changes color based on the temperature. The teachers carefully considered both phenomena and voted on maglev trains as the one to pursue.

In addition to determining the focus of the next storyline, the co-design workshops were intended to orient both returning and new teachers to the second iteration of the CT-integration cycle. The group discussed lessons learned from the first iteration, and teachers were introduced to the micro:bit as the new sensor platform. Teachers engaged in a series of challenges in which they had to program the micro:bit in MakeCode, providing them with firsthand experience using the programming language as they explored the capabilities of the sensor platform.

Much like the co-design workshops in the first iteration of the CT-integration cycle, teachers created a set of questions centered around CT in the science classroom. Much like their students do in the classroom when they first begin a phenomenon-driven storyline, the teachers wrote their questions on sticky notes and then took turns reading the questions and placing them on the board. Together with the facilitator they categorized the questions into broader categories including: (a) How can we develop a shared vocabulary around CT?; (b) What does CT look like in our current curriculum and in the curriculum we make? and (c) What would CT look like in the classroom, including horizontal and vertical integration? See Figure 3.6 for a picture of the driving questions board. Generating questions, together with engaging in sensor exploration and programming activities, shed light into the participants' widely variable knowledge of CT, and stimulated ideas for future activities.

Moving into the co-design of the maglev train storyline, the participants agreed it should address the question of how maglev trains work and carefully considered each of the focal issues described earlier in this chapter. As returning teachers, Trent and Carolyn took on a leadership role by sharing their experiences, relating their enthusiasm, and offering suggestions throughout the storyline development process. Once the group created a detailed outline and sequence of lessons for the storyline, the research

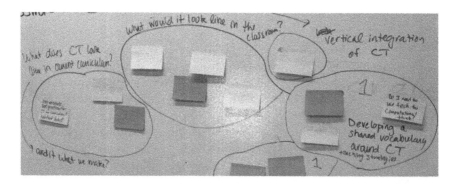

Figure 3.6 Driving questions board around computational thinking created by teachers.

team created lesson plans and other instructional materials. The teachers then had multiple opportunities to give feedback and suggest revisions prior to storyline implementation.

Implementation

All five teachers implemented the maglev train storyline in their classrooms in Spring 2019. In all classes, groups of approximately four students received micro:bits. Researchers were present for each teacher's launch, their first lesson using the micro:bit, and lessons that focused on electromagnets and incorporated the micro:bit. Students ranged from fifth grade to eighth grade, were evenly split between girls and boys, and over 50% self-identified as Hispanic. Below we detail the implementation and student experience of the two case study teachers introduced above.

Trent case study: The Maglev train storyline in a science class. Trent transitioned from teaching seventh grade science to eighth grade science at the same school, meaning that many students who had experienced the mold growth storyline then also experienced the maglev train storyline. The maglev train lessons allowed students more time to engage in scientific experimentation than the mold growth lessons and had a strong focus on fixed magnets, which the students spent about two-thirds of the unit investigating. Trent reflected that by the end of the storyline "students understood the concept of magnetism very well, but the aspects of electricity and circuits were a bit harder for them within this unit." As far as CT, Trent noted that the process of programming the micro:bit to collect and analyze data about magnetic fields "allowed the students to see something that was invisible by assigning a measurement to the magnetic field."

Although Trent highlighted science concepts and CT practices (especially computational problem solving and data analysis) in more depth compared to the mold growth storyline, he had less emphasis on "place" during the maglev unit. At the beginning of the storyline, Trent's students discussed the potential benefits of having a maglev train in their city, but this type of local connection was not brought up again. Trent ran out of time for the culminating lessons, which would have brought in a stronger emphasis on place-based learning. The lack of emphasis on personal and community relevance can be seen in his students' survey results where the number of students who answered "What we did today *does not* matter to people in my city" increased from 7% at the unit launch to almost 20% in the middle of the unit. Trent regretted not maintaining an emphasis on place throughout the storyline and noted that in the future he would highlight place in the majority of the lessons.

Trent commented that "student engagement was high [and] students were asking a lot of questions right from the beginning of the unit and were eager to participate in the investigations we planned and conducted."

This reflection is supported by his survey results as almost 80% of students reported that they understood how today's class ties to the bigger picture of what they're studying in the unit. Additionally, over 70% of students responded that they learned more in class today because other students shared their ideas and opinions.

Carolyn case study: The Maglev train storyline in an integrated STEM class. Similar to the mold growth storyline, Carolyn implemented the maglev train storyline with her 5th grade integrated STEM class, however during the 2018–2019 school year she saw her students for an entire week every 3 weeks (instead of once every 3 days). Like Trent, Carolyn felt that her students developed a good understanding of magnetic fields and how to measure them as they engaged in the storyline. However, she felt less confident about their knowledge of electromagnetism, explaining "students will need more time and exposure to deeply understand the concepts of magnetism as related to electricity."

Carolyn worked hard to motivate the use of the magnetometer on the micro:bit, including leading a class discussion of whether and how tools can make the invisible visible. Carolyn encouraged her students to draw connections to concepts they were already familiar with, such as how temperature and humidity are reported by weather forecasters. Carolyn asked her students to think about the difference between saying it is warm or damp outside versus tying specific numbers to those verbal descriptions. This discussion led students to think about the iron filings experiment they had recently completed and the possibility of using a tool to describe the magnetic field quantitatively. When Carolyn announced that the magnetometer could serve as such a tool, her students cheered and clapped!

As with Trent's implementation of the maglev train storyline, the consideration of place as a locally relevant feature did not play as large of a role as it had during the mold growth storyline. Carolyn explained, "We had discussions to constantly remind them of the potential benefits to [our city] and the surrounding areas, but the real-life examples seemed too far away." Correspondingly, the amount of Carolyn's students who reported "What we did today *does not* matter to people in my city" increased from 3% to 23% from the unit launch to the middle of the unit. Carolyn remarked that in the mold growth storyline "the physical place of school made parts of the data discussion especially exciting for kids. Parts of the maglev as a distant idea made it intriguing but ultimately difficult to connect with."

At the same time, Carolyn felt her students were highly engaged in the storyline. These impressions are supported by survey data which showed that, throughout the unit, over 90% of Carolyn's students "felt like scientists" and over 65% reported the material was interesting to them. Additionally, her students engaged frequently with one another and over 90% said that they learned more in class today because other students shared their ideas or opinions.

Reflection Workshops

Teachers attended a workshop to share and reflect on how their implementation of the maglev storyline went. Much like the first iteration of the CT-integration cycle, teachers viewed and analyzed video clips from their classrooms, engaged in written reflections and discussions, and considered aggregated survey data that highlighted their students' experiences. For example, teachers viewed videos of students sharing questions they had about maglev trains and noted differences in their approaches to facilitating this process. Teachers also thought carefully about whether the amount of CT in the storyline was appropriate and how future storylines could better incorporate the sensor platform and involve more programming.

As part of this discussion, teachers were asked to choose whether they thought the unit had adequate sensor usage and programming or whether the unit needed more sensor usage and programming. One teacher argued, "It (the micro:bit) is an intro tool for this unit, and in the future [future units] they can learn more programming." Another teacher countered that the programming in the unit should be less scaffolded and more time spent on how to program the micro:bit to collect data stating that the "coding part was heavily scaffolded. It would be good for the students to have more thought behind how to code, planning for their code, troubleshooting, and debugging their code." The discussion concluded with the challenges of finding the right balance between the science and CT with one teacher remarking that "here is a lot going on in this unit, with science content, practices, micro:bits, programming. So there's a need to figure out what the goals are and how to find the right balance." This was one of the most detailed discussions of CT that occurred within the PD to date, with teachers enthusiastically debating whether and how to increase their classroom integration of CT and science.

A final workshop served to wrap up the cycle and transition to the upcoming third iteration. Because several new teachers had joined the group, the returning teachers were asked to provide overviews of the mold growth and maglev train storylines and to facilitate a lesson from each storyline that integrated CT. Carolyn led the discussion and facilitated a lesson related to the mold growth storyline, and Jacob (a teacher who joined the project for the second iteration) did the same for the maglev train storyline. These activities provided the researchers an opportunity to see teachers' growth in their understanding of CT and sensor usage, as well as their capacity to take on a leadership role. Further, the returning teachers' eagerness to integrate CT and take part in the collaborative processes utilized in the CT-integration cycle encouraged the new teachers to begin envisioning the possibilities for engaging their students in phenomena driven, CT-integrated science learning.

Lessons Learned From Iteration 2

Lessons learned from the second iteration of the CT-integration cycle include knowledge about the PD activities and support structures that teachers deemed especially helpful. For example, teachers reported gaining a better understanding of what CT is and how CT can be integrated in a complementary manner alongside science content in their middle school classrooms. Teachers appreciated the opportunity to alternate between wearing a "student hat" and a "teacher hat" as they experienced CT-integration firsthand. By engaging in CT-integrated science learning from a student perspective and then discussing those experiences from a teacher perspective, the teachers became increasingly motivated to brainstorm new ways to integrate CT into their curriculum and instruction.

Another valuable lesson was about the increased capacity of returning teachers like Trent and Carolyn to lead workshop activities and contribute to co-designing storylines. Through their participation in the CT-integration cycle, teachers appeared to gain meaningful experiences with CT integration leading to both an increased thoughtfulness and an enthusiasm to share their experiences with colleagues. Including both returning and new teachers in the PD helped to generate a strong support network that moved beyond their relationship with the research team and shifted more of the burden to teachers themselves. As teachers became more knowledgeable, empowered, and valued they seemed especially keen to develop productive collaborative relationships amongst themselves.

Additionally, through participation in the CT-integration cycle, teachers' interest in and capacity to use sensor technology, including programming, increased markedly. Likewise, teachers reported that their students expressed more of an interest in using the sensor platform and were increasingly capable of using and programming the micro:bits to collect and analyze data during investigations to answer their scientific questions. Teachers expressed a desire to create more opportunities for their students to learn using CT practices and the sensor platform. At the same time, the teachers recognized how challenging it is to foreground all of the focal issues in a given storyline, and especially to find a good balance between emphasizing science ideas and CT practices/sensor usage.

NEXT STEPS

The CT-integration cycle appears to be a promising approach to support the professional learning of teachers who seek to engage in NGSS-aligned science instruction as well as incorporating new sensor technologies and exposing their students to CT practices as part of their disciplinary classes.

Based on our research team's experience, the PD model works well for a range of teachers, including those who are more and less familiar with NGSS, sensor platforms, and CT or computer science. The CT-integration cycle is intended to be an iterative and ongoing form of PD, providing teachers the opportunity to co-design or adapt a variety of storylines during each new iteration with a focus on different aspects of CT. Taking part in the workshops over one or more school years has the potential to expand teachers' knowledge and expertise in multiple domains and increase their students' exposure to CT-integrated science learning. The CT-integration cycle is flexible in the sense that teachers can utilize various and changing sensor technologies to promote CT practices, it can be adapted to account for teachers' unique classroom contexts, and CT integrated storylines can be generated to fit any science content area.

At the same time, participating in the CT-integration cycle does place a number of demands on teachers, including allocating the time needed to learn new technologies and classroom practices, as well as having the instructional time necessary to implement a CT- integrated storyline. Our experience in developing and implementing the PD has been with teacher volunteers, meaning they are highly motivated and have the professional support required to use new curriculum and make instructional shifts. It is unclear how well this PD would scale to much larger groups or to teachers who were required to participate.

The study described in this chapter involved only a small number of teachers from a single district, enabling us to look closely at a few individual cases over time. Next steps for our research team include scaling the PD to include more teachers and school districts, developing and revising additional storylines, and updating the sensor platform. We are also working to design a condensed version of the CT- integration cycle that can serve as an initial introduction to CT-integrated science instruction for teachers who may not have the time or administrative support to participate in the full cycle. Furthermore, our current work has been limited to supporting in-service teachers, but it seems clear that there are avenues to bring this type of professional learning to preservice teachers, in particular through supporting the development of teacher educators and by providing a framework for incorporating CT into mainstream science classes through co-designing and preparing to teach CT integrated storylines.

NOTES

1. All names used are pseudonyms.
2. https://makecode.microbit.org/

REFERENCES

Anastopoulou, S., Sharples, M., Ainsworth, S., Crook, C., O'Malley, C., & Wright, M. (2012). Creating personal meaning through technology-supported science inquiry learning across formal and informal settings. *International Journal of Science Education, 34*(2), 251–273.

Blumenfeld, P. C., Soloway, E., Marx, R. W., Krajcik, J. S., Guzdial, M., & Palincsar, A. (1991). Motivating project-based learning: Sustaining the doing, supporting the learning. *Educational Psychologist, 26*(3–4), 369–398.

Borko, H., Jacobs, J., Koellner, K., & Swackhamer, L. E. (2015). *Mathematics professional development: Improving teaching using the problem-solving cycle and leadership preparation models.* Teachers College Press.

Buxton, C. A. (2010). Social problem solving through science: An approach to critical, place-based, science teaching and learning. *Equity & Excellence in Education, 43*(1), 120–135.

Gendreau Chakarov, A., Biddy, Q., Recker, M., Jacobs, J., Sumner, T., Hervey, S., Van Horne, K., & Penuel, W. (2019). *Designing and implementing sensor-based science units that incorporate computational thinking.* Research Presentation at AERA International Conference 2019: Leveraging Education Research in a Post Truth Era: Multimodal Narratives to Democratize Evidence. Toronto, Canada: AERA.

Grover, S., & Pea, R. (2013). Computational thinking in K–12: A review of the state of the field. *Educational Researcher, 42*(1), 38–43.

Kazemi, E., & Hubbard, A. (2008). New directions for the design and study of professional development: Attending to the coevolution of teachers' participation across contexts. *Journal of Teacher Education, 59*(5), 428–441.

Krajcik, J. S., Codere, S., Dahsah, C., Bayer, R., & Mun, K. (2014). Planning instruction to meet the intent of the Next Generation Science Standards. *Journal of Science Teacher Education, 25(2)*, 157–175.

Margolis, J., Estrella, E., Goode, G., Holme, J. J., & Nao, K. (2008). *Stuck in the shallow end: Race, education, and computing.* MIT Press.

National Academies of Sciences Engineering and Medicine. (2018). *How people learn II: Learners, cultures, and contexts.* National Academies Press.

National Research Council. (2012). *A framework for K–12 science education: Practices, crosscutting concepts, and core ideas.* National Research Council.

NGSS Lead States. (2013). *Next Generation Science Standards: For states by states.* The National Academies Press.

Penuel, W. R., & Reiser, B. J. (2018). *Designing NGSS-aligned curriculum materials* [Paper prepared for the Committee to Revise America's Lab Report]. National Academies of Science, Engineering, and Medicine.

Penuel, W. R., & Watkins, D. A. (2019). Assessment to promote equity and epistemic justice: A use-case of a research-practice partnership in science education. *The ANNALS of the American Academy of Political and Social Science, 683*(1), 201–216.

Reiser, B. J. (2014, April). *Designing coherent storylines aligned with NGSS for the K–12 classroom.* Paper presented at the National Science Education Leadership Association Meeting.

Sengupta, P., Kinnebrew, J. S., Basu, S., Biswas, G., & Clark, D. (2013). Integrating computational thinking with K–12 science education using agent-based computation: A theoretical framework. *Education and Information Technologies, 18*(2), 351–380.

Severance, S., Penuel, W. R., Sumner, T., & Leary, H. (2016). Organizing for teacher agency in curricular co-design. *Journal of the Learning Sciences, 25*(4), 531–564.

Shwartz, Y., Weizman, A., Fortus, D., Krajcik, J., & Reiser, B. (2008). *Middle school science curriculum: Coherence as a design principle.* National Association of Research in Science Teaching.

Tisue, S., & Wilensky, U. (2004, May). Netlogo: A simple environment for modeling complexity. *International Conference on Complex Systems, 21,* 16–21.

Tzou, C. T., & Bell, P. (2010). Micros and me: Leveraging home and community practices in formal science instruction. In K. Gomez, L. Lyons, & J. Radinsky (Eds.), *Proceedings of the 9th International Conference of the Learning Sciences* (pp. 1135–1143). International Society of the Learning Sciences.

Voogt, J., Laferrière, T., Breuleux, A., Itow, R. C., Hickey, D. T., & McKenney, S. (2015). Collaborative design as a form of professional development. *Instructional Science, 43*(2), 259–282.

Weintrop, D., Beheshti, E., Horn, M., Orton, K., Jona, K., Trouille, L., & Wilensky, U. (2016). Defining computational thinking for mathematics and science classrooms. *Journal of Science Education and Technology, 25*(1), 127–147.

CHAPTER 4

TEACHERS' KNOWLEDGE AND SKILLS IN COMPUTATIONAL THINKING AND THEIR ENACTMENT OF A COMPUTATIONALLY RICH CURRICULUM

Irene Lee
Massachusetts Institute of Technology

Ling Hsiao
Massachusetts Institute of Technology

Emma Anderson
Massachusetts Institute of Technology

Professional Development for In-Service Teachers, pages 85–120
Copyright © 2022 by Information Age Publishing
www.infoagepub.com
85

ABSTRACT

The integration of computer science (CS) and computational thinking (CT) in science classes has been promoted as a strategy to engage all students in CS education. This approach aims to level inequities in access to computing education by placing CS education within compulsory science classes. Project GUTS' *CS in Science* curriculum supports the integration of CT-rich computer modeling and simulation activities into middle school science classrooms. It has been promoted to serve the dual goals of exposing students to CS as a powerful tool for understanding scientific phenomena while simultaneously promoting students' understanding of modern scientific practices. Yet full implementation of this curriculum that promotes the use, modification, and creation of computer models of scientific phenomena has been challenging for many middle school science teachers. In this chapter, we describe the National Science Foundation funded Teachers with GUTS program that investigated the supports and experiences needed to prepare middle school science teachers as computational thinkers capable of implementing the *CS in Science* curriculum. We discuss the professional development (PD) program, the learning objectives of the program, and how it sought to expand teachers' knowledge and skills as computational thinkers over the course of 1 year. Using a mixed methods approach, we first describe correlations between teachers' PD participation hours, their knowledge and skills in CT, and the number of *CS in Science* activities they implemented. Subsequently, we present two case studies that illustrate how teachers of varying levels of CT knowledge and skills enacted the curriculum to meet their instructional goals. Finally, we discuss the implications of these findings on teacher professional development programs that aim to prepare in-service science teachers to infuse CS and CT into middle school science classrooms.

As technological advances and scientific innovations are reshaping the ways we live and the kinds of problems we can pose and solve, there has been increasing interest in engaging K–12 students in CS and CT (Bailey & Borwein, 2011; Foster, 2006; Henderson et al., 2007; Papert, 1996; Wing, 2006). The integration of CS and CT in science classes has been promoted by both national computer science education and science education associations (Computer Science Teachers Association, 2011; National Governors Association, 2010; National Research Council, 2012; NGSS Lead States, 2013). This strategy aims to bypass some of the difficulties associated with offering stand-alone CS courses and adding additional subjects to an already crowded school day while addressing new standards in science education. Thus researchers and educators alike have embarked on projects to engage students in CS and CT through integration in core subjects as early as elementary school as a means to prepare students with the knowledge, skills, and practices for future endeavors in science and computing fields (Basu et al., 2016; Lee et al., 2011; Schanzer et al., 2018; Sengupta et al., 2013; Swanson et al., 2019).

The approach of integrating CS and CT into core subjects has many potential benefits. Since science classes are mandated for all students, integrating CS and CT in science classes serves as a way to introduce all students to CS in an equitable fashion (Lee et al., 2017). Interjecting CS and CT into science classes drives the modernization of science curriculum to reflect modern scientific practices such as computer modeling and simulation (Foster, 2006; Sengupta et al., 2013; Tedre & Denning, 2016; Weintrop et al., 2016). Additionally, the integration of CS and CT in science has potential to deepen students' understanding of scientific processes through investigation of mechanisms abstracted in computer models (Arastoopour Irgens et al., 2020; Schwarz et al., 2014, Wilkerson et al., 2015, Wilkerson et al., 2018). The integration also aspires to raise teachers' and students' awareness of the relevance of CS and CT in science and how CS and CT have been key to scientific discovery. While there are numerous potential benefits, there are also several substantial challenges to this new approach. Science teachers have difficulty finding instructional time in a crowded science curriculum to teach CS content and CT practices. Furthermore, since these topics and skills are not yet tested in standardized assessments, their value is not measured or used to assess teaching. And perhaps most importantly, there is a significantly steep learning curve for teachers to be able to engage students in CT-rich activities.

This chapter reports on the "Teachers with GUTS" research project that aimed to prepare science teachers with knowledge and skills in CT and CS in order to implement a CT-rich modeling and simulation curriculum in middle school science classrooms. During the cohort year, the project worked with middle school science teachers across two school districts in the Southwestern region of the United States. The project, in collaboration with curriculum developers, middle school science teachers, researchers, and facilitators, iteratively refined and adapted the Project GUTS *CS in Science* curriculum that integrates CS and CT in science. CT was integrated into existing earth science, life science, and physical science content through abstracting, automating, and analyzing agent-based models and running simulation experiments. CS was integrated through the programming and debugging of computer models.

The project's broader research addresses the need to understand how best to prepare science teachers for the integration of CS and CT into science classrooms. In this study, we sought to understand the impact of the PD on teacher learning. We analyzed data on teachers' knowledge and skills in CT at baseline and exit. We investigated if there was a relationship between the number of Project GUTS activities implemented, PD participation hours, and change in knowledge and skills. We also sought to understand *how* teachers implemented the curriculum; we analyzed classroom observation data and described two ways in which teachers were able to incorporate CT into their science classrooms. Finally, in the discussion section, we addressed a programmatic concern; we considered how strengths and limitations in a teacher's CT knowledge and skills may impact the implementation of our CT-rich curriculum.

BACKGROUND

CS, the foundation for all computing, is defined as "the study of computers and algorithmic processes, including their principles, their hardware and software designs, their [implementation], and their impact on society" (Tucker et al., 2003, p. 6). CT is the thought process involved in formulating problems such that their solutions can be expressed as computational steps or algorithms to be carried out by a computer (Aho, 2012; Cuny et al., 2010a; Lee, 2016). As such, CT can be seen as the connective tissue (Martin, 2018) that links CS to many disciplines. In particular, CT connects CS with science. Others suggest that integrating CT enables students to develop models and simulation of problems that they are trying to study and solve. (Denning, 2017; Lee et al., 2019; Weintrop et al., 2016) This link between CT and modeling is further supported by the importance of all three pillars of CT—abstraction, automation, and analysis (Cuny et al., 2010a, 2010b)—in developing, using, and assessing models.

Developing computer models and using them to run simulation experiments is a key component of modern scientific practice (PITAC, 2005). Increasingly scientists engage in making models and running experiments using computer models for the purpose of conducting fundamental research (Gilbert, 1991; Schwarz & White, 2005). Using a computer model as an experimental testbed, scientists are able to run multiple "What if" scenarios quickly, collect and analyze large amounts of data, test theories, illuminate core dynamics within a system, discover new questions, understand the landscape of outcomes, and build intuition about complex systems (Epstein, 2008). As explicit representations of the modeler's abstractions and assumptions, computer models can serve as artifacts around which to focus dialogue, train practitioners, and educate the general public. Reflecting changes in modern scientific practices, the Next Generation Science Standards (NGSS Lead States, 2013) promoted "mathematical and computational thinking" and "developing and using models" as key scientific practices that all students should learn in K–12 science education.

In the Teachers with GUTS program, computer models are treated as "objects to think with" or "artifacts that bridge the gap between the physical world and the abstract inner world" (Papert, 1980, p. 11). Computer models are explicitly recognized as imperfect proxies for the real world phenomenon being modeled. As executable objects, computer models can be used to visualize how the local interaction of objects called agents, following simple rules, can generate patterns seen in the real world phenomena. Additionally, because computer models embed scientific processes in code, they can be used to test hypotheses about the generator(s) of the phenomena (Bundy, 2007; Ulrich Hoppe & Werneburg, 2019). For example, one can test whether the mechanisms included in a model are sufficient to reproduce the behavior of real-world systems.

A computational thinker in the realm of modeling and simulation is operationalized for participants in Teachers with GUTS program as one who can

- decode and understand models,
- modify and create models,
- use model for scientific inquiry,
- think of real-world phenomena in terms of how they can be modeled and studied, and
- analyze models.

This operationalization encompasses Cuny et al.'s (2010a) notion of the three pillars of CT: abstraction, automation, and analysis, and situates these constructs in concrete tasks for working with computer models in a scientific inquiry context (see Table 4.1). Abstractions are uncovered in the decode and understand models task, and new abstractions are constructed prior to modification of the model in the modify and create models task. Automation is utilized both in running simulation experiments (that can sweep the parameter values) in the use of models for scientific inquiry tasks and in encoding new behaviors in the modify and create models task. Thinking of real-world phenomena in terms of how they can be modeled and studied engages learners in considering both abstraction (what to include in the model) and automation (how the processes will be encoded and how automation will be used to run controlled experiments). Finally, analyze models task refers to ascertaining the extent to which a model reflects the real world phenomenon it models. This can be achieved by comparing mechanisms in the model to processes in science and by comparing the data produced by running the model to patterns seen in the real world phenomenon.

"Decoding" or understanding the CT of the model's designer is a critical step that was previously under-emphasized in the use-modify-create trajectory (Lee et al., 2011). It involves inspecting a model's abstractions, assumptions, and mechanisms embedded in code. Initially, in Project GUTS (2007–2011), decoding was framed as understanding a mechanism in code in terms of agents' behavior from a computational perspective: "How were the agents moving?" and "What were the agents' interactions with the environment and other agents?" Later, the conceptualization of

TABLE 4.1 CT in Computer Modeling and Simulation

	Abstract	Automation	Analysis
1. Decoding to understand models (made by others)	Uncovering abstractions and assumptions.	Uncovering mechanisms encoded in the model.	
2. Modifying and creating models	Modifying or adding new abstractions.	Encoding new processes and/or behaviors.	
3. Using models for scientific inquiry		Automating parameter sweeping experiments.	
4. Thinking of real-world phenomena in terms of how they can be modeled and studied	Abstracting the phenomena as agents and environment.	Abstracting processes as agent behaviors, and interactions between agents and environment.	
5. Analyzing the model's validity (in terms of what the student knows about the scientific phenomenon being modeled)	Assessing the validity of the model in terms of what it includes and leaves out.	Assessing the validity of the model in terms of how mechanisms were programmed.	Assessing the validity of the model in terms of the data it produces.

decoding was expanded to encompass an explicit link to the scientific phenomenon being modeled: "What scientific process does this mechanism represent?" and "To what extent is the representation accurate?" The inspection and analysis of mechanisms in the model provides opportunities for students to (a) learn how models encode scientific processes; (b) develop mechanistic reasoning about phenomena (Hsiao et al., 2019); (c) reinforce understandings of scientific processes; and (d) assess the face validity of computer models.

It is notable that, in Teachers with GUTS, computer models are treated as idea models or minimal conceptual models and not as "truth." We promote a stance that the abstractions and automations in computer models may limit their validity and thus "all models are wrong, but some models are useful" (often attributed to statistician George Box, 1976). Importantly, we state that computer models are not to be used as predictive engines until their validity has been ascertained. Often, the thorough validation of models required prior to using them for predictive purposes, is beyond the scope of middle school students and teachers within the regular school day science classroom.

The integration of CT in K–12 science is a challenging endeavor for both teachers and students. It involves learning new literacies (e.g., programming, simulation environments, computational science processes) as well as disciplinary core ideas (Basu et al., 2016; Dickes et al., 2020; Guzdial, 2006; Pierson et al., 2020; Sherin et al., 1993). Despite these challenges, the integration of CT in K–12 science through computer modeling and simulation has shown benefits. Engaging in computer modeling allowed students to build deeper understandings of the causal mechanisms underlying phenomena and deepen learning in science (National Research Council, 2010). Complementarily, science provided a context in which CT was shown to be applicable, useful, and meaningful (Weintrop et al., 2016).

Research on integrating computational modeling and simulation with K–12 science curriculum has largely focused on interventionist approaches, as opposed to naturally occurring or ad hoc integrations. An analysis of CT activities from projects funded by the NSF-funded two-part workshop on Developing a Framework for Computational Thinking From a Disciplinary Perspective (Lee & Malyn-Smith, 2019) found that recent attempts to integrate CT into science classrooms fall along a continuum from the addition of "coding" activities that provide little if any support of science learning; to the integration of CT to support science content knowledge as it currently exists in science classrooms; to the integration of modern uses of computation aligned with the work of professional scientists (Lee et al., 2019).

Teacher preparation has been noted as a critical factor in the integration of CT into K–12 subject areas (Barr & Stephenson, 2011; Voogt et al., 2015; Yadav et al., 2016; Yadav et al., 2017). Key features of effective PD are known from the research literature. To be effective, PD should be grounded in teachers' needs and their work environments, and address core areas of teaching: content, curriculum, instruction, and assessment. Common features of effective teacher PD programs include opportunities to (a) gain new knowledge, (b) reflect on changes in teaching practice, and (c) increase abilities and skills. Additionally, effective PD focuses on student learning outcomes and models learner-centered instruction such that teachers experience and reflect upon learning activities that they will ultimately lead for their students (Gaible & Burns, 2005; Hassel, 1999). In addition to what is known about PD generally, Yadav et al. (2016) suggested that effective PD in CT should be tied to teachers' curricular needs, explicitly describe overlaps between learning objectives in the subject area and CT, promote the development of a community of practice among teachers, and be continuous rather than episodic.

With these understandings of the research literature on the current state of CS integration, we explore the following research questions:

1. What CT knowledge and skills did teachers gain through the Teachers with GUTS PD?

2. How did teachers incorporate the Project GUTS curriculum into their science classroom practices?

METHODS AND DATA COLLECTION

The Project GUTS CS in Science Curriculum

Project GUTS' *CS in Science* curriculum was designed to serve the dual goals of exposing students to CS as a powerful tool for modeling systems in science while simultaneously promoting students' understanding of modern scientific practices. The curriculum consists of five modules— each module is designed to be implemented over the course of five to six 1-hour class periods. The curriculum design was based on learnings during the previous 7 years of implementing Project GUTS' after school program (Lee, 2011, pp. 29–32). The challenges of moving to the school day included developing modules that aligned with school day science learning objectives, moderating pacing to fit within a 1 hour time block (that proved unrealistic for most teachers who had less than a full hour per class period), and preparing teachers to offer the CT-rich activities without the in-class support of facilitators.

"Module 1: Introduction to Computer Modeling and Simulation," lays the foundation for the following four modules and thus was designed to be implemented first. In Module 1, each lesson consists of a hands-on activity that engages the student in a new concept followed by a build activity in StarLogo Nova. The sequence of activities constructs an epidemic model by creating agents, programming agent movement, and then interaction between agents. Once the model was built, the next activity was to design and conduct experiments using the model as an experimental testbed. Finally, learners were able to modify their models to reflect a scenario or local instantiation of the phenomenon studied. This sequence exposes students to the key CS commands and constructs (instructions/commands, sequences, looping, and conditionals), modeling and simulation concepts (randomness, initialization, simulation, output), and science concepts (experimental design, experimentation, variables, data collection, and analysis) that they will use in subsequent modules.

Modules 2 through 5 follow a different pattern closely aligned to the use-modify-create progression (Lee et al., 2011) that has been shown to support and deepen youth's engagement in CT. The first lesson in these modules grounds the phenomenon studied in students' existing knowledge or experience and engages the student in *using* the base model to run initial experiments. The second lesson focuses on *decoding* and understanding the code, abstractions, and assumptions in the model. Subsequent lessons engage students in *modifying* the model to be able to answer new questions, reflect what students know about the real world, and/or serve as a vehicle to test theories about the generators of the phenomenon. Modifications to the model and *using the model as an experimental testbed* to run parameter sweeping experiments that produce data follows. The amassed data can be *analyzed* to draw conclusions about the impact of the modification on the behavior of the system studied.

StarLogo Nova was the agent-based modeling and simulation platform used in this study. StarLogo Nova is a rich computational environment (Lee et al., 2014) in which the underlying abstractions and mechanisms of a model can be inspected, manipulated, and customized. A learner can "look under the hood" and inspect the causal relationships and abstractions that are embedded in a model. It has been demonstrated to lower the threshold for engaging novices in computer modeling (Klopfer, 2003) and offers the learner a means to develop CT skills and transform from end-user to creator.

The Teachers With GUTS Professional Development Program

The Teachers with GUTS PD program aims to support teachers' integration of CT-rich computer modeling and simulation activities into science classrooms, specifically those encapsulated within the Project GUTS *CS in Science* curriculum. The PD program focused on preparing science teachers, new to CT, for in-school implementations of the *CS in Science* curriculum. The target goals for implementation were to implement Module 1 during the fall semester and at least one other module during the spring semester. The PD program consists of a 5-day face-to-face summer intensive workshop followed by quarterly 1-day face-to-face follow up workshops (in fall, winter, and spring) and interstitial webinars offered online in months when no other workshops were offered (see Figure 4.1).

Day One
On the first day of the summer workshop teachers were given an introduction to the project's goals, CT, and the NGSS. Computational science was described as the integration of computational tools and techniques into scientific fields that offered a new way to understanding large complex systems through computer modeling and simulation. Furthermore, we stressed that the understanding of large complex systems is critical to mitigating problems such as climate change, loss of biodiversity, energy consumption, and virulent disease. CT was positioned as the thinking that goes into making the computer models of complex systems. Specifically,

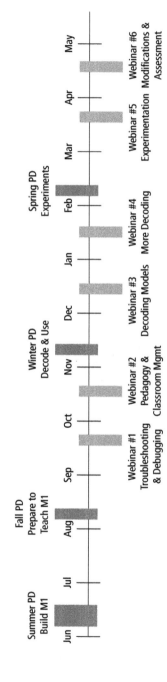

Figure 4.1 Teachers with GUTS PD workshops and webinars over the cohort year.

abstraction entailed deciding what to include in a model; automation entailed developing algorithms for how the model will run and generate outcome data; and analysis entailed assessing the face validity of the model.

Next, participants were introduced to (a) the agent-based modeling paradigm of agents, environment, and interactions; (b) adding instrumentation to models; and (c) running experiments using models as testbeds. Additional CT exercises included practice in abstracting a real world phenomenon and asking what would be needed to model the phenomenon. For example, one of the prompts used was, "What would you include in a model of traffic jams?" The discussion was followed by examining a StarLogo Nova model of traffic jams to see how another modeler conceptualized the problem. This activity also provided teachers with a first exposure to emergent patterns being formed by local interactions in models of complex systems.

To gain a foundation in algorithms and automation, participants played the "My Robotic Friends" activity in which one of a pair of participants created instructions for a "robot" to stack cups in a certain pattern, and the other participant attempted to follow the instructions. After playing the activity, the debrief focused on reflecting on the thinking skills and processes that were used in generating and following instructions. Repeated behaviors and patterns were noted and "making shortcuts" akin to counted loops and encapsulating repeated behaviors into procedures were suggested by participants and reinforced by the facilitators who provided the CS terms "loops" and "procedures." Towards the end of the first day, a "mystery model" activity was used to reinforce CT. A "mystery model" is a model in which the title does not say what the model represents, and the sliders or variables have generic names to hide what they represent. The mystery model was presented as a proxy for a real-world phenomenon and participants were tasked with applying CT to decipher the model and to guess what phenomenon it was modeling.

Day 2 Through Day 5

On Day 2 of the summer workshop, teachers engaged in each of the activities in Project GUTS *CS in Science* Module 1 playing the role of students. They experienced building a simple StarLogo Nova epidemic model in stages: first programming agent movement, then programming interactions between agents, and next using their model to run controlled experiments with the variables of population density and transmission rate of the disease. Subsequently, participants customized their models to test their ideas about the spread of disease, or to model the spread of a specific disease. Through this experience they gained an appreciation of the capabilities of StarLogo Nova, an understanding of the ways agent movement and interaction can be used to model real world phenomena, and of how a learner's agency in scientific inquiry can be harnessed by positioning the learner as the driver of the computational investigation. This experience of Module 1 set the stage for the review of three following modules on water resources, ecosystems, and chemical reactions over the next 3 days of the PD workshop. When reviewing the subsequent modules, teachers first read over the first lesson that grounds the phenomenon in student experiences and accesses prior knowledge, then they primarily focused on decoding and making modifications to the associated base model then running experiments to see the impact of their modifications. Additionally, PD activities included lesson review, targeted practice of pedagogy, equity activities developed by the Tapestry program (Cohoon, 2011), and implementation planning.

Follow-Up One-Day Workshops

The subsequent 1 day fall PD workshop (in August) provided teachers with the opportunity to review the content, practices, and pedagogy for implementing Module 1. Teachers in small groups reviewed specific lessons and practiced teaching them to one another. A community webinar in September offered support with troubleshooting technical issues and debugging StarLogo Nova projects. A webinar in October reviewed pedagogy and best practices in classroom management when teaching with computer models and simulation. The 1-day winter PD workshop (in November) focused on decoding and using models to run experiments. In this workshop teachers practiced teaching decoding with fellow teachers acting as students. Webinars in December and January provided time for teachers to discuss how they were leading decoding lessons and "making sense of" models. In the 1-day spring PD workshop (in February) teachers practiced designing and running multivariate parameter sweeping experiments to understand phenomena. In the March and April webinars, teachers discussed the struggles encountered and potential solutions to supporting students' making modifications to models and designing experiments to detect the impact of those modifications. Each of the webinars utilized the TeacherswithGUTS.org practice space as a venue for posing prompts to participants, uploading responses, and reflecting on the discussion.

The flow and sequencing of PD experiences were intentionally designed to support teachers in the scientific uses of modeling and simulation: the practice of modeling through abstraction and automation (coding and decoding models); the designing and running of experiments to generate data on the dynamics of complex systems; and finally, the analyses of those data to assess the face validity of the models. The design of the PD aimed to provide teachers with experiences of how CT can be used to develop understandings of complex systems and connect those understandings with middle school science content and practice standards, and with examples of how CT can be connected to studying and solving problems in everyday life.

In total, 70 contact hours were offered with contact between participating teachers, staff, and facilitators provided on a monthly basis. Additionally, Teachers with GUTS offered an online teacher PD network, TeacherswithGUTS.org, to serve as the community of practice for Project GUTS using teachers.

Context and Participants

Eighteen middle school and upper elementary science teachers from a large urban district and a smaller suburban/urban district in the Southwestern United States participated in this research study. Both districts serve a population with a high percentage of students from underrepresented groups in STEM (83.8% and 78.1%, respectively), and a high percentage of students qualifying for Federal free and reduced lunch program, a proxy for low socioeconomic status (74.3% and 68.2%, respectively). Within the large district, a prevailing pattern is the high mobility and high dropout rates of the student population with roughly 25% of students changing schools each year and 52% of students graduating from high school within 4 years. Within the smaller district, the high school graduation rate was 69.6% in 2018.

Data Sources

Several data sources were used to answer our research questions: a knowledge and skills survey, a count of hours of participation in PD, a count of the number of activities implemented, and classroom observations. The survey, the "Knowledge and Skills in Computational Thinking" instrument (KS-CT), was used to evaluate the contributions of the PD components to teacher's acquisition of CT knowledge and skills. The KS-CT is a 17-item multiple choice survey that consists of items from the KS-CT previously developed by New Mexico Computer Science for All (NSF CE21 CS10K Award #1240992) that was shown to have face validity and was assessed for internal consistency (Cronbach's alpha coefficient was 0.893 for the post-test). The modified KS-CT contains four scales corresponding to learning objectives in complex adaptive systems, modeling and simulation, computer science constructs, and program tracing and decoding. The instrument was also modified to use StarLogo Nova blocks rather than NetLogo code in program tracing and debugging questions.

In the KS-CT, the complex adaptive systems scale consists of three items that assess teachers' ability to select a defining characteristic of a complex adaptive system, pick out an example of a negative feedback loop, and pick out an example of a complex adaptive system (see Figure 4.2).

The KS-CT modeling and simulation scale consists of three items that assess teachers' ability to identify a feature of models necessary to run controlled experiments, the cause of different experimental results generated from a computer model, and the definition of model validation (see Figure 4.3).

The programming and CS concepts scale consists of three items. They are definitional and ask teachers to select the behavior generated by loops, the components of expressions, and use of conditional statements (see Figure 4.4).

The trace and debug scale consists of eight items. The first four items ask teachers to read a set of instructions and predict the outcome of running the instructions (see Figure 4.5).

1. Complex Adaptive Systems can be described as which one of the following?

○ a. mechanical like clockwork

○ b. having many interactions between parts

○ c. predictable

○ d. none of the above

Figure 4.2   KS-CT sample item on characteristics of a complex adaptive system.

9. To validate a model means to check the model to see that ____

○ a. it runs without crashing the computer

○ b. it produces outcomes that match the real-world system it is modeling

○ c. it has been run multiple times

○ d. it does not have bugs

Figure 4.3   KS-CT sample item on the definition of model validation.

6. When programming, a conditional block/statement (if/then/else) is used to

○ a. select an instruction depending on the answer to a question

○ b. make a comparison

○ c. confuse the robot

○ d. give more than one direction at a time

Figure 4.4   KS-CT sample item on the use of conditional statements.

The second set of items in this scale asks about the impact of randomness on agent movement. The teacher is to determine which piece of code was used to make each path (see Figure 4.6).

In summary, the KS-CT captures teachers' understanding of basic concepts and skills that may impact their decoding and interpretation of

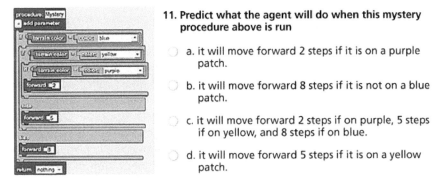

11. Predict what the agent will do when this mystery procedure above is run

    a. it will move forward 2 steps if it is on a purple patch.

    b. it will move forward 8 steps if it is not on a blue patch.

    c. it will move forward 2 steps if on purple, 5 steps if on yellow, and 8 steps if on blue.

    d. it will move forward 5 steps if it is on a yellow patch.

Figure 4.5 KS-CT sample item on predicting the outcome of running a procedure.

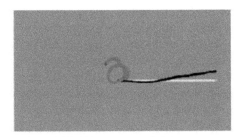

Some of the code snippets labeled 1, 2, 3, and 4 below were used to create the red, yellow, and black paths above.

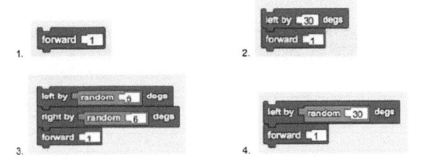

Figure 4.6 KS-CT sample item on the impact of randomness.

models, their use of models as experimental testbeds, and their interpretation model outcomes. The KS-CT was not designed to capture epistemic beliefs about modeling and simulation or CT or how well a teacher is prepared to teach abstraction or automation in a modeling and simulation context. The KS-CT's four scales relate to Weintrop et al.'s (2016) Computational Thinking in Mathematics & Science Taxonomy (see Table 4.2). The KS-CT assesses knowledge across three of four categories of the taxonomy and skills aligned with one of the categories (data practices are not covered in the KS-CT).

Classroom observations while teachers were implementing the *CS in Science* curriculum were captured by trained field investigators. Teacher enactments were captured in written observation field notes collected throughout the implementation of a module. One or two observers documented classroom activities, teacher facilitation, and student responses. At the end of the session, observers debriefed with teachers about their experience of implementing the lessons in a short interview. Across the cohort, all teachers were observed at least twice during the implementation of a *CS in Science* module. Over the third cohort year, 154 classroom observations were captured. Other data sources included PD and webinar attendance data and teachers' logs of dates when *CS in Science* activities were implemented. Teacher supplied implementation data were triangulated by field investigator observations and by student end of module survey data.

In the Winter of 2018, eight teachers participated in a 30-minute semi-structured interview exploring their teaching of the *CS in Science* curriculum, their conception of the role of modeling in science, and their understanding of the term CT. The protocol included questions about the teacher's experience with the implementation of the *CS in Science* curriculum ("What parts of the curriculum were challenging to implement?"; "What are some constraints you faced with implementation?"); teacher's conception of the role of modeling in science ("What do you think is the role of modeling in science education?"; "What do you think is the role of computational modeling in science education?"; "How does the curriculum help you meet

TABLE 4.2 Scales in the KS-CT Survey and Corresponding Categories in Weintrop et al.'s Computational Thinking in Mathematics and Science Taxonomy

KS-CT Scales	Weintrop et al.'s CT Taxonomy Category
Complex Adaptive Systems (3 items, 1–3)	Systems Thinking Practices
Modeling and Simulation (3 items, 4–6)	Modeling and Simulation Practices
Computer Science constructs (3 items, 7–9)	Computational Problem-Solving Practices
Program Tracing, Debugging, Predicting Outcome (8 items, 10–17)	Computational Problem-Solving Practices— Programming and Debugging

your science instruction goals, if at all?"); and teacher's understanding of CT ("In your own words, what is computational thinking?").

Analytical Methods

A quantitative approach was used to characterize teacher change in knowledge and skills. Data from the KS-CT scores of 13 of the 18 teachers who completed the KS-CT at baseline and exit were analyzed for number of correct answers at baseline and exit, and change in percentile correct. Subsequent linear regressions were conducted to explore the relationship between the exposure variables of hours of PD attendance and number of lessons implemented, and the relationship between teachers' understanding of CT as measured by the KS-CT and the number of lessons implemented. In order to investigate if a teacher's understanding of CT as determined by the KS-CT impacted how teachers implemented the *CS in Science* curriculum, two teachers were purposely selected for case studies. These two teachers were selected because they scored very differently on the KS-CT; one teacher had the largest gains in KS-CT understanding and the second teacher had little to no change in his KS-CT score. These teachers were also chosen because they both taught *CS in Science* Module 1 in the fall and Module 4 in the spring. Both taught eighth grade.

For each of the two teachers used in the case studies, we focused on a subset of five classroom observations, the corresponding post-observation interviews, and semi-structured interviews. Iterative rounds of open emergent coding were conducted (Saldaña, 2012). First we coded the classroom observations for the kind of tasks students were assigned (i.e., explore model, modify model, create model) and how teachers facilitated these tasks in lesson activities. We then examined teacher debriefings (captured in post-observation interviews) to understand how they thought about their implementations and explanations of their instructional strategies. Our second level of emergent coding was thematic and captured unique teacher instructional approaches. In particular, we were interested in how these two teachers framed the Project GUTS activities and lessons for their students.

Two main thematic codes emerged from our data. The first emergent code was "linking" in which the teacher made links between the different Project GUTS activities to help students make meaning of the task at hand or of the sequence of activities taught thus far in the overall module. Linking entails bridging between contiguous activities looking deeply at how the teacher pulls the various project GUTS activities together. "Linking" describes how the teacher is able to make sense of the relationship between the various Project GUTS activities and *not* about how the activity fits within a teacher's regular science curriculum. A teacher's "linking" between activities may highlight an effort to incorporate specific CT skills, for example, the encoding of processes in computer models.

The second code to emerge from the data was "connecting." This code was used to characterize how a teacher was able to draw connections between the Project GUTS activities and the larger science content knowledge or scientific practices that the teacher is aiming for their students to learn in their science class or should have already learned. "Connecting" concerns the relationship that the teacher is able to make between a Project GUTS activity and other aspects of learning in their science classroom and in their students' lives. In terms of the interview analysis, we were most interested in how each teacher thought about the role of modeling within their science classroom. The teachers' responses to the question, "What do you believe is the role of modeling in science education?" were analyzed for how they described the role of modeling.

These two themes, linking and connecting, are orthogonal to one another and do not represent ends of a single spectrum. Rather they emerged as two salient features of teachers' enactments of the curriculum: "linking" was prevalent when teachers pedagogical goals were to teach the programming or coding of models whereas "connecting" was prevalent when teachers pedagogical goals were to situate models in the contexts of science and daily life.

FINDINGS

Teachers' Gains in Knowledge and Skills Through PD

To address Research Question 1—"What knowledge and skills did teachers gain through this PD?"—we analyzed teacher KS scores. Participants' number of correct answers improved significantly from baseline to exit (from 50% to 60% correct, $n = 13$, signed rank test $p = 0.019$). The mean score change for teachers in Cohort 3 was 1.615 points (see Figure 4.7).

Participant teachers answered 60% of the items correctly on the exit survey, with the highest scores on the *Computer Science Constructs* scale (74% correct on the exit survey, normalized mean change of .23, $p = 0.031$) and the *Modeling and Simulation* scale (74% correct on exit survey). Participants had the lowest scores on the exit survey on the scales for *Tracing, Decoding, and Predicting* (27% correct on exit survey). A very high percentage of participating teachers answered the two items on the *Complex Adaptive Systems* scale correctly on the baseline survey (96%), leaving very little room for improvement. In fact, by the exit survey, the percentage answering correctly in this scale had decreased.

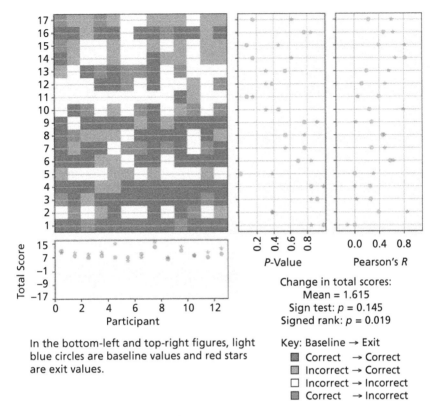

In the bottom-left and top-right figures, light blue circles are baseline values and red stars are exit values.

Change in total scores:
Mean = 1.615
Sign test: $p = 0.145$
Signed rank: $p = 0.019$

Key: Baseline → Exit
■ Correct → Correct
■ Incorrect → Correct
□ Incorrect → Incorrect
■ Correct → Incorrect

Figure 4.7 Comparison of Cohort 3 Knowledge and Skills at Baseline and Exit Showing Response Pattern (top left); Change in Total Score (bottom left); and *P*-Value and Pearson's *R* (top right).

PD Participation, Knowledge and Skills, and Implementation

PD participation hours of each teacher were plotted against change in KS-CT score and KS-CT score at exit (see Figures 4.8a & 4.8b). Linear regression was performed and R-squared value computed to determine the percentage of the dependent variable variation the linear model explains. The results suggested that the greater the number of PD participation hours, the higher the KS score at exit. But the authors make no claim of the direction of causality (that is to differentiate between, "Did more PD hours result in greater KS gains?" or "Did greater KS gains lead to continuation in the PD program?"). We also investigated the relationship between the number of Project GUTS activities implemented by each teacher and the KS change scores (see

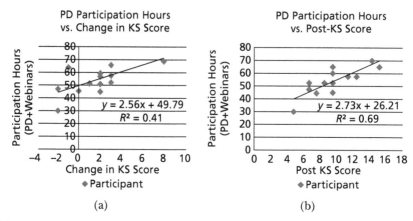

Figures 4.8 PD Participation versus change in KS score (a) and versus KS Score at exit (b).

Figure 4.9a) as well as the number of Project GUTS activities implemented by a teacher and the number of hours a teacher participated in PD workshops and webinars (see Figure 4.9b). The number of activities implemented by a teacher was loosely correlated with their change in KS score (all standard deviations were too large to have confidence in these correlations). Four teachers implemented between zero and eight lessons (less than a full module) and had KS change scores between –2 to +3 (average change in score of 0.75 with standard deviation of 2.22). Three teachers implemented between nine and sixteen lessons (completing up to two modules) and had KS change scores ranging from –2 to +3 (average change in score of 1.0 with standard deviation of 2.65). The six teachers who implemented between 17

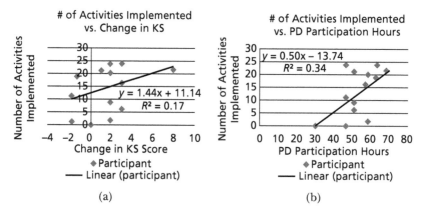

Figures 4.9 Number of activities implemented versus change in KS score (a) and versus total PD participation hours (b).

and 24 lessons (more than two and up to three modules) had KS change scores ranging from +1 to +8 (average change in score of 3.2 with standard deviation of 3.02). The number of activities implemented by a teacher was only loosely correlated to the number of hours a teacher participated in PD workshops and webinars. A missing piece of data in relation to the number of hours focused on learning CT (i.e., number of PD hours) is the number of hours a teacher spent on their own time learning the material. We were not able to capture this piece of data.

Among the teachers who implemented between 9 and 16 lessons one teacher gained significantly more between baseline and exit than the other teachers (8 point gain). Other outliers were identified: two teachers with almost no change in KS implemented more than two modules; and one teacher with a high baseline and exit KS scores (11 and 13 points, respectively) only implemented two lessons. This suggests that other factors influenced how many lessons teachers implemented.

In a previous study of Teachers with GUTS Cohort 1, Prescott et al. (2019) found that teachers' self-efficacy and beliefs in student capabilities were mediating factors in teachers' enactments of the Project GUTS *CS in Science* curriculum. This finding confirms previous research that showed teachers' self-efficacy beliefs are related to their instructional practices (Ashton & Webb, 1986; Ekmekci et al., 2018; Garet et al., 2001). Those with low self-efficacy tended towards a more traditionalist style (direct instruction) whereas those with higher self-efficacy tended towards more open-ended inquiry driven approaches (Lim & Chan, 2007). It also confirms a finding by Haney et al. (2002) that teachers who believe their students have low capabilities for learning offer a less rigorous level of content and limit their approach to direct instruction rather than inquiry-based or student-driven approaches. Unfortunately, the compounding of beliefs in students' capabilities and choice of instructional style can create feedback loops that impact student engagement and learning as described by Prescott et al. (2019):

> If a teacher believes their students' have low capabilities for learning, they will offer less rigorous content and will limit students' engagement to directed interactions. These modifications of curriculum and pedagogical moves result in lower student engagement and a poorer student learning outcome reinforcing the teacher's belief that students are incapable of learning the content or practice. On the other hand, a teacher who believes that her/his students have high capabilities for learning may offer a more rigorous level of content and engage students in more student-driven and inquiry-based interactions with content. This approach may result in greater student engagement and learning thus reinforcing the teacher's beliefs that their students have high capabilities for learning. These reinforcing feedback loops model how teacher beliefs may serve as a "critical filter" that ultimately divides teach-

ers into two categories: those who will and those who will not enact a CT-integration curriculum with fidelity to an inquiry-based approach.

Prescott et al. (2019) pointed to one case study in particular of a teacher with a high KS score who chose not to implement the *CS in Science* curriculum because they did not believe their students were capable of higher order thinking (creating and analyzing models) in the activities.

In Teachers with GUTS Cohort 2, Anderson et al. (2019) encountered teachers' hesitancy to engage students in solving complex, ill-structured problems, and discomfort with needing to help students move beyond moments of struggle when coding. Teachers' hesitancy to engage students in open-ended problem solving during coding derived from several sources: an inability to assess students' knowledge and understanding in a new context (coding) to then provide supports such as guiding questions; a lack of instructional strategies to support productive struggle; and a lack of expertise in coding. Teachers often expressed that they felt they needed to be expert in coding in order to support their students in coding even though the program promoted a view that teachers' role was to be co-learners and facilitators of knowledge building, not experts.

While the KS-CT findings give us hope that our PD is supporting teachers' knowledge and skills in CT, we realize that teachers' implementation of the *CS in Science* curriculum likely entails more than developing CT knowledge and skills; teachers must also learn how the new curriculum ties to curricular needs and how learning objectives overlap between the subject area and CT. Further, they need to gain confidence in using pedagogies and best practices for implementing computer modeling and simulation and our specific curriculum in their classroom setting. To understand how teachers implemented the curriculum, exemplifying the ties they found between the *CS in Science* curriculum and their curricular objectives and goals for student learning, we look to the field observations.

Case Studies

Our teacher cases highlight two different approaches to integrating CS into middle school science through the Project GUTS curriculum (see Table 4.3). Peter and Michael were eighth grade teachers new to CS who taught "Module 4: Chemical Reactions," as their second Project GUTS *CS in Science* module. Although they both taught in schools situated in large urban centers, they had differing teacher background characteristics. In the initial KS-CT survey assessment in the summer, they scored similarly within the lower quartile. But in the exit survey administered in late spring, Peter scored the highest post-test difference in his cohort (+8 points) whereas

TABLE 4.3 Case Study Teachers' Characteristics		
Teacher Characteristics	"Peter"	"Michael"
Grade Taught	8th	8th
Module Observed	Module 4	Module 4
District Type	Urban Large	Urban Large
Years of Teaching Experience	15+	10
Pre-KS Score	7	6
Post-KS Score	15	7
PD Participation Hours	69 Hours	52 Hours

Michael showed little gain (+1 point). Peter also attended more school year PD offerings than Michael, participating in 69 hours of PD versus Michael's 52 hours of participation. Peter was a veteran teacher of more than 15 years of teaching experience while Michael had been teaching in the classroom close to 10 years.

Although the two teachers gained different levels of knowledge as measured by the KS-CT from baseline to exit, we found in their semi-structured interviews (in Winter of 2018) that Peter and Michael had similar views on the role of modeling in their science classrooms. When asked, "What do you think is the role of modeling in science education?" Michael responded,

> When we model in science, we're trying to take all of those considerations of data as well as what would be considered text learning and it gets us to apply and manipulate...And when we're able to translate that to computer, not only is it safe for students, it's more cost-effective for teachers. It utilizes the tool to leverage...When we add the computational piece or that computer piece, it allows us to unleash the power that's within this calculating machine. Some of my students feel like it's an email machine or it's a video machine, or you know. But it does all of those things and more. So again, that was the takeaway that I wanted a lot of my students to experience in that you have an incredible machine in front of you. And if you know how to ask, it will give you tremendous answers.

We interpret Michael's remarks to mean that the role of modeling in science education is to engage students in applying what they learn from texts and in considering data when they make models, and that the models become safe and cost-effective tools for classroom use. Further, incorporating modeling in the science classroom raises students' awareness of the affordances of computers in answering scientific questions. Peter responded,

> I thought it was very important that we did a lab using our models that we built...They've used the experimental design form, they made predictions

on what was gonna happen [*sic*], they made the adjustments, they were able to run the model 10 times per variable that we changed, relatively quickly. And that was a good teaching point of; this is why we use models...we can do a model and run it a bunch of times.

He then added,

To go through different scenarios and learn about how we should react to different scenarios. Epidemics is a good example, traffic jams, traffic flow, engineering design of how do we build our roads and bridges and things like that in order to...So all those things, I think...And just more and more computer science is being involved in all careers. So, I think just having the experience and being able to go through the process, but also understanding that it has real-world applications.

From each of their answers we can surmise that both Michael and Peter view the role of modeling in science education as a way to explore phenomena through applying knowledge and data when building models, and a way to conduct experiments by manipulating variables and utilizing automation. Despite this shared view on modeling, as will be shown below, they each approached framing the Project GUTS activities in Module 4 differently.

Both teachers were observed implementing *CS in Science* "Module 4: Chemical Reactions" in Spring of 2019. The progression of the module is as follows. Students begin by observing a live or video demonstration of the reaction and subsequently are introduced to a rudimentary (base) model of the chemical reaction in StarLogo Nova (SLN). The model is used to run simulation experiments to get a sense of how the behavior of the system changes over time (by viewing the simulation window). Then, the focus of attention turns to decoding the model or translating the programming blocks into agent actions and interactions, and identifying similarities and differences between the real-life experiment and the simulation. After noticing the processes and features missing in the simulation (such as the hydration of copper ions that turns the solution blue), students modify the base model to add features of the real-world chemical reaction that were missing in the computer model. After completing the modeling and programming portions and verifying their hydration code by seeing a resultant color change, students run experiments to discern the factors that impact the rate of chemical reaction. Two additional activities invite students to model and study the impact of heating and mixing the solution on the rate of reaction. These activities are open-ended and offer students agency in deciding how to implement each feature and in developing their own experimental designs.

Within this module teachers led students through investigations of the rate of reaction of silver nitrate and copper using a StarLogo Nova computer model as an experimental testbed. Through modifying the model, students consider the evidence of a chemical reaction; the impact of limiting reactants; and identify when the chemical reaction stops. Unfortunately, neither teacher was able to reach the last two activities of the module in the 5 days of instruction they had allotted for implementation. Thus students missed the opportunity to express agency in deciding how to implement the new conditions (to add heat and stirring) and in developing their own experimental designs.

Peter

In debriefings, Peter shared that, in his regular science curriculum, students had just learned about balancing chemical equations (Observation December 6, 2018). During Peter's implementation of Module 4, his students spent 3½ of the 5 days coding the silver nitrate and copper reaction model using the chemical equation to guide their understanding of when they had completed modeling the full reaction. Due to an issue with the delivery of chemicals, Peter could not perform a live demonstration of the chemical reaction at the start of the module as was recommended in the curriculum. Instead he showcased the live demonstration on the last day of implementation. As a result, his students had limited knowledge of how the reaction progressed and what it looked like during their model construction.

To help students understand what constitutes a complete chemical reaction model, Peter *linked* student coding tasks to build the model across many sessions, and each task corresponded to coding a subcomponent of the overall model. Students explored the chemical reaction in small chunks, coding, running, and testing their model to see how each new change impacted the overall simulation. On the whiteboard, Peter listed the incremental coding tasks. He explained that everyone's end goal was to "have hydrogenated copper [*sic*]" but that coding this model was a "multi-step process" (Observation December 16, 2018). Importantly, Peter chose not to use the base model of the chemical reaction as a starting point, rather he had his students build the base model from scratch.

Peter focused on coding; he described how the chemicals interacted using SLN programming terms to help students understand the coded mechanics behind the chemical reactions. For example, when a pair could not figure out how to make a new breed of hydrated copper, he drew three different forms of copper agents and explained: "You need three collisions...When silver nitrate collides with copper, you create copper nitrate. When copper nitrate collides with water, it creates hydrated copper 1" (Observation January 16, 2019). Peter leveraged students' prior knowledge of coding "collisions" (interactions between agents) in Module 1 to explain how the silver nitrate interacts with copper and later the copper with water, generating hydrated copper with 1, 2, and 3 water molecules. To provide challenges for students at different levels, he presented various versions of the model as "Parsons problems," models in which all the necessary code blocks were present but were not connected into a sequence of instructions. Peter also created paper copies of partial solution codes that he judicially provided to students when they were stumped and/or frustrated. In some cases, Peter and his student groups increased the camera zoom in the simulation window of SLN to watch carefully how silver nitrate agents interacted with copper when they "wiggle-walked" into the copper strip. In this way, Peter focused his students on the mechanisms in the model: the behavior and interactions of agents, to anticipate the characteristics of a chemical reaction they saw in the live demonstration he offered on the final day of implementing the module.

Michael

While Peter *linked* together coding activities that built up to modeling the behavior of components in the chemical reaction, Michael took a different approach. He began with a demonstration of the chemical reaction on Day 1, then connected to his science curriculum before drilling down into the details of the mechanisms in the model. Michael helped his students make *connections* between the larger science curriculum in his classroom and the Project GUTS module on chemical reactions. This was evident in how Michael framed each Module 4 lesson *connecting* it to his larger science curriculum goals and the scientific process of modeling. For example, Michael began every lesson of Module 4 by showing a video connecting the day's lesson to a science concept or practice. On the first day, when watching a video demonstration of the silver nitrate and copper reaction, Michael pointed out the value of a virtual model and related it to why they were building computer models:

> These materials are not compounds we can't get. But they are expensive. With the virtual lab, we don't have to buy them . . . What is good about a virtual lab? We can speed it up . . . this experiment will take 9 hours to complete. That's another reason to do a computer model. We don't have to wait the 9 hours. (Observation March, 18, 2019)

Here Michael was articulating to his students why they might want to build a computer model of this particular chemical reaction.

Another connection to which Michael devoted a large portion of his class' instructional time was the concept of conservation of mass. For example, on the third day of the module he began the class by asking his student, "Do you remember that I kept asking you what is missing in the model that was [seen] in the video?" The student responded, "The water turning blue." Michael commented, "That blue is a reactant. Nothing gained or lost. The blue is copper nitrate [*sic*]" (Observation March 20, 2019). Michael explicitly connected the video the class watched, to the model his students were building, to a missing element in their model, pointing out that "nothing is gained or lost." In this conversation Michael reinforced the connection between conservation of mass and the computer model the students were building. We see this in how Michael highlighted the progression of blue in the video of the chemical reaction: "Was the blue a progression or did it just appear? Think about it..." He asked his students to remember back to the various demonstrations he had shown them and to "remember that the blue was a progression. What we are going to do is have the different steps have a progression of blues. Dark blue is last" (Observation March 21, 2019). Michael made it clear to his students why their models needed to include three different blue breeds to represent where the copper ion was in the hydration processes. In each of these examples Michael focused on a larger concept (in one case, "Why model?" and in the other, the conservation of mass) and connected these concepts or skills to the coding the students were working on during the particular lesson.

Both Peter and Michael worked toward developing CT practices through building models of scientific phenomena in their classrooms. However, Peter approached the integration focused on student mastery of programming skills, moving students from small coding tasks toward larger understanding about the phenomenon being modeled. Peter *linked* coding activities together to deepen student understanding about the full chemical reaction model, incrementally developing knowledge from smaller components. In contrast, Michael provided many opportunities for students to think about the larger context of the phenomenon before engaging in coding agent interactions in the model of the phenomenon. Michael *connected* the model to larger scientific practices and extant curriculum goals, shaping the overall understanding about the phenomenon before students grasped the finer details. Both Peter and Michael were able to align and embed Project GUTS "Module 4: Chemical Reactions" into their instructional goals. This capacity to incorporate the Project GUTS *CS in Science* module and computational modeling practices into their larger science curricular objectives demonstrated a deeper awareness and understanding of how CS ties into science learning. Both teachers essentially took ownership of these new instructional concepts and skills introduced in the module. This owning of one's curriculum is rendered uniquely in each teacher's approach to helping guide their students to begin to be computational thinkers.

DISCUSSION AND CONCLUSIONS

Strengths and limitations in teachers' CT knowledge and skills were seen to influence their enactments of the curriculum. Peter, who had the largest pre- to post- difference in score on the CT-KS survey (+8 points gained), placed greater emphasis on developing coding fluency in his classroom. He opted to provide students more opportunities to code and modify building towards a computational model of a natural phenomenon. Doing so allowed his students to build, "see" the reaction up close in the simulation, and think about the relationship between reactants and products, a key goal in Peter's regular science instruction. Peter's enactment can be characterized as placing a greater emphasis on having his students learn to problem solve when faced with programming challenges as a pathway to becoming computational thinkers. His greater knowledge and skills in CT as measured by the KS-CT, in particular his ability to decode and analyze students models quickly, enabled him to rapidly diagnose students' bugs and provided students with the relevant code snippets or hints, a strategy that a teacher less competent in CT might not be able to employ.

Michael improved by one point on his KS-CT survey and remained in the lowest quartile of CT knowledge and skills as measured by the KS-CT. He focused less on coding fluency but more on *connecting* the Project GUTS activities to his larger science curriculum. Michael placed greater emphasis on understanding the abstractions in the model being built as a pathway for his students to begin to be computational thinkers. He was able to *connect* computer modeling and simulation to the chemistry concepts he sought to teach, such as conservation of mass, and *connect* metamodeling ideas such as why it would be useful to conduct experiments using a computer model (cheaper, easy to speed up or slow down the simulation). Though his students may not have received the depth of experience in creating models as Peter's, he too was able to provide them with exposure to how models encapsulate scientific concepts and processes through abstraction. Importantly, his limitations in CT as measured by the KS-CT *did not* prevent him from implementing the curriculum to meet his curricular objectives.

Michael's ability to explain to his students the abstraction of agents of different shades of blue representing copper ions at different stages in the hydration process and the conservation of mass in the chemical reaction model despite a low score on the baseline and exit KS-CT is puzzling. There is a discrepancy between what he is able to do (recognize and explain the representations and processes in code) and what his scores show (that he has not mastered any CT skills or gained CT knowledge). There can be several explanations: The KS-CT may not be measuring this ability to connect between coded mechanisms and scientific processes; the teacher's CT understanding may be supplemented by his knowledge of chemical reactions; or the context of teaching elicited the teacher's reflective abstraction (Piaget, 2001) and reorganization of understanding whereas the KS-CT assessment did not. This finding suggests that there are missing dimensions in the KS-CT if it is to be used as a single measure to gauge teachers' level of CT understanding. Furthermore, it is unclear whether there is a threshold of teacher CT understanding as measured by the KS-CT that is necessary for implementation of the Project GUTS curriculum.

Both teachers approached the Project GUTS curriculum from different pedagogical starting points, yet each was able to help students begin to see science through a CT lens. The two teachers targeted different categories of CT as described by Weintrop et al. (2016). Peter's enactment focused on computational problem solving practices, specifically programming and debugging, while Michael's enactment focused on modeling and simulation practices, specifically meta-understandings of models and modeling as a practice. It is possible that Peter was able to incorporate "linking" between activities because he spent more time learning how to code and therefore could understand how the coding activities "linked" together. On the other hand, Michael's focus on meta-modeling concepts "connecting" to his larger classroom science curriculum goals may indicate that this is where he felt most knowledgeable. In the above cases it is evident that both Peter and Michael understood how the *CS in Science* curriculum can help teach science concepts. Our analysis highlights how "linking" and "connecting" are not only different ways of framing a lesson, but also require the development of different sets of instructional skills and the understanding of different dimensions of modeling.

In terms of the common variants of CT integrations in science classrooms, both teachers integrated CT to support science content knowledge as it currently exists in science classrooms. Peter, the teacher with stronger CT skills tended towards the addition of "coding" activities and Michael, the teachers with weaker CT skills, tended towards exposing and questioning the abstractions that may limit the validity of computer models thus aligning with the work of professional scientists. Both enactments have strengths and weaknesses and ultimately their value must be assessed within their unique context framed by curricular objectives and teacher preparation.

Implications for Teacher Professional Development Programs

In this section we will discuss the implications of these findings on teacher PDt programs that aim to prepare in-service teachers to integrate CT and CS into K–12 curricula.

As more middle school science teachers are being asked to integrate CS and CT into their science classrooms, it is important to understand that teachers' learning of CS and CT knowledge and skills, as well as teachers' development as computational thinkers, builds over time and thus their implementations of a CT integrated curriculum may shift accordingly. In particular, as teachers' skills in decoding and analyzing students' models grow, the more the teacher might be comfortable leading students in model creation. Thus, supporting different enactments of an integration curriculum may be a necessary and realistic feature of PDs focusing on CT integration. It remains an open question as to how to provide this differentiated support.

Curricular objectives were also seen to shape teachers' enactments of CT integration curricula. Thus, when considering new curricula that integrate CT into science, we recommend evaluating curricula in terms of meeting teachers' curricular objectives as well as for its ability to accommodate differing levels of teachers' knowledge and skills in CT.

Next Steps

For the future, in response to the findings above, we are considering the modification of the *CS in Science* summer PD workshop to offer differentiated strands aligned with teachers' curricular objectives to meet their immediate goals and needs (see Table 4.4). For example, we could offer three strands: (a) modeling and abstraction, (b) coding and automation, and (c) experimentation. Though each teacher would be placed in the strand that aligns with their instructional goals, across all strands, teachers would eventually receive the same content but in a different order. The first segment of each strand aligns with the teachers' immediate curricular goals and ends with a motivation or a reason why the teacher might want to expand their goals to include other CT practices. The two subsequent segments will address those concepts and practices. The motivation for expanding their goals could be in the form of discrepant findings. For example, in the experimentation strand, two models purporting to model the same phenomenon produce vastly different outcomes. Why? This question will motivate the need to "look under the hood" and inspect the models to see what they included and how they were made. The goal of engaging teachers in all of the segments is to show how each practice alone is insufficient to produce holistic understanding of the model and the extent to which it mirrors the scientific phenomenon being modeled. This approach aims to intentionally shift teachers' initial beliefs about the role of modeling in the science to include a broader set of practices and thus, perhaps, shift teachers' instructional goals.

A potential benefit of this PD redesign is that it would provide teachers with a model of how to sequence their instruction first focusing on the CT practices most aligned with their instructional goals then extending into other CT practices. A potential drawback of this PD redesign is that it would require significant resources, specifically instructors and facilitators, to support the multiple strands. A danger of this approach is that some teachers may stop attending or actively participating once they have learned to meet

	Proposed Order of Segments and Motivation to Move to Other
TABLE 4.4 Teachers With GUTS PD—Summer Workshop Re-Imagined	
Strand	**Segments**
Modeling & Abstract Centric	1st Segment: Decode existing models to assess the models' validity in terms of what was included or left out, and how it was made.
	Motivation to go deeper: Another way to assess models' validity is to check if the data they produce reflects patterns seen in the real world.
	2nd Segment: Design & run experiments and analyze data.
	3rd Segment: Program your own model of an epidemic.
Coding & Automation Centric	1st Segment: Program a model of an epidemic.
	Motivation to go deeper: How do I know if the model I programmed is realistic and/or valid scientifically?
	2nd Segment: Design & run experiments and analyze data. Check to see if the patterns generated by your model reflect the real world.
	3rd Segment: Decode other epidemic models to inspect the abstractions within.
Experimentation Centric	1st Segment: Design & run experiments with existing models & analyze data.
	Motivation to go deeper: Two models of the same phenomenon produce vastly different outcomes. Why?
	2nd Segment: Decode existing models to assess the abstractions and automations within. Uncover why the two models are producing different outcomes.
	3rd Segment: Program your own model of an epidemic.

their original instructional goal. This has happened in the past—a teacher who's instructional goal was to introduce some CS during a science class stopped attending PD once they learned what they came for—a few lessons that teach CS, and stopped implementing the *CS in Science* curriculum after teaching those lessons.

Further, we suggest an augmentation of the use-modify-create trajectory inspired by Michael's enactment of the curriculum. The use-modify-create progression, first described in Lee et al. in 2011, provided a pedagogical frame to deepen students' computational thinking across many domains. It can be augmented to better correspond to the CT approaches used within the realm of scientific uses of computer modeling and simulation. In particular, we found decoding, a form of analysis, to be a key aspect of CT that has potential to strengthen ties between coded abstractions and the real-world phenomenon being modeled. Even a teacher with low confidence and skills in programming may be able to lead students in the decoding of models as exemplified by Michael's case. The inspection of abstractions and assumptions embedded within models can be used as the focus of argumentation about the validity of models and the data they produce. A more fitting pedagogical progression for integrating CT in science becomes use-decode-modify/create-experiment. We feel this new progression may better capture the variation of teachers' enactments of curricula that integrate CS and CT into science and should be promoted in future professional development programs.

ACKNOWLEDGMENTS

This work was funded by the National Science Foundation award DRL-1503383 and 1639069. We thank the teachers and students who participated in our research study and the school district partners, field investigators, and program facilitators who supported this research. The views expressed are those of the authors and do not necessarily represent the views of the National Science Foundation or Massachusetts Institute of Technology.

REFERENCES

Aho, A. (2012). Computation and computational thinking. *The Computer Journal, 55*(7), 832–835. https://doi.org/832-835.10.1093/comjnl/bxs074

Anderson, E., Hsiao, L., & Lee, I. (2019, April 5–9). *Exploring teachers' instructional choices for promoting productive failure within a computational modeling and simulation curriculum.* Annual Conference of the American Educational Research Association.

Arastoopour Irgens, G., Dabholkar, S., Bain, C., Woods, P., Hall, K., Swanson, H., Horn, M., & Wilensky, U. (2020). Modeling and measuring high school students' computational thinking practices in science. *Journal of Science Education and Technology, 29*(1), 137–161.

Ashton, P. T., & Webb, R. B. (1986). *Making a difference: Teachers' sense of efficacy and student achievement.* Longman Publishing Group.

Bailey, D., & Borwein, J. M. (2011). Exploratory experimentation and computation. *North American Math Society, 58*(10), 1410–1419.

Barr, V., & Stephenson, C. (2011). Bringing computational thinking to K–12: What is involved and what is the role of the computer science education community? *ACM Inroads, 2*(1), 48–54.

Basu, S., Biswas, G., Sengupta, P., Dickes, A., Kinnebrew, J. S., & Clark, D. (2016). Identifying middle school students' challenges in computational thinking-based science learning. *Research and Practice in Technology Enhanced Learning, 11*(13), 1–35.

Box, G. (1976). Science and statistics. *Journal of the American Statistical Association, 71*(356), 791–799. https://doi.org/10.1080/01621459.1976.10480949

Bundy, A. (2007). Computational thinking is pervasive. *Journal of Scientific and Practical Computing, 1*(2), 67–69.

Cohoon, J. M. (2011). Perspectives on improving the gender composition of computing. *International Journal of Gender, Society, and Technology, 3*(2), 525–535.

Computer Science Teachers Association (2011). *K–12 computer science standards.* http://csta.acm.org/curriculum/sub/k12standards.html

Cuny, J., Snyder, L., & Wing, J. M. (2010a). *Computational thinking: A definition* [Unpublished manuscript].

Cuny, J., Snyder, L., & Wing, J. M. (2010b). *Demystifying computational thinking for non-computer scientists.* [Unpublished manuscript]. http://www.cs.cmu.edu/~CompThink/resources/TheLinkWing.pdf

Denning, P. J. (2017). Computational thinking in science. *American Scientist, 105*(1), 13–17. www.americanscientist.org/article/computational-thinking-in-science

Dickes, A., Farris, A., & Sengupta, P. (2020). Sociomathematical norms for integrating coding and modeling with elementary science: A dialogical approach. *Journal of Science Education and Technology, 29*(1) 35–52. https://doi.org/10.1007/s10956-019-09795-7

Ekmekci, A., Parr, R., & Fisher, A. (2018). *Results from Rice University WeTeach_CS: A computer science teaching collaborative serving teachers with different needs through variety of pathways.* Paper presented at the Society for Information Technology & Teacher Education International Conference.

Epstein, J. M. (2008). *Why model? Journal of Artificial Societies and Social Simulation, 11*(4). http://jasss.soc.surrey.ac.uk/11/4/12.html

Foster, I. (2006). A two-way street to science's future. *Nature, 440,* 419. https://doi.org/10.1038/440419a

Gaible, E., & Burns, M. (2005). *Using technology to train teachers.* http://www.infodev.org/en/publication.13.html

Garet, M. S., Porter, A. C., Desimone, L., Birman, B. F., & Yoon, K. S. (2001). What makes professional development effective? Results from a national sample of teachers. *American Educational Research Journal, 38*(4), 915–945.

Gilbert, S. W. (1991). Model building and a definition of science. *Journal of Research in Science Teaching, 28*(1), 73–79.

Guzdial, M. (2006). Software-realized scaffolding to facilitate programming for science learning. *Interactive Learning Environments, 4*(1), 1–44.

Haney, J. J., Lumpe, A. T., Czerniak, C. M., & Egan, V. (2002). From beliefs to actions: The beliefs and actions of teachers implementing change. *Journal of Science Teacher Education, 13*(3), 171–187.

Hsiao, L., Lee, I., & Klopfer, E. (2019). Making sense of models: How teachers use agent-based modeling to advance mechanistic reasoning. *British Journal of Educational Technology, 50*(5), 2203–2216.

Hassel, E. (1999). *Professional development: Learning from the best.* North Central Regional Educational Laboratory.

Henderson, P. B., Cortina, T. J., & Wing, J. M. (2007). Computational thinking. *ACM SIGCSE Bulletin, 39,* 195–196.

Klopfer, E. (2003). Technologies to support the creation of complex systems models—using StarLogo software with students. *Biosystems, 71*(1–2), 111–122.

Lee, I. (2011). *Final project report for NSFAYS Award #0639637 Project GUTS: Growing up thinking scientifically.* https://tinyurl.com/ProjectGUTS-finalreport2011

Lee, I. (2016). Reclaiming the roots of CT. *CSTA Voice – Special Issue on Computational Thinking, 12*(1), 3–5.

Lee, I., Grover, S., Martin, F., Pillai, S., & Malyn-Smith, J. (2019). Computational thinking from a disciplinary perspective: Integrating computational thinking in K–12 science, technology, engineering, and mathematics education. *Journal of Science Education and Technology, 29*, 1–8. https://doi.org/doi:10.1007/s10956-019-09803-w

Lee, I., Martin, F., & Apone, K. (2014). Integrating computational thinking across the K–8 curriculum. *ACM Inroads, 5*(4), 64–71.

Lee, I., Martin, F., Denner, J., Coulter, B., Allan, W., Erickson, J., Malyn-Smith, J., & Werner, L. (2011). Computational thinking for youth in practice. *ACM Inroads, 2*(1), 32–37.

Lee, I., & Malyn-Smith, J. (2019). Computational thinking integration patterns along the framework defining computational thinking from a disciplinary perspective. *Journal of Science Education and Technology, 29*, 9–18. https://doi.org/doi:10.1007/s10956-019-09802-x

Lee, I. A., Psaila-Dombrowski, M., & Angel, E. (2017). Preparing STEM teachers to offer computer science for all. In *Proceedings of the 2017 ACM SIGCSE Technical Symposium on Computer Science Education* (pp. 363–368). SIGCSE. https://doi.org/10.1145/3017680.3017719

Lim, C. P., & Chan, B. C. (2007). MicroLESSONS in teacher education: Examining pre-service teachers' pedagogical beliefs. *Computers & Education, 48*(3), 474–494.

Malyn-Smith, J., Lee, I., Martin, F. G., Grover, S., & Pillai, S. (2020). Computational thinking from a disciplinary perspective. *Journal of Science Education and Technology, 29*(1), 1–8.

Martin, F. (2018). Rethinking computational thinking. *CSTA–The Advocate.*

National Governors Association Center for Best Practices, Council of Chief State School Officers. (2010). *Common core state standards for mathematics.*

National Research Council. (2010). Report of a workshop on the scope and nature of computational thinking. *National Academies Press.* https://doi.org/10.17226/12840

National Research Council. (2012). A framework for K–12 science education: Practices, crosscutting concepts, and core ideas. *The National Academies Press.* https://doi.org/10.17226/13165

NGSS lead states (2013). Next generation science standards: For states, by states. *The National Academies Press.*

Papert, S. (1980). Mindstorms: Children, computers, and powerful ideas. *Basic Books.*

Papert, S. (1996). An exploration in the space of mathematics educations. *International Journal of Computers for Mathematical Learning, 1*(1), 138–142.

Piaget, J. (2001). *Studies in reflecting abstraction.* Psychology Press.

Pierson, A. E., Brady, C. E., & Clark, D. B. (2020). Balancing the environment: Computational models as interactive participants in a STEM classroom. *Journal of Science Education and Technology, 29*(1), 101–119.

Prescott, P., Lee, I. A., & Tyson, K. (2019). Teacher beliefs in student capabilities as a mediating factor in a novel understanding of enactment of CT curriculum. In *Proceedings of the 50th ACM Technical Symposium on Computer Science Education* (pp. 1277–1277). ACM. https://doi.org/10.1145/3287324.3293841

President's Information Technology Advisory Committee. (2005). *Computational science: Insuring America's competitiveness.* National Coordination Office for Information Technology Research and Development. https://www.nitrd.gov/pitac/reports/20050609_computational/computational.pdf

Project GUTS' CS in Science. (2018). (projectguts.org) https://bit.ly/2MByoOV

Saldaña, J. (2012). *The coding manual for qualitative researchers* (2nd ed.). SAGE Publications.

Schanzer, E., Fisler, K., & Krishnamurthi, S. (2018). Assessing bootstrap: Algebra students on scaffolded and unscaffolded word problems. In *Proceedings of the 49th ACM Technical Symposium on Computer Science Education—SIGCSE '18* (pp. 8–13). ACM Press. https://doi.org/10.1145/3159450.3159498

Schwarz, C., Lee, M., & Rosenberg, J. (2014). *Developing mechanistic explanations of phenomena: Case studies of two fifth grade students' epistemologies in practice over time.* International Conference of the Learning Sciences, ICLS.

Schwarz, C. V., & White, B. Y. (2005). Metamodeling knowledge: Developing students' understanding of scientific modeling. *Cognition and Instruction, 23*(2), 165–205.

Sengupta, P., Kinnebrew, J. S., Basu, S., Biswas, G., & Clark, D. (2013). Integrating computational thinking with K–12 science education using agent-based computation: A theoretical framework. *Education and Information Technologies, 18*(2), 351–380.

Sherin, B., diSessa, A. A., & Hammer, D. (1993). Dynaturtle revisited: Learning physics through collaborative design of a computer model. *Interactive Learning Environments, 3*(2), 91–118.

Swanson, H., Anton, G., Bain, C., Horn, M., & Wilensky, U. (2019). Introducing and assessing computational thinking in the secondary science classroom. In S.-C. Kong & H. Abelson (Eds.), *Computational thinking education* (pp. 99–117). Springer.

Teachers with GUTS Professional Development Network. (n.d.). Teacherswith GUTS.org

Tedre, M., & Denning, P. (2016). The long quest for computational thinking. In *Proceedings of the 16th Koli Calling International Conference on Computing Education Research* (pp. 120–129). Koli Calling. https://doi.org/10.1145/2999541.2999542

Tucker, A. (2003). *A model curriculum for K–12 computer science: Final report of the ACM K–12 Task Force Curriculum Committee.* CSTA.

Ulrich Hoppe, H., & Werneburg, S. (2019). Computational thinking—More than a variant of scientific inquiry! In S. C. Kong & H. Abelson (Eds.), *Computational thinking education* (pp. 13–30). Springer. https://doi.org/10.1007/978-981-13-6528-7_2

Voogt, J., Fisser, P., Good, J., Mishra, P., & Yadav, A. (2015). Computational think-ing in compulsory education: Towards an agenda for research and practice. *Education and Information Technologies, 20*(4), 715–728.

Weintrop, D., Beheshti, E., Horn, M., Orton, K., Jona, K., Trouille, L., & Wilensky, U. (2016). Defining computational thinking for mathematics and science class-rooms. *Journal of Science Education and Technology, 25*(1), 127–147.

Wilkerson-Jerde, M. H., Gravel, B. E., & Macrander, C. A. (2015). Exploring shifts in middle school learners' modeling activity while generating drawings, anima-tions, and computational simulations of molecular diffusion. *Journal of Science Education and Technology, 24*(2–3), 396–415.

Wilkerson, M. H., Sharref, B., Laina, V., & Gravel, B. (2018). Epistemic gameplay and discovery in computational model-based inquiry activities. *Instructional Science, 46*, 35–60. https://doi.org/10.1007/s11251-017-9430-4

Wing, J. M. (2006). Computational thinking. *Communications of the ACM, 49*(3), 33–35.

Yadav, A., Hong, H., & Stephenson, C. (2016). Computational thinking for all: Peda-gogical approaches to embedding 21st century problem solving in K–12 class-rooms. *Tech Trends, 60*(6), 565–568.

Yadav, A., Good, J., Voogt, J., & Fisser, P. (2017). Computational thinking as an emerging competence domain. In M. Mulder (Eds.), *Competence-based voca-tional and professional education* (pp. 1051–1067). Springer.

CHAPTER 5

LOOMING CODE

A Model, Learning Activity, and Professional Development Approach for Computer Science Educators

Heidee Vincent
University of North Texas

Victor R. Lee
Stanford University

Aubrey Rogowski
Utah State University

Mimi Recker
Utah State University

ABSTRACT

As school librarians are asked to take on more responsibilities outside of their regular duties, teaching coding is one such responsibility that falls outside their area of expertise. In response to these challenges faced by school librar-

Professional Development for In-Service Teachers, pages 121–139
Copyright © 2022 by Information Age Publishing
www.infoagepub.com

ians, this chapter proposes a model for designing computer science activities and instruction called Expansively-framed Unplugged. The chapter describes this model (also known as EfU) and demonstrates how it can be used to design activities such as Looming Code, a coding activity where students use Scratch to model existing patterns in a weaving as well as create new ones. This chapter describes the experience of an elementary school librarian as she attended professional development sessions to learn the activity and implemented it in two of her elementary school classes.

As providing equitable access to computer science (CS) education becomes a greater priority for many school districts throughout the United States, administrators are struggling to find additional time for scheduling learning in an already-packed school day. Because of this lack of available instructional minutes in the school day, many school librarians at the elementary and middle school levels are increasingly being asked to take on CS education responsibilities in their libraries, often in spite of their lack of training and familiarity with the subject (Martin, 2017). While school districts may sponsor professional development (PD) sessions and provide curricula, these districts are looking to librarians to teach computer coding when they have never been a student of this topic. In addition, due to budget constraints, many elementary school librarians begin working as part-time aids and are later hired as full-time librarians without ever completing a degree or certification as a school librarian or teacher. All together, these are challenging conditions for librarians to overcome in offering quality CS instruction in addition to performing their regular duties.

In this chapter, we describe a model, instructional activity, and PD approach to help school librarians or other educators with limited coding background to learn to lead coding activities in their libraries. The activities are comprised of both coding as well as "unplugged" computing activities—ones that do not require a digital computer (e.g., Bell et al., 2009). As librarians typically lack specific coding knowledge, the professional development takes a teachers-as-learners approach in which librarians are first involved as participants in the instructional activity. In this way, they first draw upon their knowledge of a familiar domain, the unplugged activity, and learn how this applies and transfers to coding concepts.

Our work begins with an observation that many of the librarians we have worked with engage in crafting as a hobby and are familiar with several different crafting media, such as paper, fabric, and paint (Lee & Vincent, 2019). Even if some librarians do not identify themselves as having a particular talent for crafting, we propose that physical crafting materials provide a concrete and tangible medium in which to explore coding concepts, and familiar media such as paper, markers, and yarn offer a low threshold to those who may be wary of learning computer programming. These aspects form the unplugged portion of our model and instructional activity.

The theoretical model underlying our approach draws upon a situated account of transfer, called expansive framing (Engle et al., 2012). This model suggests that students need extra support to fully expand the use context for new knowledge from the learning context to the transfer context, and that instructors can make that transition smoother by making multiple and frequent connections back and forth between the social context at learning and the social context at transfer. Expansive framing informed the design of the instructional activities to produce learning environments where coding is framed in real-world and authentic contexts, so that students more easily learn and retain new skills and educators (here, the librarians) are able to draw on and transfer their existing knowledge from a different yet familiar domain. Although coding connects to numerous fields and domains, the goal is for educators to make those connections explicit and frequent to both help their own learning as well as counter the risk of teaching content that their students see as only usable or applicable in one particular context.

By combining expansive framing and the unplugged approach, we propose an instructional model for introductory CS education called Expansively-framed Unplugged (EfU) (Lee & Vincent, 2019). It begins with a tangible unplugged activity, moves to paper and pencil and then digital representations of the activity (using a block-based coding language like Scratch, e.g.), and culminates in using the digital model to produce a new version of the original unplugged activity. This model informed an instantiation of an instructional activity, called Looming Code (see Table 5.1).

In the next sections, we first describe the theoretical motivation for our approach, its instantiation in Looming Code, and our approach to PD. We then describe one school librarian's experiences as she participated in our PD structured around EfU. The PD consisted of her participating in the Looming Code activities first as a student to draw upon her crafting knowledge to better understand and feel more comfortable with the specific coding activities. The librarian then implemented Looming Code with two classes of elementary school students in her school library.

BACKGROUND

Our EfU model combines ideas from both unplugged computing and the situated model of transfer, called expansive framing. Unplugged CS is a practice for teaching CS concepts and principles without a computer (e.g., Bell et al., 2009). These kinds of unplugged activities have been demonstrated in several domains, including beading (Eisenberg, 2010) and playing tabletop board games (Berland & Lee, 2011).

One of the main ideas of unplugged computing is to teach learners CS skills and concepts outside of the realm of a specific programming language. Students who shy away from actual computer coding may enjoy using those same skills and strategies in a different context, and the same skills used in coding, such as debugging and composition, can be learned and practiced in other types of tasks and contexts. This approach is similar to other long standing cognitive approaches for supporting transfer of learning through the use of analogies (Gentner, 1998) or metaphors (Videla, 2017).

For those who do enjoy actual coding, unplugged activities give them a way to practice concepts and strategies outside of a single programming language and to recognize contexts outside of the computer in which those skills could be useful. Another argument in favor of unplugged computing is that it provides a more tangible way for learning abstract CS concepts (Eisenberg et al., 2009; Kafai & Vasudevan, 2015). Students who may have a hard time understanding an abstract sorting algorithm, for example, may benefit from hands-on activities in which they sort items with paper, cards, or other tangible materials.

Unplugged activities are also appealing to teachers because, as they do not require 1–1 computing, they usually have a lower cost. However, teachers who implement unplugged activities exclusively run the risk of the learners' knowledge remaining situated in the medium of a specific unplugged task. Transfer of knowledge is problematic for instructors of all subject areas, as the learning context (environment in which the knowledge is learned) and transfer context (environment in which the knowledge will be needed) are not always similar (Bransford et al., 2000). If learners successfully practice a CS concept, such as algorithm building in a board game, they still may not be able to transfer that practice to an actual coding interface.

To address this problem, we turn to the model of expansive framing that is designed to create a more favorable environment for knowledge transfer (Engle et al., 2012). This model has been used by others to design more broadly appealing computational thinking curriculum and assessments (Grover et al., 2014).

This model posits that by making several, frequent connections back and forth between the social context of learning and the social context of transfer, teachers can help learners create an encompassing context that aids in knowledge transfer (see Figure 5.1 adapted from Engle et al., 2012). Thus, if students are able to understand the larger context into which the learning context and the transfer context fall, it will be easier for them to retain and use their knowledge in that transfer context.

Engle et al. (2012) identify five specific types of ways in which expansive framing connections can be made to create and strengthen that encompassing context. The first two involve connecting settings. First, if students understand how the skills learned will be useful for them in a future setting,

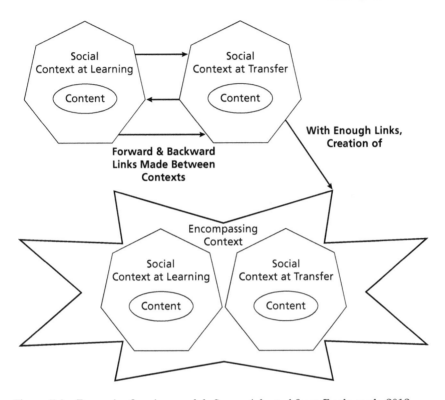

Figure 5.1 Expansive framing model. *Source:* Adapted from Engle et al., 2012.

they may learn and remember them better. Second is a focus on connecting settings in order to access prior knowledge. Besides encouraging students to look forward to future settings, this type of connection encourages students to look backwards and see how prior experience and learning may be applied to the current situation. This helps students link their current knowledge to prior knowledge, reducing the risk that current knowledge will become inert or obsolete (Bransford et al., 2000).

The next three connections involve authorship. The third type of connection suggested is that authorship leads to connecting prior knowledge in ways that support later transfer-out. This is similar to the second type in that teachers are encouraging students to use prior knowledge but emphasizes that authorship itself encourages students to do so. Engle et al. (2012) explain that students in these types of learning settings "sometimes brought in their own outside examples to form generalizations about the topics they were learning," and that "data showed that these students were also more likely to transfer certain facts, principles, and a learning strategy to a new context" (p. 224).

Fourth, authorship promotes accountability to particular content. If a student completes a creative project for some content, as opposed to passively learning about that same content, the very nature of the task encourages students to master the content in order to create. Finally, the fifth type of connection is that authorship as a practice promotes generation and adaptation of knowledge in transfer contexts. Instead of attempting to fill students' heads with knowledge, offering them a chance at authorship encourages them to be more than just consumers of knowledge and to strive to add something to the collective body of knowledge.

Eglash and Bennet (2009), for example, use the context of cornrows as a hairstyle and students' cultural capital in that area to stimulate connections to mathematics and coding. In their Cornrow Curves activity, students learn about the history of cornrows and use a computer program to create their own design. While many such connections between unplugged tasks and other non-digital contexts are desirable for transfer, we also want students to be able to use skills learned in unplugged tasks in an actual coding environment. In order to lessen the risk of students' knowledge remaining situated in unplugged tasks, our EfU model starts with unplugged activities and then encourages expansive framing to connect those tasks to actual coding tasks.

The EfU model consists of three domains and three movements across domains (see Figure 5.2). The three domains are physical artifact, paper and pencil, and digital. The first movement across domains is the movement from physical artifact to paper and pencil, where the learner creates a paper and pencil representation of the physical artifact. The second is from paper and pencil to digital, where learners use their paper and pencil representation to inform their code and create a digital model of the physical artifact. Last is the movement from digital back to physical, where learners use customized code to create their own physical artifact. Specific instantiations of the EfU model may contain steps where learners move deeper into a single domain, called submovements.

The three domains are informed by unplugged ideas. Learners and teachers who may be intimidated by starting in a digital format are eased into the process by starting with the physical artifact, then moving to paper, and finally coding digitally. Paper and pencil are also more accessible than the other two domains; it is often easier for a novice to fix a mistake on paper than it is to undo it in a physical product or in code.

The three movements are informed by the expansive framing model and serve to make connections back and forth between domains. Although students can learn to make physical artifacts or code independently of each other, the goal is for students to achieve transfer of knowledge so that their learning does not stay accessible only in the context in which it was gained. The five aspects of expansive framing mentioned earlier can be seen in different parts of the EfU model, as seen in Columns 1 and 5 of Table 5.1

in the following section. The movements from physical artifact to paper and pencil to digital offer connections of different settings for both future transfer and access to prior knowledge. Students who have done the particular unplugged activity or a similar one have prior knowledge they can draw on, and students who feel the knowledge presented might be useful in future contexts may achieve better transfer. The movement from digital back to physical artifact uses authorship of a new artifact to support later transfer out, promote accountability to particular content, and promote the generation and adaptation of knowledge.

Although the ideas behind expansive framing are focused on a situated view of student learning and transfer, they also apply to educators with little coding background. It is important to note that, unlike the other topics they may teach, they too are learners in this content area, and every aspect of EfU designed to help students learn may benefit them as well. Work by Putnam and Borko (2000) has shown that using a teacher-as-learners model for PD helps improve teacher learning. Thus, we propose that teachers prepare to teach and lead the activity by participating in it as their students will. Using unplugged ideas to inform the medium and tasks and using expansive framing to inform the interactions and conversations, will lead to an activity with a low threshold for both teachers and learners, and will help teachers with little coding background to successfully lead and support such activities.

TABLE 5.1 Levels in Looming Code and Connections to EfU				
Looming Code Level & Description	CS Concepts and Skills	EfU Model Movement	EfU Model Sub-Movement	Expansive Framing Connection
1 color grid based on physical weaving	Decomposition	Physical artifact to paper-and-pencil		FT, PK
2 make box pattern	Abstraction Loops		Paper-and-pencil	FT, PK
3 basic code in Scratch	Algorithms Abstraction	Paper-and-pencil to digital		FT, PK
4 shorter code in Scratch	Efficiency		Digital	FT, PK
5 customize design in Scratch	Debugging, Iteration		Digital	APK, APA, APG
6 create weaving from new design	Enacting code	Digital to physical artifact		APK, APA, APG

Key: FT—connecting settings for future transfer; PK—connecting settings to access prior knowledge; APK—authorship leads to connecting of prior knowledge in ways that support later transfer-out; APA—authorship promotes accountability to particular content; APG—authorship to promote generation and adaptation of knowledge.

Having teachers approach the content from the learners' perspective not only helps them become familiar with the content, but also gives them opportunities to experience firsthand the areas where students will struggle, which will help them as they lead the program themselves. This teacher-as-learner PD model has been shown to help improve teacher learning as well as shift their beliefs about teaching and learning to one more grounded in student thinking (Putnam & Borko, 2000).

EXEMPLARS

Looming Code in the Context of EfU

Looming Code consists of several levels in which learners examine example weavings, color the design on a grid, create a readable pattern of the design, code that pattern in Scratch, design a custom weaving in Scratch, and then make the design with physical materials. Table 5.1 summarizes each level and links each level to relevant CS concepts. We developed a set of Level Cards, which break down the steps of each level and offer tips and reminders, along with the student worksheet and the Scratch program used.

Level 1

In Level 1, learners are given a weaving, such as the one in Figure 5.2, and asked to examine the pattern and transfer it to a paper grid. This helps learners practice decomposition, as they move from looking at the weaving as a whole to looking at the individual parts and how they fit together. The facilitator can ask learners to think about other areas of their lives where they have to take a task or problem and divide it into smaller parts, and connect this level to coding skills by talking about decomposition explicitly.

Level 2

Once they move to Level 2, the learners make a box pattern from their grid pattern, as shown in Figure 5.3. With a completed and colored grid of the design, learners can start decomposing it further. When weaving, designs are made by using different combinations of up and down for the vertical strings, called the warp. These strings are either up or down, forming a sort of binary system in which infinite designs can be created. Learners will start with the first line of the weaving and create a box pattern for that line. This is essentially a row of boxes, with each box shifted either up or down to represent the position of a particular string. Learners will create a box pattern row for each unique row of their pattern. After creating the individual rows, learners will write the sequence of rows, for example, 1 2 3 4 3 2 1. This creates a readable pattern from which the design could be

Figure 5.2 Example weaving given to students to decode.

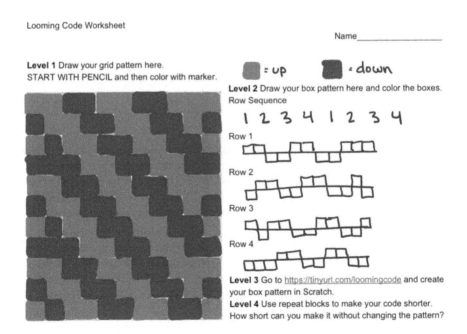

Figure 5.3 Example looming code student worksheet, levels 1 and 2.

recreated. This encourages learners to look for repeating patterns in and within rows. Some weaving designs will have a 1 2 1 2 1 2 sequence, while others include 1 2 3 4 1 2 3 4 and 1 2 3 4 3 2 1. In the classroom or library, the teacher can talk with students about abstraction as well as repeat loops.

The facilitator can also start a conversation about notation. The librarian who participated in our PD sessions stated that her students had just finished a unit in poetry, where they learned to notate poem lines by their ending rhymes, using letters to represent unique rows. Like the weaving designs, poems can have many different rhyming sequences, such as A B A B, A B A C, and others. Thus, the instructor can explain to students that it does not really matter whether they use numbers or letters or even shapes to create written notations of patterns, but it is important that they are consistent with their notation and that they make the notation clear to others who might want to understand or recreate the design and pattern.

At this point, learners can also discuss how the grid pattern from Level 1 and the box pattern from Level 2 are similar and different, and whether both are useful or necessary. Both patterns contain an accurate and complete representation of the weaving design. They both show which colored strings are visible in different parts of the weaving, but the grid pattern shows a complete visual depiction of the design as completed, whereas the box pattern is a deconstructed version. The grid pattern could be used when creating a new design to visualize the result, or to show someone else what a particular design will look like. The box pattern is more for someone who is making the design. When weaving, using a complete visual of the design requires weavers to keep track of the row they are on, as well as count boxes in a small colored grid, which could easily lead to errors. Using a more deconstructed representation, such as the box pattern allows them to see one row at a time as well as how to move their warp strings to make each row.

Level 3

In Level 3, learners are coding their pattern in Scratch. Using their box pattern and a skeleton program in Scratch, learners code each unique row with Up or Down blocks that map to the position of the boxes in their box pattern rows. Once the learners code their rows, they then move to code the sequence of rows for their design. Learners have this already written in their box pattern, so they simply need to transfer that to a row of code with the same numbers. Once they are finished coding, learners can run their code to create a visual representation of the design. The skeleton program has code in the background that creates a colored grid based on the sequence of Up and Down blocks in each row and the sequence of rows. Learners can change the colors of the boxes to match the design they are using. Ideally, the colored grid in Scratch should match their grid pattern on paper exactly. Of course, errors can be made in the process of transferring the design to a paper grid, then to a box pattern, and then to Scratch, but the visual model in Scratch allows students to compare their digital and physical designs to check for accuracy. If errors appear, the facilitator can talk to the learners about debugging, and how important it is to be able to identify whether or not there is an error, how to find it, and how to fix it. The facilitator can help learners debug or ask individual learners to help each other.

Level 4

Once learners debug their patterns and code and the visual model presented in Scratch is acceptable, they start looking for repeating patterns inside their code of the individual rows and sequence of rows. This constitutes Level 4. At this point, the facilitator can ask the learners to make their code as efficient as possible without changing the design. Code such as "Up Up Up" can be rewritten with a repeat block, using only two blocks instead of three. The result of this level depends on both the pattern a learner is using and how they decide to use the repeat blocks in their code.

Level 5

After the learners work through the first few levels with the given weaving design, they have the opportunity to create their own design in Level 5. Learners can modify their existing code or wipe everything and start afresh. If learners are having a hard time thinking of what to do for a new design, they can always keep the rows they have already coded and simply rearrange them into a new design.

Level 6

Once learners finish creating their design in Scratch, they begin Level 6 and read the pattern in their code to create their design with pipe cleaners. Instead of using real looms and yarn to weave, we use pipe cleaners and large combs. Real looms are either expensive to purchase for a whole class or difficult for younger children to operate, and we discovered that wide-toothed combs hold the pipe cleaners just enough to give students a sturdy base on which to start their weaving. Using pipe cleaners allows students more room for creativity, as it is cheaper to provide a wide variety of colors in pipe cleaners than it is in yarn. Students can also change the colors in the weft or the warp very easily with the pipe cleaners. Weaving with pipe cleaners is less time consuming than weaving with yarn, since it is not necessary to have a very tight weave and frustrating tangles are much less likely. At the end of Level 6, students complete the Looming Code sequence. If time permits, the facilitator can provide students an opportunity to try others' designs and create patterns that will stay in the library (or classroom) for future use.

As students move through the levels of the Looming Code activity, they also progress through the domains of the EfU model and make more and more connections between contexts. Table 5.1 lists each level of Looming Code with its associated movement or submovement. Table 5.1 shows how Looming Code involves the five types of connections suggested by the expansive framing model to promote transfer. The first four levels (Levels 1–4) focus on connecting settings for both access to prior knowledge and future transfer. The type of tasks students will be doing, such as taking apart a bigger problem into smaller pieces and writing and reading step-by-step instructions, can be applied to many situations and may be tailored to student interest and experience at the discretion of the teacher.

The last two Levels of Looming Code (Levels 5 & 6) focus on authorship. According to the expansive framing model, allowing students to use their creativity to take what they learned in the first half and create a new design will draw on prior knowledge, promote accountability to what they are learning, and give them a sense of having generated and adapted knowledge rather than passively consuming information.

As mentioned earlier, the three domains of the EfU model are informed by unplugged ideas, and the three movements are informed by expansive framing (see Figure 5.4). Some students and teachers have prior experience with Scratch or other block-based coding platforms, but many have none. If learners not familiar with Scratch start on the computer right away, trying to code a pattern as they decipher it, they would be learning new content and a new interface simultaneously. In order to reduce this cognitive

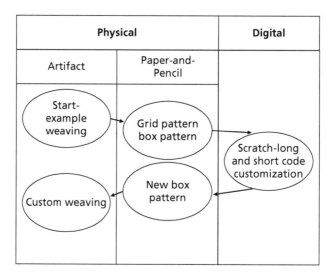

Figure 5.4 Domains and movements within EfU model with associated looming code levels.

load, learners use both physical artifacts and paper and pencil work to become familiar with the content—the weaving design—before being introduced to a new interface—Scratch. By the time learners finish their paper and pencil representations of the pattern, they are simply re-instantiating the pattern in Scratch.

Professional Development: Teacher as Learner

In addition to developing Looming Code as an instantiation of the EfU model to help both student and teacher learning, we also designed accompanying PD, using a teacher-as-learner approach. Instead of simply presenting the program materials to the librarians and talking through the program, we set up a space with all the materials needed for librarians to participate in Looming Code just like students.

This served three purposes. First, the librarian, who would later be the instructor for the program, was able to learn new and unfamiliar content she would later be required to teach. This is unlike most PD approaches where teachers are assumed to have the necessary background knowledge. Second, she had the opportunity to sit in the students' place and see the program from the learner point of view. This helps her recognize places where students will struggle and prepare for questions and scaffolding opportunities. Finally, she gets to see the instruction modeled as we teach the program. All three purposes help prepare the librarian to successfully implement the program with students and create successful learning environments.

METHODS/DATA COLLECTION

As part of a larger design-based research study in the Rocky Mountain region of the United States, one public school media and technology teacher, Rachel (a pseudonym), participated. Rachel had her elementary education teaching license, a master's degree in gifted education, and an administrative endorsement. This was Rachel's first year as the media and technology teacher, but she had several years of teaching experience. At the time of data collection, she was teaching Grade K–5 media and technology courses in the library, working with students for 90 minutes each week. Rachel was responsible for teaching both the library media and computer classes for all students in the school.

Rachel and her fifth grade students were participants in early iterations of our PD and Looming Code program. Her participation and feedback during PD sessions helped to inform our subsequent iterations and implementations of the program. Prior to participation in our Looming Code program, Rachel had been teaching her fifth grade students Scratch so they were familiar with the basics of the Scratch interface prior to beginning this project. In addition, Rachel had pursued looming as a personal hobby and was familiar with weaving techniques and patterns.

Rachel attended two PD sessions, taught by our team, each lasting around 1 hour, in which she participated in the program as a learner, with the understanding that she, in turn, would implement the program with two fifth grade classes in the library during their media and technology class time. In addition to the PD sessions, she was provided with the necessary program materials and supplies.

Rachel implemented the Looming Code activity with two of her classes, and each class spent two class periods on the activity. Each class period was ninety minutes, however both classes experienced some interruptions that prevented them from using the entirety of their time on the activity. There were 30 students total between the two classes who participated in the activity. We observed the activity and only directly interacted with them when Rachel asked us for clarification on something she was doing. The data described in the next section was collected in the PD sessions and classroom implementations in the form of observational field notes and photographs.

RESULTS AND DISCUSSION

During our first PD session with Rachel, we gave her a copy of the level cards, which included the instructions for each level and the worksheet and had her participate in the program as a student. We asked questions and pointed out things to watch for as she worked. After completing the first two levels, Rachel suggested a small change to the format of the worksheet and had several ideas on how she would teach this portion of the activity to her students. While working in Scratch, she deleted some of the background code needed to create the visual, but then realized her mistake. She was able to successfully transfer her box pattern to Scratch to produce a digital representation of the pattern. Then she customized the code to create her own pattern and began weaving it on a loom. Due to time constraints, she was not able to finish her weaving. During the second session, we gave her all the materials and resources she would need to teach the program and reviewed the program flow. She felt comfortable with the material and was excited to start the program with two of her fifth grade classes.

Throughout Rachel's implementation of the Looming Code program in her library and computer lab, she engaged in various activities we considered to be good teaching practice, or habits developed by teachers with her level of experience. She managed the behavior and focus of her classes well, asked probing questions to check for understanding, and was able to provide support and scaffolding for individual students or the whole class when help was needed. Besides Rachel's scattered comments on how she would teach certain sections of the program, none of these pedagogical behaviors were discussed in the PD sessions. We found that once Rachel was comfortable with the content of the program, she used knowledge of teaching and facilitating to adjust and augment the program to fit the needs of her students and space.

To begin the program, Rachel gave the students an overview of all the levels, and then started on a three-column chart, labeled, "Something I wonder about," "Something I learned," and "How I felt about the activity." She had the students share thoughts for the first column. While sharing thoughts about the "Something I wonder about" section of the chart, one student asked why they were doing this activity. Rachel responded by saying, "That's a good question. What does life have to do with code?" She let the students think about that for a moment, and then asked if there are no rules that we have to follow in life. One student pointed out that we should follow the rules but do not have to, and Rachel said that just like life has certain rules, so does code. She then asked, "What does code have to do with life?" The students thought, and she asked them if they have ever played a computer or video game and said that is a good example of code. She also pointed out that the fact that their parents' eye and hair color determine their eye and hair color is actually a form of code, genetic code. The students thought that was neat. One student shared that he wondered how they will be able to fix their work if they mess up, Rachel asked, "Even if it doesn't turn out exactly the way we wanted, is that really a failure?" and pointed out that some of the best learning experiences come from failures.

During levels one and two, Rachel passed two example weavings around the class for the students to hold and examine. When they were coloring their grids, she passed around boxes of crayons that included only the colors of crayons they needed to match the example weavings. Before moving to Level 3, Rachel moved all the students to the computer lab. She pulled up the Scratch project on the projector and showed the students the code (see Figure 5.5).

She pointed out that all the blocks currently on the screen need to stay where they are and they should not delete any of them, something she had done the first time she used the project. Rachel also modeled for the students how to code their rows and run their program, and asked questions to check their understanding. While modeling code, she purposely coded something incorrectly, ran the program, and asked her students why it did not work. The students were able to spot the bug in the code and fix it with Rachel's help.

As the students worked on their code, Rachel walked around, monitoring their behavior and looking for opportunities to provide support to

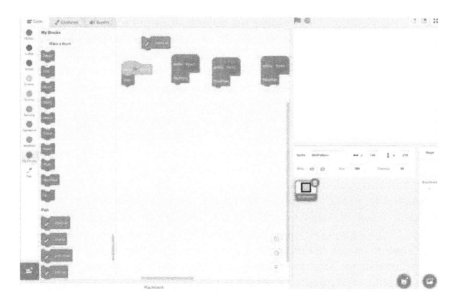

Figure 5.5   Skeleton code students used to build their patterns in scratch.

struggling students. While walking around, she was able to clarify misconceptions the students had, such as one student who believed the pattern could not be bigger than a certain length. Near the end of class, students chatted about the possibilities of coding in Scratch. Rachel mentioned that they could do some geometry work in Scratch, since they were learning about geometry in another class, and asked the students if they thought they could code a rhombus or other geometrical shape.

As the class progressed to later levels of the program, Rachel used printouts of the level cards taped to the whiteboard to help students see what they had done so far and what they would be doing next. She modeled how to set up the comb with the pipe cleaners and how to start and complete the weaving. For the rest of the time, there were students at different stages of progress. Some were coding the example pattern, some were coding their own pattern, and some were weaving their own pattern. As Rachel circled the room and talked to individual students, she was able to answer their questions no matter what step they were on. Near the end of class, she noticed an incorrect practice that had started spreading across the room and called everyone's attention to the front so that she could point it out and correct it. After explaining the correct method, she helped students who had made that error to fix their weaving.

After completing the program, we conducted a 20 minute, recorded, semi-structured interview with Rachel to find out how she felt the program had gone. We asked ten questions regarding the implementation of the program and use of the resources and materials. She said that the biggest takeaway for the students had been that they could use Scratch to make something real, and that the biggest takeaway for herself was to make sure she could do each part of the program herself before she taught it. She had shared with us when we first started working with her that she was familiar with weaving, but during the interview explained that she had never followed any specific patterns and had done what she called free looming. She told us that the Looming Code program really got her thinking about the intentionality of executing a specific pattern in a design.

Rachel also shared with us that she appreciated having both the learner's and the teacher's perspective of the program, and that it helped her see where her students would need help. She knew how she would further tweak and improve the activity if she did it again, and said that overall, she really enjoyed it. Seeing the kids sitting on the floor weaving and chatting makes her think of a quilting bee (a social activity where people gather to make quilts).

Overall, our observations show that the EfU model, Looming Code program, and teacher as learner PD approach helped Rachel gain enough content knowledge in a new activity to be able to adapt it to her particular students and use her good teaching practices to create a fun, successful learning environment.

NEXT STEPS

This chapter described a conceptual model, instructional activity, and PD approach designed to prepare school librarians or other educators with limited coding background to learn to lead coding activities and lessons in their libraries. The conceptual model, EfU, is based on a situated account of transfer, in which backward and forward connections between known unplugged contexts and new coding contexts are made salient and authorship is emphasized. EfU informed the design on an instructional activity, Looming Code, which links weaving, as its familiar and unplugged context, to the new context, coding patterns in Scratch, and back to weaving again. Similarly, the PD design is influenced by EfU and the teacher as learner approach, in that librarians first participate in Looming Code as students, and draw upon their existing knowledge of crafting to help understand and feel comfortable with the subsequent coding activities.

We note that while the example described in this chapter uses crafting, specifically weaving, as its unplugged activity, the EfU model is not limited in its scope of possible unplugged activities. In current work, we are using EfU to inform an instructional unit that uses computationally-rich board games as the familiar context. Students play these games, learn computational thinking concepts, and then create their own board games in a digital coding environment (Lee et al., 2020). In using the EfU conceptual approach, a key goal is to identify familiar contexts for students as well as teachers that serve as useful unplugged "funds of knowledge" (Moll & Greenberg, 1990) to support learning in the digital environment. A key assumption is that a well-chosen unplugged context may offer a means to broadening participation in coding to students who may otherwise lack interest. In order to avoid replicating patterns of participation in CS that exclude certain groups of students, we seek contexts (e.g., weaving, board games) that are both rich in computation and offer many trajectories for more inclusive participation. We believe that many such fruitful contexts still remain to be explored.

Future work should investigate to what extent this provides enough of a bridge for teachers who are new to coding to support and scaffold coding activities in their instructional context. This model is not proposed as a way to create content experts in CS but rather to enable non-experts to feel comfortable in hosting activities in which the students become engaged and interested in coding. While this instantiation was implemented with one educator, the model as well as the Looming Code program are certainly scalable. Similarly, future work should examine to what extent this approach moves beyond simply sparking initial interest in students and encourages a growing level of involvement and persistence in CS.

ACKNOWLEDGMENTS

This work was supported by the Institute of Museum and Library Services grant number RE-31-16-0013-16. We thank our partnering librarians, their students, and the school district.

Resources for the Looming Code activity can be found at https://slli .usu.edu/looming-code/

REFERENCES

Bell, T., Alexander, J., Freeman, I., & Grimley, M. (2009). Computer science unplugged: School students doing real computing without computers. *The New Zealand Journal of Applied Computing and Information Technology, 13*(1), 20–29.

Berland, M., & Lee, V. R. (2011). Collaborative strategic board games as a site for distributed computational thinking. *International Journal of Game-Based Learning, 1*(2), 65–81.

Bransford, J. D., Brown, A. L., & Cocking, R. R. (2000). *How people learn* (Vol. 11). National Academy Press.

Eglash, R., & Bennett, A. (2009). Teaching with hidden capital: Agency in children's computational explorations of cornrow hairstyles. *Children, Youth and Environments, 19*(1), 58–73.

Eisenberg, M. (2010). Bead games, or, getting started in computational thinking without a computer. *International Journal of Computers for Mathematical Learning, 15*(2), 161–166.

Eisenberg, M., Elumeze, N., MacFerrin, M., & Buechley, L. (2009, June). Children's programming, reconsidered: Settings, stuff, and surfaces [Conference session]. In P. Paolini (Chair), *The 8th International Conference on Interaction Design and Children* (pp. 1–8). ACM.

Engle, R. A., Lam, D. P., Meyer, X. S., & Nix, S. E. (2012). How does expansive framing promote transfer? Several proposed explanations and a research agenda for investigating them. *Educational Psychologist, 47*(3), 215–231.

Gentner, D. (1998). Analogies. In W. Bechtel, G. Graham, & D. A. Balota (Eds.), *A companion to cognitive science* (pp. 107–113). Blackwell.

Grover, S., Pea, R. D., & Cooper, S. (2014, June 23–27). Expansive framing and preparation for future learning in middle-school computer science [Conference session]. In J. L. Polman, E. A. Kyza, D. K. O'Neill, I. Tabak, W. R. Penuel, A. S. Jurow, K. O'Connor, T. Lee, & Laura D'Amico (Eds.), *11th International Conference of the Learning Sciences* (pp. 992–996). International Society of the Learning Sciences.

Kafai, Y., & Vasudevan, V. (2015, June 21–24). Hi-Lo tech games: Crafting, coding and collaboration of augmented board games by high school youth [Conference session]. In M. Umaschi Bers & G. Revelle (Co-Chairs), *The 14th International Conference on Interaction Design and Children* (pp. 130–139). ACM.

Lee, V. R., & Vincent, H. (2019, March). An expansively-framed unplugged weaving sequence to bear computation fruit of the loom [Conference session]. In P. Blikstein & N. Holbert (Co-Charis), *FabLearn Conference 2019* (pp. 124–127). Association for Computing Machinery.

Lee, V. R., Poole, F., Clarke-Midura, J., Recker, M., & Rasmussen, M. (2020). Introducing coding through tabletop board games and their digital instantiations across elementary classrooms and school libraries [Conference session]. In J. Zhang & M. Sherriff (Co-Chairs), *ACM Technical Symposium on Computer Science Education* (pp. 787–793). ACM. https://doi.org/10.1145/3328778.3366917

Moll, L. C., & Greenberg, J. B. (1990). Creating zones of possibilities: Combining social contexts for instruction. In L. Moll (Eds.), *Vygotsky and education: Instructional implications and applications of sociohistorical psychology* (pp. 319–348). Cambridge University Press.

Martin, C. (2017). Libraries as facilitators of coding for all. *Knowledge Quest, 45*(3), 46–53.

Putnam, R. T., & Borko, H. (2000). What do new views of knowledge and thinking have to say about research on teacher learning? *Educational Researcher, 29*(1), 4–15.

Videla, A. (2017). Metaphors we compute by. *Communications of the ACM, 60*(10), 42–45.

PART II

PROFESSIONAL DEVELOPMENT APPROACHES
FOR HIGH SCHOOL TEACHERS

CHAPTER 6

RE-MAKING EDUCATION IN STEM CLASSROOMS WITH COMPUTATIONAL MAKING

Brian E. Gravel
Tufts University

Maria C. Olivares
Boston University

Eli Tucker-Raymond
Boston University

ABSTRACT

Increased attention to computational thinking and its relationship to STEM teaching and learning has surfaced opportunities to explore and complicate fundamental assumptions about computation in disciplinary inquiry. Particular attention to how systematic patterns of exclusion and oppression persist in STEM and computer science requires consideration of expansive notions of computation, making, and disciplinary inquiry. This chapter describes computational making, drawing from architecture, computer science, and

Professional Development for In-Service Teachers, pages 143–170

engineering, to define and explore ways of incorporating computation in STEM classrooms through the iterative explorations of phenomena using different tools and materials. Our goals are to support teacher learning through designs that center computational making as a means of integrating computation into STEM classrooms. We present a model for re-making STEM through professional learning by asking teachers to (re)negotiate relationships to tools and materials, to disciplinary thinking, and to students through computational making. The chapter describes the theoretical rationale for the approach, the four phases of our professional learning model, including computational play, co-learning with students, reflection, and curricular design and enactment. Examples of teachers negotiating their relationships between disciplinary activity and making are presented to show how the model supports teachers' efforts to re-make STEM learning in their classrooms.

This volume explores how best to prepare in-service teachers to teach computer science (CS). With the inclusion of computational thinking (CT) in framework documents like the *Next Generation Science Standards* and the *K–12 CS Framework*, coupled with the demands of an increasingly computational world, the teaching of CS in K–12 schools deserves the attention it is receiving (Smith, 2016). One way to integrate computational ideas and practices more broadly is to position computation as inquiry in disciplinary classrooms, such as science and mathematics. At the same time, we argue the field must pay particular attention to how systematic patterns of exclusion and oppression persist in CS (Margolis, 2008; Vakil, 2018) and in STEM broadly. This chapter describes a model of teacher professional learning that is designed to study how mathematics and science teachers integrate computational practices into their classrooms in ways that invite students from Black, Latinx, and other groups underrepresented in high quality CS and STEM classes.

We position computational practices as opportunities for disrupting structures and relationships of power in the historically exclusionary spaces of math and science. In our work, we partner with teachers and school districts to think about how students engage in compelling, authentic inquiry with computational practices to open our eyes to new forms of participation and learning in STEM classrooms. A critical dimension of our approach is the intentional consideration of *making*—the exploration and manipulation of physical and digital materials for the purposes of expressing ideas, exploring phenomena, or solving problems (see Peppler et al., 2016)—as a means for expanding notions of participation. The combination of making, computation, and disciplinary inquiry, which we call *computational making*, requires teachers to renegotiate their relationships to disciplinary and teaching practices. Our design research suggests that the core of this challenge is directly related to how teachers, new to ideas of CS, computation, and making, must re-establish their relationships to disciplinary forms of inquiry they teach, the tools of that inquiry, and to their students.

In this chapter, we first explore a vignette of teachers modeling ideas in mathematics through making. Their modeling illuminated critical issues of how teachers came to think about integrating making and computational practices into their mathematics and science classrooms. We then present a theoretical perspective that specifically outlines the notion of computational making and how it can serve as a context for teachers' (re)negotiations of their relationships to disciplinary inquiry, to tools and materials, and to students. The central feature of the chapter is the presentation of the model for professional learning. It includes illustrative examples from the first two phases of the model, describing how relationships are renegotiated in service of bringing computation into STEM classrooms through making.

Our Motivation: Modeling to Make Meaning of Mathematics

Two high school geometry teachers, veterans of over 20 years each, are sitting at a table in a converted woodshop. The workshop is now a making space with a laser cutter, CNC mill, 3D printers, and other digital fabrication and electronics tools alongside the old woodworking machine, all located in the basement of a large urban high school. They are two of six people participating in a professional learning workshop on integrating making into their classrooms (Tucker-Raymond & Gravel, 2019). Of the six, they are the only two who want to learn how to use the 3D printer. The others have gone off to make wooden stools with the power saws.

After being introduced to the software program TinkerCAD, through tutorials provided in the software, the researcher asks the two teachers, Georgia and Kim, what they might want to make. Kim recalls that they give their geometry students a problem in which the students are given a (theoretical) hexagonal prism with a cylindrical hole in the middle (imagine a nut that would tighten on a screw) and they must determine the volume of the remaining material of the hexagonal prism when the diameter of the hole is the same as the diameter of the hexagon. Kim suggests they print this object with the 3D printer and Georgia agrees. In their contemplation of the object, they realize that if the hole were to touch the sides of the hexagon, as in the problem they give their students, the sides of the hexagon would not be continuous:

    Georgia: It will be too thin.
    Researcher: Yes, too thin.

Kim: So smaller, okay (touches keyboard). But now we run into the other problem because the actual calculation of the volume should be actually touching here. [What we do in class] is not realistic. It's not realistic, I know that. Actually, now I see it. Actually, when we talk about it, this one, we have to be more realistic now. Because usually we calculate it [as it] touches the hexagonal side. We always teach [it this way]. We forgot that if you touch the side, actually, the side there, [is] cut off. It becomes disconnected.

Georgia: But probably if you leave more [of the hexagonal] and take it out it won't touch.

Kim: This is the reality now though. I realize we never [thought] about that before this year. This is the diameter of the cylinder so that will also be the radius of the hexagonal. But now we forgot we have to leave space in order to hold the volume (smiles and laughs quietly). By design, I realize. All these years I didn't realize that.

Exploring new technologies together, Kim and Georgia set about translating a familiar mathematics problem that they both assigned to their high school students into this new modality, modeling software and 3D printing. The problem asked students to subtract a cylinder from a hexagonal prism as part of a volume calculation in geometry. Here, Kim had a major realization that the problem they had been assigning made little sense in the physical world. "By design, I realized," Kim offered, admitting that engaging in 3D design that involved transposing the problem into the modeling software illuminated a discrepancy. If the cylinder diameter was the same width as the hexagon, then the edges would touch; a 3D printer would not be able to produce such an object, because there must be "space in order to hold the volume." We interpret this to mean she realized the problem they had assigned to students, who completed it on paper with numerical equations, makes little sense when applied to physical objects. Kim admitted, "All these years I didn't realize that." Exploring the problem through processes of design and working with new tools exposed a discrepancy she had not identified in over 20 years of teaching. This is not a criticism of the teachers. It suggests that making can surface moments where teachers might revisit the disciplinary content they teach and the tools they use to teach it.

The teachers wanted to make a three-dimensional object using mathematical ideas that they taught. Kim and Georgia worked within a modeling environment that supported their efforts to project a flattened one-dimensional mathematical expression into a new three-dimensional representation. Producing this model using digital fabrication technologies, the 3D printer transformed the problem from computing on paper to computing with things (Knight & Stiny, 2015). In that way, engaging computation tools, like the modeling software and printer, supported a course of inquiry manifested in their making. This opened space for them to "realize" discontinuities in the ways they were relating to disciplinary ideas (e.g., translating between representations) as well as how they were teaching these ideas to their students. Yet, considering the integration of these kinds of making activities in their classrooms surfaced doubt and skepticism. Georgia later said, "I don't see how that is going to fly in a 30 student class," and Kim added, "30 students, so how do you actually get them to the same place?" While the teachers had reconsidered the relationships between mathematics and tools through making, the challenge of bringing making into their classrooms required complimentary reconsideration of their relationships to students. This integration of new tools and approaches meant paying attention to multiple, cooperative relationships at the heart of teaching and learning (Hawkins, 1974). In the workshop, the teachers focused on their making and did not discuss the learning and teaching roles that were routine in their classrooms. We learned that when teachers engaged in making they were encouraged to learn new tools and to see content in new ways. However, we had not asked them to reconsider how integrating computational forms of making might necessitate paying attention to a full range of relationships in their classrooms, including repositioning students as knowers and doers.

This story of making and mathematics catalyzed our current work, and we build on this story to describe our research using a model of professional learning for K–12 STEM teachers that emphasizes play in the space of computational making. Computational making integrates physical materials and processes, representative of "making" and the broader "maker movement" (Halverson & Sheridan, 2014) with engineering design and CT practices. Our model is designed to support teachers' explorations of computation as implicated in: (a) the disciplinary inquiry they teach; (b) the tools, for computation or not, they use with their students to engage in disciplinary practices; and (c) the ways in which they understand their students as knowers and doers. Our research seeks to understand how teachers (re)negotiate their relationships to disciplinary inquiry, tools and materials, *and* to their students, and how the shifting relationships might contribute to restructuring the pedagogies and participation structures in STEM classrooms.

BACKGROUND

Like others interested in computational activity, we are excited by the possibilities of computation for authentic inquiry in K–12 classrooms. Specifically, we subscribe to a generative perspective on computation, an expansive view of CT practices, and a mode of engagement through computational making that connects computation to heterogeneous forms of disciplinary practice. Our goal is teacher learning, and thus we connect prior research on making and computation to theories of teacher learning to show how the professional learning model creates the space for teachers to shift their relationships to disciplinary inquiry, tools, and students.

Making the Case for Re-Making STEM

Re-Making STEM emphasizes the generative importance of expanding notions of practices, participation, and engagement. Critically examining the assumptions and privileges grounding dominant descriptions of disciplinary activity requires addressing the "settled expectations" (Bang et al., 2012; Harris, 1993) that drive research and practice in educational contexts. These expectations—born from dominant positions of power, and normative visions of practice—shape how we understand tool use, language use, and the fundamental structures of inquiry. We propose a working definition of computation that supports a critical examination of the expectations that figure current conversations about CT, and offer an expansive perspective on computational inquiry that centers the role of materials and making to support disciplinary learning.

A Working Definition of Computation

Computation has long been central to how philosophers, cognitive scientists, and computer scientists have explored knowledge creation and representation (Humphreys, 2004; Minsky, 1974). Debates about the central importance of algorithms, abstraction, and the fundamental relationships between mathematics and computation date back almost a century (Copeland, 1996). These debates embody the search for elegant definitions of both the fundamental acts of a computer, but also how all learners can enact forms of thinking that resemble the logical processes of computational machinery (Yadav et al., 2016). In this chapter, we build on these attempts to define computation by considering computation from the perspective of *making*. Like others, we find prior descriptions of computing narrowing and constraining (Denning, 2009). Decoupling our thinking about computation from programming, coding, or even computers, can address this challenge. To this end, we find Knight and Stiny's (2015) definition of computation provocative. They approach computation from the perspective of architectural studies, introducing "making grammars" to illustrate the relationships between making, materiality, and certain kinds of "logic" that can govern our actions with shapes. With making grammars, Knight and Stiny (2015) propose that computation means defining a set of rules for combining elements of a system. The specific combination produces result-ing behaviors—the outcomes of those rule configurations—which present either expected or surprising effects. This suggests that establishing a set of rules for how elements are related and combined, assessing the behavior that these combinations produce, and revising those combinations are core practices of computation. One of their examples highlights how designers can combine two shapes recursively using a specific set of rules governing those combinations. We extend this idea—of rules and combinations—to think about materials and techniques for manipulating those objects in making activities, like with paper automata (e.g., Eisenberg et al., 2004), which we term *computational making*.

To illustrate this definition of computation within computational mak-ing, consider the rotating cam and follower in Figure 6.1. A cam and fol-lower mechanism involves a rotating piece, called the cam, spinning on an axle to translate rotary motion into linear motion, where the follower is a rod moved up and down by the spinning cam. In the example, the heart-shaped object is the cam that spins around, and the follower is the stick with a block at the bottom that rests on top of the heart. There are many ways to consider the rules governing the device's behavior: speed and direction of how the heart-shaped cam is rotated, the interaction between the shape of the cam and the shape of the follower, and the various points where the object is constrained (i.e., held into place), for example.

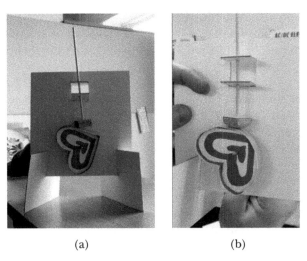

(a)   (b)

Figure 6.1 The "Heart Cam" project where the heart spins on axis to move the follower. Original design (a) with sharp edges and a loosely constrained follower, and the iterated version (b) with a rounded heart shape, tape along the interface, and a more securely constrained follower.

As the cam is rotated, the follower reacts and behaves in a particular way, in other words, the physical assembly is comprised of a set of rules—or relationships between the elements of the device—and those constituent rules combine to produce the behaviors the system exhibits. While the maker has a vision of how they would like the machine to act—the heart spins, and the follower drives the attached shaft up and down—in the first iteration, their design does not operate quite as they had hoped. The cam and follower often "stick," as these makers noticed, where all motion stops. This somewhat unexpected behavior presents an opportunity to make some decisions about where to go next with the making and inquiry. They could opt to spend time making sense of why it works this way, or change the rules of the system (i.e., iterate on the design) to make it operate more like what was envisioned, or explore a new direction altogether because the behaviors they observed sparked some new interest in the materials or mechanisms. In this example, one of the participants, Ruth, commented that she was "just overwhelmed at the number of ways it doesn't work," further wondering "how we can debug enough of what I called the wobbles in our movement machine to make it work, sort of." These makers chose to try and get the contraption to work as they imagined, and they engaged in a series of iterative adjustments to different components of their project. They rounded the edges of the heart to create fewer sharp corners. They added scotch tape to the edge of the heart to reduce friction between it and the follower. And, they adjusted the follower by changing the shape of the block on the bottom and better securing the wooden skewer so that it could move up and down with less side-to-side wiggle (Figure 6.1). The outcome was a project that spun much more smoothly, a result achieved through attending to the "rules" of the system and altering them to produce changes in its behavior.

Interpreting this example through the lens of Knight and Stiny's (2015) idea of computing with materials, the heart-cam makers' process amounts to a form of computational inquiry. The decisions about how to assemble the contraption, how to secure different elements, and how to operate it all amount to conjectures about how these materials and rules of engagement fit together. The prescription and adjustment of rules are manifestations of the maker's conjectures with materials—what they built became a computational system—and the ways that system behaved became moments to learn from. As Ruth noted, she was "overwhelmed" by the ways this system did not "work," yet they engaged in an iterative process of building, operating, and refining this device to improve its performance. This is a learning process, organized by these material conjectures embedded in the maker's craft. Whether that learning is directed at refining rules to produce desired behaviors or taking the opportunity to shift the thread of inquiry toward an emergent point of interest, computation helps us understand different ways of learning with tools and materials (see Champion et al., 2020).

Re-Thinking Computational Thinking Practices

The history of attempts to define what computation means for thinking and learning (e.g., Bers, 2017; Grover & Pea, 2013; Papert, 1980; Wing, 2006) are collective efforts to articulate what it means to think *like* and *with* a computer. These conversations about CT relocate "thinking" from the machine to be instead distributed between the people, the machines, and the languages that mediate conversations between them (Vygotsky, 1978). CT from this stance is about how humans think, together or alone, in ways that amplify the power of computational tools to ask questions, make expressions, represent ideas, or gather information. While efforts to define and expand CT (e.g., "CS Unplugged," Caeli & Yadav, 2020) offer valuable insights about forms of human thinking with tools and materials, we argue too little attention has been paid to the inherent presumed coupling of CT with the origins of CS as a discipline (Denning, 2017). Denning (2009) argues that the construct of CT is one too closely tied to the field of CS. That is to say, the same social, political, and intellectual orientations that structure CS and its interpretation of computation have come to predominantly structure and restrict our notion of what it means to think computationally. While this framing of CT affords an ability to draw from a theoretical and practical repertoires rooted in the field of CS, it has also delimited and discouraged the conception and pursuit of a more profound, disciplinarily dynamic, and cross-cutting understanding of computation. To this point, Denning (2009) writes, "A growing number of scientists are now saying that information processes occur naturally (e.g., DNA transcription) . . . Computation is present in nature even when scientists are not observing it or thinking about it" (p. 30). Indeed, the current conversation and related frameworks organize the space of CT using principles foundational to CS, which places specific constraints on attempts to define and advance computation. We hope to complicate the "settled" (Bang et al., 2012) nature and origins of the current debates about CT with a conscious decoupling of the ideas of "thinking computationally" from CS in order to imagine expansive possibilities for learning in computation.

Underlying these discussions of CT appears to be an assumption that computation, in its current form and within its current delineations, has somehow already arrived, we know precisely what it looks like, we can name the practices, and we can imagine the possibilities that this established line of thinking and practice create. While theoretical and empirical work has given some shape to notions of computation in particular contexts, we argue this assumption requires further examination to unearth and transform powered systems deeply entrenched in how we conceive of and realize computation. As an example of the blackboxing that has taken place at the hands of a technophilic society, we briefly take up the case of the d-c algorithm paradigm.

Abstracted from social phenomena and initially adapted informally in mathematics and computing as an idea used "to help with the explanation of an algorithm" (Aho et al., 1974, p. 1), the d-c paradigm was adapted as a "control abstraction" program for rapid problem-breakdown and automation (Horowitz & Sahni, 1978). The d-c paradigm—where *d-c* is shorthand for divide-and-conquer—has evolved in outwardly neutral and mechanistic disguise through the process of shorthand encoding and rapid utilization and proliferation within a quickly evolving CS. Divide-and-conquer algorithms are foundationally driven by a paradigm that aims to recursively and perpetually identify a problem, break it down into sub-problems more easily solvable/domitable, and "conquer" or "solve" them. In a society founded on the American imperialistic doctrine of manifest destiny and the subjugation, exploitation, and elimination of Native and African peoples it necessitated, it is critical that efforts toward educational equity and broadening participation in STEM interrogate and reconceive of what is possible, what is known, what can still be known as it relates to computation, human thought, and attempts at CT integration in educational settings. Further, treating computation as a settled or well-understood activity erases the consequential reality of stark and unjust differential access to computational skills, tools, and practices for people based on racial, gender, and socioeconomic differences (for example, see Margolis, 2008). The conversation around "what counts as computational thinking" has limited interaction with conversations about equity and the endemic marginalization of historically underrepresented groups in STEM, including CS (Vakil, 2018). These are conversations that must be had in parallel, to inform one another, if we are to provide access and achieve equity in STEM education. The field's current understanding of CT is predicated on the purposes and practices of dominant groups and their understandings of computation, not unlike traditional STEM disciplines (Bang et al., 2012). This means that we have yet to understand what different forms of computation look like and how it functions for marginalized groups who have been excluded from conversations that have defined the dominant meanings of CT.

We seek to build on, refine, and possibly expand definitions of CT. We want to know what learning is possible with computation, but we choose to center the overlooked issues of power, exclusion, and preservation in discussions of how computation should and can contribute to more equitable STEM classrooms. We do this by imagining computation as a way of inquiring, where the concurrent and collective exploration of ideas, tools, materials, through forms of making, becomes a way to explore more expansive notions of what "counts" as computational work. To do this with teachers and students is to encourage an examination of the relationships to disciplinary inquiry, tools, and each other through computational activity.

Computational Making Practices

Our professional learning model builds from a central high-level conjecture: By participating in a professional learning program that provides opportunities to incorporate computational making practices (CMPs) through interdisciplinary exploratory play, co-making with students, and attention to heterogeneity, teachers will learn how to effectively incorporate computational learning opportunities into their disciplinary classrooms and change their relationships to tools, disciplinary inquiry, and students (see Sandoval, 2014). This conjecture supposes that there are certain practices for making and thinking computationally that create the space for teachers to renegotiate relationships; these practices define computational making as an activity.

Our framework for CMPs was based on prior research and theory as well as our own empirical work in computational making settings (e.g., Grover & Pea, 2013; NRC, 2012; Weintrop et al., 2016; Wing, 2006). Through practices drawn from CT frameworks coupled with science, mathematics, and engineering disciplinary practices, as well as making practices (Honey & Kanter, 2013; Tucker-Raymond & Gravel, 2019), we designed a space to give learners opportunities to conduct their own inquiries, provide authentic contexts for their learning, and engage their identities in science and engineering.

The composite framework of CMPs in Table 6.1 operates as a constellation of practices that support inquiry across different contexts. Situated perspectives on learning (Lave & Wenger, 1991) place particular attention on the contexts where learning happens, acknowledging that the particulars of each context shape the learning there. A situated perspective is central to how we imagine CMPs are enacted in classrooms, where teacher's individual situations, disciplinary foci, and relationships are seen as intertwined with the practices they enact with their students in the classroom.

Our focus on these CMPs leverages the affordances of physical computing and digital fabrication as well as the values and characteristics associated with making practices. At the same time, it takes seriously the ways in which computation can most effectively serve disciplinary investigations. The examples presented in Table 6.1 highlight the interconnectedness of these practices, and the ways they are used for particular activities and disciplinary goals. At the same time, the CMPs are considered a lens through which to look more expansively at forms of computational activity, ways of seeing computation that create space for teacher learning organized around their multiple relationships of practice.

TABLE 6.1 Computational Making Practices With Examples From Participant's Projects

Practice	Definition	Example
Identifying an initial phenomenon	Understanding the scope of a phenomenon and its constituent factors	Simplistic public perception of social movements, like Black Lives Matter
Identifying emergent phenomena	Identifying phenomena that arise in the process of making	Negotiating the many personal relationships to social movements and how to represent that
Decomposing an initial phenomenon	Breaking down a phenomenon into parts that can be more easily solved	Trying to understand why youth do not use the public parks
Transforming a phenomenon	Translating a phenomenon for different contexts, tools, and computational devices	Prototyping a mobile "app" using Micro:bit radio signal functionality
Iterating design	Prototyping, making multiple revisions and improvements of designs and products	Reconfiguring the wiring pathway through an interactive pi
Abstracting	Represent real phenomena and generalize through computational means	Building a small "greenhouse" to test temperature monitoring systems for growing plants inside
Modeling	Developing and using models to understand the world and test theories and solutions	Relating slow Internet speeds in schools to the number of students trying to access the network at any time
Debugging and troubleshooting	Systematically figuring out why something is not working	Testing multiple different servos with the Micro:bit to see which behaves as expected
Attending to precision	Considering the (high or low) importance of precision	Moving from scissors to a dye cutter to make precise cuts for a pop-up card
Brainstorming with materials	Thinking through and generating ideas with materials and their specific properties	Wrapping paddle wire around a dowel to create a spring
Selecting tools, materials, and processes	Awareness of affordances and constraints to make informed decisions for use	Moving from scissors to a laser cutter to make gears out of mounting board
Communicating to audiences	Sharing with others. Using networks for help, discussion, and dissemination	Creating video "pitches" of prototype designs for feedback

Teacher Learning: Renegotiating Relationships to Disciplinary Inquiry, Tools, and Students

We have argued that computation is a means for learning with tools and materials, but here we are specifically talking about teachers. Computational making is a central component of the framework guiding our design, but we must also consider how teachers learn to shift their practices, and what they might shift their practices towards: teacher learning as disciplinary inquiry (Ball & Cohen, 1999), and teacher learning organized around heterogeneous ways of knowing (Nasir et al., 2006). We will describe how teacher learning through collective, disciplinary activity, and a perspective on the heterogeneity of disciplinary inquiry and classrooms shapes classroom practice, which grounds the design of our model focused on shifting relationships.

Teacher Learning as Disciplinary Inquiry

Successful models of teacher professional development that support teacher change provide opportunities for collective inquiry among participants in ongoing communities of practice that are closely tied to classroom practice (Ball & Cohen, 1999). At the same time, opportunities that engage teachers in disciplinary inquiry, highlighting the multiple, heterogeneous ways of knowing both in disciplinary thinking and in their classrooms, change teachers' relationships to their classroom teaching, the disciplines themselves, and their students' sense-making (Rosebery et al., 2017). Moreover, learning opportunities in which teachers conduct their own inquiries and develop classroom materials related to those efforts make those materials resources for reflecting on their own thinking (Pappas & Tucker-Raymond, 2011). As teachers work together and talk, "peer interaction provides important opportunities for teachers to express, test, and revise their artifact *and* their ways of thinking about teaching and learning as related to the artifact" (Zawojewski et al., 2008, p. 221). The work of professional learning is one of examining and renegotiating relationships that connect people, ideas, and things.

Heterogeneous Ways of Knowing

Human sense-making and activity are fundamentally diverse, dynamic cultural processes (Cole, 1996; Rogoff, 2003), and teaching needs to be responsive to this heterogeneity. Nasir et al. (2006) offer that "culture" means "the constellations of practices historically developed and dynamically shaped by communities in order to accomplish the purposes they value" (p. 489). Practices are formed, shaped, and affirmed through the ways communities use tools and materials and organize activity. These wide-ranging "constellations of practice" comprise the foundation of heterogeneous ways of knowing and being, and we draw this perspective to understand learning as the continual acquisition and refinement of diverse repertoires of heterogeneous cultural practices (Gutierrez & Rogoff, 2003), including learning with computational tools in disciplinary activities.

Studies of mathematics and science learning have likewise documented the fundamentally heterogeneous nature of students' sense-making (Calabrese Barton & Tan, 2009; Rosebery et al., 2010; Warren et al., 2001). In our view, designing for heterogeneity has the potential to expand the territory of sense-making away from what has conventionally been highlighted in schools to include more wide-ranging, intellectually powerful practices like those outlined in NGSS and discussed above (Bang et al., 2012; NGSS Lead States, 2013). To do this effectively, however, entails that teachers learn to recognize and attend to their students' diverse sense-making repertoires as intellectually generative in science and math (Rosebery et al., 2017) and that they are oriented toward students' sense-making in a relationship of "actively responsive understanding" (Bakhtin, 1986). Designing for heterogeneity will help both teachers and students expand the limits of what is perceived as possible (Heath, 1986) for meaningful engagement in STEM.

EXEMPLAR: THE RE-MAKING STEM PROJECT

In a partnership between learning scientists, critical scholars of education, computational mathematicians and physicists, engineering and computer educators, and two school districts, the Re-Making STEM project's centerpiece is a model for sustained multidisciplinary professional learning. This professional learning model consists of a four-phase design that draws from extensive literature on teacher learning, teacher inquiry, and heterogeneous ways of understanding disciplinary thinking and students (Rosebery et al., 2017; Russ et al., 2016; Warren & Rosebery, 1995).

The Professional Learning Model of Re-Making STEM

The model is a four-phase structure for professional learning. Phase 1 was a 5-month period of playing with craft and digital materials, which we called *computational play*. Phase 2 asked teachers to become *co-learners* and *co-makers* with their students, beginning with after-school sessions to explore problems, tools and materials, and ways of working together as learners. This phase culminated in week-long summer workshops where teachers and students explored the theme of movement, both social movements and issues of access and equity in the public spaces they inhabit (e.g., playgrounds and parks). Phases 3 and 4 involved supporting teachers to co-design and implement their own curricular units featuring computational making. We present each of the phases, with descriptions of participation structures and grounding examples of how relationships were (re)negotiated as teachers engaged in computational play and co-learning activities.

Phase 1: Computational Play

Play involves taking risks and exploring new configurations (Bruner, 1972), it fosters role-playing (Kavanaugh, 2011), it is deeply cultural (Rogoff et al., 1993), and it can create moments where people "bump up against the world"—where the world does not behave in the ways people might expect—which can be powerful catalysts for learning (Bransford & Schwarz, 1999). In this first phase, teachers are asked to be playful with tools and materials, each other, and ideas, as a means of beginning to explore their relationships to tools, materials, and disciplinary inquiry. Phase 1 play sessions are organized around prompts, domains of materials that became increasingly unfamiliar over time, and participation structures. The opening prompt is, "Make something move." Teachers use card stock, mounting board, and tools for cutting and assembling to begin making something move. Drawing inspiration from semi-functional models (e.g., the heart-shaped cam in Figure 6.1), websites like papermech.net, and books are encouraged. Together, teachers build objects that are whimsical, exploratory, and playful using paper and craft materials, things most individuals are familiar with. The second prompt is, "Make something that interacts," where new tools are introduced: geared-down hobby motors, simple circuit materials, piezo buzzers, and LEDs. Motors might be added to existing prototypes to drive their motions, or copper tape and LEDs may be used to create a circuit within the object. Digital fabrication tools are introduced as the expressed needs of the teachers warrant their use, for example, if teachers want to make gears out of mounting boards and scissors are not working well. Finally, the third prompt asks teachers to "Tell a story" with their creations and the optional addition of digital tools like the Micro:bit and digital design software. Throughout this progression of prompts and projects, teachers move from mechanical ("Make something move") to electrical ("Make something interact") to digital modalities ("Tell a story"). All along, their creations evolve, shift, dissolve, and morph as new tools, materials, and ideas are introduced into the space of computational possibilities.

Participation Structures

Over the course of this ~30 hour exploration, a complimentary set of participation structures supports teachers in drawing out computational ideas, reflecting on making, and discussing emergent disciplinary questions. Each session includes *circle time*, where participants sit in a large circle and each person is asked to share a reflection on the session in response to one of four prompts: (a) "What was a success you experienced today?"; (b) "What was a frustration you experienced today?"; (c) "What was something you learned from someone else today?"; and (d) "What connections do you see to STEM?" Everyone shares at circle time, so that all voices are heard

Figure 6.2 Cupid project, involving the wound rubber band which spun an arrow in circles.

and themes are surfaced. Circle time is consistently conducted each session in order to establish it as a practice, both to support teachers reflecting on their own relationships and to model the practice for teachers to bring to their classrooms.

Example 1: Renegotiating a Relationship to Mathematics in Making

During Phase 1, Tom and Cara, both middle/high school math teachers participating in the first enactment of the model, worked together to "make something move." In their first project, they built "Cupid" using a wound-up rubber band attached to an arrow. The user spins the arrow around to a certain point, and the rubber band unwinds it when the user releases it, eventually pointing at one of the people sitting around a circle (see Figure 6.2). Elsewhere, we have described how disciplinary questions emerged in this project, as the teachers wrestled with questions of friction, probability, and momentum with their colleagues (Gravel et al., 2019). While we observed moments of disciplinary inquiry, Cara still questioned the relationships between math and making Cupid:

> I was saying when we made Cupid, like, we didn't, we hadn't really done a whole lot of math to help us make the project. We did some math after, we tried to fit math to it. We talked about, like, do we think it's better or worse, or does it matter, to use the math to make the thing, or to try to fit the math to the thing.

Cara's question positions math and making as relatively discrete entities. Mathematics is known, it is something she knew how to identify in her work, at least, a form of mathematics that she was accustomed to using. In building Cupid, they had not done the kinds of things that she associated with mathematics. She raised the questions of when math might be happening, before or after (e.g., to "fit math" to the project), in the processes of making. Parsing the activities of math and making reveals aspects of her relationships to these activities, maintaining them as generally separate entities. Yet, her question also places the relationship between them at the center of her curiosity, "Do we think that it's better or worse, or does it matter?" This is evidence of her early-stage negotiations of the structure of the relationship between math and making in the context of her project. Her wonderment signifies an attempt to understand inquiry in computational making relative to mathematics as she knows it, a familiar activity. Mapping the structures of computational making (e.g., "math to make" or "fit math to the thing") to her own ideas about disciplinary practice opened space for her to begin negotiating ideas about what it means to "do math" (in its recognizable forms) as compared with other activity.

With Cupid, the teachers explored the relationships between winding and unwinding of the arrow. They wondered, does winding up the arrow five times produce a proportional number of spins? This was a mathematical question for them, and they recorded data on different attempts in a table, collected using the high-speed camera on their iPhone to take careful measurements. A curious observation emerged: for small numbers of winds, the resulting spins were slightly less; for example, 4 winds produced 3.5 spins. However, for larger winds, Cupid would spin *more* than the number of winds; for example, 10 winds produced 12 spins. The observation sparked a fruitful discussion about friction, momentum, and how they might model this phenomenon. For Cara, the Cupid project did not present as obviously mathematical, yet it surfaced questions about the relationships between mathematics and making, including where and how mathematics contributed to the larger inquiry in which she and her colleagues were engaged. Later, we see Cara further wonder about a different structural configuration in terms of how math is situated in the making processes.

In another round of inquiry, Tom and colleagues built a small version of the game "Operation." Tom reflected on this project, specifically contemplating the roles of abstraction and modeling—ideas central to mathematical practice—as he described the kinds of thinking their project demanded:

> I think we kind of did two very different kinds of thinking. Where the one kind of thinking was building a circuit that was gonna work, and like, make things light up and make noise, and stuff... when, you know, you complete the circuit. So that was, like, one kind of thinking that wasn't so much spatial. We were drawing a lot of little, like, circuits in our notebooks and stuff like that, and playing with these pieces. Um. And then the other kind of thinking we were doing was very spatial, it was like the layout of the pieces, how

big are they gonna be, how are we gonna cut them out, like, we, we did, like, a mockup of the little monster guy...here [grabs and older example]. So, mock up for a little monster guy...so this kind of stuff was very, looking at it, laying it out. And then the circuit stuff was more like serial, like putting this stuff in order, like, do we have enough batteries, that kind of stuff. So, there was two very different kinds of thinking that I think was going on.

Tom named two "kinds" of thinking that he noticed in different aspects of their project: As he calls it, the "serial" thinking required to wire a circuit, where step-by-step decisions are made in ways reminiscent of algorithmic forms of thinking; and the "spatial" thinking required to arrange different pieces of the project. Tom's curiosity explored the nature of the thinking that went into different aspects of their computational making project. This was less about the large scope relationship between math and making, but rather it was his attempt to refine descriptions of the different kinds of thinking that certain tasks, tools, and materials seemed to require. Designing so that circuits are "gonna work" shaped their thinking in some ways, and organizing and arranging elements shaped their thinking in other ways. This relates to the tools and materials under consideration, but also the nature of the tasks themselves, making something work compared with making decisions about how something should look. We interpret his focus on "kinds" of thinking as negotiating his relationships between making, tools, and characteristics of thinking—"serial" and "spatial"—that map onto mathematical ideas. Cara placed mathematics and making in comparison with each other. Tom focused more on finding corresponding structures between the two. Both orientations offer substantive evidence of the relational work happening within this context as teachers considered, and expanded, notions of disciplinary inquiry.

Both reflections came in response to asking the teachers to relate the CMPs to their making in this computational play phase. Cara and Tom represent different ways teachers negotiated the relationships of their work—to disciplinary inquiry, tools, and materials through these playful engagements. Specifically, Cara was responding to the "modeling" CMPs as she mapped the structure of making to recognizable forms of mathematics (e.g., using tables to record the number of winds compared to the number of unwinds). Whereas Tom, thought about the materials at hand (e.g., circuits, laser cut board game pieces), specifically "selecting tools, materials, and procedures," and how certain materials and tasks may influence the forms of thinking required to engage in computational making. Naming these forms of thinking provided space to begin mapping what emerged in making to forms of mathematical practice, like using algorithms and representing ideas spatially.

Phase 2: Co-Making, Co-Learning

This phase expands the focus on teachers' relationships to disciplinary inquiry and tools to include their relationship to students, as partners in learning. The explicit consideration of student-teacher relationships in making is central to our goals of addressing equity and inclusion in computational spaces. As the teachers in our opening vignette experienced, bringing computational making to classrooms requires consideration of what we expect students can do. Through making, we see possibilities in how teachers might develop relationships to students' as knowers and doers. In this phase of the model, teachers and students operate as co-makers to identify and address problems or issues in the world.

This phase asks teachers to intentionally explore their relationships to students' heterogeneous knowledge practices. We framed this as an inquiry into students about whom the teachers had questions—about their strengths, brilliance, barriers to engagement—and what might be possible in a new relational dynamic (Ballenger, 2009). Teachers were asked to specifically consider students from nondominant communities, and in our workshops all of the participating youth identified as students of color. The teachers expressed reservations about how to address the stable roles of teacher and student that they occupied in their classrooms. At the same time, they expressed excitement about using unfamiliar territory—computational making—as grounds to explore their relationships to their students in new ways.

This co-learning phase begins with the introduction of specific co-learning principles, which included: (a) Don't say "no" to ideas—say "yes" and build on them; (b) Just try it; (c) This is *one way* to do it, not *the* way; (d) Play, and have fun with making! With co-learning as a goal, careful selection of tools, materials, and tasks was required to protect against inadvertently positioning the adults as more knowledgeable than youth—a powered dynamic we are explicitly trying to disrupt. To this end, the introductory activity is to "take something apart." Teachers and students take apart broken electronics like old camcorders, laptops, VCRs and DVD players, small kitchen appliances, and computer peripherals (e.g., keyboards, mice), exploring the components and finding elements that intrigue them. While potentially "technocentric" (Blikstein, 2013), this activity places an unknown object at the center of the shared inquiry, where neither the student nor the teacher knows what they will find inside. This shared space to wonder about what things are, how they work, and how to take things apart creates the conditions for teachers to express intellectual humility (Olivares et al., 2019). Openly expressing curiosity, uncertainty, and respect for students' ways of inquiring is critical to the renegotiation of teachers' relationships to their students (Olivares & Tucker-Raymond, 2020). In our workshops, some co-makers were inspired to learn more about how these electronics worked. One group was fascinated by large capacitors they found inside an old computer—exploring the symbols on the components and making sense of their possible functions in the devices they disassembled. Others were encouraged to build something new from the components they harvested, including using found buttons or motors to control or power kinetic sculptures. Following these initial activities, there is a week-long summer making workshop where the same students and teachers work together to scope problems and design responses or solutions.

The week-long computational making workshops are the centerpiece of Phase 2. The theme of the workshop is, "Movement: Of People, Machines, and Nature." Movement connects broadly to various disciplinary ideas and social issues, for example, the modeling of systems of energy flow on playgrounds or representations of change in public opinion over time. The theme is situated within a larger charge to "make your community a better place to be." The teachers and students spend significant time framing the problem, developing prototypes, playing with materials, and receiving feedback. The youth are experts when it comes to their own communities, and thus their contributions to understanding the problem and designing solutions are recognized and valued. Embedded in the workshops are engineering and design activities intended to help participants shape and refine their projects. These include problem scoping and framing activities, structures for prioritizing tasks, and different ways of offering and receiving feedback. Teachers and young people work together in teams of 4–6, and the culminating event invites parents and community members to a showcase of the projects.

Participation Structures

As with Phase 1, participation structures are critical in facilitating how participants negotiate different kinds of relationships. Phase 2 focuses on teachers' re-negotiating relationships to students, alongside continued negotiations of their relationships to disciplinary inquiry and tools. In this co-making, we encourage free-choice grouping and fluid role constructions. Participants have agency to organize as they choose, and to reorganize as they see fit. This flexibility is critical to supporting the exploration of new directions and it requires supporting participant's attempts to get "unstuck" when certain configurations prove challenging. Where possible, teachers and students have access to "technical support" for specific tool workflows, programming within specific coding environments, and design advice to address impasses. In our first enactment, the participants jokingly asked for an hour of "Ask Amon," where one of the PIs sat at a table and fielded questions like a helpdesk. Circle time remains a constant practice in Phase 2, where students and teachers reflect together and identify themes and threads of their experience. The final structure is an exhibition, where friends, family, and community members are invited to see the work, ask questions, and engage with students' and teachers' co-learning from the week.

Example 2: Rethinking Mathematics, Students, and Making

At the conclusion of a second summer workshop week in Phase 2, Cara reflected on co-learning with her students after they had worked on a few different projects together:

> We're all learning, it's not like I could show them how to use the CNC. I don't know. I didn't know how to use the Micro:bit to do what we wanted to. I didn't know how to make that box. So [the students] felt like on an even playing field with all the adults I think. Which was cool.

Cara positioned everyone as learners in this phase, students and teachers alike. The students learned to use the CNC and laser cutter to make parts for their project while she learned to code the micro:bit. Neither the students nor Cara had done either task before. Co-making on large projects involves many tools, processes, and problems, and different collaborators assume roles and conduct tasks in ways that are distributed and cooperative. That way, they are all "learning" together. The acknowledgement of students as knowers and doers emerged in their shared work, and it appears as evidence of how relationships can be understood in new ways through computational making. Following this co-making, Cara described mathematics operating in a way that seems different from her earlier comments:

> But I think the big idea...is what math do we need to use when, and why do we need to use it? And so even if you're just talking about basic operations, my biggest deal issue with students is they have all those tools, Pythagorean theorem, graphing, blah blah blah, but they don't know how to figure out which tool they need to use at what point. And that's what I'm trying to teach them. It's, "You know all this" and I'll be, "Okay, what's the next step?" And they'll be, "Add" and if I don't react, they'll go "Subtract. No. Divide."...So, do I think [computational making] is useful? Yeah, because there is something tangible now they are seeing it and they're feeling it and they're trying to apply it though. It's still hard for those students that struggle to pick what they're applying, but I think it is easier and that's a skill that I think who cares how hard the actual math is. It's about do you know what you need to do now?

Cara discussed how her teaching goal is "What math do we need to know when, and why do we need to use it?" She related that challenge to her experiences with making, where the "tangible" materials became the focus of mathematical inquiry. Compared with her earlier treatment of math and making it as relatively distinct entities, here she framed math as a tool used to address problems or needs in particular moments. No longer positioning math and making as discrete activities, computational making served to re-frame the mathematical work in terms of problem solving with "tangible" objects, where making and mathematics are integrated and mutually informing.

Designing and fabricating objects on the CNC, or on the laser cutter, requires different forms of mathematical computation (e.g., laying out objects equally in space, comparing measures and scales). Cara noticed her students engaging with math in these ways as they worked alongside her. Their mathematical practices were directed toward their needs for the CNC and the laser cutter. The same students she had in class, who "don't know how to figure out which tool they need to use and at what point," were now doing exactly that, within the context of computational making. Cara realized that some mathematical practices may still pose challenges for students, but within the context of making, math becomes a tool for conducting the kinds of design and inquiry required by the problem or phenomena at hand. And that students can demonstrate their own ways of making math useful as a tool in their work.

In these exemples, both related to Phase 1 and Phase 2 of the model, teachers actively negotiated relationships to different elements of their practice. Cara mapped her early experiences with making onto what she knew about mathematics while Tom articulated different forms of mathematical thinking required when engaging different tools and materials. Further, Cara witnessed her students, as co-learners and co-makers, approaching math as a heuristic in their shared project. Shifting relationships between math, materials, and students is precisely the goal of the Re-Making STEM model. The design, which leverages aspects of play, exploration, and collaboration, situates computation and making as contexts for teacher learning. Teacher learning involves shifting relationships in order to see computational making as a new approach to engaging their students, and their heterogeneous ways of knowing, in authentic inquiry in STEM classrooms. While the analysis is preliminary, the exemplars show how these shifts in relationship involve re-mappings, refined definitions, and coming to see students' resources in new ways. However, while the evidence of the desired shifts is present in Phases 1 and 2, we argue that it is also crucial to explore how these shifts play out in classroom settings, which are the focus on Phases 3 and 4 of the model.

Phases 3 and 4: Reflection, Curricular Planning, and Implementation

Teachers convene in Phase 3 to reflect on the first two phases of work and to begin planning for a computational making curricular unit. Reflection begins with a careful analysis of the various roles that participants played during Phase 2. Teachers are asked to map the roles they experienced at different times, and the relative length and centrality of their positions in those roles. In the first enactment, the role of "learner" appeared in every single teacher's map—both centrally, and in relation to other roles like "follower," "facilitator," and "put together-er." The prominence of teachers listing learner in different kinds of ways, especially in relation to the co-learning structure, suggests that Phase 2 created space for teachers to examine ways of relating to their students around learning in computational making activities. Teachers build on discussions of roles as they considered "big ideas" for their classroom units. Over a series of meetings, curricular plans are developed that include computational making activities to engage students in the CMPs. Researchers and teachers are partners in this work, co-designing the units with feedback from colleagues. Included in this reflection and planning phase are the development of assessments specific to each teacher's classroom context.

Phase 4 is implementation, and the duration, cycles, and intensity of implementation will obviously vary. Central to this phase is design flexibility along critical dimensions: duration, complexity of problems, alignment with content standards, and roles for teachers and researchers in the enactments themselves. By co-designing, and allowing for a broad range of flexibility, teachers are able to modify existing project ideas, create new ones, or even explore ideas together with their students over long periods of time before coming to see a possible computational making project that could enhance the work. All along, teachers and researchers debrief the classroom sessions, centered on the relationships between people, tools, and ideas.

FUTURE DIRECTIONS FOR RE-MAKING STEM

The Re-Making STEM professional learning model has illuminated some exciting features of how computation and making can impact teacher learning and practice. The model foregrounds the importance of play and adopting roles as learners in exploring new materials and tools, activities teachers unfortunately have little time to do in their professional lives. In computational making, the complexity of relationships to disciplinary inquiry, to tools, and to other people are made available for reconsideration. We saw teachers changing how they map disciplinary thinking and activities (i.e., making) onto each other, how they define different forms of thinking as it relates to materials and tasks, and we saw teachers acknowledge students' mathematical prowess in new ways. Phases 1 and 2 created the space for these complex relationships to surface, and to become the objects of reflection and reconsideration. At the same time, more careful analysis of teacher planning and implementation will hopefully reveal more about how these relationships shifted, the dynamics of those shifts, and ways to more securely build computational making into STEM teachers' practice.

We share this model in hopes that it can inform the field's desire to design for and study transformative ways of bringing computation, CS, and CT into K–12 schools. We must also expressly state the need for explicit consideration of power in the relationships we are trying to interrogate and the structures we are trying to disrupt. As we articulated above, we call for an expansive view of computation, one that is not solely coupled with the discipline of CS, but rather one that opens our eyes to how people learn with disciplinary practices, new tools, and other people, be it together with colleagues, or students and teachers working collaboratively as co-learners. To intentionally question the origins of frameworks like CT allows us to center issues of equity in the design of teacher professional learning. Our model consequentially addresses issues of power by striving for a renegotiation of pivotal relationships in teachers' practice. To shift ways of thinking about disciplinary inquiry, tools, and materials is to take an expansive view of what is possible in computational activity. Therefore, our model's core objective is to bring computation into the classroom in ways that broaden ideas about who can participate in STEM and what that participation might look like.

Looking forward, the model demonstrates possible pathways for STEM teachers to bring computation into their classrooms. We acknowledge that other researchers and educators may want to address this goal from within more dominant conversations about computation. We hope our approach is seen as complementary, as all domains should embrace persistent challenges to the settled notions of computational approaches to disciplinary activity. When taking a more expansive view of computation—computational making—we might better understand what computational activity can do for youth and teachers alike. The expanded perspective offers new insights into how they approach new tools and materials, frame problems and phenomena they are knowledgeable of and passionate about, and express their stances or identities relative to social movements, tools, and disciplinary inquiry. We hope this model serves as an on-ramp to more formalized computational paradigms, connecting to CS principles that are grounded in approaches that value the funds of knowledge and heterogeneous practices that youth bring to moments of inquiry. We ask researchers of CS and CT to center the role of equity, and to work toward dignifying approaches to STEM and CS teacher professional learning.

ACKNOWLEDGMENTS

This material is based upon work supported by the National Science Foundation under Grant Numbers DRL–1742369, DRL–1742091. We would like to acknowledge the support and collaboration of Amon Millner, Aditi Wagh, Dionne Champion, Ezra Gouvea, Ada Ren, David Benedetto, and Ann Rosebery, whose brilliance is central in this work. Any opinions, findings, and conclusions or recommendations expressed in this material are those of the author(s) and do not necessarily reflect the views of the National Science Foundation. Part of this project was originally carried out at TERC in Cambridge, MA.

REFERENCES

Aho, A. V., & Hopcroft, J. E. (1974). *The design and analysis of computer algorithms.* Pearson Education India.

Bakhtin, M. M. (1986). *Speech genres and other late essays.* University of Texas Press.

Ball, D. L., & Cohen, D. K. (1999). Developing practice, developing practitioners: Toward a practice-based theory of professional education. In L. Darling-Hammond & G. Sykes (Eds.), *Teaching as the learning profession: Handbook of policy and practice* (pp. 3–22). Jossey Bass.

Ballenger, C. (2009). Puzzling moments, teachable moments: Practicing teacher research in urban classrooms. *Practitioners Inquiry Series.* Teachers College Press.

Bang, M., Warren, B., Rosebery, A. S., & Medin, D. (2012). Desettling expectations in science education. *Human Development, 55*(5–6), 302–318.

Bers, M. U. (2017). *Coding as a playground: Programming and computational thinking in the early childhood classroom.* Routledge.

Blikstein, P. (2013). Digital fabrication and 'making' in education: The democratization of invention. *FabLabs: Of machines, makers and inventors, 4,* 1–21.

Bransford, J. D., & Schwartz, D. L. (1999). Chapter 3: Rethinking transfer: A simple proposal with multiple implications. *Review of Research in Education, 24*(1), 61–100.

Bruner, J. S. (1972). Nature and uses of immaturity. *American Psychologist, 27*(8), 687–708.

Caeli, E. N., & Yadav, A. (2020). Unplugged approaches to computational thinking: A historical perspective. *TechTrends, 64*(1), 29–36.

Calabrese Barton, A. C., & Tan, E. (2009). Funds of knowledge and discourses and hybrid space. *Journal of Research in Science Teaching, 46*(1), 50–73.

Champion, D., Tucker-Raymond, E., Millner, A., Wright, C., Gravel, B., Likely, R., Allen-Handy, A., & Dandridge, T. (2020). Designing for computational STEM and arts integration in culturally sustaining learning ecologies. *Information and Learning Sciences, 121*(9/10), 785–804.

Cole, M. (1996). *Cultural psychology, A once and future discipline.* The Belknap Press of Harvard University Press.

Copeland, B. J. (1996). What is computation? *Synthese, 108*(3), 335–359.

Denning, P. J. (2009). Beyond computational thinking. *Communications of the ACM, 52*(6), 28–30.

Denning, P. J. (2017). Remaining trouble spots with computational thinking. *Communications of the ACM, 60*(6), 33–39.

Eisenberg, M., Buechley, L., & Elumeze, N. (2004, December). Computation and construction kits: Toward the next generation of tangible building media for children. In Kinshuk, D. G. Sampson, & P. Isaías (Eds.). *Proceedings of the IADIS International Conference on Cognition and Exploratory Learning in Digital Age* (pp. 423-426). IADIS Press.

Gravel, B. E., Olivares, M. C., Tucker-Raymond, E., Wagh, A., Gouvea, E., Millner, A., & Ren, A. (2019, March 31–April 3). *Teachers' emerging disciplinary questions in the context of computational play* [Paper presentation]. The National Association of Research on Science Teaching Annual International Conference.

Grover, S., & Pea, R. (2013). Computational thinking in K–12: A review of the state of the field. *Educational Researcher, 42*(1), 38–43.

Gutiérrez, K. D., & Rogoff, B. (2003). Cultural ways of learning: Individual traits or repertoires of practice. *Educational Researcher, 32*(5), 19–25.

Halverson, E. R., & Sheridan, K. (2014). The maker movement in education. *Harvard Educational Review, 84*(4), 495–504.

Harris, C. I. (1993). Whiteness as property. *Harvard Law Review, 106*(8), 1707–1791.

Hawkins, D. (1974). I, thou, and it. In D. Hawkins (Ed.), *The informed vision: Essays on learning and human nature* (pp. 48–62). Agathon.

Heath, S. B. (1986). The functions and uses of literacy. In S. de Castell, A. Luke, & K. Egan (Eds.), *Literacy, society, and schooling: A reader* (pp. 15–26). Cambridge University Press.

Honey, M., & Kanter, D. (2013). *Design, make, play: Growing the next generation of STEM innovators.* Routledge.

Horowitz, E., & Sahni, S. (1978). *Fundamentals of computer algorithms.* Computer Science Press.

Humphreys, P. (2004). *Extending ourselves: Computational science, empiricism, and scientific method.* Oxford University Press.

Kavanaugh, R. D. (2011). Origins and consequences of social pretend play. In A. D. Pelligrini (Ed.), *The Oxford handbook of the development of play* (pp. 296–307). Oxford University Press.

Knight, T., & Stiny, G. (2015). Making grammars: From computing with shapes to computing with things. *Design Studies, 41*, 8–28.

Lave, J., & Wenger, E. (1991). *Situated learning: Legitimate peripheral participation.* Cambridge University Press.

Margolis, J. (2008). *Stuck in the shallow end, updated edition: Education, race, and computing.* MIT press.

Minsky, M. (1974). *A framework for representing knowledge.* MIT Press.

National Research Council. (2012). *A framework for K–12 science education: Practices, crosscutting concepts, and core ideas.* National Academies Press.

Nasir, N., Rosebery, A. S., Warren, B., & Lee, C. D. (2006). *Learning as a cultural process.* In K. Sawyer (Eds.), *The Cambridge handbook of the learning sciences* (pp. 489–504). Cambridge University Press.

NGSS Lead States. (2013). *Next generation science standards: For states, by states.* The National Academies Press.

Olivares, M. C., & Tucker-Raymond, E. (2020, March 28). *Critical relationality.* Medium. https://medium.com/@mariaco_87227/critical-relationality-a-justice-oriented-approach-to-education-and-education-research-8bf911c381b4

Olivares, M. C., Tucker-Raymond, E., & Gravel, B. (2019, March 31–April 3). *Intellectual humility: Desettling teacher-student relationships to knowledge in STEM* [Paper presentation]. The National Association of Research on Science Teaching Annual International Conference.

Papert, S. (1980). *Mindstorms: Children, computers, and powerful ideas.* Basic Books.

Pappas, C. C., & Tucker-Raymond, E. (Eds.). (2011). *Becoming a teacher researcher in literacy teaching and learning: Strategies and tools for the inquiry process.* Routledge.

Peppler, K., Halverson, E., & Kafai, Y. B. (Eds.). (2016). *Makeology: Makerspaces as learning environments* (Vol. 1). Routledge.

Rosebery, A., Ogonowski, M., DiSchino, M., & Warren, B. (2010). "The coat traps all your body heat": Heterogeneity as fundamental to learning. *Journal of the Learning Sciences, 19*(3), 322–357.

Rosebery, A., Warren, B., & Tucker-Raymond, E. (2017). Developing interpretive power in science teaching. *Journal of Research in Science Teaching, 53*(1), 1571–1600.

Rogoff, B. (2003). *The cultural nature of human development.* Oxford University Press.

Rogoff, B., Mistry, J., Göncü, A., Mosier, C., Chavajay, P., & Heath, S. B. (1993). Guided participation in cultural activity by toddlers and caregivers. *Monographs of the Society for Research in Child Development, 58*(8), i–179.

Russ, R., Sherin, B. L., & Sherin M. G. (2016). What constitutes teacher learning? In D. Gitomer, & C. Bell (Eds.), *Handbook of research on teaching* (pp. 391–438). American Educational Research Association.

Sandoval, W. (2014). Conjecture mapping: An approach to systematic educational design research. *Journal of the Learning Sciences, 23*(1), 18–36.

Smith, M. (2016, January 30). *Computer science for all.* https://obamawhitehouse .archives.gov/blog/2016/01/30/computer-science-all

Tucker-Raymond, E., & Gravel, B. E. (2019). *STEM literacies in makerspaces: Implications for learning, teaching, and research.* Routledge.

Vakil, S. (2018). Ethics, identity, and political vision: Toward a justice-centered approach to equity in computer science education. *Harvard Educational Review, 88*(1), 26–52.

Vygotsky, L. S. (1978). *Mind in society: The development of higher mental processes.* Harvard University Press.

Warren, B., Ballenger, C., Ogonowski, M., Rosebery, A. S., & Hudicourt-Barnes, J. (2001). Re-thinking diversity in learning science: The logic of everyday sensemaking. *Journal of Research on Science Teaching, 38*(5), 529–552.

Warren, B., & Rosebery, A. S. (1995). *"This question is just too, too easy!": Perspectives from the classroom on accountability in science.* National Center for Research on Cultural Diversity and Second Language Learning.

Weintrop, D., Beheshti, E., Horn, M., Orton, K., Jona, K., Trouille, L., & Wilensky, U. (2016). Defining computational thinking for mathematics and science classrooms. *Journal of Science Education and Technology, 25*(1), 127–147.

Wing, J. M. (2006). Computational thinking. *Communications of the ACM, 49*(3), 33–35.

Yadav, A., Hong, H., & Stephenson, C. (2016). Computational thinking for all: Pedagogical approaches to embedding 21st century problem solving in K-12 classrooms. *TechTrends, 60*(6), 565–568.

Zawojewski, J., Chamberlin, M., Hjalmarson, M., & Lewis, C. (2008). Developing design studies in mathematics education professional development: Studying teachers' interpretive systems. In, *Handbook of design research methods in education: Innovations in science, technology, engineering, and mathematics learning and teaching* (pp. 216–245). Routledge.

CHAPTER 7

CULTURALLY RESPONSIVE METHODS FOR ENGAGING ALL STUDENTS IN COMPUTER SCIENCE PRINCIPLES

S. Megan Che
Clemson University

Rhoda Latimer
Clemson University

Eileen Kraemer
Clemson University

Murali Sitaraman
Clemson University

ABSTRACT

This chapter discusses insights from the implementation of a week-long professional development experience for prospective computer science teachers.

Professional Development for In-Service Teachers, pages 171–187
Copyright © 2022 by Information Age Publishing
www.infoagepub.com
171

The professional development experience was framed by a culturally responsive pedagogical perspective. We present findings of ways prospective computer science teachers perceived culturally responsive pedagogy and their implementation of culturally responsive computer science during the ensuing academic year. Findings indicated that this cohort of teachers' perceptions and implementations of culturally responsive computing included three facets: belief in students' academic potential, affirming student realities, and critical self-reflexivity.

Fields of study are strengthened when those who influence the field (participate in, engage in, contribute to, enhance, define, push) are not only themselves diverse across a range of factors but are also active in expanding and seeking to be generatively responsive to emergent diversities in the field. The importance of diversity is emphasized across rural (Han & Leonard, 2017) and urban educational settings (Graham, 2018), from preschool (Reid & Kagan, 2015) to secondary schools (Boser, 2011), and particularly for arenas such as STEM fields (Smith-Doerr et al., 2017) and the PK–12 teacher workforce (Boser, 2014) who are under-diversified compared to local and/or national demographic contexts. There are many particular affordances from increased diversity (Intemann, 2009), including creativity (Smith-Doerr et al., 2017), openness to novelty, and the innovations that this novelty can spark (Smith-Doerr et al., 2017); a closed field often becomes an echo chamber largely impervious to both different perspectives and to its consciousness of its own constraints. Fortunately for emerging fields like K–12 CS education and K–12 CS teacher education in the United States, the public school student population in the United States is now nearly majority-minority (de Brey et al., 2019), a context that provides a wealth of opportunity for expansion of thought that most nations lack. Thus, it is an especially opportune moment for CS educators and CS teacher educators—a much less diverse population than the students they teach (Boser, 2011, 2014)—to thoughtfully prepare to engage their students in socially just CS teaching and learning.

With the purpose of illuminating an instructional approach seeking to cultivate affordances of diversity, this chapter situates one generative pedagogy, culturally responsive computer science (CRCS), within frames of social justice, equity, and culturally relevant teaching (CRT). Drawing on our experience engaging 17 prospective high school CS teachers in professional development aligned with CRCS, we offer illustrative pedagogical moments for richly implementing CRCS. The questions central to our preparation of high school CS teachers are: (a) What are prospective computer science (PCS) teachers' perceptions of CRCS by the end of the PD? and (b) How do teachers implement CRCS throughout the ensuing academic year?

BACKGROUND

Culturally responsive pedagogy (Gay, 2002) is a relatively recent iteration of bodies of research and thought around culturally relevant pedagogy (Ladson-Billings, 1995, 2014) and efforts towards sustaining, equitable, humanizing pedagogies with the goal of social justice (Howard, 2003). In this section we trace the emerging threads of CRCS education, beginning with conceptions of equity and social justice in education and CS education. We subsequently discuss culturally relevant pedagogy and culturally responsive pedagogy, and end with the primary critical framing for this study, culturally responsive computing.

Socially Just and Equitable Educational Processes

Several features (partially) characterize socially just contexts from our perspective: expansiveness, plurality, multiplicity, and reflexivity. Drawing on Bell's (2016) articulation of theoretical foundations underpinning social justice education, our view is that expansiveness in the sense of being open to possibility, humbly curious about one's worlds, and to finding peace with uncertainty, is critical to socially just societies. In fact, these characteristics of expansiveness can disrupt dogmatic, inflexible intrusions of one individual's particular notions of morality and reality on another individual. To be open to change and to be open to challenge—that is, to avoid becoming stagnant and lifeless—one must first admit that one does not know everything and even possibly that one might know (in the sense of absolute certainty) nothing. In our view, socially just contexts, whether societies, families, classrooms, schools, or communities, encourage expansiveness because of the generative potential inherent in the possibility (if not the responsibility) of thinking anew.

Likewise, socially just contexts not only value but seek plurality because of the catalytic role diversity—in its various instantiations—can often play in maintaining our expansiveness. Because of the innovative potential of diversity (Smith-Doerr et al., 2017), we are less likely to sink into rigidity and mind-numbing routine when we surround ourselves with diversity. Attendant to diversity, socially just contexts value multiplicity, in the senses of seeking multiple perspectives on issues (particularly complex and confounding social issues) as well as seeking courses of action that stand to benefit multiple parties (Bell, 2016). Finally, in our view, a continual critical reflexivity—trying to locate, question, and perturb one's relative position(s) of power in various social and cultural fields (in the Bourdieusian sense of field; see Bourdieu, 1986) is important for disrupting pathways through which power operates.

In education specifically, Hackman (2005) offers several active processes for educators to consider as they prepare to facilitate socially just classroom environments. Crucially, Hackman's (2005) first focus is on developing strong and deep familiarity with the content; socially just education refrains from watering down curricular expectations for certain students, thereby limiting their access to deep and rich learning opportunities. A corollary to deep content understanding is the development of critical thinking; engaging students in analyzing and evaluating is essential to their ability to participate in creating more socially just communities (Hackman, 2005). Hackman (2005) includes the process of personal reflection (similar to what we and Scott et al. [2015] think of as critical self-reflexivity) as an important aspect of socially just teaching.

Equity, in our perspective, is a precondition for a socially just society. We see equity as a society-scale condition in which every person has access to what they require to engage in forming socially just contexts (Bell, 2016). Some requirements for equity include material (stable housing, food, physically safe surroundings) and nonmaterial (love, nurture, self-esteem, psychologically safe surroundings) necessities. A context or situation striving to be socially just aims to ensure that all people, particularly those who have been historically or are currently marginalized, have viable and sustaining ways of providing for their sound physical and psychological health.

Our view of equity in CS education is informed by Ryoo et al.'s (2014) consideration of the question of what equity pedagogy looks like in introductory (i.e., exploring computer science) CS classrooms. Ryoo et al. (2014) assert that equity-based CS classrooms include asset-based approaches to students' lived experiences and cultures by utilizing pedagogical strategies that make CS relevant—culturally and socio-politically—to students. Additionally, equitable CS teachers hold high expectations for students and disrupt stereotypical notions of who can and should succeed in CS.

While we see equity and social justice more as characteristics—ways of being, or circumstantial conditions—than as static nouns, or things that are (and presumably always will be), we see culturally relevant and culturally responsive pedagogies as actions and processes that put effort into bringing the characteristics of equity and social justice into daily social and community living. In our view, equity and social justice are descriptive indicators of specific ways of being (they work for us like adjectives) and culturally relevant and culturally responsive pedagogies are sets of actions we can take (for us, they function as verbs) to direct our energies towards bringing equitable and socially just ways of being into lived experience. Though both culturally relevant and culturally responsive pedagogies may work towards shared, similar aims, we, with respect, depart from many scholars by distinguishing between culturally relevant and culturally responsive pedagogies, as we detail below.

Culturally Relevant and Culturally Responsive Pedagogies

Culturally relevant and culturally responsive pedagogies share many common traits, including a genesis from—and inextricable connection to—critical race theories that examine and uncover systemic and structural racism in society and in schools (Brown-Jeffy & Cooper, 2011). Another shared trait is a concern for incongruities between many students' out-of-school daily lived contexts and the formal classroom environment (Brown-Jeffy & Cooper, 2011; Howard, 2001). From a Bourdieusian perspective, many students' habitus (norms, perspectives, attitudes, values, culture) are not aligned as closely with the expectations of the field (of school) as privileged students' habitus. Formal schooling processes are disposed to benefit students whose habitus aligns more closely with that of formal school because those students have access to greater social capital and valued networks (Zevenbergen, 2003).

Both culturally relevant and culturally responsive pedagogies respond to this mismatch by asserting that the formal school context needs to value, connect with, and build upon students' diverse lived realities rather than expecting students to bear the responsibility of translating from their home context to the relatively removed school environment (Gay, 2010; Ladson-Billings, 1995, 2006). In other words, if spaces exist between home and school environments, the onus is on the responsible adult actors in schools (not the children) to modify the formal school environment so that these spaces are bridged. One way both culturally relevant and culturally responsive pedagogies advocate that this narrowing of spaces occur is through teachers' engagement in critically-minded examinations of their positions of privilege in society (Gay, 2010; Ladson-Billings, 1995).

For us, the distinction between culturally relevant and culturally responsive pedagogies arises in the consideration of specifically how a formal school environment, like a classroom, is altered so as to value and connect more closely to more students' lived realities. Our concern arises from our experiences with teachers and colleagues in which the practice of incorporating or including culturally specific contexts suffices for culturally relevant pedagogy. As both Ladson-Billings (1995) and Howard (2001) point out, a static application on the part of teachers of a cultural context onto academic content is largely insufficient to fostering an empowering social classroom atmosphere, absent additional, responsive teacher actions. Limiting or centering one's approach to a series of teacher-selected applications of specific context in an attempt to recognize and honor diverse socio-historical student backgrounds is partial. We emphasize the "dynamic and synergistic" characteristics of Ladson-Billings' (1995) articulation of culturally responsive pedagogy as "a more dynamic or synergistic relationship between home/community culture and school culture" (p. 467).

Thus, our view of the potential of culturally responsive pedagogy is that teachers are prepared to notice, acknowledge, and legitimize students' home and cultural contexts through affirming organic and emergent classroom interactions. Teachers and students, together, build trust by sharing aspects of their lives and their communities as they engage in seeking to understand content. Culturally responsive teachers can then pick up on or "pull" from students' divulged interests and community life to construct and highlight connections between content, culture, and community in ways that validate and affirm what students themselves have offered.

Our primary motivation for making and maintaining this distinction between what we see as culturally relevant pedagogy's tendency to "push" relevant task contexts and culturally responsive pedagogy's tendency to "pull" from students' expressed lived cultural realities is grounded in processes of critical self-reflection with respect to ours and teachers' relatively privileged social status. Being aware of this status imbalance between teachers and diverse students, we hesitate to prepare teachers to engage in processes that—though enacted with affirming intent—may, with validity, be viewed by students and their parents as stereotyping and as cultural appropriation and may be viewed by ourselves as a reductive essentialism. This is the rationale for our focus on culturally responsive pedagogy in our CS PD project.

Culturally Responsive Computing

Different academic disciplines in education are formulating the nature and instantiation of culturally responsive approaches in their particular contexts (Aguirre & del Rosario Zavala, 2013; Hernandez et al., 2013; Moje & Hinchman, 2004). In CS education, scholars are investigating and elaborating connections between CS, community context (Eglash et al., 2013; Leonard et al., 2018), culturally-based knowledge, and classroom experience. Scholars are also contributing to our understandings of critically oriented, socially minded potentials within culturally responsive computing (CRC) to rebuild communities and societies (Lachney, 2017; Lachney & Yadav, 2020).

Employing a perspective centralizing the importance of student and teacher transformational social agency in CS education, Scott et al. (2015) outlined and elaborated five tenets essential for CRC:

1. All students are capable of digital innovation.
2. The learning context supports transformational use of technology.
3. Learning about one's self along various intersecting sociocultural lines allows for technical innovation.

4. Technology should be a vehicle by which students reflect and demonstrate understanding of their intersectional identities.
5. Barometers for technological success should consider who creates, for whom, and to what ends rather than who endures socially and culturally irrelevant curriculum (pp. 420–421).

This perspective of culturally responsive computing resonates and aligns with our emphasis on dynamic, emergent, affirming classroom interactions that critically question our relative social capital. Further, this perspective simultaneously avoids reducing culturally responsive pedagogy to the act of pasting specific contexts onto academic content. For these reasons, Scott et al.'s (2015) frame for culturally responsive computing guides this study.

METHODS/DATA COLLECTION

Description of the PD

To better understand PCS teachers' understandings and implementations of CRCS, we conducted PD explicitly focused on CRCS to 17 PCS teachers during a week-long PD course designed to prepare teachers to teach an introductory high school CS course. Additionally, our culturally responsive PD continued during the academic year with four follow-up Saturday workshop sessions. Though the bulk of the content of the PD was predicated by a nationally scaled provider of CS teacher PD, the research team for this project developed and implemented a CRCS module which was delivered during the summer week-long PD. Further, we collaborated with one of the national PD facilitators for the academic year follow-up sessions to responsively highlight and connect teachers' words and actions to elements of CRCS in what became, at times, a near-co-teaching model with the first author and the national PD facilitator in discussion sessions with the cohort PCS teachers.

The intensive week-long PD that occurred in the summer focused on inquiry pedagogy, CS content, and issues of equity in teaching and learning. Infused into the PD activities were discussions of (in)equity and culturally relevant pedagogy. The additional CRCS PD module we developed for this teacher cohort introduced the notion of CRCS by asking teachers to ponder some of the affordances and limitations of setting CS content in a teacher-selected, culturally specific context. Most of the teachers, including both Black and non-Black teachers, voiced concerns about the risk of stereotyping their students by assuming what those students' interests were likely to be. The PCS cohort teachers, though affirming the idea of connecting CS content to students' interests, articulated a hesitation connected to reductive generalizations implicit in choosing particular contexts—whether rap songs, fishing tournaments, or fashion shows—for students, especially without prior knowledge of the students' interests and experiences. The first author, who facilitated this two-hour seminar-style CRCS PD introductory module, then posited the question: Given the importance of the task context and the goal of connecting to student interests, how can we honor student individuality while attending to the social and cultural context? In other words, how we can pull from students' experiences rather than push what we think their interests are onto them.

As we pondered this question, the lead author briefly touched on three of Scott et al.'s (2015) tenets of culturally responsive teaching: reflection, asset building, and connection. We highlighted the tenet of asset building because as a team we had decided to prioritize our CRCS module according to what might make the most immediate impact for students. This decision was based on our view that once the asset building tenet was firmly established, we could build on that foundation in future sessions to develop the tenets of reflection and connection. Nonetheless, one might argue that the module just described began with reflection, since teachers were immediately asked to reflect on their socio-cultural position with respect to the act of selecting particular racialized and gendered contexts for students. The lead author and several PCS teachers shared, from their classroom experiences, specific instances of asset building, or as we also termed it, *contribution-seeking* approaches to students. We—the lead author and the PCS cohort teachers—also discussed the role of genuine curiosity in effective teaching through the connection between students feeling valued (a requisite for socially just classrooms) and teachers being genuinely curious about how their students are thinking and reasoning. Finally, we articulated the notion of critical reflexivity as moving beyond reflecting on one's instruction to reflecting on one's positionality and what it means to be generative in the face of unearned privilege.

During the week-long summer PD and the academic year follow up sessions, the research team and PD facilitator sought opportunities to notice and publicly acknowledge connections between teachers' shared experiences, insights, and questions to the framework of CRC. It was through this process that we sought to deepen and affirm, through emergent and organic connections arising from teachers' contributions about their experiences in their CS classrooms, the PCS teachers' familiarity with and understandings of CRC.

Participants

This cohort of 17 PCS participants were experienced teachers from across a state in the Southeast. Almost all participants completed an alternative certification to teaching route with a focus in business education.

Most participants were new to CS—78% of them had not taught a CS class previously, and only one of the 17 teachers had taught the specific course for which the PD was designed. Further, 83% of these teachers identified as female, 50% identified as Black, and 56% identified as White. On average, the home high schools of these teachers included a student population that was 26% Black and with an average subsidized student lunch rate of 46%. The research team included the lead author, a White female mathematics education professor, the second author, a Black female mathematics education doctoral student, the third author, a White female computer scientist, and the fourth author, an Indian male computer scientist.

Data Collection and Analysis

Because this study includes one cohort of PCS teachers and explores in a naturalistic setting their perspectives of and implementations of CRCS, it falls within the method of case study research (Yin, 2017). Specifically, the case in this study is the week-long PD experience. The unit of analysis is the 17 PCS teachers' meanings for and instantiations of CRCS. These individual contributions were shared (and collected as data by the research team) over the span of one academic year, during both the summer week-long PD and the four follow-up sessions during the year. The data we collected included teachers' narrative responses to open-ended survey items on pre- and post- summer PD surveys as well as teachers' narrative responses to an end-of-academic-year survey. These questions asked teachers about their characterizations of and implementations of culturally responsive pedagogy, among other items. Additionally, several members of the research team took field notes during all PD sessions (summer and academic year). Finally, the research team debriefed after each PD session to construct analytic memos of our observations and field notes.

All of these data were coded using Scott et al.'s (2015) tenets for CRC and culturally responsive pedagogy as a priori themes. Specifically, we coded for any instance of any of the CRC tenets, although not all of the tenets actually materialized in our data, as discussed below. We independently coded a subset of survey responses and field notes and then met to compare and refine our coding processes. This iterative refinement of our application of our a priori themes, resulted in all of the data being coded by more than one research team member.

RESULTS AND DISCUSSION

Our analysis of these PCS teachers' perceptions and implementations of CRCS revealed three regularities which comprise a subset of the CRC tenets

(Scott et al., 2015) and which were not equally prevalent: *belief in students' academic potential, affirming student realities,* and *critical self-reflexivity.* This PCS teacher cohort, as evidenced in their pre-PD survey free responses, even initially tended to hold a belief that all students can learn meaningful CS. This initial confidence in students likely primed many PCS teachers to readily align with and incorporate several of the tenets of CRC even in their first year of teaching an introductory CS course.

Belief in Students' Academic Potential

The most prevalent way in which teachers operationalized CRCS was by exhibiting trust in their students' abilities to engage meaningfully in CS content. The PCS teachers participating in this study often and repeatedly connected their belief that all of their students could and would learn in response to teachers' reliance on inquiry pedagogy as an instructional strategy. Thus, a high expectation of students' academic potential was not only a typical stated perspective, but this expectation was also often brought into classroom reality through the implementation of pedagogical strategies that engaged students in active construction of knowledge rather than merely passive reception of information.

For instance, during the academic year PD follow-up sessions, one PCS teacher spontaneously described how she conducted a CS lesson by posing a challenging task to students and then giving them the time, space, and trust to progress in their approach to the task. In another session, as several teachers shared their challenges and successes in navigating through the curriculum, the taken-as-given pillars of belief in their students' potential and the provision of an inquiry-based learning environment through which students exhibit their potential were clear. For instance, in response to a question to the cohort posed by a research team member about what a typical day was like in their classrooms, most teachers responded that they prepared by seeking out thought-provoking tasks connected to CS standards, launched the task in class with minimal direct instruction, and, when students were ready, discussed the strategies they attempted and their outcomes.

To share one further illustrative experience from the academic year follow-up PD sessions that is replete with CRCS, we focus on two teachers' implementation of a planned lesson on robotics. The teachers had co-planned their lesson, in which the rest of us were going to engage as "students," earlier in the day. This opportunity gave the research team time to scan the contents of the lesson plan, which was part of the national-level teacher support materials that the PD facilitator provided for the teachers' use. The two teachers made several modifications to the provided lesson materials that increased both the cultural responsiveness and the inquiry of the lesson. First, they vocabulary words presented in the provided lesson as statements into questions. For instance, rather than informing us what computer programming is or the reasons memory is important, these teachers asked us to generate and contribute ideas around this content ourselves. They then built on our contributions towards a class-level shared understanding of these vocabulary concepts. Secondly, these teachers asked for multiple responses even when the first response was correct. These instructional moves communicated to us that our teachers were confident that we, individually as students and socially as a class, were capable of undertaking the cognitive work of thinking, reasoning, and analyzing. Rather than immediately evaluating a student response and taking the opportunity (away from students themselves) to decide on the viability of that response, these teachers sought a variety of responses that became the focus of the ensuing analysis—that we, as students, undertook to figure out which responses made more sense and why. This instructional rigor and the expectation that students can navigate such rigor are enactments of their belief in students' academic potential, a central tenet of CRC (Scott et al., 2015).

Thirdly, these two teachers, in their co-planning, chose to provide as few instructions as possible for operating the robot (how to get the robot to go forwards or backwards, and how to start and stop or turn). This minimal introduction to the technicalities of operating the robot sent the unspoken message that we could—and were expected to—figure out how to accomplish our goals on our own with the support of accompanying written instructions. That is, rather than demonstrate in detail each facet of the functioning of the robot, the teachers consciously planned to give us minimal such information but to provide material to which we could turn to support our efforts whenever we found we needed such support. These two teachers expected us to use available materials, without having to be told exactly which materials to use, and how and when to progress towards our goals.

After the lesson, we asked these teachers why they had made these adjustments that raised the expectations for students, and they both said, "That's just how you teach." One of these teachers had told us during the lesson that we are an advanced group of students by virtue of being in her class. She told the research team afterwards that she emphasizes to her own students that she sees them all as gifted and talented. She further asserted that, for her actual lesson with her students, she would have made available a greater variety of materials, some of which would work and some of which would not because she wants them to experience both success and failure so that they can learn how to productively navigate both.

In the last academic year follow-up session, teachers reflected on successes and struggles over the previous year, and the tone of the cohort was again affirming of students' potential. Most teachers shared that their students exceeded their initial expectations of them by, for instance, being ready to begin programming sooner than teachers had anticipated and by devoting time, energy, and efforts (more than even the teachers estimated) on course projects. Many teachers were excited (which is not to say surprised) that their diverse students, including females and underrepresented students of color, were experiencing successes to the extent of signing up for advanced CS courses. Further, some students who had not seemed particularly interested in the beginning of the year had become increasingly engaged. In general, this cohort of PCS teachers seemed pleased that their students had largely met and even exceeded their already robust expectations.

This pervasive belief in students' potential, accompanied with instructional implementation that expected students to be active in thinking and reasoning, is illustrative of CRCS because it is contribution-seeking and asset-building (Scott & White, 2013). That is, teachers expected their students to be both capable of making important contributions to the class and to actually offer these contributions to the class by participating in the inquiry-centered instructional environment. The teachers' role, as many PCS teachers themselves expressed, was to seek out their students' thinking and strategies and structure these contributions in such a way that advanced students' content understanding. In this way, the teachers were building on students' academic assets of critical thinking, questioning, and innovating. Finally, by holding high expectations of students and demonstrating—with words and actions—their belief that students can and will meet these expectations, these teachers exhibited the first tenet of CRC—that all students are capable of digital innovation (Scott et al., 2015). Simultaneously, when teachers implemented rigorous CS instruction in such a way that students were engaged in thinking, questioning, and figuring out strategies and solutions, they were also addressing the second tenet of CRC—providing learning contexts that support digital innovation (Scott et al., 2015).

Affirmation of Students' Realities and Identities

A second, though less pervasive, instantiation of CRCS from these PCS teachers was the affirmation of students' realities and identities both through the acknowledgement of their material circumstances as well as through task openness that allowed for student expression of themselves and their cultures. During the academic year follow-up sessions, many PCS cohort teachers mentioned more than once their hesitation to assign work for students to complete at home. This hesitation was not because they believed their students were incapable of working independently. Rather, they were concerned that many of their students had after-school responsibilities that contributed to the functioning of their home or community environments. For instance, teachers recognized that many students had jobs after school, were taking care of family members, or had a range of commitments that limited their access to the material requisites (quiet time, working space, perhaps collaborative peers) for completing homework. By thoughtfully considering the question of what it means for each of their students when part of their evaluation hinges on an activity (homework) in which some of them are predisposed to perform well because their out-of-school circumstances support the completion of the activity, these teachers exhibited characteristics of equitable and responsive pedagogy.

Teachers additionally affirmed students' diverse realities and identities by providing open-context tasks which allowed and indeed expected students to enrich by framing their work on the task in a situation (persona, game, song, movie, video) that was relevant and interesting to them. Though, as we discuss shortly, teachers did at times pose culturally specific tasks, many teachers also posed tasks which gave students freedom to construct, by using computational techniques and tools, solutions that were reflective of their own interests, personalities, and cultures. Open-context tasks asked students to engage in technological innovation (Scott et al., 2015) by creating, as part or all of their solution to the task, a product (avatar, code, background, website, and so on), the context of which the students selected. Further, by legitimizing, validating, and affirming these individualized products reflective of students' diversity, the teachers enacted—in action with students—their esteem of diverse perspectives, approaches, and cultures. Open-context tasks provided opportunities to iterate once more from cultural relevance and cultural responsiveness. Specifically, open-context tasks provided psychologically safe and affirming spaces for students themselves to construct connections between who they are, who their communities are, and what CS is and can be.

Critical Self-Reflexivity

A third glimmer of CRCS in teachers' instructional implementation were moments of critical self-reflexivity. To be sure, these moments were not as pervasive as we had hoped; it seems that, for this cohort of PCS teachers at least, we were more effective at supporting asset-building (outwardly focused on students) perspectives than critically self-reflexive (inwardly focused on oneself) perspectives. One of these few instances of critical self-reflexivity, however, has already been shared in the earlier discussion of one cohort teacher's assertion that she saw all of her students as gifted and talented. From a frame of CRCS, we see this teacher's action as a conscious use of her status as a teacher to disrupt messages sent to students in devalued academic tracks about who they are as students and what they are expected to achieve. That is, she was aware that she had some standing, influence, and social capital by virtue of being the teacher of these students. In turn, she chose to use that influence in an attempt to undermine dominant and delimiting messages about who these children were as students.

Another moment of critical self-reflexivity from a cohort teacher occurred when a White female teacher somewhat hesitantly shared with the lead author that, after the culturally responsive summer PD in which we discussed some of the potential risks of utilizing racialized and gendered task contexts, she was reluctant to implement one of the lessons provided by the national PD organization. She was concerned that she might offend her students if they thought she was stereotyping them. In the end, she did implement the lesson, complete with the racialized and gendered context, and her experience was that the students responded positively to both the context and the content of that lesson. Her critical self-reflexivity, in the awareness of the potential for reductively essentializing students, seems to have contributed to a sensitivity to students' reception of the task context that proved a productive combination in this instance.

Discussion

Results from this study are based on one cohort of PCS teachers; though these teachers' schools are scattered widely across one state, we want to avoid an implication that insights from our study hold in these same ways in other contexts.

The relative absence of or silence around deficit perspectives of children from this cohort of 17 PCS teachers is striking to us. Most cohort teachers seemed disinclined to afford relevance either to students' academic performance in other disciplines or to students' academic tracks (Oakes, 2005). In fact, there was a marked absence of "leveling" discourse wherein teachers articulate reduced expectations of students tracked into less rigorous academic curricular pathways. The few times teachers shared about their students' performance in other classes was when those students' engagement in their CS class rose above what some teachers might have predicted from their other academic performance. Thus, teachers largely refrained from using students' prior or other academic performance as an excuse for low student expectations in their class. Further, on the whole, teachers declined to attribute either their own expectations or the engagement of their students to any academic track; teachers rarely voiced hesitation to hold students to rigorous expectations because the students were on a "low" academic track.

These are hopeful signs, though they are not inevitable. CS education has only to turn to mathematics education, which has been rigidly tracked for decades, to understand the risks that tracking poses to generative CRCS education. Academic tracking has an insidious way of creating degenerative ruts in both teachers' and students' minds, which far too often delimit teachers' and students' perspectives of what students are capable of in those tracks. See, for instance, Boaler's and Oakes' extensive work in education on the destructive consequences of academic tracking in schooling for many students (e.g., Boaler, 2002; Boaler & Staples, 2008; Oakes, 1985; Oakes, 1986). Indications from our work with this cohort of PCS teachers are that CS education at the high school level may have thus far, for the most part, avoided academic tracking. Further, at least one cohort teacher was attempting to disrupt damaging effects of academic tracking by asserting to her students that she saw each of them as gifted and talented. As standards for high school graduates in CS grow, however, splitting CS graduation requirements into separate tracks or streams is a substantial risk to culturally responsive CS schooling and to equitable, socially just CS education in general (Ansalone, 2003; Cavanagh, 2008).

To continue to propagate and better understand CRCS, then, the field of CS education in the next few decades will likely undertake rigorous classroom-based research studies which provide empirical insights from complex and dynamic CS K–12 classrooms of students and teachers generating content understanding. To prepare teachers to locate and structure student contributions, we need more concrete understandings of what those contributions might be for specific content goals. Additionally, to support the development of a critically self-reflexive consciousness, the field of CS could benefit from studies examining the processes for supporting teachers' awareness of their socio-cultural positionings and what those positionings mean for socially just CS classrooms. While we adamantly agree with Coffey and Farinde-Wu's (2016) reiteration of the importance of teacher preparation programs supporting teachers in critically examining the role of their privilege, we look forward to the generation of insights from CS education about a variety of strategies for progressing towards this goal.

REFERENCES

Aguirre, J. M., & del Rosario Zavala, M. (2013). Making culturally responsive mathematics teaching explicit: A lesson analysis tool. *Pedagogies: An International Journal, 8*(2), 163–190.

Ansalone, G. (2003). Poverty, tracking, and the social construction of failure: International perspectives on tracking. *Journal of Children and Poverty, 9*(1), 3–20.

Bell, L. A. (2016). Theoretical foundations for social justice education. In M. Adams & L. A. Bell (Eds.), *Teaching for diversity and social justice* (pp. 1–14). Routledge.

Boaler, J. (2002). *Experiencing school mathematics: Traditional and reform approaches to teaching and their impact on student learning.* Routledge.

Boaler, J., & Staples, M. (2008). Creating mathematical futures through an equitable teaching approach: The case of Railside School. *Teachers College Record, 110*(3), 608–645.

Boser, U. (2011). *Teacher diversity matters: A state-by-state analysis of teachers of color.* Center for American Progress.

Boser, U. (2014). *Teacher diversity revisited: A new state-by-state analysis.* Center for American Progress.

Bourdieu, P. (1986). The forms of capital. In J. Richardson (Eds.), *Handbook of theory and research for the sociology of education* (pp. 241–258). Greenwood.

Brown-Jeffy, S., & Cooper, J. E. (2011). Toward a conceptual framework of culturally relevant pedagogy: An overview of the conceptual and theoretical literature. *Teacher Education Quarterly, 38*(1), 65–84.

Cavanagh, S. (2008). Keeping track: Structuring equality and inequality in an era of accountability. *Teachers College Record, 110*(3), 700–712.

Coffey, H., & Farinde-Wu, A. (2016). Navigating the journey to culturally responsive teaching: Lessons from the success and struggles of one first-year, Black female teacher of Black students in an urban school. *Teaching and Teacher Education, 60,* 24–33.

de Brey, C., Musu, L., McFarland, J., Wilkinson-Flicker, S., Diliberti, M., Zhang, A., Branstetter, C., & Wang, X. (2019). *Status and trends in the education of racial and ethnic groups 2018. NCES 2019-038.* National Center for Education Statistics.

Eglash, R., Gilbert, J. E., & Foster, E. (2013). Toward culturally responsive computing education. *Communications of the ACM, 56*(7), 33–36.

Gay, G. (2002). Preparing for culturally responsive teaching. *Journal of Teacher Education, 53*(2), 106–116.

Gay, G. (2010). *Culturally responsive teaching* (2nd ed.). Teachers College Press.

Graham, S. (2018). Race/ethnicity and social adjustment of adolescents: How (not if) school diversity matters. *Educational Psychologist, 53*(2), 64–77.

Hackman, H. W. (2005). Five essential components for social justice education. *Equity & Excellence in Education, 38*(2), 103–109.

Han, K. T., & Leonard, J. (2017). Why diversity matters in rural America: Women faculty of color challenging Whiteness. *The Urban Review, 49*(1), 112–139.

Hernandez, C. M., Morales, A. R., & Shroyer, M. G. (2013). The development of a model of culturally responsive science and mathematics teaching. *Cultural Studies of Science Education, 8*(4), 803–820.

Howard, T. C. (2003). Culturally relevant pedagogy: Ingredients for critical teacher reflection. *Theory into Practice, 42*(3), 195–202.

Howard, T. C. (2001). Telling their side of the story: African-American students' perceptions of culturally relevant teaching. *The Urban Review, 33*(2), 131–149.

Intemann, K. (2009). Why diversity matters: Understanding and applying the diversity component of the National Science Foundation's broader impacts criterion. *Social Epistemology, 23*(3–4), 249–266.

Lachney, M. (2017). Culturally responsive computing as brokerage: Toward asset building with education-based social movements. *Learning, Media and Technology, 42*(4), 420–439.

Lachney, M., & Yadav, A. (2020). Computing and community in formal education. *Communications of the ACM, 63*(3), 18–21.

Ladson-Billings, G. (1995). Toward a theory of culturally relevant pedagogy. *American Educational Research Journal, 32*(3), 465–491.

Ladson-Billings, G. (2006). Yes, but how do we do it? Practicing culturally relevant pedagogy. In J. Landsman & C. Lewis (Eds.), *White teachers/diverse classrooms: Building inclusive schools, promoting high expectations and eliminating racism* (pp. 29–42). Stylus.

Ladson-Billings, G. (2014). Culturally relevant pedagogy 2.0: AKA the remix. *Harvard Educational Review, 84*(1), 74–84.

Leonard, J., Mitchell, M., Barnes-Johnson, J., Unertl, A., Outka-Hill, J., Robinson, R., & Hester-Croff, C. (2018). Preparing teachers to engage rural students in computational thinking through robotics, game design, and culturally responsive teaching. *Journal of Teacher Education, 69*(4), 386–407.

Moje, E. B., & Hinchman, K. (2004). Culturally responsive practices for youth literacy learning. In T. L. Jetton & J. A. Dole (Eds.), *Adolescent Literacy Research and Practice,* (pp. 321–350). The Guilford Press.

Oakes, J. (1985). *Keeping track: How schools structure inequality.* Yale University Press.

Oakes, J. (1986). Keeping track, part 1: The policy and practice of curriculum inequality. *Phi Delta Kappan, 68*(1), 12–17.

Reid, J. L., & Kagan, S. L. (2015). *A better start: Why classroom diversity matters in early education.* Poverty & Race Research Action Council.

Ryoo, J. J., Margolis, J., Goode, J., Lee, C., & Moreno Sandoval, C. D. (2014). *ECS teacher practices research findings—In brief.* Exploring Computer Science Project, University of California, Los Angeles Center X with University of Oregon, Eugene. http://www.exploringcs.org/ecs-teacher-practices-research

Scott, K. A., Sheridan, M., & Clark, K. (2015). Culturally responsive computing: A theory revisited. *Learning, Media and Technology, 40*(4), 412–436. https://doi.org/10.1080/17439884.2014.924966

Scott, K. A., & White, M. (2013). COMPUGIRLS' standpoint: Culturally responsive computing and its effect on girls of color. *Urban Education, 48*(5), 657–681.

Smith-Doerr, L., Alegria, S. N., & Sacco, T. (2017). How diversity matters in the US science and engineering workforce: A critical review considering integration in teams, fields, and organizational contexts. *Engaging Science, Technology, and Society, 3*, 139–153.

Yin, R. K. (2017). *Case study research and applications: Design and methods.* SAGE Publications.

Zevenbergen, R. (2003). Mathematics, social class and linguistic capital: An analysis of mathematics classroom interactions. In B. Allen & S. Johnston-Wilder (Eds), *Mathematics education: Exploring the culture of learning* (pp. 129–143). Routledge.

CHAPTER 8

E-BOOKS FOR HIGH SCHOOL COMPUTER SCIENCE TEACHERS

Barbara J. Ericson
University of Michigan

Mark Guzdial
University of Michigan

ABSTRACT

Online computer science teacher professional learning opportunities offer advantages in time and costs, but only if they are actually effective for teacher learning. Effective learning is engaging and creates opportunities for practice, without overwhelming the learner with too much cognitive load. We describe a model for online computer science teacher development using e-books whose design is guided by principles from the learning sciences. We call our model *examples+practice* because of the emphasis on "worked examples" and "practice" at different levels of challenge. The results from our design-based research suggest that the e-books are efficient and effective for CS teacher learning.

Professional Development for In-Service Teachers, pages 189–205
Copyright © 2022 by Information Age Publishing
www.infoagepub.com
All rights of reproduction in any form reserved.

189

One solution to the challenge of preparing thousands of in-service teachers to teach computing is to provide online learning opportunities. With online learning, teachers can study where they are, rather than travel to face-to-face professional development (PD), which reduces cost. Further, asynchronous learning opportunities may fit into a teacher's busy schedule while learning online could possibly scale to reach thousands of teachers at the same time.

The problem with asynchronous online learning opportunities for teachers is making it really work effectively (Jung & Rha, 2000). The most common form of online learning for computer science (CS) teachers is the use of MOOCs (massive online open learning courses; Gray et al., 2016; Spradling et al., 2015). While MOOCS enroll many teachers, the results suggest that they might not be effective for scaling CS teacher education. MOOCs have low-completion rates (Kolowich, 2013), and typically rely on passive learning instead of active learning. However, at least one MOOC was as effective as face-to-face PD in achieving CS teacher certification (Fletcher et al., 2016). We need to be able to create online CS learning opportunities for in-service teachers that (a) have acceptable rates of retention (i.e., teachers complete the learning opportunity); (b) have impact on teacher learning in terms of subject matter knowledge and pedagogical content knowledge (PCK); and (c) lead to increased teacher confidence.

This chapter tells the story of our efforts over several years and multiple studies to create online CS teacher PD opportunities. Explicitly, our effort connects multimedia learning principles to e-book features. It serves as a model that is grounded in education research literature. Our goal is for the lessons learned from this work to be useful and adapted by other education researchers and PD providers.

We focus on three driving questions in this chapter:

- What principles of multimedia instructional design might apply to developing e-books for online CS teacher PD?
- How well do e-books work for developing teachers' CS content knowledge, CS PCK, and confidence?
- Do CS teachers use e-books differently than CS students, or could we just provide teachers with the same materials that we provide to students?

Overall, our goal is to generate evidence-supported design principles for the use of e-books for CS teacher preparation. Although the e-books that we create are useful, our larger goal is to make the e-books replicable. As a result, we conducted a series of studies in order to inform future e-book developers. We present some of our findings in this chapter.

BACKGROUND

In our work, we designed our online CS learning opportunities as a *book* in order to make it familiar to teachers. First, all teachers have experience learning from books. Second, all books share certain characteristics; they provide a structure, with well-known elements like a table of contents, chapters, sections, and questions at the end of the chapter. Third, teachers know how to pace their learning activity around books (e.g., to set a goal of completing a chapter in a week, or only having time to complete one section). Taking these elements into consideration, our goal is to create effective electronic books or e-books for CS learning.

E-books are a popular focus of research in computing education today given that traditional paper-based books cannot take advantage of interactivity, visualizations, and opportunities for practice with feedback. A 2013 working group of CS educators defined a set of requirements and research questions for "interactive computer science electronic books" (Korhonen et al., 2013) and predicted that paper textbooks would be replaced with interactive e-books. The work we describe here is part of this international movement to create a new medium for teaching and learning about computing.

Online learning is inherently a form of multimedia learning (Mayer, 2009). There is a large research literature on how to support learning with multiple media (Mayer, 2008), which we used to ground our design decisions for the e-books. By using a grounded approach in research literature, we provide a *rationale* for our design decisions that connects our design features to evidence-supported multimedia principles. Our e-books instantiations of those principles could be inspected, tested, and critiqued. Another designer may replace one of our design decisions with a different implementation of the multimedia design principles. Our experiments can be analyzed in terms of how well we implemented a given principle. As such, our e-books serve as models for *exploring* online CS teacher learning, rather than just a fixed implementation of an intervention or a curriculum.

In the rest of this section, we present a set of principles we used to develop our e-books, and then provide a description of how the designed features of our e-book implement these principles.

Principles of Multimedia Learning Design for Computer Science E-Books

Prior work on multimedia learning has identified several principles that are important for using different media as a learning tool. One of the principles is related to *cognitive load*, which describes the amount of attention and other cognitive resources needed during the learning process. High levels of cognitive load can overwhelm working memory and interfere with learning. Thus, keeping cognitive load to a low manageable level (Sweller, 1994) is a key multimedia learning principle.

Another principle is the *interactivity principle* (Mayer et al., 2003), which states that learning is most effective when learners control the pace of a multimedia presentation because a continuous presentation can overload the learner's cognitive system. A book or e-book, which does not move forward on its own, allows the learner to control the pace.

A third principle is related to *worked examples* (Atkinson et al., 2000). In our design of the e-book we used worked examples, which are an effective way to reduce cognitive load and focus attention productively during learning. A worked example is a description of a complete process from problem statement through solution. Worked examples are contrasted with worksheets filled with problems to solve, or programs to write. Completely worked out examples provide students the opportunity to learn the rules and strategies without also practicing problem-solving at the same time (as a worksheet or program assignment might). Including *similar* practice problems with the worked examples can motivate students to attend to worked examples, so the most effective instructional design is to interleave worked examples with practice problems (Trafton et al., 1993).

A fourth principle is related to the use of *multiple modalities* (Mayer & Moreno, 1998; Mousavi et al., 1995); this principle recognizes that humans are able to attend to sounds and visuals separately. For example, a text description of a diagram (where both the diagram and the text are perceived visually) is less effective for learning than an audio narration describing a visible diagram. CS tends to rely on visual components: diagrams, program code, and descriptive text. We may be able to improve learning by including more non-visual content.

Finally, our goal was to design an e-book that would also support teacher development of PCK because teachers need more than just content knowledge of CS (Yadav & Berges, 2019). An effective CS teacher also knows what students typically get wrong, what the most common misconceptions are, how to identify student misconceptions, and what activities help students to overcome challenges. CS teachers need to learn both subject matter knowledge and PCK.

Using the Principles to Design E-Book Features

Our e-books explicitly use these principles in identifying and implementing features. We call the implementation model for our e-books "examples+practice" because almost every page of the e-book is a worked example, followed by one or two practice problems. Our worked examples focus on either (a) completely working code that can be executed with the e-book (Figure 8.1), or (b) code in a visualizer that could be run forward or backward, with all variable values made visible.

Further, our worked examples are clustered into contexts (Morrison et al., 2015), such as graphics with turtles, image manipulation, or text manipulation. We build on prior work from our group about the value of contexts to motivate learning in CS (Guzdial, 2010). We explain loops, for example, by moving turtles, then manipulating all the pixels of a picture, then changing all the characters and words in a text. Examples and problems within a contextual group requires the use of background knowledge that is relevant to a context (e.g., that pictures are made up of pixels with red, green, and blue channel colors; that turtles have pens that go up and down). Thus, each problem in a contextual group requires common knowledge and does not have its own details to learn, which reduces cognitive load.

We also often highlight "subgoals" in worked examples through the use of comments as shown in Figure 8.1 (Margulieux et al., 2012). In some of our prior work, we have shown that subgoals reduce cognitive load and can lead to improved learning. Using subgoals encourages students to self-explain the problems with the text of the subgoals. Our prior work has shown that subgoals are particularly effective with K–12 teachers, even more so than with undergraduate students (Margulieux et al., 2013).

Additionally, our e-books provide several kinds of practice, which have a lower cognitive load than writing code (Morrison et al., 2015). The most common kind of practice in most CS classes is to write code. Having a range of practice types makes it more likely that we meet students at the level appropriate to their ability and interest. Types of practice include fill-in-the

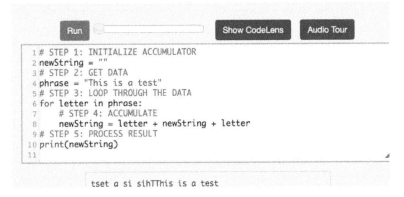

Figure 8.1 A worked example from one of our e-books.

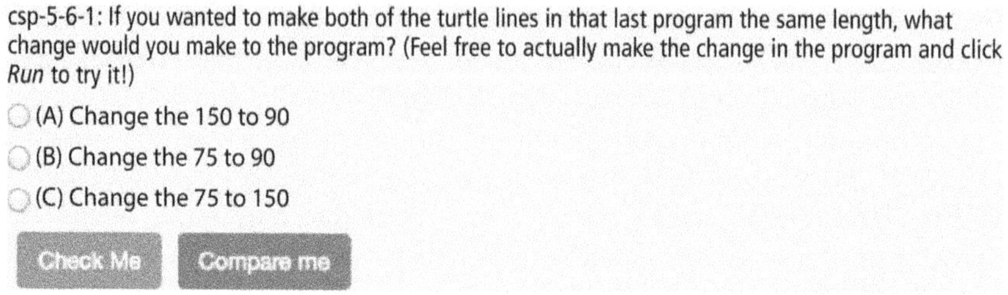

csp-5-6-1: If you wanted to make both of the turtle lines in that last program the same length, what change would you make to the program? (Feel free to actually make the change in the program and click *Run* to try it!)

○ (A) Change the 150 to 90

○ (B) Change the 75 to 90

○ (C) Change the 75 to 150

[Check Me] [Compare me]

Figure 8.2 A multiple choice practice problem that requires students to study the provided worked example.

blank and multiple-choice questions (Figure 8.2). We often directly reference the worked example in the practice problem, so that the practice problem is a prompt to study and learn from the worked example.

Our e-books feature a particular kind of practice called a "Parsons problem" (Morrison et al., 2016), which are mixed-up code problems. Students are given a problem statement, and a set of program statements that solve the problem (along the left side in Figure 8.3) that can be dragged into the correct order (on the right side). Our research shows that solving Parsons problems is more efficient but just as effective for learning gains from pretest to posttest as writing the equivalent code (Ericson et al., 2017). We predict that Parsons problems have a lower cognitive load than writing the equivalent code.

Since we know that CS learning tends to overload visual working memory, we also include videos and audio tours (Morrison, 2013) in our e-books. Videos include screencasts, teaching demonstrations, and explanations about student misconceptions. Audio tours highlight one or more lines of code as the audio explains the highlighted code.

Finally, our e-books include teacher notes, with an explicit focus on PCK content. Some of the notes demonstrate how to teach concepts, for example, physically walking through a turtle graphics program in order to use body-syntonic learning. Some of the notes identify common misconceptions that students have about programming. We continue to use an examples+practice pattern even with the teacher PCK content.

THE METHODS AND PARTICIPANTS IN OUR E-BOOK STUDIES

In the following sections, we describe four studies from our e-book research and subsequently discuss lessons learned. These studies vary from relatively small implementations with 10 teachers, to large and open studies with csp-5-1-2: The following program uses a turtle to draw a capital L as shown in the picture to the left of this text, but the lines are mixed up. The program should do all necessary set-up: Import the turtle module, get the space to draw on, and create the turtle. Remember that the turtle starts off facing east when it is created. The turtle should turn to face south and draw a line that is 150 pixels long and then turn to face east and draw a line that is 75 pixels long. We have added a compass to the picture to indicate the directions north, south, west, and east.

Drag the blocks of statements from the left column to the right column and put them in the right order. Then click on *Check Me* to see if you are right. You will be told if any of the lines are in the wrong order.

Drag from here

```
ella.forward(150)
```

```
ella.left(90)
```

```
ella.right(90)
```

```
ella.forward(75)
```

Drop blocks here

```
from turtle import *
```

```
space = Screen()
ella = Turtle()
```

Check Me   Reset

Figure 8.3 A parsons problem with mixed up blocks on the left and a partial solution on the right.

thousands of users. The scale of the study changes what we can possibly learn. With a smaller scale, we can provide greater insight and precise findings (i.e., the findings are true about individuals). With a larger scale, we know less about individuals, but we have more confidence about generalizability. The results from these studies are described in the next section.

The studies focused on our e-books that met the learning objectives of the Advanced Placement (AP) Computer Science Principles (CSP) and Computer Science A (CSA) exams. We built an e-book using Python to prepare AP CSP high school teachers first. This e-book includes teacher notes, information on PCK, and answers to the end of chapter exercises. We later built a companion e-book for AP CSP high school students, without the teacher-specific components. First author Ericson also built an AP CSA e-book using Java for high school students. These e-books have been used by Rise Up 4 CS, a project that Ericson created to help underrepresented students succeed in AP CS (Ericson & McKlin, 2018).

Studies Examining the Usability and Effectiveness of E-Books

One of the first papers on our e-books included two studies that focused on usability features of the e-book and how teachers used the book (Ericson et al., 2015). For the first study on usability, we put an open call on social media for current CS teachers to review three different e-book platforms' components and complete a usability survey on their experiences. The 18 teachers who participated in this study rated the Runestone platform components used for our e-book as more usable than either CS Circles or ZyBooks. However, this was an open online survey, so we only know that the teachers self-reported themselves as experienced CS teachers. This is a methodological theme to which we will return in the "Lessons Learned" section.

The second study was more controlled and focused on use patterns of the e-book (Ericson et al., 2015). While our participants were again recruited via social media, they completed a pretest to allow us to evaluate their existing CS content knowledge. We only accepted 10 teachers who scored low (< 40%) on our pretest so that there was an opportunity to measure learning. We also collected names and addresses of the participants, so that we could send those who completed the study a $50 gift card. We asked these participants to read eight chapters of the e-book and complete the posttests at the end of every two chapters. The data we collected included pretest and posttest scores (e.g., about CS content knowledge), surveys (e.g., about their confidence in teaching CS), and *log files*.

Log files are records of activity within the e-book. For example, we knew the time at which any participant opened a page in the e-book, clicked a button (e.g., to run a program, or to make a choice in a multiple-choice question), or edited a program to make a change. Log files can be voluminous and detailed but are only useful for answering a narrow set of questions. For example, log files can tell you *what* a participant did, but not *why* they did something (e.g., Did someone tell them what to click?) nor exactly *who* completed the action. If a participant did not log in (or, more commonly, lost the username we knew about), we would only record the Internet address of the computer used, not who the user was. Log files describe behavior, but not intentionality and not always identity.

We published a second paper where we described a series of design iterations (Ericson et al., 2016) which we characterized as design-based research. *Design-based research* is an iterative process of development, evaluation, and reflection. We consider our first iteration of the study to be the original 10 participants described earlier. For the second iteration, we made changes in the e-book to address usability problems and to expand the number and range of practice problems. Our study in the second iteration was much larger, with 229 teachers responding to be a part of the study. To qualify for the study, participants had to be at least 18 years old, hold a bachelor's degree, and could not have taught Python. While the majority of the study applicants were from the United States (75%), teachers also applied from the United Kingdom, Spain, Mexico, Australia, England, Scotland, Thailand, Germany, Greece, New Zealand, Canada, France, Russia, The Netherlands, Finland, China, Pakistan, Belgium, Brazil, and the Philippines.

Again, we only accepted teachers who did not have prior CS knowledge, which we defined as scoring less than 70% correct on the pretest (seven or less questions correct out of 11). However, there is great demand for CS teacher PD opportunities, and many teachers wanted to see our e-book even if they had too much knowledge to qualify for the study. We can tell from log file data that some teachers took the pretest, scored (too) well, and then retook the test to score below 70%, presumably in order to qualify for the study. Of the 229 teachers who applied for the study, 130 teachers qualified for the study by scoring less than 70% on the pretest. Of these only 45 (35%) took the first end-of-chapter test (after Chapter 2) and only five people took the test after Chapter 17 (the final chapter). For this study, we again had pretest and posttest scores, survey responses, and log file data. We also identified three of the participants for phone interviews to gain a more in-depth understanding of their e-book experience.

This was our last study looking at the e-book as a whole. We had evidence that the e-books were effective. To inform future designers and developers, we wanted to answer specific questions about how and why the e-books worked. Our overall goal was to provide a set of design principles, not just create a single platform.

Studies Examining How and Why E-Books Worked

One study examining how and why e-books worked compared whether behavior differed between the teacher and student e-book users for the student and teacher version of the AP CSP e-book (Parker et al., 2017). As mentioned earlier, the teacher e-book included PCK (e.g., how to diagnose and correct common student misconceptions and how to teach turtle geometry) and all the exercise solutions. If there was no difference in how students and teachers used the e-book, we might recommend that developers only create a single set of materials. There is obviously less design and development in creating only a single e-book, rather than two. We had 445 teachers and 516 students who used the teacher and student e-books, respectively. Our only source of data was the log files on the open Internet; that is a methodological challenge, which means that we cannot be entirely sure of the identity of the users. For instance, student e-book users may have included some teachers. The teacher e-book required a login, so most of that data was probably from teachers, but we cannot be sure.

A key open-ended question in this series of studies is related to what the users (teachers or students) wanted to learn from reading the e-book—in other words, what did they *want* to learn? We presume that the goal for both sets of users was to learn content knowledge, for example, about programming in Python. If the e-books were used essentially the same way, then an argument might be made that we do not need two e-books. We might just give the teachers the student e-book, perhaps providing PCK learning opportunities in some other way. Building and maintaining only one e-book would reduce costs.

Ericson (2016) conducted a more focused study comparing learners solving (a) adaptive Parsons problems versus (b) non-adaptive Parsons problems versus (c) writing the equivalent code. Ericson invented two types of adaptation for Parsons problems: intra-problem and inter-problem adaptation. In intra-problem adaptation, if the user is struggling to solve the current problem it can dynamically be made easier by disabling distractors (unneeded code blocks), providing indentation, or combining blocks. In inter-problem adaptation, the difficulty of the next problem is modified based on the user's performance on the last problem. If the user solved the last problem in just one attempt, then the next problem is made harder by using all available distractors and mixing the distractors in randomly with the correct code. If the user took six–seven attempts to solve the last problem, then half of the distractors are removed and the remaining distractors are shown paired with their corresponding correct code blocks on the next problem. If the user took more than seven attempts to solve the last problem then all distractors are removed from the next problem.

Ericson's final study used mixed methods that helped us understand what we could and could not assume from log file analyses (Ericson et al., 2019). One part of her study was a think-aloud interview study where she observed teachers using adaptive and non-adaptive Parsons problems and asked them questions about their experience. The second part of the study was a between-subjects study of 126 undergraduate students who were randomly assigned to one of four conditions: (a) solving on-task adaptive Parsons problems, (b) solving on-task non-adaptive Parsons problems, (c) writing the equivalent code, or (d) solving off-task Parsons problems. The final part was a pure log file analysis. Thus, we could compare detailed studies of participants in laboratory conditions to studies of thousands of users whose identity was unknown to us. On the open Internet, does user behavior match what is seen in the between-subjects study?

LESSONS LEARNED

In this section, we describe some of our lessons learned across the above studies.

Participation Led to Greater Confidence and Performance on the Posttests

In the first two studies described (Ericson et al., 2015), we found that teachers who made active use of the e-book features scored better on the posttests and reported an increase in their self-efficacy for teaching CS. Recall that in both studies, we attempted to screen teachers who already knew the content. Teachers who spent a significant amount of time in the e-book chapters and attempted almost every practice problem had higher scores on the posttests, while teachers who completed few practice problems did not have similar outcomes. For example, one teacher in our first study ran code in the e-book 153 times, edited code 93 times, and made it through Chapter 8 of the e-book with 66% correct on the posttest for that chapter. Another teacher ran code only 19 times, never edited code, and also made it through Chapter 8, but did not get anything correct on that posttest.

Results from our studies also indicated evidence of sustained use and increased confidence over time. As one teacher in our second study told us, "I have been told that I will teach computer science next year—and I am completely overwhelmed and intimidated—but this course is helping to put my mind at ease" (Ericson et al., 2016). In a later chapter, the same teacher wrote on a survey, "I feel as if I am slowly adding on to my knowledge of the Python language. It is helpful to 'build' my knowledge."

Heterogenous, Low Cognitive Load Practice Activities Led to Sustained Use

CS classes typically require students to practice by mostly writing code. In our e-books, there are various kinds of practice, many with a lower cognitive load than writing code. What we found is that more participants attempt to solve Parsons problems rather than respond to multiple-choice questions or edit code, even when instructed to edit code in the e-book. Since sustained participation leads to increased learning and self-efficacy, the teachers get more value the longer we can sustain their engagement. By having a heterogenous collection of practice activities, we can get greater use and longer engagement than if we just had teachers edit and run code.

Practice Is Key for Facilitating Understanding

We have already described how participation led to greater confidence and performance on posttests, and how having a range of practice activities led to sustained participation. What we learned from log file analysis is that practice sometimes *drove* learning. Even in our initial study (Ericson et al., 2015), we documented that some teachers would attempt the practice problem, get it wrong, and *then* go back to run the code and study the worked example. While we named our model "examples+practice," we sometimes saw practice => examples. Teachers are careful time managers; some of them did not study the worked examples and instead jumped straight to the practice problems, and they only went back to the examples if they needed to.

The implication is that the practice problems have to be carefully designed to require understanding of the worked examples. Examples have low-cognitive load, but they only lead to learning if the learners actually study them. Practice problems can encourage that study. Getting the practice problem wrong can actually drive understanding and learning.

Success Depends on Saving Teachers Time

From the very beginning, our goal was to fit the e-books into the time constraints of busy in-service teachers. We understood that teachers would only use the e-book if they could fit it into their busy schedule. From our log file analysis, we found that most teacher learning sessions were between 7 and 22 minutes. That is a small window of time to teach CS, including programming. We have worked to make learning as efficient as possible, like opening the e-book to where the teacher left off last, to mark sections as completed, and to provide answers to practice problems to reduce frustration. From our teacher surveys and interviews, we are confident that paying attention to learning efficiency is critical for successful in-service CS teacher learning.

Teachers and Students Use the e-Book Differently

Teachers are more expert learners than high school students as shown by their learning behaviors in the teacher e-book. The teachers' activities reflected a greater ability to monitor and regulate their learning. For example, when a teacher got a Parsons problem wrong a few times, they recognized that it was not worth investing more time and moved on. On the other hand, students were more likely to keep at the problem for many more attempts—and still not get it right. Another example is that students would more likely run a program example multiple times without any changes to the program between runs, as if they expected the output to be different without changing the program. Teachers rarely did this.

These results suggest to us that students need more low-level guidance than we currently provide. For example, we might need to point out to students when they are engaging in behaviors that are unlikely to lead to more learning. Teachers, on the other hand, could likely use more high-level navigation support. A table of contents is useful for the teachers, but is not finely grained enough. They could use a more detailed breakdown of a list of topics and specific kinds of practice in each section. This would provide teachers with a more nuanced view of the resources from which they might pick what to work and focus on. Our log files suggest that teachers can productively monitor and guide their own learning, while students need a different level of support.

Adaptive Parsons Problems Are More Efficient and Just as Effective

Students in the adaptive and non-adaptive Parsons problem conditions solved the problems significantly faster than those in the write code condition (Ericson, 2016). There was no statistically significant difference in completion time between the adaptive and non-adaptive conditions, though the average time was higher for the adaptive condition than the non-adaptive condition (e.g., the variance was large in the groups). All conditions showed a significant increase in scores from pretest to posttest, even the control group. This is likely due to repeated exposure to the same questions. The adaptive Parsons condition had a significantly higher learning gain from pretest to posttest than the control group.

Studying Online Learning Creates Methodological Challenges

The most open and accessible form of our e-books is to simply let anyone come and use them. Freely available e-books, without requiring even a free registration and login, eliminates barriers to entry. However, we then know nothing about participants or their goals. We can describe behavior, and even show learning (e.g., as the user at the same Internet address performs better on exercises due to use), but those claims are still hollow if we do not know if we met the learners' goals.

As we require registration, or require a certain threshold score on a pretest, we can make some greater claims about the learners. But users can lie on registration (e.g., claim to be a teacher or a high school student when they are not), or can fake test results to gain access. These problems are not specific to e-books. These are methodological challenges for any Internet-based online learning. We need to be aware of these challenges as we evaluate research findings about online learning for CS teachers.

NEXT STEPS

Our results echo the finding from Fletcher et al. (2016) that blended approaches are most likely to have the greatest success. Face-to-face learning reduces the methodological challenges and increases motivation. MOOCS alone and e-books alone will likely not be as effective as a combination of online, self-paced materials with in-person PD that can provide community and motivation.

In our interview studies, we talked with teachers who were using the e-book in combination with PD, and we learned how the two modalities supported each other. We asked one teacher how much the e-book contributed to her confidence and she replied, "Quite a bit really. I mean, I probably would have been lost without it. When I took the professional development workshop and was introduced to the e-book at the beginning, I really was lost." She mentioned feeling that PD instructors were initially "talking above my head." However, she told us that the e-book allowed her to better understand the face-to-face professional learning: "I mean, I know that sounds awful, but it was just like overwhelming. Then as I went on throughout the summer and I took some other courses and as I was exposed to e-book, I could understand things."

Perhaps the biggest gap in our understanding of the e-book is the lack of knowledge about the effectiveness of the supports for PCK. While we have evidence that teachers are increasing in confidence, we do not know if they are learning from the PCK supports we are providing. We are interested in using techniques for measuring CS PCK (Yadav et al., 2016; Yadav & Berges, 2019) to determine if the e-books are having an impact on teachers' CS PCK.

As we have been developing these e-books over several years, we recognize both how much we learn from the log file analysis and yet how difficult it is to interpret the data in the log files. We are interested in providing tools to e-book designers and authors that would analyze the log file data and provide summary visualizations, so that they can see how their e-books are being used, in order to improve the quality and test the design hypotheses. We are also interested in providing similar dashboard tools to teachers, so that they can get a sense of how their students are progressing and where the group or individual students need more help by analyzing the log files and providing summary statistics.

Finally, we are exploring the use of our e-book technology to develop new e-books for specific purposes. One of those purposes is helping teachers who teach one CS course (e.g., AP CSP) to develop the skills for another (e.g., AP CSA). In this case, we have specific learning goals towards which we can assess progress. Ericson is also creating new e-books for undergraduate computing courses. We plan to use our same principled approach in these new e-books and continue to enhance our design principles through evaluation of the new e-books. We think interactive e-books are the future and are excited to be contributing to their development.

ACKNOWLEDGMENTS

This material is based on work supported by the National Science Foundation under Grants No. 1138378 and 1432300. Any opinions, findings, and conclusions or recommendations expressed in this material are those of the author(s) and do not necessarily reflect the views of the National Science Foundation.

REFERENCES

Atkinson, R. K., Derry, S. J., Renkl, A., & Wortham, D. (2000). Learning from examples: Instructional principles from the worked examples research. *Review of the Educational Research, 70*(2), 181–214.

Ericson, B. J. (Eds.). (2016). Dynamically adaptive parsons problems. In *Proceedings of the 2016 ACM conference on international computing education research* (pp. 269–270). ACM. https://doi.org/10.1145/2960310.2960342

Ericson, B. J., Kantwon, R., Parker, M., Morrison, B., & Guzdial, M. (Eds.). (2016). Identifying design principles for CS teacher EBooks through design-based research. In *Proceedings of the 2016 ACM conference on international computing education research* (pp. 191–200). ACM. https://doi.org/10.1145/2960310.2960335

Ericson, B. J., Margulieux, L. E., & Rick, J. (Eds.). (2017). Solving parsons problems versus fixing and writing code. In *Proceedings of the 17th Koli calling conference on computing education research* (pp. 20–29). ACM. https://doi.org/10.1145/3141880.3141895

Ericson, B., McCall, A., & Cunningham, K. (Eds.). (2019). Investigating the affect and effect of adaptive parsons problems. In *Proceedings of the 19th Koli calling international conference on computing education research* (pp. 1–10). ACM.

Ericson, B., & McKlin, T. (Eds.). (2018). Helping underrepresented students succeed in AP CSA and beyond. In *Proceedings of the 49th ACM technical symposium on computer science education* (pp. 356–361). ACM.

Ericson, B., Moore, S., Morrison, B., & Guzdial, M. (Eds.). (2015). Usability and usage of interactive features in an online EBook for Cs teachers. In *Proceedings of the workshop in primary and secondary computing education* (pp. 111–120). ACM. https://doi.org/10.1145/2818314.2818335

Fletcher, C., Monroe, W., Warner, J., & Anthony, K. (Eds.). (2016). *Comparing the efficacy of face-to-face, MOOC, and hybrid computer science teacher professional development.* Paper presented at the Learning with MOOCs conference.

Gray, J., Corley, J., & Eddy, B. P. (Eds.). (2016). An experience report assessing a professional development MOOC for CS principles. In *Proceedings of the 47th ACM technical symposium on computing science education* (pp. 455–460). ACM.

Guzdial, M. (2010). Does contextualized computing education help? *ACM Inroads, 1*(4), 4–6.

Jung, I., & Rha, I. (2000). Effectiveness and cost-effectiveness of online education: A review of the literature. *Educational Technology, 40*(4), 57–60.

Kolowich, S. (2013, August 8). The MOOC 'revolution' may not be as disruptive as some had imagined. *The Chronicle of Higher Education.* https://www.chronicle.com/article/the-mooc-revolution-may-not-be-as-disruptive-as-some-had-imagined/

Korhonen, A., Thomas, N., Boisvert, C., Crescenzi, P., Karavirta, V., Mannila, L., Miller, B., Morrison, B., Rodger, S. H., Ross, R., & Shaffer, C. A. (Eds.). (2013). Requirements and design strategies for open source interactive computer science eBooks. In *Proceedings of the iticse working group reports conference on innovation and technology in computer science education-working group reports* (pp. 53–72). ACM.

Margulieux, L. E., Guzdial, M., & Catrambone, R. (Eds.). (2012). Subgoal-labeled instructional material improves performance and transfer in learning to develop mobile applications. In *Proceedings of the 9th annual international conference on international computing education research* (pp. 71–78). ACM. https://doi.org/10.1145/2361276.2361291

Margulieux, L. E., Guzdial, M., & Catrambone, R. (2013). Subgoal labeled worked examples improve K–12 teacher performance in computer programming training. In M. Knauff, M. Pauen, N. Sebanz, & I. Wachsmuth (Eds.), *Proceedings of the 35th Annual Conference of the Cognitive Science Society* (978–983). Cognitive Science Society.

Mayer, R. (2009). *Multimedia learning* (2nd ed.). Cambridge University Press.

Mayer, R. E. (2008). Applying the science of learning: Evidence-based principles for the design of multimedia instruction. *American Psychologist, 63*(8), 760–769.

Mayer, R. E., Dow, G. T., & Mayer, S. (2003). Multimedia learning in an interactive self-explaining environment: What works in the design of agent-based microworlds? *Journal of Educational Psychology, 95*(4), 806–812.

Mayer, R. E., & Moreno, R. (1998). A split-attention effect in multimedia learning: Evidence for dual processing systems in working memory. *Journal of Educational Psychology, 90*(2), 312–320.

Morrison, B. B. (Eds.). (2013). Using cognitive load theory to improve the efficiency of learning to program. In *Proceedings of the 9th annual international acm conference on international computing education research* (pp. 183–184). ACM. https://doi.org/10.1145/2493394.2493425

Morrison, B. B., Margulieux, L. E., Ericson, B., & Guzdial, M. (Eds.). (2015). Subgoals, context, and worked examples in learning computing problem solving. In *Proceedings of the eleventh annual international conference on international computing education research* (pp. 21–29). ACM. https://doi.org/10.1145/2787622.2787733

Morrison, B. B., Margulieux, L. E., Ericson, B., & Guzdial, M. (Eds.). (2016). Subgoals help students solve parsons problems. In *Proceedings of the 47th ACM technical symposium on computing science education* (pp. 42–47). ACM. https://doi.org/10.1145/2839509.2844617

Mousavi, S. Y., Low, R., & Sweller, J. (1995). Reducing cognitive load by mixing auditory and visual presentation modes. *Journal of Educational Psychology, 87*(2), 319–334.

Parker, M. C., Rogers, K., Ericson, B. J., & Guzdial, M. (Eds.). (2017). Students and teachers use an online ap cs principles eBook differently: Teacher behavior consistent with expert learners. In *Proceedings of the 2017 ACM conference on international computing education research* (pp. 101–109). ACM. https://doi.org/10.1145/3105726.3106189

Spradling, C., Linville, D., Rogers, M. P., & Clark, J. (2015). Are MOOCs an appropriate pedagogy for training K–12 teachers computer science concepts? *Journal of Computing Sciences in Colleges, 30*(5), 115–125.

Sweller, J. (1994). Cognitive load theory, learning difficulty, and instructional design. *Learning and Instruction, 4*(4), 295–312. https://doi.org/http://dx.doi.org/10.1016/0959-4752(94)90003-5

Trafton, J., Reiser, G., & Reiser, B. J. (Eds.). (1993). The contributions of studying examples and solving problems to skill acquisition. In *Proceedings of the 15th annual conference of the cognitive science society* (pp. 1017–1022). Lawrence Erlbaum Associates.

Yadav, A., & Berges, M. (2019). Computer science pedagogical content knowledge: Characterizing teacher performance. *ACM Transactions on Computing Education, 19*(3), 1–24. https://doi.org/10.1145/3303770

Yadav, A., Berges, M., Sands, P., & Good, J. (Eds.). (2016). Measuring computer science pedagogical content knowledge: An exploratory analysis of teaching vignettes to measure teacher knowledge. In *Proceedings of the 11th workshop in primary and secondary computing education* (pp. 92–95). ACM.

CHAPTER 9

IMPLEMENTING A PROFESSIONAL DEVELOPMENT FRAMEWORK TO ASSIST THE ROLLOUT OF COMPUTER SCIENCE IN SECOND-LEVEL SCHOOLS IN IRELAND

Oliver McGarr
University of Limerick

Merrilyn Goos
University of Limerick

Clare McInerney
University of Limerick

Keith Johnston
Trinity College Dublin, The University of Dublin

Una Fleming
University of Limerick

Professional Development for In-Service Teachers, pages 207–222
Copyright © 2022 by Information Age Publishing
www.infoagepub.com
207

ABSTRACT

This chapter describes the rollout of a computer science (CS) subject in secondary schools in the republic of Ireland and details the professional development framework implemented to support its rollout. A central component of this framework is the establishment of teachers' communities of practice. Examining the professional development of out-of-field CS teachers through the lens of subject identity using social identity theory (SIT), the chapter questions whether such communities of practice can be readily established. In addition, it also questions the assumptions regarding the homogeneity of out-of-field CS teachers and their motivations for adopting the subject. The implications of viewing the professional development of out-of-field teachers as an identity project is subsequently examined.

This chapter outlines the recent introduction of a computer science (CS) subject at upper secondary level (16–18 years) in Ireland. It first outlines the background of CS efforts in Ireland before examining the literature in relation to teacher professional development (PD) for out-of-field teachers in the area of CS. Following this, the chapter describes the PD framework used to support teachers in the introduction of CS in Ireland. The final section examines the establishment of communities of practice through the lens of social identity theory (SIT) and in doing so raises questions about the organic growth of communities of practice amongst this diverse group of out-of-field teachers.

There is a growing interest in CS education globally, particularly in attempts at broadening participation among under-represented populations (Menekse, 2015). This has resulted in an increase in the introduction of both primary and secondary school CS curricula (Falkner et al., 2018; Yadav et al., 2016). Ireland has followed these international trends and has recently seen the introduction of CS initiatives at both lower (12–15 years) and upper secondary school (16–18 years) levels. However, despite only recently being introduced, there have been attempts to include CS as a subject in Ireland as far back as the late 1970s when there were calls for the establishment of a CS subject as a result of the rise in interest in microcomputers (McGarr, 2009). At that time CS was introduced as an optional area of study in upper secondary school mathematics but it had little uptake in the following years (O'Shea, 1983). Instead, the study of computer applications, such as word processing, dominated computer use in Irish schools during the following 2 decades (McKenna et al., 1993; DES, 1997) largely reflecting patterns of use in other countries (Menekse, 2015).

At the turn of the millennium there were renewed calls to introduce a dedicated CS subject in Ireland and this resulted in research by O'Doherty et al. (2004), commissioned by the National Council for Curriculum and Assessment (NCCA), into the feasibility of introducing the subject. This feasibility study concluded that, while there was interest and merit in including the subject, there was a general reluctance to introduce a specialized CS subject at a time when not all students had access to a basic Information and Communication Technology (ICT) skills experience in schools. As a result, the interest in the introduction of the subject receded.

Influenced by international trends in the past decade, there was renewed interest in introducing CS in schools and this resulted in a number of initiatives. The first was the introduction of a short course in coding introduced into lower secondary schools (Grades 7–9). This has been very successful with over 100 schools introducing it with approximately 3,000 students currently studying the subject in school. In addition to this initiative, in 2017, the NCCA commissioned a report on the provision of courses in CS in upper second-level education internationally (Keane & McInerney, 2017). This report found that CS subjects were established across many countries and that there was a large degree of commonality in terms of the content of the programs. The report also found that teacher PD was a considerable challenge.

Following the publication of this report and in parallel to the rollout of a short course in coding in lower secondary level, plans were put in place in 2017 for the introduction of CS as a subject in upper secondary schools (Grades 10–12) and its introduction was accelerated through the curriculum design process for roll out in 2018. As part of the selection process for the initial pilot phase, schools were invited to submit expressions of interest. At present, there are 40 schools participating in the introduction of the subject. These schools are geographically dispersed across the country and include a range of the different types of post-primary schools in Ireland, including single-sex and mixed schools, comprehensive schools, community colleges and schools as well as secondary schools (see Table 9.1).

As with other jurisdictions, however, the introduction of the subject is not without its challenges as it requires a significant level of in-service teacher PD (Yadav et al., 2016), particularly as no similar subject exists within the current Irish educational system. Further, there are additional challenges related to in-service PD that are exacerbated by the unique aspects of the Irish educational system. For example, Ireland has no previous history of

TABLE 9.1 Timeline of Events	
2017	Publication of report on the provision of courses in CS in upper second-level education internationally (Keane & McInerney, 2017)
Early 2017	Formation of the subject design committee by the NCCA
Late 2017	Publication of subject specification (subject syllabus)
Early 2018	Selection of first 40 pilot schools following schools' applications
Mid 2018	Commencement of teacher professional development
Sep 2018	Launch of subject in schools

CS at upper secondary-school level and therefore many teachers without any experience of CS are tasked with introducing this subject to schools. Without access to a community of established teachers that have experience of already teaching the subject, this can be a challenge. In addition, as it is an examinable subject at upper-secondary level, performance in the subject can determine entry to third-level (university) education—hence, its assessment could be considered "high stakes" in nature. This brings added pressure from parents to ensure the subject rollout is a success from the onset to maximize their children's chances of meeting the matriculation requirements of their chosen degree programs.

A further challenge relates to the geographic dispersal of the schools. The pilot phase involves only 40 of the over 700 post-primary schools in Ireland, which has resulted in many of the schools being quite geographically isolated and the only schools in some counties delivering the subject. As a result, teacher isolation is an important issue that also needs to be addressed.

Finally, there are issues related to in-service teacher PD and isolation and issues of subject identity, which are also important. All teachers who have been selected to teach CS come from other subject backgrounds and thus how they identify with CS will be important as its introduction progresses. For these reasons the in-service PD needs to ensure that strong technical, pedagogical, and curriculum knowledge is achieved. At the same time, it must also develop a strong sense of community to address potential issues of isolation and identity in relation to CS. Before detailing the nature of the in-service PD delivered to participating teachers, the following section explores the relevant literature related to PD and CS pertinent to the Irish context.

BACKGROUND

The importance of developing strong communities of practice and providing in-service PD for out-of-field teachers (teachers qualified in one subject area but requested to teach another subject they are not formally qualified in) are critical aspects related to the Irish context. Therefore, this section explores the relevant literature on out-of-field teaching and communities of practice in in-service teacher education.

In-Service Professional Development of Out-of-Field Teachers

Probably the most significant challenge associated with the introduction of CS relates to the need for suitable PD for teachers. As Falkner et al. (2018) noted, there has been significant attention devoted to exploring effective models of teacher PD in the CS community. However, it must be noted that there are widespread concerns about the effectiveness of CS teacher PD, particularly its short-term "splash and dash" nature and its inability to adequately develop teachers' technical and pedagogical skills or change attitudes (Menekse, 2015; Yadav et al., 2016).

While Ragonis et al. (2010) argued that CS deserves designated CS teacher-preparation programs and that only teachers with formal qualifications in this field should teach the subject, internationally there has been a lack of adequate teacher certification programs for CS teachers (Yadav et al., 2016). In saying this, certification programs have been increasing. For example, in 2012 in the United Kingdom, the Computing at School (CAS) group introduced "master teachers" in computing which involved experienced in-service teachers being appointed and trained to deliver continuing professional development (CPD) to their peers (Smith et al., 2015). Ireland is also establishing formal certification both at the pre-service and in-service level to support the rollout of the new national upper-secondary level CS curricula.

PD for CS, however, is unlike PD for other subjects (Menekse, 2015) because, in most cases, CS is not a required subject and many teachers do not hold specific qualifications in the area. Therefore, there are fewer PD efforts and studies in this domain compared to more established subjects such as mathematics and science. Despite this, there are key principles that are recognized in the field. In his review of CS teacher PD studies published between 2004–2014 in the United States and drawing on the broader literature of teacher PD from Desimone (2009), Menekse (2015) outlined six fundamental factors that have the potential to influence teacher practices and student learning. They include: (a) duration of the program, (b) long term support for teachers to implement new practices and instructional methods, (c) focus on active learning strategies, (d) explicit focus on pedagogical content knowledge, (e) ongoing collaboration and communication with school leadership and district administration, and (f) student learning data.

Yet, as mentioned previously, teacher PD in the CS community is further complicated by the out-of-field nature of teachers. For example, in describing most of the CS teachers in secondary schools in a Scottish context, Cutts et al. (2017) noted that the teachers are "often teachers from another subject, e.g., mathematics or business studies, who are self-taught in CS content, and/or who have learned how to teach the subject by trial and error in the classroom" (p. 31). Similarly, Falkner et al. (2018) offered a similar insight into primary teachers in Australia, noting that the majority had never taught CS before. Hobbs (2013) observed that while out-of-field teaching was an increasingly common practice across the wider educational sector, the issue was not widely researched. It is, therefore, not surprising that within the CS literature, the out-of-field nature of CS teaching appears to have been largely overlooked.

Teachers' personal and professional identity is intertwined with their knowledge and appreciation of their subject matter (Beijaard et al., 2000). As a result, moving to a "new" subject area can result in feelings of discontinuity. At the same time, it can provide opportunities for identity expansion and a reconceptualization of practice. It is for this reason that Hobbs (2013) viewed out-of-field teaching as a "boundary-crossing" event. In Hobb's (2013) research into out-of-field teachers in Australia she conceptualized three groups of factors that influence the identity construction of out-of-field teachers, namely: (a) contextual factors (the location of the school, including its rurality and its size); (b) support mechanisms (the degree to which a teacher felt supported); and (c) personal resources (including their adaptive expertise, knowledge, confidence and commitment). Du Plessis et al. (2014) also wrote on the issues of identity for out-of-field teachers commenting that: "When teachers are assigned to positions for which they are not suitably qualified this often results in the lived experiences of not feeling 'at home' or a struggle to experience 'belongingness' in specific out-of-field subjects or year levels" (p. 91).

To support out-of-field teachers, access to a wider community of professionals that helps address feelings of vulnerability is evident within the CS literature, echoing the wider teacher PD literature. For example, Cutts et al. (2017) noted that the vast majority of CS teachers were "singletons" in their schools and hence lacked immediate access to other CS teachers to share experiences and practice. This finding was also empirically supported by research; exploring the experiences of CS teachers in the United States, Yadav et al. (2016), for example, found that over half of the 24 teachers interviewed reported feeling isolated. They noted:

> Teachers in this study also commented on how teaching computer science can be a lonely enterprise in schools where there are few computer science teachers, or often only one per school. Computer science teachers typically work independently and often rely on virtual communities to stay in touch with colleagues, rather than through the continual collaborations that in-house teachers may have. (p. 247)

Given the solitude of the CS teacher's work, Yadav and colleagues (2016) concluded that communities of practice are critical in CS teachers' development to address both content and pedagogical needs. A similar view was put forward by Ryoo et al. (2015) who argued for the professional learning communities to develop strong professional cultures that teachers could associate with. In their research into CS teachers in a Los Angeles school district, Ryoo et al. reported that teachers described increased understanding, confidence, and application of inquiry and equity-based teaching practices as a result of engagement in a professional learning community.

As this brief overview has highlighted, the communal element of teacher PD is critical for CS teachers as most are entering the territory of a new subject area, which can bring feelings of vulnerability and a sense of being out of place. This need for professional communities dovetails with the "boundary crossing" (Hobbs, 2013) literature in relation to identity development, as previously mentioned, where engagement with the emerging community can help develop a new or hybrid professional subject identity. The following section aims to outline the in-service PD framework provided for the teachers as part of the rollout of the CS subject in the 40 pilot schools in Ireland.

EXEMPLARS: THE PROFESSIONAL DEVELOPMENT FRAMEWORK

In Ireland, curriculum development is overseen by the NCCA. This oversees a partnership approach to subject development where a subject design team is established involving representatives from a range of stakeholder groups including teachers, industry, teacher unions, and the national parent's council amongst others. This design team develops the curriculum (in Ireland called the subject specification) which is subsequently approved and implemented by the Department of Education and Skills (DES).

The subject specification for CS at upper-secondary level in Ireland (ages 16–18 years), published by the NCCA (2018), set out the focus of the subject as being constructed into three strands: practices and principles, core concepts, and CS in practice. The related learning outcomes reflected a reasonably broad agenda concerning student learning, identifying outcomes ranging from those at the contextual and social level (historical, ethical, social, and economic impacts), to core principles of CS, such as computational thinking. Problem-solving and understanding about key concepts such as abstraction, logic and algorithms, to more applications level outcomes as reflected in the ability to program and build computational artefacts are also evident in the specification. Links with language learning and the potential for the subject to facilitate the development of analytical and problem-solving skills are to the fore within the specification document.

In line with the emphasis on "key skills" (e.g., information processing, critical thinking, communication, working with others) the potential for development of transferable skills such as synthesis, evaluation, communication, time management, organization, and teamwork are also evident, giving some insight into the nature of the learning experience envisaged by the developers. This is further evident in the intended interaction between the three strands where the core practices, principles and concepts (strands one and two) are intended to be applied in practice (strand three) via collaborative learning tasks which increase in complexity and sophistication as the program progresses. This reflects an intended non-linear sequencing between the three core strands of the program. The specification sets out four key learning tasks to be completed throughout the program, each of which outputs a computational artefact and a related report detailing its development by the team members.

In line with this, the end of course assessment includes both a coursework component and a terminal examination: The coursework component being based on the development of a computational artefact and a report detailing the process and work involved. The specification is somewhat unique in that, in addition to addressing the standard areas about intended learning outcomes and assessment, it also provides significant attention to the nature of the learning experiences envisaged by the design team of developers.

The Irish government launched the new CS subject in September of 2018. In the previous spring, 40 schools and teachers were selected to be part of the initiative and the PD for teachers commenced at that time. The teachers who participated in the rollout of the subject were from a variety of backgrounds, and while some had experience with CS from personal interest and from teaching coding at lower secondary school level, the majority fit the description of out-of-field teachers.

As with the introduction of all new school subjects in Ireland, teacher PD was provided by the Professional Development Support Service for Teachers (PDST). The PDST was established by the DES in 2010 as a support service to oversee and run the PD of teachers in the primary and second level sectors. In order to deliver the PD to participating teachers, a team of three full-time staff were assigned to the implementation team, and their role was to plan and deliver the PD to support the implementation of CS. Specifically, the PD for the teachers was planned to run over a 2-year time period and aimed to address teachers' CS content knowledge, their pedagogical knowledge, and awareness of their knowledge of the subject specification (curriculum).

THE PROFESSIONAL DEVELOPMENT FRAMEWORK

From the onset, the PD framework adopted a community of practice philosophy (Wenger, 1999; 2011) where communities of practice are "groups of people who share a concern or passion for something they do and learn how to do it better as they interact regularly." The PD infrastructure contained a number of elements as outlined in Figure 9.1 and subsequently explained.

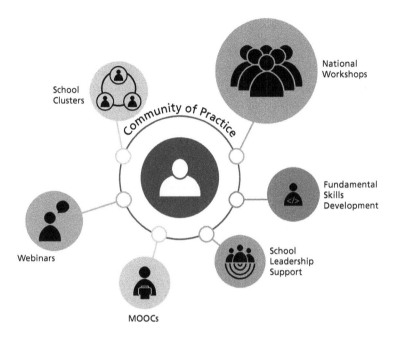

Figure 9.1 Overview of professional development framework (PDST, 2018).

National Workshops

The first aspect of the PD infrastructure put in place was a series of national workshops delivered by the PDST support team of trainers delivered once per semester. These national workshops were normally 2 days in duration and hence had a residential element to them. The workshops focused on developing the teachers' pedagogical knowledge and skills and their understanding of the subject specifications. They were normally facilitated by the team of three PDST officers employed to oversee the implementation of the PD program. These officers were school teachers with expertise in the area of CS that had been seconded from their teaching posts as part of the project rollout. These sessions also employed guest speakers and experts during the year to address specific aspects. These were "hands-on" type workshops where the entire cohort of teachers could share experiences, discuss practices, and problem solve in relation to classroom practices. As residential workshops which took place in a hotel in the centre of the country, they also aimed to facilitate informal interactions, thus contributing to the development of the community of practice.

Webinars and the SLACK Platform

The second component of the PD infrastructure consisted of different forms of virtual supports including an online collaboration platform (using the SLACK software; see https://slack.com) and additional webinars. The online collaboration platform was a password controlled collaborative forum which acted as an extension of the national workshops as it enabled teachers to continue the conversations that took place in the workshops. This online forum also acted as a resource sharing platform and a space to raise questions both with the PDST support staff and other teachers. Given the geographical dispersion of the members, this forum also acted as an important cohering function to enable the teachers to maintain contact throughout the teaching terms in between the formal workshops. In the first year of the program, this online space was primarily used as a platform to share resources and experiences and was used to varying degrees by the participating teachers. Webinars were delivered during the year by members of the PDST team and these addressed issues related to the teaching of CS (such as pedagogical approaches to problem solving, female participation and managing student project work).

School Clusters

The participants were also arranged into regional clusters and meetings of these clusters, facilitated by a member of the PDST team, were arranged on a regular basis (normally twice per semester). These regional meetings consisted of six to eight teachers. Being a smaller gathering, these meetings had both a social and professional function. From a social perspective, they provided teachers with an opportunity to meet and talk about their experiences in a more intimate and perhaps less intimidating environment than the national workshops. Therefore, they had a supportive, collegial aspect to them. From a professional perspective, they also facilitated the sharing of practice and aimed to contribute to the teachers' emerging new subject identity. While topics to discuss were planned in advance of these meetings, these topics were generated by the group members. In relation to school leadership support, school principals were also provided with information on the program rollout and how best to support its provision in the schools in order to enhance the school leadership support dimension.

Massive Open Online Course (MOOC) and Fundamental Skills Development Workshops

The final aspect of the PD infrastructure established was access to online MOOCs in CS and additional fundamental coding skills development workshops. These supports were provided to complement the work within the national workshops but were primarily provided to enable teachers to up-skill and address deficiencies they had in their CS content knowledge. These supports were not compulsory, and it was anticipated that as the teachers had a wide range of previous knowledge of CS, there would be significant varia-tion amongst the group in relation to their use. However, their provision was important in catering for the wide variation of subject knowledge within the group. As participation in these online training courses and additional work-shops was more individual in nature, it also enabled teachers to upskill and address their deficiencies in subject content in a less public forum while also having access to the other elements of the PD infrastructure.

PEDAGOGICALLY FOCUSED WITH AN EMPHASIS ON COMMUNITIES OF PRACTICE

Armoni (2011) noted that as CS in schools was relatively new, there was scant literature on CS teacher education and for that reason many pro-viders had established CS PD frameworks that are not situated within par-ticular models that exist in the literature. While this is the case in CS, the PDST has established a strong expertise in the delivery of PD for teachers in Ireland, and from the onset the design of the PD infrastructure had at its core a strong emphasis on reflective practice. In addition, the need to have a strong pedagogical focus to the national workshops was also seen as essential. For that reason, the infrastructure established, and its underlying philosophy, aligns with the existing literature in the area. For example, the strong focus on active learning and classroom pedagogy are two of the fun-damental factors necessary for effective PD identified by Meneske (2015) in his review of existing PD programs in CS.

In addition, the extended and multi-dimensional aspect of the PD archi-tecture, that mixes both formal and informal PD opportunities, reflects the "ecosystem" approach outlined by Falkner et al. (2018). Similarly, the em-phasis on reflective practice and the strong undergirding of communities of practice, which the online platform and the regional meeting clusters aim to achieve, proliferate the CS PD literature (see, e.g., Armoni, 2011; Cutts et al., 2017; Ryoo et al., 2015; Yadav et al., 2016).

DISCUSSION AND NEXT STEPS: COMMUNITIES AND IDENTITIES

In outlining the approach taken to the in-service PD of CS teachers in Ire-land, this chapter has highlighted the emphasis placed on ensuring the PD was pedagogically focused while simultaneously emphasized the development of teachers' CS content knowledge. In addition, it has also highlighted the importance of reflective practice and highlighted how informal communities of practice could be facilitated in the overall PD infrastructure. CS communities of practice are also being established outside the in-service PD of CS teachers in Ireland, such as the Computer in Education Society of Ireland Community of Practice[1] initiative. Looking specifically at the development of communities of practice, the extent to which these communities have formed and are established is not known as yet (at the time of writing the PD is in its early stage and the research tracking its development has not been completed). That being said, we argue that the success of this curriculum initiative will largely hinge on whether these communities of practice are effectively established as they play an important role in the development of teachers' subject identity.

To further this perspective on identity, and in particular the PD of out-of-field teacher identities, it is worth exploring this issue from a psychological perspective. SIT (see Turner et al., 1979) can be a worthwhile lens to examine this issue of identity and help unpack some of the important issues teacher educators need to be cognisant of in the CS PD field. According to SIT, one's identity is not only individual, but it is also social in nature in that we align and associate with particular groups and in doing so also distance ourselves from other groups. Therefore, who one feels they are, is as much about who they feel they are not. The social status of a group is, therefore, critical in determining whether one decides to associate with it, as one's self-esteem will be subsequently tied to the esteem of the social group. For that reason, aligning one's identity with a new group is largely dependent on the status of the group. The status and prestige of the new subject needs to be higher, or at least equal to, one's current group, in order for one to consider identifying with it. Therefore, if the group is seen in a more positive light, in comparison to the group the individual previously associated with, movement to the new group and association with it is desirable. This in SIT terms is known as *social mobility*. Phoenix (2007) described its function as follows: "According to SIT some members of subordinate groups use social mobility (e.g., through promotion in employment) to improve their position by leaving behind their (previous) social group" (p. 65). On the other hand, if the status of the new group is perceived as lower than the original group, then there will be little incentive to "move" or begin to associate oneself with the new group. Instead the individual may employ techniques to distance themselves from the new lower-status group.

Turning to the issue of out-of-field teachers, this understanding of SIT implies that the extent to which out-of-field teachers will associate with a new subject is dependent on the status of the new subject in comparison to their "home" or existing subject. This echoes Hobb's (2012) contention that taking on a new subject is as much an identity project as it is the acquisition of new knowledge. Looking at CS from this perspective, highlights the importance of its status as a subject in schools in order for out-of-field teachers to identify with it. Ni and Guzdial (2012), for example, argued that teacher identity is central to sustaining motivation, job satisfaction, and commitment. School subjects often exist in an invisible and socially accepted hierarchy where more traditional subjects with a classical humanist tradition have higher status than those that are seen as more vocationally orientated. Subject status is also frequently dependent on how difficult it is perceived and how beneficial it is for entry to particular prestigious professions (DiMaggio, 1982).

In Ireland, traditionally CS or information technology studies in schools had little status and was seen more as a time to "play" with computers and since it was not a subject examined through the state examination system, it also held little status in schools (McGarr, 2009). Similar concerns related to the status of computing in other jurisdictions have also been raised by others (Ni & Guzdial, 2012). For that reason, existing computer teachers (who taught these computer skills-type courses) but who are now engaging with the CS initiative may see opportunities for upward "social mobility" through acquiring the skills and knowledge to teach an upper secondary level examinable subject—with significantly higher prestige than the version they had previously taught. Therefore, for many of the traditional "computer studies" teachers that are involved in this out-of-field PD, they may have an interest in ensuring the establishment of the subject in school is a success as their professional status is tied to its success. Therefore, they may enthusiastically engage in new communities of practice related to CS.

On the other hand, if the subject is perceived as having a lower status than the out-of-field teacher's existing subject specialism then identification with the new subject is less likely to occur. Ni and Guzdial (2012), for example, found that some CS teachers did not identify with CS due to departmental hierarchies and its status. In their study, as CS was offered under the business department, teachers did not value what they were teaching and were not motivated to teach the courses as they were considered lower-status technical courses. For that reason, they did not see CS as part of their own professional identity and instead continued to define themselves according to their original subject specialisms. Teachers in this case are less likely to participate in communities of practice in any meaningful way.

Returning to the PD framework that has been put in place to support the implementation of the new CS subject in Ireland, there was a strong emphasis on developing communities of practice and ensuring there is ample space for both formal as well as informal opportunities for teacher engagement. Yet looking at this through the lens of SIT, there is no guarantee that such communities will be sustained, as not all out-of-field teachers will necessarily see participation in such a community as a form of upward professional mobility as the teachers are coming from a variety of different subject backgrounds. Indeed for some teachers, who already teach more "prestigious" subjects such as mathematics, taking on the role of the CS teacher could be seen as a professional demotion. We argue that greater attention needs to be given to this aspect when designing PD for out-of-field teachers in CS. In particular, PD programs that establish the infrastructure for communities of practice to form, based on the belief that they will naturally occur, need to pay more attention to teachers' existing subject identities. Assuming these out-of-field teachers are a relatively homogenous group with similar interests and motivations may be the biggest barrier to the formation of effective, and much needed, communities of practice in this area. Unpacking one's current subject identity and exploring how one perceives their new subject identity should therefore form part of such PD.

CONCLUSION

The introduction of CS into Irish schools is at its early stage and at the time of writing the teachers are now in their second year of implementation. While significant progress has been made in the first year, the extent to which the in-service PD infrastructure put in place has provided adequate support to the teachers and has helped develop a strong community of practice and subject identity will be determined in time. That being said, as this chapter has highlighted, the success of establishing a sustainable stable CS subject in Irish schools, and attracting students to it, is dependent on the extent to which the teachers identify with the subject and advocate its promotion at a school and local level. It could be argued that the subject identity is particularly important for this early "pioneering" group of teachers as, how they promote its development and nurture new teachers, will be critical to the subject's success.

In considering PD programs for teachers, this chapter has highlighted the need to see this PD in CS, particularly with out-of-field teachers, as an identity modification project and hence the micro-politics of subject subcultures and teachers' professional identities are paramount. For that reason, the assumption that communities of practice will organically develop as part of any PD provision needs to be challenged, and the necessity for supports to help nurture such communities should be recognized.

NOTE

1. http://www.cesi.ie/community-of-practice-%E2%80%A2-facilitators-guide/

REFERENCES

Armoni, M. (2011). Looking at secondary teacher preparation through the lens of computer science. *ACM Transactions on Computing Education, 11*(4), 1–38.

Beijaard, D., Verloop, N., & Vermunt, J. D. (2000). Teachers' perceptions of professional identity: An exploratory study from a personal knowledge perspective. *Teaching and Teacher Education, 16*(7), 749–764.

Cutts, Q., Robertson, J., Donaldson, P., & O'Donnell, L. (2017). An evaluation of a professional learning network for computer science teachers. *Computer Science Education, 27*(1), 30–53.

DES. (1997). *IT 2000–A policy framework for the new millennium.* Stationery Office.

Desimone, L. (2009). Improving impact studies of teachers' professional development: Toward better conceptualizations and measures. *Educational Researcher, 38*(3), 181–199.

DiMaggio, P. (1982). Cultural capital and school success: The impact of status culture participation on the grades of US high school students. *American Sociological Review, 47*(2), 189–201.

du Plessis, A. E., Gillies, R. M., & Carroll, A. (2014). Out-of-field teaching and professional development: A transnational investigation across Australia and South Africa. *International Journal of Educational Research, 66*, 90–102.

Falkner, K., Vivian, R., & Williams, S. A. (2018). An ecosystem approach to teacher professional development within computer science. *Computer Science Education, 28*(4), 303–344.

Hobbs, L. (2013). Teaching 'out-of-field' as a boundary-crossing event: Factors shaping teacher identity. *International journal of Science and Mathematics Education, 11*(2), 271–297.

Keane, N., & McInerney, C. (2017) *Report on the provision of courses in computer science in upper second level education internationally* (Dublin, NCCA).

McGarr, O. (2009). The development of ICT across the curriculum in Irish schools: A historical perspective. *British Journal of Educational Technology, 40*(6), 1094–1108.

McKenna, P., Brady, M., Bates, P., Brick, J., & Drury, C. (1993). *New information technology in the Irish school system.* Office for Official Publications (EC).

Menekse, M. (2015). Computer science teacher professional development in the United States: A review of studies published between 2004 and 2014. *Computer Science Education, 25*(4), 325–335.

National Council for Curriculum and Assessment. (2018). *Computer Science curriculum specification.*

Ni, L., & Guzdial, M. (2012). Who AM I? Understanding high school computer science teachers' professional identity. In *Proceedings of the 43rd ACM technical symposium on computer science education* (pp. 499–504). ACM.

O'Doherty, T., Gleeson, J., Johnston, J., McGarr, O., & Moody, J. (2004). *Computers and curriculum: Difficulties and dichotomies.* National Council for Curriculum and Assessment.

O'Shea, F. (1983). Computers in schools. *Education Ireland, 1*(4), 20–26.

PDST. (2018). *PDST leaving certificate computer science–National workshop 1.* https://www.compsci.ie/fileadmin/user_upload/NW1_Workshop_Manual_-_final.pdf

Phoenix, A. (2007). Identities and diversities. In D. Miel, A. Phoenix, & K. Thomas (Eds.), *Mapping psychology* (pp. 43–104). The Open University.

Ragonis, N., Hazzan, O., & Gal-Ezer, J. (2010). A survey of computer science teacher preparation programs in Israel tells us: Computer science deserves a designated high school teacher preparation! In *Proceedings of the 41st ACM technical symposium on computer science education* (pp. 401–405). ACM.

Ryoo, J., Goode, J., & Margolis, J. (2015). It takes a village: Supporting inquiry-and equity-oriented computer science pedagogy through a professional learning community. *Computer Science Education, 25*(4), 351–370.

Smith, N., Allsop, Y., Caldwell, H., Hill, D., Dimitriadi, Y., & Csizmadia, A. P. (2015). Master teachers in computing: What have we achieved? In *Proceedings of the 10th workshop in primary and secondary computing education* (pp. 21–24). ACM.

Turner, J. C., Brown, R. J., & Tajfel, H. (1979). Social comparison and group interest in ingroup favouritism. *European Journal of Social Psychology, 9*(2), 187–204.

Wenger, E. (1999). *Communities of practice: Learning, meaning, and identity.* Cambridge University Press.

Wenger, E. (2011). *Communities of practice: A brief introduction.* STEP Leadership workshop, University of Oregon. https://scholarsbank.uoregon.edu/xmlui/handle/1794/11736

Yadav, A., Gretter, S., Hambrusch, S., & Sands, P. (2016). Expanding computer science education in schools: Understanding teacher experiences and challenges. *Computer Science Education, 26*(4), 235–254.

PART III

ONGOING AND SCALING-UP
PROFESSIONAL DEVELOPMENT APPROACHES

CHAPTER 10

SUPPORTING ONGOING TEACHER CAPACITY AND DEVELOPMENT

Moving Beyond Orientation Professional Development to Support Advanced Teacher Learning

Leigh Ann DeLyser
CSforALL

Stephanie Wortel-London
CSforALL

Lauren Wright
Penn State University

ABSTRACT

Over the last 10 years, a significant number of teachers have participated in professional development (PD) in preparation for teaching computer science

Professional Development for In-Service Teachers, pages 225–242
Copyright © 2022 by Information Age Publishing
www.infoagepub.com
All rights of reproduction in any form reserved.

(CS) at the K–12 level. Most of these PD opportunities are hosted by trained facilitators who serve a geographic region and are focused specifically on a particular course, tool, or curriculum implementation. Although independent PD is common in the K–12 school system in the United States, a majority of the PD teachers' experience in their careers is directly supported by the local education agencies, schools, or districts where they work. This ongoing development is meant to build off of the preparation teachers received prior to entering the classroom by providing targeted development necessary to help teachers gain a spectrum of knowledge and skills, refine their practice, and move from novice to experienced teachers. In this chapter, we will highlight the ongoing work of school systems in supporting teachers in the development of their CS pedagogical content knowledge. The chapter will use a literature review from multiple disciplines to motivate a conceptual framework for ongoing teacher development, as data show that districts had not previously supported ongoing CS teacher development. Further, data from over 150 school districts serving over 2 million students from 20 states demonstrate (a) the current state of ongoing support for teacher development and (b) strategic goals set by districts to create supportive PD pathways for teachers of CS. Additionally, goals set by districts provide examples of using best practices for supporting teacher development in a CS education context.

The United States, among many other countries, is focused on increasing the availability of computer science (CS) education opportunities for students within formal education (Gal-Ezer & Stephenson, 2009; Hubwieser et al., 2014). A key component of increasing the number of CS courses offered is increasing the number of teachers who can teach those courses in schools. This is a broader challenge than just preparing CS teachers, as a K–12 effort must also include generalist K–8 teachers and other subject area teachers, such as mathematics teachers, who will be asked to integrate CS concepts into their subjects.

The need to increase teacher capacity for CS education has moved faster than post-secondary teacher preparation programs, creating a wealth of in-service teacher preparation models and opportunities that are shared in this book. Many of these approaches seek to close the gap by providing teachers with a quick on-ramp to a CS classroom. Some of the approaches used in the community even include ongoing support for the teacher through in-person (University of Oregon, 2019) or virtual learning communities (Cooper et al., 2014).

These in-service opportunities are orienting tens of thousands of teachers to CS education content and curriculum (Code.org, 2019). A number of chapters in this book highlight outcomes and research findings from specific professional development (PD) efforts while also offering recommended next steps for improving these opportunities for teachers to learn about CS education. Instead of focusing on a single PD opportunity or program, this chapter uses data from school districts to look at the whole picture of teacher learning for CS education. This chapter will highlight the complementary actions taken by school districts to enhance teacher professional learning beyond PD workshops. In this chapter, we use the umbrella term Local Education Agency (LEA) to represent both school districts and the few independent school or other participating education associations. All participating LEAs provided direct instruction to students over multiple grades.

The data comes from LEA teams who participated in a self-evaluation exercise named the Strategic CSforALL Resource and Implementation Tool or SCRIPT (DeLyser & Wright, 2019), regarding the support of mastery development of their teachers. The self-evaluation exercise was facilitated by CSforALL leaders and engaged LEA-based teams in identifying opportunities to support teachers' PD experiences, including participation in professional learning working groups or networks and clear support for feedback on teaching practices. DeLyser and Wright (2019) share the development of the rubrics used in the self-evaluation exercise and selection of criteria.

The LEA teams engaged in a goal setting process, creating short- and long-term goals to support teacher development. We present an analysis of the 284 goals established by these LEA teams to demonstrate how teachers in engaged LEAs are being supported in their ongoing professional learning and provide a discussion of these data for future directions in the CSforALL community.

BACKGROUND

As a field, we seem to have a continued goal of creating and delivering PD that focuses on generating more entry-level or novice CS teachers (Margolis & Goode, 2016) in order to rapidly scale up the number and diversity of students who participate in CS education. This sense of urgency combined with an extreme lack of teacher preparation programs focused on CS have perpetuated the sustained goal of orientation PD without considering more advanced PD offerings. In this chapter, we use the term "orientation professional development" or "orientation PD," to represent a teacher's first exposure to CS. Orientation PD takes many forms and, depending on the provider, can include one or more of the complex factors contributing to highly effective teaching such as fluency in assessment, differentiated instruction, and CS pedagogical content knowledge (PCK) to name a few.

Orientation PD is a critical first step for in-service CS teacher development. Any teacher without a background in CS needs introductory PD to provide the basic fundamentals of grade-appropriate CS. Teachers need to explore the tools and systems and experience activities similar to what the students will do in order to be able to troubleshoot or assist students in later classroom activities. Orientation PD, however, cannot possibly provide the depth of professional learning for novice CS teachers to attain what would be minimum entry level teacher qualification standards in other subjects.

Developing Teacher Competency and Mastery

A teacher who qualifies for certification is not a master teacher. The components of certification are often used to set a minimum bar when measuring teacher preparation and its impact on student achievement (Sykes & Martin, 2019). Neither correlation nor causation between teacher preparation and student outcomes has yet to be demonstrated in CS education literature. However, it is not hard to infer that performance relationships between teacher practices and student outcomes would be similar to those found in other STEM disciplines (Darling-Hammond & Podolsky, 2019). Therefore, an examination of the components of teacher competency in other domains can be informative. These positive relationships between teacher preparation and student performance are explored by Darling-Hammond and Podolsky (2019) as indicated below:

> We defined qualifications according to state requirements for teacher certification or licensure, which evaluate preparation to teach in terms of exposure to particular bodies of content and pedagogical knowledge, as well as passage of licensure tests—often in basic skills, subject matter knowledge, and pedagogy or teaching performance. From this perspective, the key issue is not whether there are enough warm bodies to enter teaching, but whether there are enough qualified individuals, by state's licensure standards, willing to offer their services in the specific fields and locations that currently lack an adequate supply—and whether sufficiency of supply can be achieved solely in response to the market, or will require policy interventions. (p. 3)

A large body of literature connects the components of teacher preparation to student performance. Research in other academic subject areas, such as mathematics and English language arts, has found teacher preparedness and quality to be a key contributor to student outcomes (Darling-Hammond & Youngs, 2002). Teacher preparedness and quality is not a single dimension, but a complex set of factors including content knowledge, pedagogical knowledge, PCK, and experience in classrooms contributing to the ability to adjust and adapt prepared lessons based on formative feedback and student needs (Darling-Hammond & Youngs, 2002).

Teacher mastery is an ambitious label, and modern education research encourages the idea of continuous improvement in professional learning over the more fixed idea of mastery (Harwell, 2003). Continuous improvement operates on a core principle that teams of school personnel evaluate data to constantly adjust approaches to best address challenges that arise. This practice can be applied both to individuals, where teachers reflect on the performance of their students, and institutions where schools might look at subgroups of students to identify gaps or barriers across multiple classrooms. Continuous improvement takes commitment to the ongoing collaborative process and working groups that meet regularly and work together to solve challenges. This ongoing collaborative work can also be seen as a form of PD supported by internal working groups. As CS is a relatively new subject in K–12, these working groups may also be instrumental in the development of PCK that combines what experienced teachers adapt from other subject areas into their CS classrooms (Gal-Ezer & Stephenson, 2010). This practice of ongoing reflection and iteration is a key component of modern definitions of highly effective teacher behavior (Harwell, 2003).

Teacher Preparation in CS Education

With the sense of urgency and rush to prepare CS teachers, the design of PD for new CS teachers is less developed when compared to the basic preparation of teachers in other disciplines (Gal-Ezer & Stephenson, 2010). CS teachers are often teachers from other subject areas who have been provided professional learning to add a new subject to their repertoire. Additionally, a lack of clear and coherent certification for CS teachers often allows schools to place inexperienced and minimally prepared teachers into CS classrooms (Lang et al., 2013). The combination of these factors has led to a PD landscape where a majority of the opportunities do not align with research-based best practices for PD (Menekse, 2015).

In a meta-analysis published in 2015, Menekse observed in a literature review that 43% of CS PD opportunities for teachers lasted less than a week. In addition, these PD opportunities were not spread over time but rather provided in a single one-time workshop over the summer (Menekse, 2015). In the literature, many of the PD opportunities explicitly referenced introducing CS concepts. In the meta-analysis, only 33% of the programs used an assessment that included a test to measure teacher content knowledge after the orientation PD. All PD does not necessarily need to include a content knowledge assessment, but if the primary goal of the PD is to provide CS content knowledge, how can we judge the efficacy of teachers' learning during PD without a measure of that content?

In the paper *Bringing Computational Thinking to K–12: What Is Involved and What Is the Role of the Computer Science Education Community*, Barr and Stephenson (2011) argued that we need to change the systems responsible for preparing teachers and providing learning to students (i.e., schools) in partnership with the CS education community in order to expand access to

CS and computational thinking (CT) in the K–12 environment. Barr and Stephenson (2011) explicitly stated that schools should "provide teachers with professional development and support in the form of learning communities, summer institutes, peer learning offered by teachers with computational thinking experience..." (p. 120). This suite of ongoing activities are not a single stand-alone activity to ensure teachers meet a minimum standard of content knowledge. Rather, they are a collection of tools at the disposal of policy makers, school leaders, and the CS education community to help teachers responsible for CS instruction as they continuously improve and grow toward becoming well prepared, knowledgeable teachers.

A Self-Reflective Rubric for Teacher Capacity and Development

CSforALL has created and uses a process and series of tools, called the SCRIPT (Strategic CSforALL Resource and Implementation Planning Tool). SCRIPT enables LEAs to reflect upon the state of their current CS education implementation (including PD efforts for CS teachers), self-assess against a series of rubrics built from district change literature (DeLyser & Wright, 2019), and set goals to improve their CS education implementations (Wortel-London et al., 2019). The process and rubrics were developed after studying continuous improvement literature (Hawley, 2006) and existing education reform indicators (Common Core State Standards Initiative, 2010; NGSS Lead States, 2013; United States Department of Education, 2019).

As seen in Figure 10.1, the SCRIPT has five components including (a) leadership, (b) teacher capacity and development (TCD), (c) curriculum and materials selection and refinement, (d) partners, and (e) community. A sixth subcomponent called "infrastructure" is currently under development. In this chapter, we will be exploring data from the "teacher capacity and development" section of the SCRIPT. This data includes rubric scores and goals set by LEA teams to better understand the PD landscape in CS for a sample of U.S. school districts.

Figure 10.2 shows a screenshot of the TCD section of the SCRIPT rubric. The TCD section of SCRIPT has four sub-components including orientation teacher PD, teacher working groups, advanced teacher development, and teacher feedback. These sub-components were inspired by the Next Generation Science Standards' (NGSS) Indicator #3: Professional Learning for Teachers, the *Common Core Workbook* section "Train Educators on Common Core and Assessments," and the Race to the Top indicators for Great Teachers and Leaders (Common Core State Standards Initiative, 2010; NGSS Lead States, 2013; United States Department of Education, 2019). Detailed information on how these sub-components were inspired

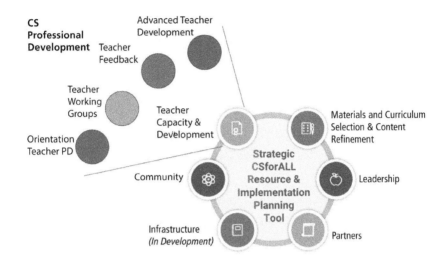

Figure 10.1 The five established components of the SCRIPT rubric, highlighting the subcomponents that refer specifically to CS Teacher PD.

Teacher Capacity and Development

All teachers have an understanding of the CSforALL initiatives in the district, and opportunities for integrated CS projects. Teachers with responsibility for CS content have clearly defined opportunities for integrated CS projects. Teachers with responsibility for CS content have clearly defined opportunities to learn computer science and expand their pedagogical fluency. There are well-defined incentives for participating in such professional development opportunities.

	Novice	Emerging	Developing	Highly Developed
Orientation Teacher PD	Teachers have not participated in CS education PD or have not had prior CS education experience.	Teachers independently identify professional development opportunites and participate in orientation PD at their own discretion.	Teachers are supported in their selection of professional development opportunities and are connected to each other for coherent pathways and grade level consistency.	Teacher orientation professional development is chosen to align with district vision and goals, and teachers are supported in the selection and attendance of the PD.
Teacher Working Groups	There is no participation by teachers in working groups focused on CS education.	Participation in Teacher working groups is entirely driven by individual teachers and mostly consists of participation in national communities such as CSTA or CSforALL Teachers.	Teachers participation in working groups both at a local and national level as a part of their professional learning network (PLN). Teachers are supported and recognized for this work with PD hours or other standard district incentives for professional learning.	There are K–12 working groups for sequential planning in the district, and outcomes from these groups are shared in district communications. Teacher working groups use student data and artifacts to drive teacher development. Meetings are scheduled and participation is part of incentive structures for teacher performance rating.

Figure 10.2 A screen shot of the SCRIPT rubric. *Note:* Full rubric available at www.csforall.org/SCRIPT

by NGSS, Common Core, and Race to the Top has been published in "A Systems Change Approach to CS Education: Creating Rubrics for School System Implementation" (see DeLyser & Wright, 2019).

In the remainder of this chapter we will describe the process by which the rubric scores and goals were collected from the participating LEAs, present an analysis of these data, and share next steps for the CS education community in light of these findings.

METHODS

The data were generated by a population of over 150 school districts and other local education authorities (LEAs) in the United States. In total, the LEAs included in this data set serve over two-million students from 20 states. These LEAs participated in SCRIPT workshops (Wortel-London et al., 2019) that consisted of a structured leadership planning experience in which an LEA administrator, school building administrators, school counselors and CS instructors worked together to chart a plan for bringing CT and CS instruction to all students served by that LEA. The holistic plans developed during the workshop take into account (a) materials and infrastructure required; (b) leadership and community buy-in development; (c) teacher capacity, development, and support; and (d) partnerships with other organizations and businesses in the community.

As a part of the workshop, the LEA teams self-rate their LEA on up to five rubric areas including teacher capacity. The teams then set short- and long-term goals related to growth within these areas for a 3-month, a 6-month, and a long-term improvement plan. CSforALL also collects information about the LEA from the National Center for Education Statistics District Search portal including enrolled student numbers and demographic information.

We used the rubric scores and goals set by the LEAs, based on a form submitted by the LEAs during the workshop. During the workshop and with guidance from the document, the five rubric areas were addressed one at a time. In each area of the rubric, LEA teams performed targeted self-reflection on rubric sub-components with ratings through an online form. The subcomponents of the TCD SCRIPT rubric included (a) orientation teacher PD, (b) teacher working groups, (c) advanced teacher development, and (d) teacher feedback. In each of these subcomponents TCD areas, LEAs were asked to consider whether they are currently operating in this area as novice, emerging, developing, or highly developed.[1] Descriptions were provided in each sub-category area of TCD to help LEAs differentiate between the different levels for each subcomponent. After completing an open-ended reflection on areas of strength and areas for growth, LEA teams were given time to set goals for each rubric area, and finalized goals were submitted via the online form. As a result of the goal setting process, 284 goals were collected from 63 school LEAs pertaining specifically to TCD.

A team of two raters, both familiar with the SCRIPT workshops and who have observed districts during the rubric reflection process, worked on independently coding these goals. The raters reviewed the goals and created a preliminary set of codes from 50 randomly selected goals. Raters discussed the initial code book and rated a second set of goals to compare for inter-rater agreement before each rater continued with individual ratings. The codes were developed with a focus on the nature of the intended action of the goal and the content of the support needed to enact the goal. The codes and definitions were enumerated in a shared code book. Among the goals analyzed, codes for the nature of the intended action in the goal included "teacher working group," "professional learning communities," "orientation teacher PD," "continuing teacher PD," and "administrator/mentoring support." A parallel code having to do with "building awareness" or "landscaping" also emerged. A statistically independent, orthogonal set of codes emerged having to do with the content addressed via each of the goals, including: (a) "content"—in reference to specific CS and CT content knowledge; (b) "pedagogy"—how to teach; (c) "pedagogical content knowledge"—how to teach the specific CS and CT content knowledge; and (d) some combination of these. Table 10.1 shows example goals with codes.

TABLE 10.1 Example Goals With Codes		
Example Goal	Type Code	Focus Code
Survey teachers to determine their computer science background	Awareness/ Landscaping	Landscaping
Conduct October visit to schools with exemplary CS programs	Continuing Professional Development (Local)	All
Middle school connection teachers identify and map out what will be taught at each grade level	Teacher Working Group	Content
At least 80% of schools will participate in the summer CS workshop to support project-based learning in K–12	Continuing Professional Development (Local)	Pedagogical Content Knowledge
Select additional CS curriculum modules for elementary and middle school based on curriculum gaps. Select teachers to complete appropriate training to teach the selected modules.	Continuing Professional Development	Content

TABLE 10.2 Coding Scheme for Goals	
Nature of Intended Action for Teacher Development	Content to Be Delivered
Teacher Working Group	Content knowledge of CS or CT
Professional Learning Communities	General pedagogy
Orientation Teacher PD	Specific pedagogical content knowledge of CS or CT
Continuing Teacher PD	A combination of any of the above
Administrator/Mentoring Support	

In Table 10.2, the coding scheme for each goal is presented visually. Each goal in the set received a code from Columns 1, and an optional code from Column 2.

To establish inter-rater agreement, a training set of 50 randomly selected goals was chosen to be rated by each rater independently. The two raters then went over the training set of 50 goals to establish rules, definitions, and norms to continue the categorization. Perfect initial agreement between the raters was established for more than half of the goals, with 100% agreement reached after a discussion of disagreements. A single rater then coded each of the remaining goals.

RESULTS AND DISCUSSION

The results start with a discussion of the rubric scores and then move to an analysis of the goals set by LEAs which they labeled as furthering their TCD work. We also present a descriptive case of a LEA supporting ongoing teacher development over a 1-year period.

LEA Self-Reflective Rubric Scores

During the workshop, LEA teams collaboratively rated themselves on the TCD rubric. Each rubric selection was translated to a numeric value (novice = 1, emerging = 2, developing = 3, and highly developed = 4). LEA size was categorized as small (less than 10,000 students) or medium to large (greater than 10,000 students) based on student enrollment numbers from the National Center for Education Statistics. Large and small districts were separated for analysis to see if any between group differences would emerge. From the 63 LEAs whose goals are analyzed, 41 of the schools were classified as small and 22 were classified as medium to large.

Table 10.3 shows the average rubric score for LEAs included in this study across the four TCD sub-components and the sum of all teacher capacity

TABLE 10.3 LEA Self-Ratings on Teacher Capacity and Development Comparing Small LEAs With Medium-To-Large LEAs

Rubric Sub-Category	Small LEAs	Medium to Large LEAs
Orientation Professional Development Score	2.1	1.9
Teacher Working Group Score	1.9	1.8
Continuing Professional Development Score	2.4	2.3
Administrative Support Score	2.0	1.4
Overall	8.4	7.3

ratings. Orientation professional development (OPD) refers to the support and coordination for teachers selecting and attending orientation PD aligned to the LEAs CS education plans. The teacher working group score indicated the availability and alignment of teacher working groups for CS education efforts. The continuing PD score, similar to OPD, assesses the support and coordination for teachers in identifying and attending aligned continuing PD opportunities. Administrative support score refers to the support for administrators, mentors, and other teacher feedback personnel (coaches, supervisory positions, etc.) for observing and providing high quality feedback for CS teachers.

The average OPD score refers to the support and coordination for teachers selecting and attending orientation PD aligned to the LEAs CS education plans. The average score for OPD was at the emerging level (2). According to the SCRIPT rubric, an emerging OPD score (2) indicates that in many LEAs there are teachers who are interested in pursuing OPD, but they are unsupported in those choices. This can yield teachers in the same school, or even the same grade teaching different curriculum or nothing at all.

Teacher working groups and continuing PD also averaged just under the emerging level. Emerging for these sub-components also indicates that there are individual teachers who are working together, or perhaps seeking out continuing PD, but are doing so on their own behalf, and not as a part of official, school-organized activities. We see the largest gap between the small and medium to large LEAs in the support for administrator's ability to provide feedback to teachers. Overall, these data reflect the reliance on individual teachers to identify PD, select options that may or may not align with what their colleagues are doing, and seek additional learning opportunities on their own.

LEA Goals for Teacher Capacity and Development

CSforALL collected 284 goals from 63 LEAs related to TCD. Figure 10.3 shows the breakdown of goals by qualitative codes. As shown in Figure 10.3,

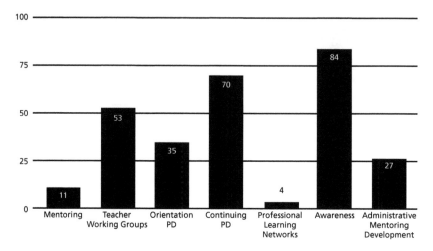

Figure 10.3   Breakdown of district goals by action.

84 of the 284 goals analyzed were focused on awareness and landscaping. Awareness and landscaping goals often focused on increasing the awareness of what CS is, communicating the plan for CS across the LEA, or understanding the landscape of current CS education efforts within schools. For example, one LEA wrote a goal that said, "Teachers will be introduced to the CS vision." This is a typical awareness goal in that the vision is not instructional content or practice, but instead more of a high-level plan for the "what" and "why" of CS education. Awareness extends beyond teachers, however, as demonstrated by this goal: "Develop a communication plan for admin, teachers, and librarians."

Landscaping goals focused more on identifying the existing CS efforts. One LEA wrote, "Identify the Computer Science teachers & what PD they need for their specific curriculum and pathway." Many LEAs have communicated that they do not have good record keeping of who is teaching CS, where it is being taught, or what curriculum is being used. Although the assumption is that most teachers would need orientation PD (OPD) or awareness and buy-in for CS education, many LEA teams thought about the way that continuing PD could identify and provide support for teachers.

Of the 284 goals, 70 focused on continuing professional development (CPD) of undefined structure, 53 focused on creating teacher working groups, and four referenced connecting teachers to larger out-of-LEA professional learning networks (such as the Computer Science Teachers Association, or CSTA). Some of the LEAs focused their CPD efforts at the local level (e.g., "At least 80% of our schools will participate in the summer CS workshop to support project-based learning K–12"), while others looked to external sources for CPD opportunities (e.g., "Put CS webinars from

NCWIT.org in My Learning Plan for guidance counselors"). Teacher working groups were described broadly as just meeting times (e.g., "Organize local working groups (in regional networks) of schools at different levels of CS implementation"), while others are more specific about the goals of the groups (e.g., "K–12 working groups for the sequential planning in the LEA and outcomes from these groups"). Overall, LEAs saw the value in creating CPD opportunities for teachers and staff.

Although the CS education community focuses on OPD, only 35 of the 284 goals set by LEAs focused on OPD. Some of the goals mentioned external vendors (e.g., "Finalize pilot agreement with CodeHS.com"), while others focused on the outcome of such PD (e.g., "All teachers have a basic knowledge of what CS is and have implemented it in their classrooms on some level"). Some of the OPD goals extended beyond teachers responsible for CS content such as, "Offer five minute CSforALL informational presentations at faculty meetings district wide." Overall, the OPD goals focused on building foundational knowledge of CS and specific CS curricula for teachers and staff.

Figure 10.4 shows the breakdown of the goals based upon the qualitative coding of the focus of the PD opportunity specified in the goal. Many of the goals (106) did not specify a focus of the activity or PD. For example, one LEA wrote, "Develop PD opportunities in Summer 2018 to prepare for 2018–2019 school year." Many of the LEAs' goals were focused on development or identification of future PD and therefore a focus could be a part of the development process. A number of goals were written in a way to indicate that content, pedagogy, and PCK would be a part of the development activity. For example, one LEA set a goal to "Train all teachers across all content areas on the what, why, and how of CS instruction."

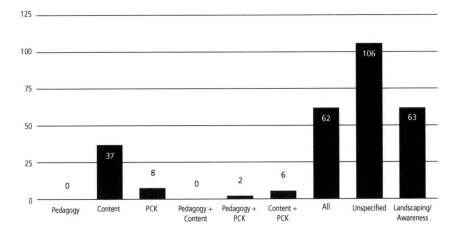

Figure 10.4   Goal focus.

Some of the goals specifically referenced CS content as an important unique component of the goal. One LEA set a goal: "All staff will be exposed to a base-level understanding of CS. This will be planned at a faculty meeting or during January PD and led by Dr. D." The content-focused goals covered the range of types of PD, including continuing PD, showing that LEA leadership recognized the need for teachers to continue to explore CS concepts even after orientation PD.

Exemplar Teacher Capacity Work

Attention to the layers of support and collaboration required to attend to ongoing PD and development of teacher leaders was a crucial element for one shared education services LEA who participated in the SCRIPT process. In addition to being a shared education services provider, this LEA also served as an educational campus unto itself, providing education to a significant special education population drawn from the region served, as well as alternative high school experiences and career technical education experiences. For the purposes of this chapter, this LEA will be referred to as Elmswood Shared Educational Services.

At Elmswood, a CS planning team was assembled to go through the SCRIPT workshop experience as well as to carry forward the work. During a values-surfacing activity at the beginning of the SCRIPT workshop, Elmswood identified social and emotional learning and career preparation as local values for incorporating CT and CS practices into the comprehensive education experience. The Elmswood team then set a goal to engage a diverse group of teachers in the ideation process to create a playbook for integrating CS practices into the individualized education plan and core content areas of the school day. Elmswood is an exemplar for the diversity of experience and responsibilities included in the membership of the planning team, which consisted of school building principals, foreign language teachers, assistive technology specialists, special education teachers, the librarian, the school counselor, and others. These diverse funds of knowledge allowed many different teachers across the campus to assume leadership in the eyes of their community—not just teachers assigned as technology integration specialists and CS teachers.

The CS planning team at Elmswood also engaged in a process of CS educational technology immersion and purposeful play to begin filling out the pedagogy playbook for the campus. They began by laying out the entire contents of their "library of things" in order to have each team member tinker and experiment with an eye to potential uses in the classroom and library. They then took notes and gathered the instructional ideas generated into the first draft of the playbook. This is an example of a teacher working group composed of various instructional staff collaborating to create locally relevant teaching resources.

The ongoing work of the Elmswood planning team involves creating a benchmark crosswalk between a locally agreed-upon list of CS practices and the social emotional learning framework for special education that had previously been adopted by the campus. The logic behind this step was that teacher colleagues would be more willing to take on the PD to incorporate CS into their teaching if they knew it was already well aligned with the existing required special education standards on campus—so they knew that they weren't being asked to do an "extra set of things." This example of cultivating teacher leader ownership and mentorship of other teachers on campus shows how a growth pathway and culture of continuous learning can be encouraged by creating durable organizational structures within an educational campus like Elmswood or another LEA.

Next Steps

The CS education community should continue to create opportunities for teachers to explore CS education for the first time, but this needs to be complemented with resources, self-assessment structures, and opportunities for teachers to continue to learn and develop after those initial experiences. Initial ratings from the SCRIPT rubric show that districts beginning to engage with this work will be supported to attain higher ratings in teacher development through access to resources, continuous self-assessment, and opportunities to expand their CS PCK. In 2010 it was considered to be an ambitious goal to provide PD for 10,000 teachers by 2015 (Astrachan et al., 2011). In 2019, not only have we surpassed that goal, the scale of needs in teacher preparation is completely different. CSforALL collected commitments for the 2018 CSforALL Summit which offered over 168,000 opportunities for teachers to engage with CS education efforts, PD, or curriculum.

We are at a tipping point where most students and teachers will no longer be in their first experience with CS, and those teachers no longer need OPD. Will first exposure, first experience opportunities still be needed? Absolutely. But the important question for the CS education community is how do we support what comes next? As we build the pipeline of reflective and experienced CS teachers, we need to recognize that the deep bench of disciplinary knowledge and experienced teachers that exists in schools for other subject areas does not exist for CS. Teacher working groups and locally owned PD may need resources and support to meet a standard of high quality. In a national education environment where CSforALL has realized its mission, high quality CS education will be an integral part of ALL student's academic experiences from K–12. That means multiple learning opportunities, with multiple instructors both in and outside of the school building. Teachers will also learn and develop through multiple opportunities for CPD. They will learn from their peers in working groups, from the larger community in professional learning networks, and from their own trial-and-error with reflection.

The CS education community is poised to continue to ensure our best practices of rigor, inclusion, and equity are not just part of the orientation, but lived values that are revisited by teachers in their quest for mastery. Researchers need to explore the development of competency in CS educators and the best practices not just for PCK and classroom performance, but also for ongoing supported professional learning in a continuous improvement cycle. The consistently low scoring sections of the SCRIPT rubric and the goals set by districts indicate that ongoing professional learning is an important component in the next phase of CS education initiatives in the United States. The research-practice partnerships funded by the National Science Foundation are well placed to study these questions with input from educators, and the RPPforCS (www.csforall.org/rppforcs) project led by SageFox Consulting and CSforALL will continue to share outcomes from the collective group of projects.

In this chapter, we have presented literature connecting the current needs in CS preservice teaching to current practices in LEAs in CS in-service teacher PD. CSforALL developed the SCRIPT workshop and rubric to help school and LEA leaders to assess the current condition of their CS PD efforts, as well as interlocking systems of support needed for PD to yield success for teachers and their students. We then presented aggregated data reflecting how LEAs are creating opportunities for teachers to learn CS. This snapshot of what LEAs are currently doing to support their teachers with CS PD points the way to next steps we can encourage LEAs to take to continuously improve the preparation of their CS teaching force. To inform these efforts, CSforALL will continue to collect and analyze LEA and systems change data in order to identify the needs of teachers and the opportunities to support local change through LEAs.

NOTE

1. A copy of the full rubrics can be found on the CSforALL website at www.cs-forall.org/SCRIPT

REFERENCES

Astrachan, O., Cuny, J., Stephenson, C., & Wilson, C. (2011, March). *The CS10K project: Mobilizing the community to transform high school computing* [Conference Session]. In *The 42nd ACM Technical Symposium on Computer Science Education* (pp. 85–86). ACM.

Barr, V., & Stephenson, C. (2011). Bringing computational thinking to K–12: What is involved and what is the role of the computer science education community? *Inroads, 2*(1), 48–54.

Code.org. (2019). What will you create? *Code.org.* https://code.org/

Common Core State Standards Initiative. (2010). Appendix A. In *Common Core State Standards for English language arts & literacy in history/social studies, science, and technical subjects.*

Cooper, S., Grover, S., & Simon, B. (2014). Building a virtual community of practice for K–12 CS teachers. *Communications of the ACM, 57*(5), 39–41.

Darling-Hammond, L., & Podolsky, A. (2019). Breaking the cycle of teacher shortages: What kind of policies can make a difference? *Education Policy Analysis Archives, 27*(34), 1–11.

Darling-Hammond, L., & Youngs, P. (2002). Defining "highly qualified teachers": What does "scientifically-based research" actually tell us? *Educational Researcher, 31*(9), 13–25.

DeLyser, L., & Wright, L. (2019, July 15–17). *A systems change approach to CS education: Creating rubrics for school system implementation* [Paper Presentation]. The Innovation and Technology in Computer Science Education Conference.

Gal-Ezer, J., & Stephenson, C. (2009). The current state of computer science in US high schools: A report from two national surveys. *Journal for Computing Teachers, 1*, 1–5.

Gal-Ezer, J., & Stephenson, C. (2010). Computer science teacher preparation is critical. *ACM Inroads, 1*(1), 61–66.

Harwell, S. H. (2003). *Teacher professional development: It's not an event, it's a process.* http://www.northernc.on.ca/leid/docs/teacher%20professional%20development.pdf

Hawley, W. D. (Eds.). (2006). *The keys to effective schools: Educational reform as continuous improvement.* Corwin Press.

Hubwieser, P., Armoni, M., Giannakos, M. N., & Mittermeir, R. T. (2014). Perspectives and visions of computer science education in primary and secondary (K–12) schools. *ACM Transactions on Computing Education, 14*(2), 1–9.

Lang, K., Galanos, R., Goode, J., Seehorn, D., Trees, F., Phillips, P., & Stephenson, C. (2013). *Bugs in the system: Computer science teacher certification in the US* [Report]. The Computer Science Teachers Association and The Association for Computing Machinery. http://csta.acm.org/ComputerScienceTeacherCertification/sub/CSTA_BugsInTheSystem.pdf

Margolis, J., & Goode, J. (2016). Ten lessons for computer science for all. *ACM Inroads, 7*(4), 52–56.

Menekse, M. (2015). Computer science teacher professional development in the United States: A review of studies published between 2004 and 2014. *Computer Science Education, 25*(4), 325–350.

NGSS Lead States. (2013). *Next Generation Science Standards: For states, by states.* The National Academies Press.

Sykes, G., & Martin, K. (2019). Equitable access to capable teachers: The states respond. *Education Policy Analysis Archives, 27*(39), 1–49.

United States Department of Education. (2019). *Race to the Top Fund.* https://oese.ed.gov/offices/office-of-formula-grants/school-support-and-accountability/race-to-the-top-district

University of Oregon. (2019). *Exploring computer science—A K–12/university partnership committed to democratizing computer science.* http://www.exploringcs.org/

Wortel-London, S. B., DeLyser, L., Wright, L., & Aguiar, J. H. (2019, June 13–16). *A goal analysis of computer science education: Setting institutional goals for CS ed* [Paper presentation]. The International Conference on Computational Thinking Education, Hong Kong.

CHAPTER 11

LEVERAGING COLLECTIVE IMPACT TO SCALE COMPUTER SCIENCE TEACHER PROFESSIONAL DEVELOPMENT AND CERTIFICATION

Carol L. Fletcher
The University of Texas at Austin

Jayce R. Warner
The University of Texas at Austin

ABSTRACT

The CS for all movement represents an ambitious effort to bring computing education to all American K–12 schools. Achieving this goal will require the rapid scale-up of educator capacity to teach computer science (CS) in thousands of schools that do not currently offer CS. This study explores the use of a collective impact approach called WeTeach_CS to address this complex

Professional Development for In-Service Teachers, pages 243–269
Copyright © 2022 by Information Age Publishing
www.infoagepub.com

problem in Texas. We describe how WeTeach_CS operationalized the five core elements of collective impact (common agenda, shared measurement systems, mutually reinforcing activities, continuous communication, and a backbone organization) to create a collaborative, multi-sector network of partners all focused on supporting in-service teachers to build the CS knowledge and skills necessary to achieve a high school CS teacher certification. To evaluate the collective impact model, we describe a quasi-experimental study using interrupted time series analysis that demonstrated empirically the effectiveness of the model in increasing the rate of CS teacher certifications. The relationship between teacher capacity and other elements of the CAPE Framework for equitable computer science education, such as access and participation, are also explored. We discuss implications for other states who may consider deploying a similar model as they develop strategic, large-scale investments in K–12 systems for computing education.

The ubiquitous influence of technology on our social, economic, and political lives has brought a great deal of attention to the way in which we address technology education in schools. Parents, educators, and politicians of both parties have begun championing technology education that goes beyond teaching students to be consumers of technology but rather developing the knowledge and skills needed to become creators and innovators of technology. This movement toward making computer science (CS) education, rather than simply technology education, a reality for all students can be generally described as the CS for all movement (CSforAll, 2020).

CS for all goals vary across localities, with some, such as those of the state of Arkansas, focusing on the goal of access to CS courses in every high school (Arkansas Department of Education, 2019) and others, such as Chicago Public Schools, focusing on ensuring every student actually completes a secondary CS course before high school graduation (Elahi, 2016). Regardless of the specifics, the movement in general requires a substantial increase in the number of educators who are equipped to teach CS (Lang et al., 2013). As more states and districts embrace the vision of CS for all, leaders are grappling with the enormous challenge of equipping the educational system with the human capital necessary to realize that vision.

Nationally, principals and superintendents cite a lack of qualified teachers as the primary barrier to offering CS (Google Inc., & Gallup Inc., 2016). From their analysis of public high schools in 39 U.S. states, the Code.org Advocacy Coalition (2019) reported that only 45% of high schools teach CS. If we were to assume that the data in these 39 states are representative of the 27,832 public high schools in America (Code.org Advocacy Coalition, 2019), our country would need to produce an additional 15,308 qualified CS teachers just to have a single CS teacher at every U.S. public high school that currently lacks one. Policies that require schools to offer CS or, even more ambitiously, those that require all students to complete a CS course for graduation, can be valuable drivers for change but will prove to be failures if schools lack trained and qualified CS educators. Currently, the ecosystem that both prepares new teachers and provides experienced teachers with ongoing support for professional learning is ill-equipped in most states to implement the rapid scaling up of skills necessary to reach every school and student. Tackling this challenge will require states and regions to implement novel approaches for growing existing educator capacity.

CS Teacher Certification Pathways: Preservice

The standard method for becoming qualified to teach at the K–12 level is through preservice programs. However, this model breaks down when applied to CS teachers. According to the 2020 State of CS Education Report, only 20 states authorized a state-approved preservice teacher program in CS (Code.org et al., 2020). Even in states where such programs were officially authorized, very few institutions actually produce certified teachers through these programs. Title II National Teacher Preparation Data indicated that only 100 teachers graduated from a CS preservice teacher preparation program in 2016–2017 (Code.org Advocacy Coalition, 2019). The lack of viable preservice pathways in Texas reflects this national trend. In our counts using data from the Texas Education Research Center, only 59 teachers completed a preservice CS teacher certification program in Texas between the 2011–2012 and 2014–2015 school years. This included both traditional university-based undergraduate programs and post-baccalaureate alternative certification programs. During the same time period, 6,582 math and 4,714 science teacher candidates completed preservice programs. Given that math and science are also cited by the state of Texas as critical shortage areas for teachers, one can see the depth of the challenge for CS.

There are several reasons why CS preservice teacher preparation may be particularly challenging. In states such as Texas, preservice teacher candidates pursuing high school certifications are required to hold or be pursuing an undergraduate degree in a discipline such as mathematics, physics, or biology, before they are able to add on a teacher certification. As such, university-based teacher certification programs often try to recruit undergraduate students from CS departments because they have a deep knowledge of CS. With average starting salaries for CS degree holders at $66,000 (Colino, 2018) and average starting salaries for classroom teachers at $40,074 (Texas Association of School Boards, 2018), the value proposition for CS undergraduates to go into education rather than industry is a major challenge.

In addition, the regulatory ecosystem within which preservice programs operate can be quite complex, with policies governed by both institutions of higher education and state regulatory agencies. For example, university-based preservice educator programs in Texas must meet 104 regulations related to the structure of the program, provide 300 hours of training, including 30 hours in field-based training in the appropriate content area, and verify that all online coursework is accredited by the Distance Education Accrediting Commission or Quality Matters (Texas Education Code, 2018). Although meeting all of these criteria makes sense for programs in other disciplines that produce large numbers of teachers, the effort required to meet all of these standards for CS certification may be prohibitive given the very small number of CS majors currently choosing this pathway. For example, of the 59 teachers in Texas whose first teacher certification was in CS between 2011 and 2015, less than 10 went through a university-based preservice program that recruits undergraduate majors in fields other than education to obtain certification.

Program length is also a barrier to rapidly increasing CS teacher capacity through traditional undergraduate programs as compared to in-service programs. Most undergraduate secondary teacher certification programs take 4 years at a minimum to complete because candidates are often exiting school with both an undergraduate degree in their discipline and a teaching certification. Four years may be a reasonable standard for undergraduate degree completion, but given the 15,000+ new CS teachers needed in the United States, it would take several decades to produce enough new CS teachers through an undergraduate pathway to meet the goal of one teacher per school nationwide.

Finally, adding preservice CS teacher certification to university offerings requires institutional changes that depend on cooperation between colleges, schools, and departments of education and CS or computer engineering. This change in institutional cooperation and structures requires the collaboration and consent of numerous individuals and entities, all of whom may lack incentives to invest departmental resources in CS teacher certification or have other reasons for maintaining the status quo. For example, the standard criteria for promotion and tenure for faculty in CS departments emphasizes publication in archival journals (Patterson et al., 2020). Even if a partnership with college of education faculty on developing preservice CS teacher preparation programs resulted in journal publications, these types of publications might not be as highly valued by tenure review committees as those more directly related to innovations in CS.

CS Teacher Certification Pathways: In-service

An alternative solution to increasing the CS teacher workforce is training in-service teachers from other disciplines to become certified in the teaching of CS. According to the National Survey of Science & Mathematics

Education (NSSME), which included CS for the first time in 2018, most CS teachers already hold teacher certification in other subjects, with 34% certified to teach mathematics and 28% certified to teach business (Gordon & Heck, 2019). Given the small number of individuals that exit a preservice teacher preparation program with a CS certification (based on Title II data cited previously), this may indicate that many secondary CS teachers start their teaching careers in another discipline and then add CS. The NSSME survey also noted that almost half of CS teachers (47%) reported teaching in K–12 for over 10 years but that only 21% reported teaching CS for over 10 years. Additionally, NSSME reports that only one in four CS teachers have a degree in CS, computer engineering, or information science. Each of these data points indicates it is likely that most current secondary CS teachers began their teaching career in a field other than CS.

One advantage to training in-service teachers of other subject areas to fill the CS teacher capacity gap is that the length of time it takes to add a certification in a new content area tends to be a lot shorter than the time required to obtain initial certifications through standard preservice programs. Forty-four states allow in-service teachers to acquire supplementary teaching credentials simply by passing the relevant exam or completing additional, requisite PD courses (Kim et al., 2021). However, a major challenge faced by most in-service teachers who want to become qualified to teach CS is a lack of administrative or PD support (Google Inc., & Gallup Inc., 2016; Lang et al., 2013). One hypothesis for this lack of support is that there are only a small number of prospective or practicing CS teachers in any school or district, making the investment of administrative time or financial resources uncompelling.

The NSSME survey supports the hypothesis that most schools have no more than one CS teacher by documenting the substantial differences that exist between math, science, and CS teachers in the percentage that have either observed other teachers of the same subject in their school (56% of math teachers, 50% of science teachers but only 36% of CS teachers) or been observed by a colleague from their school (41% of math teachers, 38% of science teachers, but only 17% of CS teachers). Such data may indicate that, unlike math and science teachers who work with colleagues in the same discipline and can observe or be observed by each other, CS teachers have few options to collaborate with other CS teachers. As a result, schools that want to add CS to their master schedule may only start with one or two sections taught by one teacher. This lack of critical mass makes creating PD or providing alternate support for new CS teachers incredibly inefficient from the perspective of district or school administrators. Individual schools, and even districts with multiple high schools, may find it difficult to create the kind of economies of scale needed to implement effective and sustainable PD programs for only a handful of teachers. This problem is compounded by the fact that school districts often lack administrative personnel with computing expertise, which makes the mentoring of new teachers and the informed vetting of resources to grow a CS program especially challenging for administrators.

The path to realizing the vision of CS for all is complex and fraught with challenges. To overcome these challenges, we need innovative models of teacher capacity building that can be scaled quickly over large, geographically and culturally diverse areas. These models must be responsive to the unique needs and current assets of schools and districts while also leveraging the resources and computing expertise of partners outside the K–12 system to help "fill the gaps" in school district capacity. One type of model that fits this bill is the collective impact model, which brings together stakeholders from varying organizations to take on complex social problems and effect sustainable change at scale. This chapter will describe the key components of collective impact and how this model can create the supportive, multi-layered ecosystem needed to build CS programs in both small and large districts.

WeTeach_CS (WTCS) is a collective impact effort that has been addressing the CS educator capacity issue in Texas since 2015. From its initial implementation until now, the rate at which new CS teachers obtained certification has more than doubled. This chapter outlines how the WTCS collective impact project was designed and enacted to increase statewide capacity for K–12 computing education. We will discuss why building system-wide capacity in CS education is uniquely suited to a collective impact approach and explain the mechanisms for using collective impact to scale and sustain support for teachers. We will also address the role of the backbone organization in coordinating collective impact and the metrics used to evaluate impact on teachers, schools, and students. Other large educational systems attempting to develop an ecosystem of support for CS education should find value in the lessons learned from the WTCS model.

BACKGROUND

Collective Impact

Collective impact is an innovative model for tackling complex social problems that leverages the skills, resources, and cooperation of a diverse range of stakeholder groups in a coordinated manner. Collective impact initiatives acknowledge the challenges of focusing on isolated components of a system or symptoms of a problem and opt instead to coordinate cross-sector efforts toward addressing a specific problem of practice and tracking progress with mutually agreed upon metrics. According to Kania and Kramer (2011), effective collective impact efforts include five key components:

a common agenda, shared measurement systems, mutually reinforcing activities, continuous communication, and a backbone organization that can help to coordinate and support the work of all network participants.

Collective impact models have been successfully applied to a wide variety of social challenges, including healthcare, juvenile justice, chronic homelessness, and, as one of the most common contexts, education. In a review of collective impact efforts, Lynn and Stachowiak (2018) found that eight of 25 projects were focused on educational outcomes such as college and career readiness, college enrollment, and high school graduation. However, the majority of these studies and collective impact projects in education have focused on student outcomes rather than educator capacity issues. The work presented here involves measuring educator capacity to address an educational problem, namely, the lack of student access to and participation in CS courses. Although we are measuring educator capacity by tracking high school CS teacher certification, collective impact models could also be valuable in building CS educator knowledge and skills in states which don't require computing teachers to be formally certified.

The WTCS program is based on a collective impact framework that makes it possible to scale promising practices across a large, geographically and culturally diverse state such as Texas. With over 1,200 school districts and five million students in Texas, models that engage a variety of stakeholders to address a specific problem of practice are vital to address the wide variety of needs that teachers and communities have when it comes to computing education. The following section describes the WTCS PD network model and the components of the model that are grounded in the collective impact approach.

The mission of WTCS is to educate, inspire, and empower K–12 teachers in achieving the goal of CS for all. The WTCS effort to broaden participation in CS acknowledges the many variables, policies, cultural norms, and institutional capacity issues that all impact the experiences of students in high school computing. Although there is value in specific student interventions, such as after school programs, mentoring, and coding camps, focusing on teachers and school systems has greater potential to effectively address the massive challenge of equitably scaling up access to CS education. Investing in teachers and their work within schools supports the systemic capacity-building that is needed to make long-term changes in student access and participation on a large scale. Thus, teachers and schools are the units of change in these types of broadening participation efforts. The WTCS program consists of five key levers at the teacher and school level that impact student experiences in computing:

1. growing teacher content knowledge in CS
2. building CS instructional skills

3. focusing on strategies to increase equity in CS classes
4. creating a professional community of CS educators
5. increasing CS teacher certification

WeTeach_CS Structure & Scope

WTCS PD experiences are designed to reflect the attributes of high quality PD outlined by Darling-Hammond et al. (2017). These include having a strong content focus, incorporating active learning by teachers, supporting teacher collaboration, modeling effective instruction in CS topics, and creating PD experiences that are of sustained duration.

From 2015 to 2018, the WTCS collective impact effort consisted of a backbone organization, managed out of The University of Texas at Austin (UT Austin), and approximately 30 WTCS regional collaboratives distributed across the state of Texas. Funding for the WTCS network was provided to UT Austin by the Texas Education Agency, which leveraged Title II, Part B funds from the No Child Left Behind Act to support a statewide network for STEM teacher PD. Through a grant application process managed by UT Austin, WTCS regional collaboratives were funded to recruit and support cohorts of 20–40 teachers in their respective regions. A WTCS collaborative consists of a small group of Instructional Team Members (ITMs) from a variety of institutions with expertise in areas such as CS, effective pedagogy, state standards, and K–12 PD. The ITMs create and implement a PD plan of at least 60 hours for teachers in their cohort based on a local needs assessment and their own expertise. Nonprofit, workforce development, and industry leaders often contribute to WTCS collaborative planning and training as well. Fiscal agents for WTCS collaborative grants include institutions of higher education (IHEs), education service centers, school districts, and nonprofits.

ITM teams must include at least one CS professor and one instructional specialist with experience in teacher PD. The CS professor brings CS content expertise to the team while the instructional specialist ensures the learning experiences reflect best practices in instruction and are aligned with the needs of classroom teachers as well as state course standards. Figure 11.1 illustrates the collective impact network including the relationship between UT Austin as the backbone organization and WTCS collaboratives across the state. This hub-and-spoke model, where UT Austin serves as the hub for all WTCS collaboratives while also facilitating collaboration among various collaborative leaders, has resulted in a highly engaged network that has developed the capacity of CS education leaders across the state to support teachers and districts as they grow K–12 CS programs.

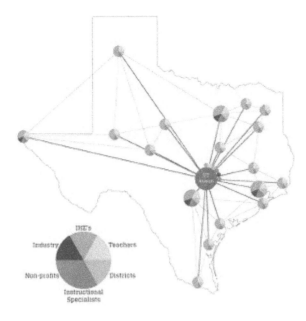

Figure 11.1   The WeTeach_CS collective impact model.

Each WTCS collaborative PD program consists of some combination of five types of learning experiences for teachers and a financial incentive as described below:

1. *Locally developed workshops* delivered by computing faculty in partnership with instructional specialists that are based on the unique needs of the teachers or districts involved and the knowledge and skills of local IHE faculty. For example, if most teachers in a WTCS collaborative are brand new to computing, PD might focus on introductory exposure to block-based programming. If most teachers have some prior experience with programming, PD might focus on Java so that teachers can prepare to teach courses like Advanced Placement (AP) CS A.
2. *Train-the-trainer* style PD offered by UT Austin in which ITMs receive training and then subsequently train teachers in their respective regions. Topics include integrated computational thinking, Scratch, Java, 3D printing, and physical computing.
3. *Online coursework* for emerging CS teachers developed by UT Austin. For example, Foundations of Computer Science for Teachers: TExES Prep is a 7-week course that can be taken asynchronously by any teacher. It was specifically designed for high school teachers to build their content knowledge in preparation for the Texas Grades

8–12 CS certification exam. This exam, termed the Texas Examination of Educator Competencies (TExES) can be taken by teachers who were previously certified in a subject other than CS to obtain a CS teacher certification. Another online course is Strategies for Effective and Inclusive CS Teaching, which focuses on equity issues and broadening participation in computing.

4. *WTCS Workshops* delivered directly by WTCS staff such as the We-Teach_CS Certification Prep course, a 2-day, in-person training that reviews all of the teacher competencies measured on the TExES. From 2015 to 2018, this workshop was delivered across the state of Texas in partnership with various WTCS collaboratives to reduce travel and expenses for teachers by bringing the resources of UT Austin directly to teachers.

5. A *CS Certification Incentive Program* (CIP) to provide a monetary incentive to teachers to gain the additional knowledge and skills needed to pass the certification exam and begin teaching CS. Unlike other professions in which employees are rewarded with raises or promotions for learning new skills or taking on new responsibilities, teachers from other disciplines who take on the challenge of becoming CS certified generally receive no monetary compensation from their employers. Although our prior research indicates that the stipend wasn't the primary motivational factor for pursuing certification (Fletcher et al., 2017), it was useful in advertising the program and helping teachers to persist in their preparation when the content became especially challenging.

The hub-and-spoke design of the WTCS collective impact network facilitates distribution of both resources and activities across a wide and diverse set of local contexts. The network supports different types of WTCS collaboratives that serve a variety of school districts (Figure 11.2). These range from single district CS collaboratives coordinated by large urban districts with multiple high schools, such as Fort Bend Independent School District (ISD) outside of Houston (Point A in Figure 11.2), with a population of 76,000 students, to networks of small, remote, and rural districts. Region 18 WTCS collaborative, for instance, in West Texas covers 37,553 square miles and serves multiple small, rural districts such as Presidio ISD (1,242 students) on the Mexican border (Point B) and Iraan-Sheffield ISD (504 students) in the high plains (Point C). During the 2017–2018 school year, WTCS served 396 school districts, 763 campuses, and 1,118 K–12 educators across the state.

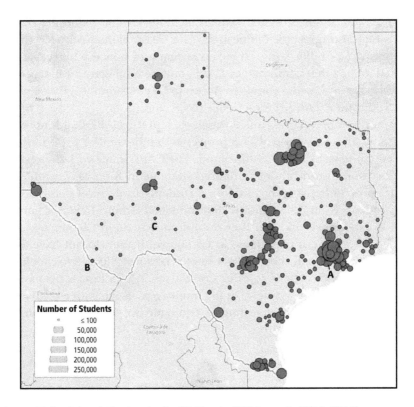

Figure 11.2   School districts in the WeTeach_CS Network (2016–2018).

Leveraging Components of Collective Impact Within WeTeach_CS

Utilizing the five key components of collective impact, WTCS is able to leverage expertise and institutional resources across a diverse range of organizations to support teachers and districts in their CS education capacity building efforts. In this section we describe how WTCS leverages key components of collective impact.

Common Agenda

Teachers, schools, universities, nonprofits, industry partners, and PD providers who participate in the WTCS program all share the common goal of broadening participation in computing in K–12 education. While the focus of the WTCS collaboratives is primarily to build teacher content knowledge and skills, this work is grounded in the larger context of the

K–12 CS education ecosystem, which includes several additional components that also impact CS education. The CAPE Framework (Fletcher & Warner, 2021), reflects this larger ecosystem and how teacher capacity is related to the other components. CAPE, outlined in Figure 11.3, stands for (a) Capacity for CS education, (b) Access to CS education, (c) Participation in CS education, and (d) Experience of CS education.

Equity is a thread that runs through each of the CAPE building blocks. The ultimate goal of the WTCS project is to improve the experiences of diverse students in K–12 CS education. The CAPE framework underscores the fact that historically marginalized students in K–12 (i.e., students of color, girls, students with disabilities, students from rural communities, and students from economically disadvantaged families) cannot have equitable experiences in CS if they do not participate in CS courses. Additionally, they cannot participate in CS courses if they do not have access to those courses, and they will not have access to CS if their schools and districts lack the capacity to offer CS courses. WTCS invests primarily in this foundational capacity level of the framework, which is an essential condition for the subsequent scaling of equitable access, participation, and experiences in CS education.

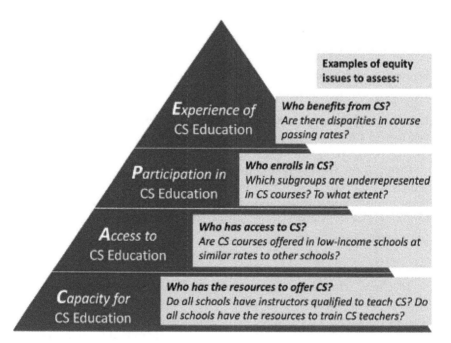

Figure 11.3 The CAPE framework.

Shared Measurement Systems

The WTCS theory of change uses capacity building as a lever to improve equitable access and participation in CS education. Each of these levels of the CAPE Framework includes measures that are consistent and scalable across schools, districts, regions, and the state. The efforts of the network as a whole and individual WTCS collaboratives are focused on four goals that can be measured objectively at all levels of the network.

- Goal #1: Increase *capacity* for CS as measured by the number of certified CS teachers.
- Goal #2: Increase *access* to CS as measured by the number of high schools offering one of 16 designated CS courses.
- Goal #3: Increase *participation* in CS as measured by the number of students completing at least one CS course.
- Goal #4: Increase *diversity* in CS as measured by the number of students completing a CS course disaggregated by gender, ethnicity, disability, and socio-economic status.

Each of these measures can be tracked in Texas through the state's Education Research Center (ERC) or at the local level by an individual school or district. These measures are tracked over time to determine progress toward broadening participation in computing, with Measures 1–3 serving as leading indicators of the fourth and final goal. Supporting coding, programming, and computational thinking experiences in K–8 is also a part of the WTCS network goals, but consistent measures for this goal have not yet been established.

Mutually Reinforcing Activities

Teachers and WTCS collaborative instructional team members contribute to and benefit from the activities of the WTCS network. All WTCS teachers have access to online and in-person PD from UT Austin. This includes a 7-week, asynchronous Foundations of Computer Science for Teachers course and a 2-day, in-person WTCS Certification Prep workshop (offered numerous times across the state). Both of these PD activities provide consistent and structured support focused on building teacher content knowledge tied specifically to the CS teacher certification exam. These resources are coupled with regional WTCS collaboratives that provide additional teacher PD which can be tailored to meet the needs of each regional cohort of teachers involved in WTCS. Other online and in-person courses are also available for WTCS teachers to take based on their individual needs. All WTCS activities focus on supporting one or more of the five key components of the WTCS model:

1. building CS *content knowledge,*
2. developing *pedagogical skills* in CS,
3. implementing *equi*table teaching *practices* and *environments* in CS,
4. supporting teachers to obtain high school CS teaching *certification,* and
5. connecting all stakeholders to the larger CS education *community.*

In addition to online courses and workshops for teachers, ITMs from each regional collaborative benefit from participation in the train-the-trainer style of PD. Building the capacity of not only classroom teachers but instructional teams as well results in a more robust and sustainable statewide network of expertise that will support K–12 CS teachers even after the grant period. Building this instructional leader capacity also facilitates cross-pollination of expertise, with leaders from different regional WTCS collaboratives sometimes traveling to provide PD to teachers in other regions. Thus, participants benefit not only from the resources of the backbone organization, but from other members of the network as well.

Continuous Communication

WTCS participants are connected through an ecosystem of communication and support. The WTCS blog serves as a weekly online newsletter to which over 1,300 stakeholders are subscribed. The blog focuses on informing teachers of new PD opportunities, policy and funding updates relevant to CS education, student learning opportunities, and instructional resources. It is the only statewide communication vehicle focused specifically on K–12 CS. WTCS also maintains Facebook and Twitter feeds to which over 2,400 people are subscribed. Each WTCS collaborative project director regularly communicates with his/her teacher participants regarding their regional PD program, and teachers meet together regularly within each WTCS collaborative. Project directors receive ongoing support from UT Austin staff through in-person and virtual meetings, CS workshops, and train-the-trainer opportunities that they can subsequently implement in their regions. During WTCS project director meetings, leaders discuss grant management strategies, resources for CS PD, and state and local policies that might impact the teachers and districts they serve.

Backbone Organization

From 2015 to 2018, UT Austin served as the backbone organization for WTCS, coordinating all CS collaborative funding and support, state level PD, network communications, data collection, and convening of teacher and leader participants. One key responsibility of the WTCS staff is to support the ITMs who lead each of the WTCS regional collaboratives. Many of the CS faculty members serving as ITMs have deep content knowledge in

CS but lack background or experience in K–12, course standards, teacher PD, or effective pedagogical practices. Instructional specialists partnered with CS faculty members generally have extensive backgrounds in these areas but lack depth in CS. Helping each of these types of ITMs to learn from each other and develop an engaging and coherent experience for their teachers is a prime objective of the WTCS team at UT Austin.

In addition, UT Austin hosts an annual WTCS summit, a multi-day event that was attended by over 400 educators in 2018. The purpose of the summit is to provide PD and build community across the statewide network. The summit engages nationally recognized speakers and workshop leaders but also relies on WTCS teachers and ITMs as workshop presenters. Building the leadership capacity of the WTCS network through events like the WTCS summit is another strategy for sustaining the positive outcomes of the collective impact network beyond the specific grant funding window.

Evaluating Collective Impact

Despite the recent popularity of collective impact efforts among funders and social entrepreneurs (Kania et al., 2014), limited peer-reviewed research has been published to evaluate the efficacy of collective impact efforts to date. In a recent search for empirical studies of collective impact models in three major social science/education research databases (i.e., Academic Search Complete, ERIC, and PsycINFO), we found no peer-reviewed publications that addressed the influence of collective impact in educational settings. If practitioners, policymakers, and researchers are going to continue to tout the value of collective impact, more rigorous research and, according to U.S. Deputy Secretary of Education Jim Shelton, "proof points," are needed to validate the utility of this approach (Edmondson & Hecht, 2014, p. 7).

One reason that the effectiveness of collective impact models has not been substantiated by rigorous research may have to do with the difficulty in conducting experimental studies at such large scales. Studies that randomize participants into treatment and control conditions simply are not very feasible at the scale that collective impact models are implemented. Furthermore, by its very nature, collective impact does not identify a specific treatment a priori that is to be applied under controlled conditions. Rather, the collective impact model is designed, like other continuous improvement models, to bring to bear multiple resources and potential interventions that meet the needs of a diverse range of teachers and school settings. Acknowledging the variation that occurs in schools and designing a support system that specifically addresses problems of practice across these diverse settings is a hallmark of continuous improvement models like collective impact.

Although traditional experimental designs may not be practical for evaluating the effectiveness of collective impact models, many quasi-experimental designs are well-suited for that purpose. One goal of our research is to test out a method for empirically demonstrating the effectiveness of a collective impact model. While the overall mission of the WTCS project is to broaden participation in K–12 computing, we have focused this study specifically on the teacher capacity component of this effort. The problem of practice we are addressing is the lack of certified high school CS teachers across the state of Texas. Specifically we examine the following question: "Can a collective impact model like WTCS substantively increase the number of CS-certified teachers in the state across a broad range of diverse schools and communities?"

METHOD

To test whether the WTCS program impacted the number of certified CS teachers in the state, we utilized a quasi-experimental design called interrupted time series (ITS) analysis. This type of analysis is designed to determine whether an intervention had an effect on the target outcome across time by comparing measures of the outcome before and after the start of the intervention. The period of time before the onset of the intervention is termed the pre-intervention phase, whereas the period of time spanning the start of the program and afterward is called the intervention phase. For the WTCS program, the pre-intervention phase spanned the 2013–2014 and 2014–2015 school years and the intervention phase lasted throughout the 2015–2016 and 2016–2017 school years. ITS allows for two distinct causal effects to be estimated (Huitema, 2011). One is a change in *level* and the other is a change in *slope*. A statistically significant level change would indicate that there was a change in the total number of licensed CS teachers from immediately before the start of the program to immediately after that could not be attributed to the overall trend. The presence of a change in slope would indicate, simply, that the slope of the intervention phase differed from the slope of the pre-intervention phase or, in other words, that the rate at which teachers became certified was different between the two phases.

To help strengthen claims to causal inferences of any observed effects, that is, claims that any differences between the two phases could be attributed to the WTCS program, we repeated the same analysis for a comparison group. For this comparison to be valid, it was important to select a comparison group that would likely be affected by the same unobserved confounding factors—should any exist—but that would not be influenced by the intervention. Similar results between the treatment and comparison groups would then signify the presence of confounding factors not accounted for and thus preclude attributions of cause to the intervention. We chose technology applications teachers to serve as the comparison group because their field more closely resembles that of CS teachers than any other discipline for which there is a K–12 educator certification in Texas. While most CS courses in Texas require a teacher to hold a Grades 8–12 CS certification, there are some introductory courses that can be taught with a technology applications certification as well. These include AP CS Principles and a course called Fundamentals of CS, which is a survey course that can be considered as a non-AP version of CS Principles given the similar standards for the two courses.

Using the technology applications certification as a comparison helps rule out the possibility of the introduction of AP CS Principles in 2017 as a reason for any significant change in the number or rate of teachers becoming certified in CS. Thus, our analysis was designed to test: (a) whether there were statistically significant differences between the two phases in the number of certified CS teachers immediately following the start of WTCS (level change) and the rate of increase in the number of certified CS teachers over the course of the intervention phase (slope change); and (b) whether such differences were present when conducting the same analysis for certified technology applications teachers. Because the WTCS program is designed to train and support teachers over time, we did not expect the results to show any significant change in level, but we did anticipate that there would be a statistically significant, positive change in slope. We expected neither the level change nor the slope change to be statistically significant for technology applications teachers.

To count the number of certified teachers in the state, we used data from the Texas Education Research Center (ERC), which serves as a data clearinghouse for all public education data in the state. Within the ERC database, we were able to access the certification and employment records for all CS and technology applications teachers in the state for a 4-year period beginning with the 2013–2014 school year through the 2016–2017 school year. Thus, our samples for both CS and technology applications included all teachers certified to teach at the secondary level during these school years. Counts of certified teachers were calculated for each month during that time frame, provided that the teacher held an active certification in the relevant field and was employed as a teacher of record during that month.

Before specifying the regression models to be used, we inspected the data for potential irregularities and found there to be serial dependency among the time points. Specifically, we noticed a systematic drop in the number of certified teachers every 12 months. This was most pronounced in the data for technology applications teachers (see Figure 11.4).

We presumed these recurring drops to be the result of some teachers allowing their certifications to expire before taking the necessary steps to renew them. To account for this serial dependency in the model, we included

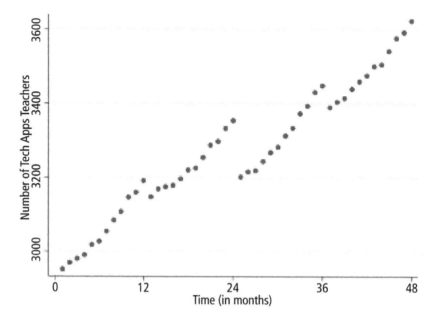

Figure 11.4 Number of teachers certified in technology applications over time.

11 dummy-coded variables representing the months of the year. To account for autocorrelated errors, we used the Prais-Winsten (Prais & Winsten, 1954) estimation method. The resulting regression model assumed the form:

$$Y_t = \beta_0 + \beta_1 \, T_t + \beta_2 L_t + \beta_3 S_t + \beta_4 M1_t + \ldots + \beta_{15} M11_t + \varphi_1 e_{t-1} + u_t,$$

where

Y_t is the number of certified teachers at time t;

β_0 is the intercept;

β_1 is the pre-intervention slope;

β_2 the level-change at the time of the intervention;

β_3 is the change in slope from the pre-intervention to the intervention phase;

β_4 through β_{15} are the coefficients for the month dummy variables;

$M1_t$ through $M11_t$ are the months of the school year at time t;

T_t is the value of the time variable at time t;

L_t represents the level-change variable and is a dummy-coded variable that denotes the phase at time t;

S_t represents the slope-change variable and is defined as $(T_t - (n_1 + 1))L$;

φ_1 is the first-order autoregressive coefficient;

e_{t-1} is the residual at time $t-1$; and

u_t is the residual at time t.

RESULTS AND DISCUSSION

Computer Science Teachers

Results of the analysis for the number of certified CS teachers showed a statistically significant change in slope between the pre-intervention and intervention phases (Table 11.1). The average number of teachers who became certified in CS each month after the start of the WTCS program was higher than the monthly rate of teachers during the period of time prior to the program by about 13 teachers. Before WTCS, approximately five teachers per month became certified across the state in CS compared to approximately 18 teachers per month after the program began. As expected, the level change was not statistically significant. These patterns can be seen in Figure 11.5.

TABLE 11.1 Interrupted Time Series Analysis Results for Certified CS Teachers				
	B	*SE*	*t*	*p*
Pre-intervention slope	5.21	0.70	7.45	.000
Level change	−7.70	13.01	−0.59	.558
Slope change	13.38	1.13	11.79	.000
Constant	379.91	12.22	31.10	.000

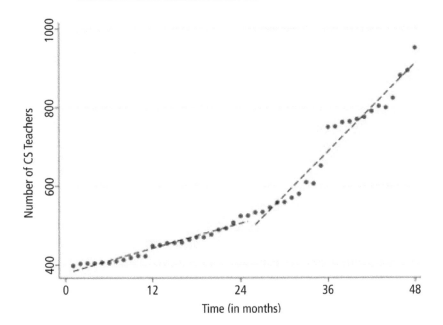

Figure 11.5 Number of CS teachers in Texas who were certified and employed from the 2013–2014 through the 2016–2017 school years.

Parameters for Counting Certified Teachers

It is worth noting the parameters for counting teachers that were used in designing this study. The counts of CS teachers represented in Figure 11.5 include the total number of teachers each month who were both certified in CS and employed as a classroom teacher. This is not the only way we could have counted teachers. We could have conducted a similar analysis where, rather than using the total number of CS-certified teachers each month, we used counts of the total number of new, initial certifications. However, only counting new certifications would prevent us from determining whether the total number of certified CS teachers was truly increasing or whether the newly certified teachers were simply replacing teachers who had been certified previously. Similarly, we could have counted all certified teachers rather than those who were certified and employed. This would have provided a more accurate count of the total number of individuals certified in CS. However, the ultimate goal is to benefit students by increasing their access to CS courses taught by qualified teachers, and a certification in CS does not help in this way unless the individual holding the certification is employed as a teacher. To ensure that the results of this study were meaningful in terms of intended outcomes, we limited the sample to individuals who were employed as classroom teachers.

Newly Certified CS Teachers

Nevertheless, examining the number of initial certifications over time and including all teachers rather than only those employed as classroom teachers can provide additional insight into what is happening and thus enrich the results of this study. Figure 11.6 displays these data while also distinguishing between in-service and preservice teachers. For each school year, the chart shows the number of initial CS certifications obtained by in-service and preservice teachers. For in-service teachers, an average of 57 teachers each year became certified in CS during the 2 years prior to the start of the WTCS program compared to an average of 229 teachers each year during the 2 years since the program began. In contrast, the average numbers of newly certified preservice teachers were 22 per year before the program and 24 per year after the start of the program. As the WTCS program only targeted in-service teachers, these data provide further support of the program's impact by showing that the increases in the number of certified CS teachers could not have been the result of preservice teacher programs. These data also underscore what we mentioned previously regarding the persistent challenges facing preservice programs for prospective CS teachers. In a state that turns out approximately 25,000 new teachers

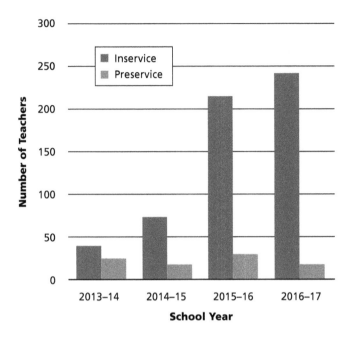

Figure 11.6 Number of newly certified CS teachers.

through preservice programs each year (Ramsay, 2019), 24 total CS preservice teachers is a staggeringly small number.

Comparing to Technology Applications Teachers

To help control for potential confounding factors, we conducted the same interrupted time series analysis for a comparison group of teachers who obtained certification in technology applications. Technology applications was chosen for the comparison group because it most closely aligns with CS in terms of the courses taught and the content knowledge required to teach the courses. In fact, some introductory CS courses can be taught in Texas by a teacher who holds a certification in either CS or technology applications.

Results of the ITS analysis of the number of certified technology applications teachers revealed no differences between the pre-intervention and intervention phases in terms of either slope or level (Table 11.2). A visual of these data is shown in Figure 11.7. These null results provide counterfactual evidence that supports a causal link between the WTCS program and the increase in the number of certified CS teachers in the state.

TABLE 11.2 Interrupted Time Analysis Series Results for Certified Technology Applications Teachers

	B	SE	t	p
Pre-intervention slope	11.55	1.39	8.32	.000
Level Change	−18.77	18.87	−0.99	.327
Slope Change	1.69	2.44	0.69	.493
Constant	2960.64	24.30	121.83	.000

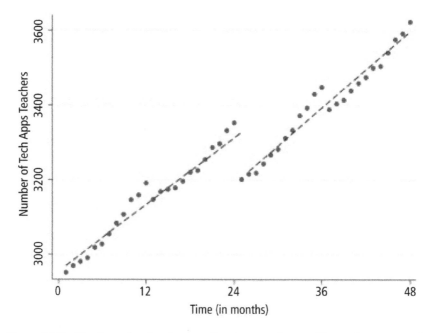

Figure 11.7   Number of technology applications teachers in Texas who were certified and employed from the 2013–2014 through the 2016–2017.

The fact that there was a change in the rate of newly certified CS teachers but no such change in the rate of newly certified technology applications teachers helps rule out the possibility that the increase in CS teachers was the result of some other factor, such as an increase in the overall number of teachers. This difference occurred in spite of the fact that AP CS Principles was launched in 2016–2017 and Texas teachers could teach that course with a certification in technology applications, even if they did not hold a certification in CS. This lower certification requirement applies to both AP CS Principles and one other introductory CS course in Texas. Other courses such as Computer Science I, Computer Science II, and AP CS A all require a CS certification. It is likely that the introduction of AP CS Principles did help generate more interest in offering CS in high schools. However, since AP CS Principles teachers were not required to be certified in CS, and we did not see notable increases in the less rigorous technology applications certification, it is not likely that the launch of the new course was a contributing factor in the increase in certified CS teachers.

Causal Inference

We should note that the results of the comparison group do not rule out any potential causal influences that are specific to CS, such as other programs designed to train teachers to get certified in CS. However, two other points of evidence exist that refute the possibility of CS-specific confounders. The first is that the WTCS program was designed and implemented beginning in 2015 precisely because no such in-service teacher training program existed in the state at the time. That does not preclude the possibility that a change in preservice CS programs resulted in the overall increase in certified CS teachers. However, that possibility can be ruled out by comparing the data from this study with the data obtained through the WTCS program. As shown in Figure 11.6, the data from this study show that the total number of in-service teachers newly certified in CS during the intervention phase was 457. During that same time period, WTCS documented a total of 386 teachers who got certified specifically through the WTCS program, comprising 84% of the all in-service teachers certified during the intervention phase of this study. Thus, even if there was some other factor that positively impacted the number of in-service teachers certified in CS during this time, that factor could have independently accounted for no more than 16% of the total increase. Taken together, these data and the results of this study provide strong causal evidence that the WTCS collective impact model positively impacted the number of certified CS teachers in the state.

Estimating Effect Size

Standardized measures of effect size (e.g., Cohen's d, Hedge's g) are often used in experimental and quasi-experimental studies as a means of quantifying the extent of an intervention's impact on the outcome. Although such measures could be computed for interrupted times series analyses, scholars (e.g., Huitema, 2011) have cautioned against doing so because the fact that time series data utilizes timepoints, rather than individuals, as the unit of analysis makes standardized effect sizes prone to misinterpretation. As an alternative, examining the coefficients for the pre-intervention slope and slope change variables can provide a good description of the extent to which the WTCS program impacted the number of certified CS teachers in the state. As noted previously, the average number of newly certified CS teachers each month during the intervention phase was about 18 teachers. Comparing this to the rate of newly certified teachers in the pre-intervention phase (approximately 5 teachers) tells us that the WTCS program increased the rate of newly certified CS teachers by 357%. Similarly, comparing the 951 total teachers who were CS-certified and employed at the end of the study's time period to the 645 total teachers who would have been certified and employed at that time if the pre-intervention slope's trajectory had continued, tells us that the WTCS program increased the total number of newly certified CS teachers by 147% over a 2-year time period.

NEXT STEPS

This examination of the WTCS model has several policy implications for CS education leaders and policymakers who face similar challenges in trying to quickly scale the capacity of their educator communities to offer CS courses. This research indicates that developing and implementing a collective impact model can be an effective approach to rapidly increasing educator capacity through in-service teacher training. Policymakers should consider whether investing in a coordinated, collaborative, collective impact network is a more viable model for increasing capacity than the traditional policy solution of a competitive grant program administered by the state in which only a handful of winning districts reap the benefits of the investment. Although this research indicates a collective impact approach can be effective, conducting an actual comparison of the collective impact approach with the competitive grant approach is a logical next step in determining how we can best support CS education.

Another related consideration worth further examination is whether the collective impact model is able to increase capacity and opportunity for a wider, more diverse range of schools and students rather than just increasing capacity overall. In short, does a collective impact model increase teacher capacity and diversify student participation and experiences in CS education? Longitudinal data indicate that increased teacher capacity has coincided with an increase in the percentage of high schools offering CS courses in Texas (from 35% of high schools in 2014–2015 to 47% of high schools in 2018–2019). Texas has also seen significant improvements in the diversity of students enrolled in CS over that same time period. While overall high school CS course enrollment increased by 53%, enrollment increased by 72% for economically disadvantaged students, by 71% for students with disabilities, by 67% for Black students, and by 70% for

Hispanic/Latino students. Only female enrollment, which increased by the same percentage as overall (53%) failed to change markedly and remains the most persistent gap for historically marginalized students in the state (Texas Advanced Computing Center, 2020). These improvements in both access and participation for the state overall could potentially be attributed to the WTCS collective impact approach but a more rigorous analysis that compares WTCS schools to non-WTCS schools across the state would be necessary to determine with clarity the impact of the model on diverse participation rates.

In addition, qualitative research should be conducted to determine why the collective impact model was successful at increasing CS teacher capacity. Our hypothesis is that the collective impact model is able to serve teachers and schools that, either because of small size, lack of administrative resources, or other unknown factors, are far less likely to land a competitive grant designed to support CS teacher growth or effectively access external resources for growing CS teacher capacity on their own. The vast majority of schools that participated in the WTCS project had one or no CS teachers. It is likely that most of these schools and districts would not or could not invest the administrative resources in applying for a grant to support a solitary teacher or evaluating resources for growing a CS program even if they were free. Unlike PD grant programs for subjects such as mathematics, which is taught in every school regardless of size due to federal testing and accountability requirements, many schools lack the internal administrative expertise to design their own CS teacher PD or evaluate the quality of external PD in CS education. Given that almost all principals were previously classroom teachers, the lack of CS expertise at the school administration level is a natural byproduct of the general lack of individuals with CS degrees entering the teaching profession upon college graduation. By using the collaborative approach in which multiple stakeholders and experts bring all of their resources to the table and proactively reach out to hundreds of schools to participate, smaller schools and districts potentially benefit through access to resources that they would not otherwise have.

In another study (Warner et al., 2019), we tested the above hypothesis and found that, indeed, smaller, rural schools experienced greater growth as a result of participating in a collective impact network than schools in urban and suburban areas. Additional research should be conducted to determine empirically whether schools that increased teacher capacity through collective impact also were more likely than schools that did not participate in the WTCS collaboratives to increase other components of the CAPE framework, such as increased access to courses, increased diverse participation, and improved experiences for historically marginalized students.

The CS education community and future research should also consider how this model transfers to other states and contexts. Can collective impact prove effective in states whose models for gatekeeping CS teacher certification differ from that used in Texas? We expect that the general structure of the collective impact model can be applied to the problem of practice of CS teacher certification and capacity building, regardless of the specific regulatory policies which govern certification in other states, but this has yet to be tested empirically. This will become possible as additional states begin to develop and implement strategic plans for scaling up CS teacher capacity.

While it is important to work on expanding CS teacher preservice programs, the immediate demand for new CS teachers requires us to look for potential solutions in addition to CS teacher preservice programs. Lessons learned from investigating the impact of the WTCS program on improving teacher capacity at scale in Texas provide pathways for productive development and measurement of collective impact programs and for realizing the vision of CS for all.

REFERENCES

Arkansas Department of Education. (2019, June 10). *Summit report: A report from the 2019 National Computer Science Summit for State Leaders.* https://dese.ade.arkansas.gov/Files/20201217110410_Report_from_the_2019_CS_for_State_Leaders_Summit.pdf

Code.org Advocacy Coalition. (2019). *2019 State of computer science education.* https://advocacy.code.org/2019_state_of_cs.pdf

Code.org, CSTA, & ECEP Alliance. (2020). *2020 State of computer science education: Illuminating disparities.* https://advocacy.code.org/2020_state_of_cs.pdf

Colino, S. (2018, September 11). *Eight college majors with great job prospects.* U.S. News & World Report. https://www.usnews.com/education/best-colleges/articles/2018-09-11/8-college-majors-with-great-job-prospects

CSforALL. (2020). *About CSforALL.* https://www.csforall.org/about/

Darling-Hammond, L., Hyler, M. E., & Gardner, M. (2017). *Effective teacher professional development.* Learning Policy Institute.

Edmondson, J., & Hecht, B. (2014, Fall). Defining quality collective impact. *Stanford Social Innovation Review.* https://ssir.org/articles/entry/defining_quality_collective_impact

Elahi, A. (2016, March 1). CPS to roll out computer science requirement. *Chicago Tribune.* https://www.chicagotribune.com/business/blue-sky/ct-computer-science-graduation-cps-bsi-20160225-story.html

Fletcher, C., Garbrecht, L., Warner, J. R., & Monroe, W. (2017, April). *Analyzing the impact of teacher perceptions of computer science on computer science certification success* [Poster presentation]. American Educational Research Association Annual Meeting, San Antonio, TX.

Fletcher, C. L., & Warner, J. R. (2021). CAPE: A framework for assessing equity throughout the computer science education ecosystem. *Communications of the ACM, 64*(2), 23–25. https://doi.org/10.1145/3442373

Google Inc., & Gallup Inc. (2016). *Trends in the state of computer science in U.S. K–12 schools.* http://goo.gl/j291E0

Gordon, E. M., & Heck, D. J. (2019). *2018 NSSME+: Status of high school computer science.* Horizon Research, Inc.

Huitema, B. E. (2011). *The analysis of covariance and alternatives: Statistical methods for experiments, quasi-experiments, and single-case studies* (2nd ed.). John Wiley & Sons.

Kania, J., Hanleybrown, F., & Juster, J. S. (2014). Essential mindset shifts for collective impact. *Stanford Social Innovation Review, 12*(4), 1–5.

Kania, J., & Kramer, M. (2011). Collective impact. *Stanford Social Innovation Review, 9*(1), 36–41.

Kim, J., Edwards, K., Childs, J., Fletcher, C., Leftwich, A., & Hendrickson, K. (2021). *Landscape of computer science teacher qualification pathway* [Poster presentation]. SIGCSE'21, 52nd ACM Technical Symposium on Computer Science Education, Virtual Event, USA.

Lang, K., Galanos, R., Goode, J., Seehorn, D., Trees, F., Phillips, P., & Stephenson, C. (2013). *Bugs in the system: Computer science teacher certification in the U.S.* Computer Science Teachers Association.

Lynn, J., & Stachowiak, S. (2018). *When collective impact has an impact: A cross-site study of 25 collective impact initiatives.* https://www.orsimpact.com/DirectoryAttachments/10262018_111513_477_CI_Study_Report_10-26-2018.pdf

Patterson, D., Synder, L., & Ullman, J. (2020). *Evaluating computer scientists and engineers for promotion and tenure.* Computer Research Association. https://cra.org/resources/best-practice-memos/evaluating-computer-scientists-and-engineers-for-promotion-and-tenure/

Prais, S. J., & Winsten, C. B. (1954). Trend estimators and serial correlation. *Cowles Commission Discussion Paper, Statistics, 383.* https://cowles.yale.edu/publications/archives/ccdp-s

Ramsay, M. C. (2019). *Certified teacher demographics by preparation route 2014–2018.* SBEC Online Data. https://tea.texas.gov/Reports_and_Data/Educator_Data/Educator_Reports_and_Data/

Texas Advanced Computing Center. (2020). *Texas CS Profile 2018–19.* https://tacc.utexas.edu/epic/research/cs-regional-data

Texas Association of School Boards. (2018). *Teacher salaries, pay raises stagnant for 2017–2018.* https://www.tasb.org/services/hr-services/hrx/compensation-and-benefits/teacher-salaries,-pay-raises-stagnant-for-2017–201.aspx

Texas Education Code. (2018). *Requirements for educator preparation programs.*

Warner, J. R., Fletcher, C. L., Torbey, R., & Garbrecht, L. S. (2019). Increasing capacity for computer science education in rural areas through a large-scale collective impact model [Conference session]. In *SIGCSE: The 50th ACM technical symposium on computer science education* (pp. 1157–1163). ACM. https://doi.org/10.1145/3287324.3287418

EXPANDING COMPUTER SCIENCE OPPORTUNITIES

A Personalizable, Flexible Model for Professional Learning

Dave Frye
Code.org

Mark Samberg
NC Department of Public Instruction

Ha Nguyen
North Carolina State University

ABSTRACT

The past 5 years has seen a rapid growth in teacher professional learning programs at scale to address the significant shortage of computer science (CS) teachers (Code.org, 2017a; Cuny, 2011). The focus has been primarily on intensive face-to-face workshops aligned with a specific curriculum (Code.org, 2019a). The long-term success of a broad-scale CS initiative, however,

Professional Development for In-Service Teachers, pages 271–294
Copyright © 2022 by Information Age Publishing
www.infoagepub.com

requires a more flexible, personalizable approach to professional learning that will attract, retain, and support new CS teachers beyond an initial week of workshops (Zhao, 2018). In this chapter we present a model for effective, personalizable CS professional learning that has been designed and successfully implemented in North Carolina. The program brings together effective professional learning activities, including online courses, web-based learning resources, and communities of practice to supplement widely-used face-to-face workshops. We discuss barriers that limit teacher engagement in CS as well as the underlying principle components of the model for effective, personalizable CS professional development. Finally, opportunities for further development and study across research, practice and policy are offered with a lens toward scaling to other states and refining the model to adapt to the rapidly changing field of CS education.

In the past 5 years, rapid growth in national and state movements for expanding opportunities for students in computer science (CS) education has created a significant demand for and shortage of CS teachers (Code.org, 2017a, 2017b, 2019c; Cuny, 2011). To address the immediate need for CS teachers in early-adopter schools and to meet state mandates, a number of professional learning programs have been launched at scale throughout the country, with a focus on intensive face-to-face workshops aligned with a specific curriculum (Code.org, 2019a). The long-term success of a broad-scale CS initiative, however, requires a more flexible, personalizable approach to professional learning that will attract, retain, and support new CS teachers beyond an initial week of workshops (Zhao, 2018). In particular, support for teachers in rural, underserved, and under-resourced areas are needed to overcome barriers that limit their participation and that result in fewer CS opportunities for students in these communities (Committee on Underrepresented Groups and the Expansion of the Science and Engineering Workforce Pipeline, 2011).

In this chapter we present a model for effective, personalizable CS professional learning that has been designed to bring together effective professional learning activities, including online courses, web-based learning resources, and communities of practice to supplement widely-used face-to-face workshops. Currently, the model has been implemented in North Carolina, where rural, underserved, and/or under-resourced areas account for a large portion of the state (Code.org, 2017a; Eanes, 2020). We subsequently discuss barriers that limit teacher engagement in CS and present the underlying principal components of the model for effective, personalizable CS professional development (PD). Finally, opportunities for further development and study across research, practice and policy are offered with a lens toward scaling to other states and refining the model to adapt to the rapidly changing field of CS education. Throughout the chapter, PD and professional learning are discussed at four levels as shown on Table 12.1.

TABLE 12.1 Definitions Used in This Book Chapter	
Terms	**Definition**
Professional Learning *Activity*	A workshop, course, or other individual engagement by a teacher to improve teaching practice.
Professional Learning *Program*	A prescribed set of activities developed by PD providers to address the needs of teachers.
A Teacher's Professional Learning *Experience*	The long-term, sustained set of activities that a teacher engages in for professional growth and mastery of their teaching practice.
A *Model* for Professional Learning	An overarching conceptual framework for designing and structuring a teacher professional learning experience.

BACKGROUND

In recent years, many professional learning programs have claimed that new CS teachers who have no CS experience can attend 5 to 10 days of workshops and be prepared to teach CS (Cho et al., 2014; Liu et al., 2012; Menekse, 2015). This has resulted in unprecedented growth in the CS teacher workforce in schools and districts at scale, in diverse communities and school settings throughout the country (Code.org, 2021). The rapid growth of new CS teachers engaging in professional learning programs over the past 3 years is essential to attain the widely shared goal of creating opportunities for every student, in every school, to learn CS (Code.org, 2019a, 2019c; CSForAll, n.d.). Initial professional learning programs often train teachers of other subject areas to teach a specific CS curriculum rather than help teachers develop a comprehensive set of CS teacher content knowledge and skills (CSTA, n.d.). Therefore, to support continued professional learning for all CS educators, personalizable pathways of CS professional learning are needed to address three essential shortcomings of initial CS professional learning programs: (a) Lack of depth in content knowledge and pedagogical skills, (b) Barriers that limit engagement in the hardest to reach schools, and (c) Lack of support beyond initial professional learning toward professional growth and mastery (Gray et al., 2015; Zhao, 2018).

Lack of Depth in Content Knowledge and Pedagogical Skills

While in-service teachers often transition from one course to others within their discipline or content area (e.g., transitioning from teaching algebra to teaching pre-calculus), the transition to CS from another content area introduces new difficulties that are not necessarily addressed through initial professional learning programs (Gray et al., 2015). Since there are very few undergraduate or graduate programs for CS educators (Delyser et al., 2018), nearly all teachers attending CS professional learning programs were either prepared to teach in a different subject area (most often math, science, or business) or were professional computer scientists who transitioned to teaching (Liu et al., 2012). The fundamental, sustained engagement and learning of both content and pedagogy found in a 4-year undergraduate program is simply missing from this type of CS educator preparation (Gray et al., 2015). This shortcoming is often addressed by states, districts, and schools piecing together a variety of CS professional learning activities throughout the year from the abundant number of curriculum and professional learning programs (Delyser et al., 2018). Without clearly stated flexibility or thoughtful planning, these system-wide solutions can lack continuity and create confusion about how the different activities align, what is required or optional, and how much time and commitment is needed, especially for a teacher learning a new content area such as CS (Delyser et al., 2018).

In short, transitioning to teaching a new subject area is overwhelming even with initial intensive professional learning activities and ongoing support programs. Additionally, many teachers who are new to teaching CS are also teaching other subject areas while attempting to learn the new content and pedagogy of CS (Sadik et al., 2020). Coupled with limited structures for mentoring and planning, the transition to teaching CS can be challenging for even the most motivated teachers (see Gray et al., 2015). A personalizable model shifts professional learning from "Many things I must do" to "Choosing what would be most helpful to me, now and in the future." In doing so, it gives teachers flexibility in obtaining the content knowledge, pedagogical skills, and networks of resources they need to develop their expertise, at their own pace, and as appropriate for their teaching environment (Zhao, 2018).

Barriers That Limit Engagement

Face-to-face workshops are a core component of many initial CS professional learning programs (Darling-Hammond et al., 2017). Such synchronous, in-person professional learning activities are an efficient solution to learn new content and create early peer networks (Brooks & Gibson, 2012). In particular, they are highly effective when local capacity for teacher support exists, including available financial support, a large cohort of local teachers (Penuel et al., 2007; Tondeur et al., 2016), and sufficient, sustained time made available for these activities (Darling-Hammond et al., 2017; Desimone, 2009; Garet et al., 2001). However, this type of professional learning becomes challenging when used to engage peers from small schools across larger geographic regions. In the hardest to reach areas, including under-resourced, small, and rural schools, teacher engagement in these programs is limited by a combination of geographic, financial, and time-based barriers (Gray et al., 2015).

Face-to-face workshops are often located in centralized areas in a state or region to ensure greatest reach to the largest number of teachers in each workshop (Hansen-Thomas et al., 2016). However, by locating events centrally for greatest impact, more extensive travel, time investment, and expense is placed on those teachers coming from remote areas. Travel is a significant barrier both in terms of time investment and financial support (McConnell et al., 2013). For distant and rural teachers, a 6-hour workshop located multiple hours away may simply be an unreasonable investment of travel time to attend a single day event. Longer activities, such as week-long workshops, are more reasonable in terms of travel time investment, but require greater travel expenses. If these longer activities are not subsidized, the additional expenses can be cost prohibitive, especially in under-resourced schools (McConnell et al., 2013).

Scheduling for face-to-face workshops across multiple schools and districts can also be a barrier, as teachers all have varied daily and yearly schedules, demands, and opportunities for PD (Wei et al., 2010; Wynants & Dennis, 2018). Small schools have greater limitations around staff schedule flexibility and substitute teacher availability and funding. Districts or schools are more apt to seek the greatest scale with their professional learning activities and host or invest in a workshop for a larger group of teachers than for a single teacher in a content area. Finally, the limited number of teachers is also problematic for the development of peer support and networks (Wei et al., 2010). Many CS teachers are singletons in their schools and must seek support from other teachers in other schools in their districts. However, in cases where under-resourced, rural, and small counties offer a CS class, the CS teacher is often the only one in the entire district. Thus, there is no access to a local peer group or professional community that can provide support such as peer mentoring, shared resources, and informal professional learning activities. For example, if all schools in North Carolina had a sufficient number of teachers to provide at least one CS course to all middle and high school students, the 20 smallest, rural counties would have, on average, five CS teachers throughout the county compared to 287 CS teachers on average in each of the two largest urban counties (Friday Institute for Educational Innovation, 2020a, 2020c).

In summary, the barriers to teacher engagement in current CS professional learning activities means fewer CS teachers, courses and opportunities, especially in small, rural, and underserved schools. This results in fewer student enrollments in these districts (Eanes, 2020). Figure 12.1 shows a side-by-side comparison of CS course enrollments, economic prosperity, and community types in North Carolina (Frye et al., 2017). In the CS

Figure 12.1 CS enrollments, economic prosperity, and community types in NC.

enrollment map, the lightest colored counties are those with the smallest number of students in CS courses. Low-enrollment counties align closely with the lightest-colored Tier 1 economically disadvantaged counties on the second map, as well as the rural counties in green in the third map. In other words, the lowest CS enrollments can be found in economically distressed and disadvantaged counties, and rural counties in North Carolina.

In the context of these barriers and the varied landscape of resources available to CS teachers, current CS professional learning programs that focus on synchronous, in-person workshops need to be expanded to meet the needs of the hardest to reach schools, especially those in small, rural, and under-resourced areas (Google & Gallup, 2020). PD providers are adding online and asynchronous options for professional learning activities, and new programs are being offered that are completely online. Many of these workshops are offered by the creators of tools, such as Sphero, Wonder Workshop, Apple, Google, and Microsoft. While these additions create more engagement opportunities, they are not a silver bullet to the barriers for all teachers. Teachers need a personalizable model of professional learning that helps them (a) make sense of the growing number of programs available; (b) alleviate their environmental and contextual barriers (place, time, etc.); (c) support their content and pedagogical needs; and (d) develop their own sustained professional learning experience.

Lack of Supports Beyond Initial Professional Learning

High-quality implementation of new and changing content also requires ongoing reflection, coaching, and mentoring (Joyce & Showers, 2002; Showers & Joyce, 1996). As new CS teachers complete their first year teaching a new subject or course, they are best prepared to reflect on their experience and work with peers and colleagues to develop a plan for improving their teaching practice. Mentors and local communities of practice play a critical role in helping new teachers focus on specific needs and make the most of their limited time to engage in meaningful activities that are specifically valuable to them (Goode et al., 2014). In large, urban districts, we can assume a CS teacher is more likely to have access to a local network of CS peers, industry partners, and university-based subject matter experts to engage in communities of practice and work with local mentors. Without this local network, new CS teachers in small districts can get lost in the many professional learning activities that may not align with their development needs, their interests, or may be beyond their expertise.

By using a model that could be personalized, teachers have greater flexibility to sample some activities, work on what they specifically need, and choose which activities to engage in and which ones to skip (Zhao, 2018). A flexible, personalizable model is most critical for teachers after the first year of teaching CS, when they have gained experience implementing CS in their classroom. With scaffolding and guidance, it is a time when teachers can address their individual needs, interests, and opportunities, which in turn could result in longer engagement and greater satisfaction in their professional learning experiences.

A Model of Effective, Personalizable CS Professional Development

Many professional learning opportunities are presented to teachers in the form of one-time workshops, focusing on a specific set of content or approach regardless of teachers' needs and capacities (Wynants & Dennis, 2018). While this approach can meet many of the immediate needs of a new teacher, it does not offer the time and resources necessary to lead to deep learning and transformative change (Bickerstaff & Cormier, 2015). In the past 2 decades, a significant body of research has identified the critical components of effective PD (Desimone, 2009; Garet et al., 2001). Highly effective PD has been defined as "structured professional learning that results in changes in teacher practices and improvements in student learning outcomes" (Darling-Hammond et al., 2017, p. v). Most recently, Darling-Hammond and colleagues (2017) identified that effective PD includes most or all of the following seven features:

- *Content focused:* Discipline-specific content and pedagogies in teachers' classroom contexts.
- *Active learning:* Teachers engage directly in designing and trying out teaching strategies through interactive activities that are connected to their classrooms and students.
- *Supports collaboration:* Space for teachers to share ideas, feedback, and collaborate, often in job-embedded contexts.
- *Models of effective practice:* Teachers view examples from peer teachers, and video or written cases to support a clear vision of what best practices look like.

- *Coaching and expert support:* Experts can share their knowledge of content and evidence-based practices that focus directly on teachers' individual needs.
- *Feedback and reflection:* Built-in time to reflect, receive feedback, and revise to help teachers thoughtfully move toward the models of effective practice (above).
- *Sustained duration:* Adequate time to learn, practice, implement in class, and reflect.

Although this PD framework is comprehensive, it works best when sufficient local capacity and supports are available for teachers to engage in sustained, connecting activities such as professional learning communities (PLCs) to not only bring together many of these elements of effective PD, but also impact greater change at a school or district level (Darling-Hammond et al., 2017; Goode et al., 2014). As such, large scale professional learning programs, especially those that target small, rural, and under-resourced communities may be limited in success as a result of the distributed participants and the lack of connection to a central point of impact, such as a school or district. Therefore, to meet such standards of effective PD, a more flexible, personalizable approach is needed to support all teachers' professional learning while still engaging with peers, experts, and a broader community. As a result, the seven elements of effective PD presented above are more effectively addressed when professional learning programs incorporate principles of personalizable education (Zhao, 2018):

- *Teacher Agency:* Varying degrees of ownership over time to design aspects of their own learning experiences in the context of personal interests, needs, strengths, and resources.
- *Shared ownership:* Beyond agency for their own learning, teachers own their learning choices and also contribute to decisions about professional learning activities.
- *Flexibility mindset:* Belief in the value of adapting professional learning plans to address unexpected issues, change, and emerging opportunities in a field that is changing quickly.
- *Value creation:* Individual value and purpose through the collection of long-term, sustained professional learning activities in which they engage.
- *Enhancing Strengths:* Instead of ensuring that all teachers simply learn the same content, focus on enhancing individual strengths and interests.

The model for effective, personalizable CS PD discussed in this chapter (see Exemplar) includes the features of highly effective PD

(Darling-Hammond et al., 2017) while incorporating the five principles of personalizable education (Zhao, 2018). The core components of the professional learning activities are designed to improve teaching practice and student learning, and the personalizability allows opportunity for all teachers to navigate their own path to greater mastery of their craft. Teachers engage with peers and experts, opt-in and opt-out of professional learning activities, take ownership for their learning, grow from mentorship and coaching, apply flexibility to adapt to changes, and focus on enhancing their strengths over time through sustained professional learning (Butler et al., 2004; Hall & Trespalacios, 2019).

Personalizable PD models help teachers create their own, customized professional learning pathway (Zhao, 2018), thus allowing them to adapt to policy changes, grow beyond initial workshops, and shift to new curricula and tools, while building on strengths, rather than simply checking boxes or covering all of the required topics dictated by professional learning workshops. In the exemplar section below and throughout this chapter, the model for personalizable CS professional learning discussed includes five PD activities: (a) initial face-to-face CS workshops, (b) massive open online course for educators (MOOC-Ed), (c) un-facilitated online learning modules, (d) communities of practice, and (e) micro-credentials. These five activities are offered as a comprehensive menu of choices to allow flexibility and customization to support the diversity of CS teacher expertise and professional learning needs. In a field that is changing as quickly as CS education, the integration of both effective practices and personalizability provides an innovative approach to meet teachers at all stages of development and provide the flexibility needed to address unique strengths, barriers, and professional learning needs in diverse schools and communities.

EXEMPLAR

In this section we present an example of a CS PD model developed and implemented in North Carolina, which combines elements of effective PD with personalizable education. The cornerstone of the model is *personalizability*, which for the purposes of this work, is defined as *personalizable professional learning* where the medium, content, duration, and goals of the professional learning activities can be customized by each teacher based on needs. The starting and ending points are variables based on the specific support needed for each teacher. Teachers have the opportunity to craft their own professional learning experience by engaging in a selection of varied supports that meet their learning needs and preferences. In contrast, more widely implemented *personalized professional learning* approaches typically involve a series of prescribed pathways for teachers to choose from based on their needs. The starting point or ending competencies are usually fixed, as are the supports available in moving a teacher from the beginning to the end of a professional learning program (Schifter, 2016).

The model of effective, personalizable CS PD presented here is designed to provide a framework that brings together *existing* professional learning opportunities for CS teachers, leveraging strengths from each, while assessing gaps to help fulfill characteristics of effective PD and components of personalizable education. The advantages of this approach are two-fold. First, different types of professional learning programs can be utilized and connected to each other to meet teachers' unique needs. Second, it helps break down the silos between professional learning programs thereby reaching teachers where they are—physically or developmentally. Siloed programs can be redundant for teachers, and they can waste their time as the expectation is that they will complete the entire program even if they do not need all aspects of it.

In the following sections, we review the strengths and weaknesses of five different professional learning activities that comprise our model including: workshops, massive open online courses (MOOCS), online learning modules, communities of practice, and micro-credentials. We simultaneously analyze how these activities incorporate features of effective PD (see Table 12.2) while contributing to personalizable teacher learning (see Table 12.3).

Initial CS Teacher Workshops

For the purpose of this chapter, initial CS teacher workshops represent multi-day, face to face summer workshops that prepare in-service teachers for their first CS class, often focused on a specific curriculum or set of classroom resources. Initial CS teacher workshops are one of the most commonly implemented and impactful types of CS professional learning programs (Menekse, 2015). Face-to-face in design, this professional learning provides a hands-on, dedicated time with content and pedagogy, and it is effective for getting many new CS teachers started in teaching CS. In addition to providing an immersive hands-on instructional experience, face-to-face workshops provide an opportunity for participants to construct peer networks of other CS teachers, many of them in their region or state.

As mentioned previously, face-to-face programs require teachers to travel to a centralized location for approximately a week, and often include follow-up meetings throughout the year (Garet et al., 2001). For example, the primary method of professional learning for the most widely used AP CS curricula, Code.org, is a 5-day face-to-face workshop held during the summer plus four Saturday meetings throughout the academic year. Since face-to-face models are designed for teachers who are or will be teaching their CS courses for the first time, this time commitment and intense immersion is an effective way to start a CS teacher's professional learning experience (Brown, 2018).

This approach incorporates six of the seven features of effective PD (Darling-Hammond et al., 2017). It offers an immersion in CS content and supports active learning as teachers engage in simulated lessons as both learners and instructors (Goode et al., 2014). Finally, initial workshops support collaboration as activities include teachers working together with peers and facilitators to design, assess, and explore effective CS teaching practices. While this is an effective way for a new CS teacher to gain content knowledge, the content taught can be limited or too focused because it is associated with a specific curriculum.

Another important feature of effective PD is providing models and modeling of effective practice. For example, in the Code.org professional learning program, teachers engage in eight different teach, learn, observe (TLO) activities throughout the 5 day session where they role play as a teacher, learner, or observer (Goode et al., 2014; Code.org, 2019b). In doing so, they see examples of CS teaching from peer teachers, and they have the opportunity to experience, observe, give feedback, and discuss how to make improvements during the workshop. Similar approaches are used in other CS professional learning programs that prepare new teachers for their initial teaching of this new content area.

Initial CS teacher workshops provide coaching and expert support as well. For example, when CS teachers attend workshops, they interact with a facilitator who is an expert on the content and curriculum. Facilitators not only provide training on upcoming units that teachers will teach in their new class, but they also provide coaching and feedback on questions that participants may have from their teaching experience so far that year. In combination, these activities within the initial workshop provide CS teachers with the opportunity to receive feedback, reflect upon initial activities, and revise their plan for classroom practice.

Initial workshops have many strengths that make them effective for new CS teachers, they also present several limitations. First, while instruction focuses on authentic activities a teacher will be implementing in CS, professional learning takes place over the summer and before teachers enter the CS classroom. As a result, teachers do not have an opportunity to apply their work to real-world practice until the following academic year. In addition, the current face-to-face workshops that are available to CS teachers are not of a sustained duration. These programs are designed for first year CS teachers only, and follow-up options are limited and prescribed in ways that may not align with the needs of individual teachers who want to continue their professional learning and growth.

Initial CS teacher workshops incorporate nearly all of the features of effective PD, and as such they are a core component to an effective, personalizable model for PD. Face-to-face workshops, such as the one described above however, do not necessarily contribute to a personalizable model, as they are often prescribed around an individual curriculum, including the content and pedagogy needed to deliver the curriculum (Goode et al., 2014). As such, other types of activities are necessary to supplement workshops and create a CS professional learning path that allows for efficient and effective professional learning over time.

Massive Open Online Courses for Educators

Massive open online courses for educators (MOOC-Eds) were created by the Friday Institute in 2013 in order to provide at-scale virtual professional learning to educators throughout the world. As MOOCs were rising in popularity, the Friday Institute aimed to create a MOOC experience specifically designed for educators, applicable in schools and districts, and informed by features of effective professional learning. MOOC-Ed courses are time-bound (with defined start and end dates) and teachers can participate asynchronously from any device with an internet connection anywhere in the world. Since 2013, MOOC-Eds have reached over 40,000 educators in all 50 states and over 130 countries (Friday Institute for Educational Innovation, 2020b).

MOOC-Eds are designed specifically to meet the needs of professional educators through four design principles that support personalizability (Kleiman et al., 2015):

- *Self-directed learning:* Teachers are free to move around the course in a way that makes the most sense to them, accessing learning resources in any order, moving out of order through course units, or even skipping units if they wish to do so.
- *Peer-supported learning:* Participants in a MOOC-Ed course engage in theoretical and applied discussions with educators around the world in the discussion forums that are at the core of the MOOC-Ed experience.
- *Job-embedded learning:* Course content is immediately applicable to course participants' jobs, and discussions focus on teachers applying learning to their classroom and returning to share their experiences in discussion forums.
- *Multiple voices:* MOOC-Ed courses invite and facilitate a variety of voices that focus on theoretical applications, classroom applications, and real-world applications.

Along a spectrum of MOOC instructional designs that range from cMOOCs that focus on community, connectivism and communal inquiry (Bond, 2015; Daniel, 2012; Downes, 2012; Siemens, 2004) to traditional teacher–student instruction in xMOOCs (Daniel, 2012; Rodriguez, 2013), MOOC-Eds can be seen as a middle ground or hybrid of these instructional approaches. Sometimes described as "social constructivist MOOCs" (Ferguson & Sharples, 2014; Kleiman et al., 2015), MOOC-Eds employ instructional elements that facilitate individual consumption (e.g., readings and videos), reflection and sensemaking activities in course community spaces (e.g., such as discussion forums), and instructor participation in the forums in ways that leverages the experiences of all participants to best apply new content to existing teaching practice.

To supplement initial CS teacher workshops, help to reduce barriers, and support a more personalizable model for CS PD, the Friday Institute has created two CS-focused MOOC-Ed courses for new CS teachers: Teaching the Beauty and Joy of Computing (BJC) Curriculum and Teaching Computer Science Discoveries (CSD)—both launched in the Spring of 2019. These courses add to the menu of professional learning options available to teachers. Since the courses are online, the simulated classroom experiences in face-to-face workshops are replaced with videos of middle and high school students engaged in CS tasks in the BJC and CSD courses. Learners are asked how they would address certain situations seen in videos, including student misconceptions, struggles, or initial instruction. In the discussion forums, learners are encouraged to share and critique approaches and work with peers to discuss best approaches.

To ensure personalizability, a teacher can take a MOOC-Ed course in-lieu of the initial CS teacher workshops, take it in parallel with these workshops, or take it later in the school year as a supplement or a refresher to the initial CS workshops. CS teachers can also choose components of the MOOC-Ed course that support their individual interests or professional learning needs. Because of this personalizable approach, it is not necessary for a participant to complete a MOOC-Ed and earn a certificate of completion. In support of personalizability and the MOOC-Ed design principles, participants are asked to identify their learning goals at the outset of a MOOC-Ed course, and then asked if they have met their learning goals at the end of the course. Many participants indicate that their goal for the course is not to earn a certificate of completion (Kleiman et al., 2015) and therefore, course completion is an invalid metric to use to determine successful engagement.

MOOC-Ed courses support six of the seven features of effective PD (see Table 12.2). They are content focused and built around a specific curriculum in order to provide opportunities to extend or replace face-to-face workshops. These courses also encourage active learning, as teachers are

TABLE 12.2 Features of Effective PD Found in CS Professional Learning Activities in This Model

	Content Focused	Active Learning	Supports Collaboration	Models of Effective Practice	Coaching and Expert Support	Feedback and Reflection	Sustained Duration
Initial CS Teacher Workshops	Yes	Partially	Partially	Yes	Yes	Yes	No
MOOC-Ed Courses	Yes	Yes	Yes	Yes	Yes	Yes	No
Online Learning Modules (Unfacilitated)	Yes	Yes	No	Yes	No	Yes	No
Communities of Practice	Yes	Yes	Yes	Yes	Yes	Yes	Partially
Micro-Credentials	Yes	Yes	No	No	Yes	Yes	No

presented with videos and real-world scenarios and are asked to reflect upon and apply what they would do as a teacher or how they would support students in their classroom in a similar scenario. Videos and supplemental resources such as case reports of effective practice also provide teachers with exemplars of effective CS teaching methods (Kleiman et al., 2015).

All MOOC-Ed courses include a discussion board where CS teachers can interact with other teachers by posting assignments, practices, reflections, and feedback. Like face-to-face workshops, active learning and collaboration in MOOC-Ed courses are not necessarily job embedded. The time-bound nature of the course does not ensure that CS teachers are able to directly connect the right CS content to their students and classroom. Nonetheless, by using MOOC-Ed courses along with face-to-face workshops, we are able to provide more sustained professional learning experience. While CS workshops are 1-week long, for instance, MOOC-Ed courses can last anywhere from 6 to 8 weeks (Kleiman et al., 2015). Further, although teachers can take the MOOC-Ed course multiple times, currently, there is no progression of course content that would make it a long term and sustainable professional learning experience.

MOOC-Ed courses contribute a sense of agency, shared ownership and a value in flexibility to support personalizability (see Table 12.3). The courses explicitly encourage teachers to take agency by allowing them to choose the learning components that are most interesting or valuable. Additionally, as flexibility is a hallmark of the MOOC-Ed model, teachers are encouraged to go back to past lessons, skip lessons, and take lessons out of sequence to address current needs and interests. The intentional, directive nature of this approach is a critical component to helping teachers understand the value of owning their learning choices. As such, MOOC-Ed courses do not

TABLE 12.3 Features of Personalizable Learning Found in CS Professional Learning Activities in This Model

	Teacher Agency	Shared Ownership	Flexibility Mindset	Value Creation	Enhancing Strengths
Initial CS Teacher Workshops	Sometimes	No	No	Sometimes	No
MOOC-Ed Courses	Yes	Yes	Yes	No	No
Online Learning Modules	Yes	Yes	Yes	Yes	Yes
Communities of Practice	Yes	Yes	Yes	Yes	Yes
Micro-Credentials	Yes	Yes	Yes	Yes	Yes

only add new professional learning options to a menu of choices for new CS teachers, but they also provide foundational experiences in personalizable PD, while encouraging agency and shared ownership of learning.

Online Learning Modules

Online learning modules are individual units from MOOC-Ed courses made available in a self-paced, always-available format. One of the greatest strengths of online learning modules is that it is directly connected to current classroom activities. Teachers can engage in this type of professional learning when they need it rather than waiting for a scheduled workshop or course to begin. This just-in-time approach allows them to implement solutions in the classroom immediately, address knowledge gaps in real-time, refresh ideas from summer workshops, or address issues in student learning (Holmes et al., 2010).

Online learning modules only incorporate five of the seven features of effective PD. As with other methods, these modules are content-focused and built around a specific curriculum (CSD and BJC). CS teachers can take an online learning module as a way to extend their professional learning from a face-to-face workshop or MOOC-Ed and dig deeper into specific content and practices. However, online learning modules are not a standalone professional learning solution. They do not support collaboration, coaching, or reflection and feedback, as the on-demand nature of the modules means that there may not be a sufficiently large cohort at any one time to generate real discussion or opportunities for meaningful collaboration.

Online learning modules, however, contribute to all five components of personalizability (see Table 12.3). In addition to teacher agency, shared ownership, and value in flexibility previously discussed in MOOC-Eds, online learning modules also contribute to value creation and enhancing strengths. A set of shorter learning modules provides flexibility for teachers so they can customize their content, thereby removing structures seen in online courses. It also encourages teachers to take greater ownership in their professional learning experience. Teachers have to make an active choice to select and engage in the modules that create value for them. In this model, online learning modules are presented as a resource to fill content deficits, and to enhance strengths and support areas of interest and passion at a teacher's pace, time, and chosen level of engagement.

Communities of Practice

For the purposes of this chapter, communities of practice refer to online and face-to-face communities of CS teachers, CS experts, and other partners that connect around supporting CS teaching in K–12 classrooms. These communities can vary in characteristics such as geographic proximity (from locally-focused to globally open), time (longstanding or short-term), and topic focus (curriculum-specific, grade level, or open to all topics). Throughout the components of the effective personalizable PD model, both online and in-person communities of practice provide peer support to ensure collaboration and peer discussion and feedback (Lock, 2006). Teachers connect MOOC-Ed courses and online learning modules to local professional learning communities in schools and throughout districts. As an additional community of practice support, a series of teacher-driven workshops, Edcamp:Code, are provided throughout the state (Friday Institute for Educational Innovation, n.d.). Following the tenets of the widely used EdCamp model (EdCamp Foundation, 2019), these workshops focus on CS teaching, but are (a) *free + open* to educators in all subjects and all levels of CS knowledge, skill or experience; (b) *participant-driven* to encourage participants to define the agenda for the workshop based on their interests; (c) *focused on experience, not experts* to shift the sessions from pre-planned expert talks to experience-sharing discussion sessions; and (4) *incorporating the rule of two feet* to encourage teachers to get up and leave a session that may not be of interest to find something that better fits their needs (Owen, 2008).

The inclusion of three types of communities of practice (face-to-face workshops, online communities, and EdCamps) offers multiple advantages, including opportunities to overcome barriers for those that may be the only CS teacher in their school, district, or region (e.g., Carpenter, 2016; Holmes et al., 2010). Involvement in a CS community of practice provides access to peers with similar interests, environments or experiences, both within state and across the country (Conrad, 2005; Lock, 2006). As such, they provide unique access to the benefits that come with support, feedback and coaching from true peers that can relate to the strengths and barriers of an individual teacher's environment (Carpenter, 2016; Swanson, 2014).

Communities of practice incorporate seven of the seven features of effective PD (see Table 12.1). They are content focused, they promote active learning and they encourage teachers to actively share their ideas and practices, to give other teachers feedback, and to ask questions of others (Lock, 2006). The greatest strength of the community of practice approach is that it supports collaboration with true peers, and it allows the teacher to take on multiple roles as expert, novice, learner, and teacher (Goode et al., 2014). Communities of practice are also job embedded, providing an avenue for teachers to ask questions or discuss classroom practice in-line with their teaching schedule. Teachers do not need to wait for a scheduled workshop or course to ask a question or hope to find an answer in the resources of an online learning module. Communities of practice are also spaces where models of effective practice are shared in a more exploratory, informal environment that incorporates coaching and expert support as well as opportunities for feedback and reflection. Experienced peers provide insights, answer questions, and give support to novice teachers. These types of interactions happen more organically and spontaneously than those that occur in workshops and classes (Probst & Borzillo, 2008).

Communities of practice are not a stand-alone, sustainable professional learning approach, but rather, one of the components of an effective personalizable PD model. While exemplary communities have grown to be sustainable, the connection to other professional learning programs provide the foundational framework for ongoing professional learning activities needed to support teachers at all levels. Communities of practice, however, are designed with personalizability as their core (see Table 12.3) and contribute to teacher agency and shared ownership by providing many levels of short-term engagement, participation, and leadership in a community (Booth & Kellogg, 2014). While communities of practice can provide long-term engagement, a user's engagement in a community of practice may fall off if a community is not sufficiently active or "safe" (Probst & Borzillo, 2008).

Communities of practice are incredibly flexible and quick to adapt to unforeseen changes, encouraging teachers to focus on value creation, and members support to enhance strengths. By their nature and design, communities of practice are powerful professional learning activities that not only provide many options for ongoing learning, but also enhance teachers' understanding of the value of personalizable PD (Goode et al., 2014).

Micro-Credentials

For the purpose of this chapter, micro-credentials are competency-based credentials that allow CS teachers to demonstrate specific, job-embedded, performance-based skills and expertise. They provide an alternative approach to ongoing certification or licensure of in-service CS teachers where state and local policy allows (Code.org, 2019d). Within a model for effective, personalizable CS PD, acknowledgement and certification of teacher learning is also personalizable to meet the needs of each individual teacher (Ni & Guzdial, 2012). Micro-credentials are ideally suited for this approach, as they are competency-based assessments of teacher learning that can be the outcome of a professional learning activity but can also be acquired simply by demonstrating competency regardless of how that competency was obtained. In the same manner as they craft their own professional learning experience, teachers can choose which micro-credentials best fit with their professional learning experience as well as how to acquire and demonstrate competency for each micro-credential (Code.org, 2019d).

Micro-credentials contain a core question that defines a specific content or practice and ask teachers to submit one or more work artifacts to demonstrate competency in the defined area (Brown, 2019; Code.org, 2019d; see also Chapters 14 and 15 on micro-credentials). Typically, a text explanation connects the artifact to the competency being demonstrated while reflection connects the content of the artifact to the teachers' own experiences. All submissions are scored through a rubric and rated on a simple binary scale of "yes" or "not yet." Feedback is provided to support further professional learning and teachers are encouraged to engage in additional learning, make changes, and resubmit artifacts if needed to earn the micro-credential. The review and feedback process is seen as a coaching and learning opportunity as opposed to judgment. Upon earning a micro-credential, a teacher is presented with a digital badge as well as a certificate of completion for an estimated number of professional learning hours.

Micro-credentials bring a final component to the model for effective, personalizable CS professional development with four of the seven features of effective PD. Like the other four professional learning activities previously discussed in this chapter, micro-credentials are content focused. As demonstrations of teacher competency, micro-credentials promote active learning that is truly job-embedded since the artifacts that teachers submit are demonstrations of their implementation of CS content and pedagogy in the classrooms. The feedback portion of the micro-credentialing process provides CS teachers the opportunity to receive expert support and peer feedback from reviewers. That feedback can be seen as a form of coaching as it identifies gaps in the teacher's competency and includes suggestions on how to address those gaps. Teachers who engage in the micro-credentials complete a reflective question around the artifact they submit. When they receive feedback, they again reflect on the feedback around their practice, particularly if revision and resubmission is required.

On its own, the micro-credentialing process does not provide a fully effective professional learning path for teachers because it does not promote some of the key features of effective PD. The micro-credentialing process, by its nature, is not an activity that supports collaboration. Teachers create the artifact on their own which is focused on their individual practices and not on learning from models of effective practice. Micro-credentials also are not of a sustained duration because they are designed to be completed once. That being said, micro-credentials can be embedded throughout a teacher's professional learning experience and built into a portfolio that demonstrates an individual teacher's expertise.

On the other hand, micro-credentials contribute to each of the five components of personalizable learning (see Table 12.3). Much like MOOC-Eds or online learning modules, micro-credentials encourage teacher agency, ownership, and flexibility. Their strength is the value they create inherently as a credential, but also the competency-based approach which ensures teachers are demonstrating real practice rather than simply listening to an expert at a conference or checking boxes to meet ongoing credit requirements. In conjunction with the other professional learning activities discussed above, they complete a package of support for personalizable PD beginning with agency and ownership in what to learn, how to create value for one's self, who to work with to enhance strengths, how to adjust to change, and finally, how to demonstrate real improvements in the classroom and receive credit.

NEXT STEPS

The model for personalizable CS PD presented in this chapter is innovative in its approach to bring together widely-used professional learning activities that include features of effective PD. The model supports teachers in addressing individual needs, engaging in areas of interest, and overcoming barriers faced due to resources, location, time, and environment. While the model is innovative and demonstrated success by reaching over 750 beginning CS teachers in North Carolina from 2016–2019 (Friday Institute for Educational Innovation, 2020c), further research, development, and adaptation is needed to ensure its effectiveness in the rapidly changing CS education environment in states and communities throughout the country. In the short term, opportunities to advance this model can be seen around education practice, policy, and research: (a) development to reach additional teachers, including addressing the needs of more experienced CS teachers, and incorporating new effective professional learning activities to expand options (see also Chapter 10); (b) alignment with policies for CS educators, including standards, licensure, and continuing education requirements; and (c) research and evaluation of the model's impact on CS teaching practice across different demographics and school environments.

Development to Reach Additional Teachers

The current implementation of the model for effective, personalized CS PD is designed for in-service teachers in other content areas to initially transition to CS teaching, regardless of experience or content expertise. With the success in growing the CS teacher workforce since 2016, the number of experienced CS teachers will also continue to grow. Additionally, our model is implemented with currently available professional learning activities. New CS professional learning activities are being developed at a constant pace as the demand for more CS teachers and classes increases throughout the country. With a focus on personalizability for teachers and methods for incorporating many new professional learning activities, further development is needed to expand the current model to reach new audiences, such as experienced CS teachers, and address their individual interests, needs and teaching environments.

Alignment With Policies for CS Educators

As CS becomes more embedded into school systems and more classes are taught, additional policies that impact teachers will be developed or redesigned. In late 2019, CSTA released newly revised CS Educator Standards (CSTA, n.d.) that will provide structure for what teachers should know and be able to demonstrate in classroom practice. States have often leveraged these types of standards to inform their policies, which can have a significant impact on current CS teachers. Given that many new CS teachers have had limited professional learning activities (some as little as a week), it is unlikely they will be fully prepared to meet and demonstrate a comprehensive set of standards (Menekse, 2015).

The model discussed in this chapter for effective, personalizable CS professional learning provides a unique opportunity for both self-assessment and design of professional learning plans that address current teachers' needs. Additionally, it can be used to frame professional learning plans for future CS teachers so they are on a path to meet standards or any local policies that may impact them in the future. By providing a pathway to success for new CS teachers, two critical problems can be avoided: (a) CS teachers will not be simply "grandfathered" into a CS license without meeting a set of standards for high quality teaching, thereby avoiding a significant number of potentially underqualified CS teachers in the field, and (b) new CS teachers will not be pushed out of the field due to inability to meet standards or policy, thereby avoiding a shortage of teachers for all of the new CS courses recently added to schools around the country. A thoughtful, personalizable approach with sufficient time and planning can support teachers and schools to continue to expand opportunities in CS for all students.

Research on Impacts on Diverse CS Teaching Practice

Finally, additional research should be conducted to better understand the impacts of a personalizable approach as compared to other, more prescribed professional learning programs. Given that the central tenets of personalizable learning are teacher agency, ownership, value creation, flexibility, and enhancing strengths (Zhao, 2018), further research on how this model supports teachers in diverse demographic, geographic, and experiential contexts will inform understanding of how all teachers can benefit from this model. Such research on personalizable PD for CS teachers will also inform future decisions about implementation and scaling of the model, and its effect on expanding CS opportunities for all students and all schools.

REFERENCES

Bickerstaff, S., & Cormier, M. S. (2015). Examining faculty questions to facilitate instructional improvement in higher education. *Studies in Educational Evaluation, 46*, 74–80.

Bond, P. (2015). Information literacy in MOOCs. *Current Issues in Emerging eLearning, 2*(1), Article 6.

Booth, S. E., & Kellogg, S. B. (2014). Value creation in online communities for educators. *British Journal of Educational Technology, 46*(4), 684–698. https://doi.org/10.1111/bjet.12168

Brooks, C., & Gibson, S. (2012). Professional learning in a digital age. *Canadian Journal of Learning and Technology, 38*(2), 1–17.

Brown, D. (2019). *Research and educator micro-credentials.* http://digitalpromise.org/wp-content/uploads/2019/02/researchandeducatormicrocredentials-v1r2.pdf

Brown, R. (2018). *Estimating the causal effect of Code.org teacher training program on Advanced Placement outcomes.* West Coast Analytics. http://www.westcoastanalytics.com/uploads/6/9/6/7/69675515/wca_code_final_report_2018.pdf

Butler, D. L., Lauscher, H. N., Jarvis-Selinger, S., & Beckingham, B. (2004). Collaboration and self-regulation in teachers' professional development. *Teaching and Teacher Education, 20*(5), 435–455.

Carpenter, J. P. (2016). Unconference professional development: Edcamp participant perceptions and motivations for attendance. *Professional Development in Education, 42*(1), 78–99.

Cho, S., Pauca, P., & Johnson, D. (2014, March 17). *Computational thinking for the rest of us: A liberal arts approach to engaging middle and high school teachers with computer science students* [Conference session]. Society for Information Technology

& Teacher Education International Conference, Jacksonville, FL.Code.org. (2017a). *Support K–12 computer science in North Carolina.* https://code.org/advocacy/state-facts/NC.pdf

Code.org. (2017b). *Recommendations for states developing computer science teacher pathways.* https://code.org/files/TeacherPathwayRecommendations.pdf

Code.org. (2019a). *2018 annual report.* https://code.org/files/annual-report-2018.pdf

Code.org. (2019b). *2019 CS discoveries local summer workshop.* https://curriculum.code.org/plcsd-19/local/

Code.org. (2019c). *2019 state of computer science education.* https://advocacy.code.org/2019_state_of_cs.pdf

Code.org. (2019d). *Micro-credentials: A pathway for certification and professional learning.* http://advocacy.code.org

Code.org. (2021). *Code.org statistics.* https://code.org/statistics

Committee on Underrepresented Groups and the Expansion of the Science and Engineering Workforce Pipeline. (2011). *Expanding underrepresented minority participation: America's science and technology talent at the crossroads.* National Academies Press.

Conrad, D. (2005). Building and maintaining community in cohort-based online learning. *Journal of Distance Education, 20*(1), 1–20.

CSForAll. (n.d.). *About CSForAll.* https://www.csforall.org/about/

CSTA (n.d.). *Standards for CS teachers.* https://www.csteachers.org/page/standards-for-cs-teachers

Cuny, J. (2011). Transforming computer science education in high schools. *Computer, 44*(6), 107–109.

Daniel, J. (2012). Making sense of MOOCs: Musings in a maze of myth, paradox and possibility. *Journal of Interactive Media in Education, 2012*(3), Article 18. http://doi.org/10.5334/2012-18

Darling-Hammond, L., Hyler, M. E., & Gardner, M. (2017). *Effective teacher professional development.* Learning Policy Institute.

Delyser, L. A., Goode, J., Guzdial, M., Kafai, Y., & Yadav, A. (2018). *Priming the computer science teacher pump: Integrating computer science education into schools of education.* CSforAll.

Desimone, L. M. (2009). Improving impact studies of teachers' professional development: Toward better conceptualizations and measures. *Educational Researcher, 38*(3), 181–199.

Downes, S. (2012). *A true history of the MOOC* [Audio]. http://www.downes.ca/presentation/300

Eanes, Z. (2020, January 15). Business leaders seeing talent gap want to fund more computer science teachers in NC. *The News & Observer.* https://www.newsobserver.com/news/business/article239278213.html

EdCamp Foundation. (2019). *Tenets of the edcamp model.* https://www.edcamp.org

Ferguson, R., & Sharples, M. (2014, September). Innovative pedagogy at massive scale: Teaching and learning in MOOCs [Conference session]. In U. Cress, V. Dimitrova, & M. Specht (Eds.), *Proceedings of the 4th European Conference on Technology Enhanced Learning: Learning in the synergy of multiple disciplines* (pp. 98–111). Springer.

Friday Institute for Educational Innovation. (n.d.). *EdcampCode: Beyond the hour of code.* https://www.fi.ncsu.edu/event/edcampcode-beyond-the-hour-of-code -workshops-for-all-teachers/

Friday Institute for Educational Innovation. (2020a). *Computer science enrollments in North Carolina* [Unpublished raw data].

Friday Institute for Educational Innovation. (2020b). *MOOC-Ed enrollment data* [Unpublished raw data].

Friday Institute for Educational Innovation. (2020c). *CS teacher professional learning engagement data in North Carolina* [Unpublished raw data].

Frye, D., Morris, S., Samberg, M., & Keller, L. (2017). *NC computing education landscape report.* The Friday Institute for Educational Innovation. https://go.ncsu .edu/nc-cs-landscape-report

Garet, M. S., Porter, A. C., Desimone, L., Birman, B. F., & Yoon, K. S. (2001). What makes professional development effective? Results from a national sample of teachers. *American Educational Research Journal, 38*(4), 915–945.

Goode, J., Margolis, J., & Chapman, G. (2014). *Curriculum is not enough: The educational theory and research foundation of the exploring computer science professional development model* [Symposium session]. The 45th ACM Technical Symposium on Computer Science Education (SIGCSE'14), New York, NY. https://doi .org/10.1145/2538862.2538948

Google Inc., & Gallup Inc. (2020). *Moving forward: Closing the computer science learning gap: Rural and small town school districts.* https://services.google.com/ fh/files/misc/closing-computer-science-learning-gaps-rural-and-small-town -school-districts.pdf

Gray, J., Haynie, K., Packman, S., Boehm, M., Crawford, C., & Muralidhar, D. (2015, March 4–6). *A mid-project report on a statewide professional development model for CS principles* [Symposium session]. The 46th SIGCSE Symposium, Kansas City, MS.

Hall, A. B., & Trespalacios, J. (2019). Personalized professional learning and teacher self-efficacy for integrating technology in K–12 classrooms. *Journal of Digital Learning in Teacher Education, 35*(4), 221–235.

Hansen-Thomas, H., Grosso Richins, L., Kakkar, K., & Okeyo, C. (2016). I do not feel I am properly trained to help them! Rural teachers' perceptions of challenges and needs with English-language learners. *Professional Development in Education, 42*(2), 308–324.

Holmes, A., Signer, B., & MacLeod, A. (2010). Professional development at a distance: A mixed-method study exploring inservice teachers' views on presence online. *Journal of Digital Learning in Teacher Education, 27*(2), 76–85.

Joyce, B. R., & Showers, B. (2002). *Student achievement through staff development.* NCSL.

Kleiman, G., Wolf, M. A., & Frye, D. (2015). Educating educators: Designing MOOCs for professional learning. In P. Kim (Eds.), *The MOOC revolution: Massive open online courses and the future of education* (pp. 117–146). Routledge.

Liu, J., Lin, C. H., Hasson, E. P., & Barnett, Z. D. (2012, October 3–6). Computer science learning made interactive—A one-week Alice summer computing workshop for K–12 teachers. In *2012 Frontiers in Education Conference proceedings* (pp. 128–133), Seattle, WA..

Lock, J. V. (2006). A new image: Online communities to facilitate teacher professional development. *Journal of Technology and Teacher Education, 14*(4), 663–678.

McConnell, T. J., Parker, J. M., Eberhardt, J., Koehler, M. J., & Lundeberg, M. A. (2013). Virtual professional learning communities: Teachers' perceptions of virtual versus face-to-face professional development. *Journal of Science Education and Technology, 22*(3), 267–277.

Menekse, M. (2015). Computer science teacher professional development in the United States: A review of studies published between 2004 and 2014. *Computer Science Education, 25*(4), 325–350.

Ni, L., & Guzdial, M. (2012, Februar 29–March 3). Who AM I?: *Understanding high school computer science teachers' professional identity* [Symposium session]. The 43rd ACM Technical Symposium on Computer Science Education, Raleigh, NC.

Owen, H. (2008). *Open space technology: A user's guide.* (3rd ed.). Berrett-Koehler.

Penuel, W. R., Fishman, B. J., Yamaguchi, R., & Gallagher, L. P. (2007). What makes professional development effective? Strategies that foster curriculum implementation. *American Educational Research Journal, 44*(4), 921–958.

Probst, G., & Borzillo, S. (2008). Why communities of practice succeed and why they fail. *European Management Journal, 26*(5), 335–347. https://doi.org/10.1016/j .emj.2008.05.003

Rodriguez, O. (2013). The concept of openness behind c and x-MOOCs (Massive Open Online Courses). *Open Praxis, 5*(1), 67–73.

Sadik, O., Ottenbreit-Leftwich, A., & Brush, T. (2020). Secondary computer science teachers' pedagogical needs. *International Journal of Computer Science Education in Schools, 4*(1), 33–52.

Schifter, C. C. (2016). Personalizing professional development for teachers. In *Handbook on personalized learning for states, districts, and schools* (pp. 221–235). Information Age Publishing.

Showers, B., & Joyce, B. (1996). The evolution of peer coaching. *Educational Leadership, 53*(6), 12–16.

Siemens, G. (2004). *Elearnspace. Connectivism: A learning theory for the digital age.* https://citeseerx.ist.psu.edu/viewdoc/download?doi=10.1.1.1089.2000&rep =rep1&type=pdf

Swanson, K. (2014). Edcamp: Teachers take back professional development. *Educational Leadership, 71*(8), 36–40.

Tondeur, J., Forkosh-Baruch, A., Prestridge, S., Albion, P., & Edirisinghe, S. (2016). Responding to challenges in teacher professional development for ICT integration in education. *Educational Technology and Society, 19*(3), 110–120.

Wei, R. C., Darling-Hammond, L., & Adamson, F. (2010). *Professional development in the United States: Trends and challenges.* National Staff Development Council.

Wynants, S., & Dennis, J. (2018). Professional development in an online context: Opportunities and challenges from the voices of college faculty. *Journal of Educators Online, 15*(1). https://doi.org/10.9743/JEO2018.15.1.2

Zhao, Y. (2018). *Reach for greatness: Personalizable education for all children.* Corwin.

CHAPTER 13

CODE SAVVY EDUCATORS

A Professional Development Model for In-Service Educators

Lana Peterson
University of Minnesota

Cassandra Scharber
University of Minnesota

Sarah Barksdale
University of Minnesota

Andrea Wilson Vazquez
Hamline University

Tom Cozzolino
Concordia University

Professional Development for In-Service Teachers, pages 295–315
Copyright © 2022 by Information Age Publishing
www.infoagepub.com

ABSTRACT

In 2015, the non-profit organization, Code Savvy, launched Minnesota's first statewide professional development experience for K–12 in-service teachers related to computer science, called the MNCodes Educator Training Program. In this chapter, we describe this program by sharing its history, identifying its guiding framework, and outlining its professional development model. We subsequently provide considerations for others interested in designing a cohort-based professional development experience for in-service teachers.

The demand for computer science (CS) education and the integration of computational thinking (CT) into K–12 education continues to grow; however, many students do not yet have access to these learning opportunities. Female, Black, and Hispanic students continue to encounter structural and social barriers that limit access and exposure to CS (Google Inc., & Gallup Inc., 2016, 2020). According to the Pew Research Center (2018), the percentage of women in computing jobs has actually decreased since 1990; women comprised 32% of computing jobs in 1990 compared to only 25% in 2016. Within U.S. computing and mathematical careers, women are employed at 26% while Black and Latino people are employed at only 8% (Bureau of Labor and Statistics, U.S. Department of Labor, 2020). Similarly in 2019, only 29% of Advanced Placement (AP) CS exams were taken by female high school students and only 24% of AP CS exams were taken by American Indian/Alaska Native, Black, Hispanic/Latino, and Native Hawaiian/Other Pacific Islander (College Board, 2019). Research also shows that students' STEM-related career interests are largely developed before high school which makes participation in computing crucial for students in Grades K–8 (Corbett & Hill, 2015; Sadler et al., 2012). As a result, many researchers have suggested that CT and CS should be integrated across K–12 content curricula (e.g., Bocconi et al., 2016; Delyser et al., 2018).

The integration of CS and/or CT into K–12 education must be coupled with K–12 teachers and classroom/school/district environments that are cognizant of and actively address the needs of Black, Hispanic, Indigenous, English language learning, and female students within computing. Quality professional development (PD) for K–12 educators on CS and CT is crucial for a sustained shift toward student access to computing education (Barr & Stephenson, 2011; Goode, Peterson, et al., 2020; Yadav et al., 2016). PD in CS is unique as educators generally have little CS background, content expertise or prior programming experience (Bernier & Margolis, 2014; Goode et al., 2014). In a literature review of K–12 CS PD, Menekse (2015) outlined that high quality CS PD includes: (a) collaboration with other educators, (b) time for implementation and practice, (c) active learning methods that parallel classroom teaching approaches, (d) a focus on pedagogical content knowledge, (e) follow up support, and (f) professional learning communities. Barr and Stephenson (2011) also recommend the use of learning communities, peer learning, exposure to computing industries, the development of teaching tools, and the sharing of students' activities in PD.

The organization and expectations of K–12 CS education in the United States rests with state governments (Mannila et al., 2014). In the state of Minnesota, those expectations are further delineated to local governments and individual school districts. To date, at the state level, Minnesota is in the early processes of engaging in conversations and efforts related to K–12 CS education and educator training (Code.org et al., 2020; CSforAllMN, 2018). In response to the lack of training for CS teachers in the state, the non-profit organization, Code Savvy, launched the first statewide PD experience for educators related to CS in 2015 and is considered to be a leader in the state. In this chapter we describe Code Savvy's PD cohort for in-service educators and provide a list of considerations for others interested in designing cohort-based PD experiences.

BACKGROUND

State Landscape

Minnesota is currently ranked last in the country for access to CS education as only 19% of its high schools offer a foundation CS education course (Code.org et al., 2020). Furthermore, Minnesota has only enacted two of the nine recommended state-level CS policies (Code.org et al., 2020). There is not a state-level CS education plan, no state-level K–12 CS student standards, no state-level funding for CS-related educator PD, and limited as well as confusing CS teacher licensure certifications (Office of the Legislative Auditor, 2016). Due to our state context, the availability of CS education opportunities depends on individual teacher, school, or district initiatives.

While there is a long way to go in building equitable access to CS education, Minnesota is making some progress. In the Fall of 2018, Minnesota joined 23 other states and U.S. territories in seeking to increase the number and diversity of K–16 students with access to CS by becoming members of the national Expanding Computing Education Pathways Alliance (ECEP) (https://ecepalliance.org). Minnesota's ECEP alliance chapter is called CSforAllMN, and its purpose is to help shape the vision for K–12 CS education in Minnesota with a focus on policy, broadening participation, and PD (https://csforallmn.org). CSforAllMN recognizes Code Savvy as the leading Minnesota organization committed to supporting K–12 CS education.

Code Savvy Organization: History, Purpose, and Impact

Code Savvy, a non-profit organization that started in 2013, works to empower all educators and youth with the knowledge, skills, and support to create with technology while working to interrupt and counteract gender and racial gaps in computing (www.codesavvy.org). Code Savvy's portfolio of K–12 educator and youth programs impacts thousands throughout the state each year. In 2015, Code Savvy launched its MNCodes Educator Training Initiative for in-service teachers that includes professional training workshops, coaching, a year-long PD cohort, and a summit each spring. The year-long PD cohort is called the MN Coding in the Classroom Leadership Cohort, and is the focus of this chapter. The goals of this cohort are to develop teachers' CS content knowledge, increase teachers' confidence in teaching and integrating CS in their classroom, and examine inequities that persist within CS education. Over the past 5 years, the cohort estimates to have partnered with 140 educators in over 80 Minnesota school districts, impacting over 37,000 students.

Code Savvy and the LT Media Lab at the University of Minnesota have been engaged in a research practice partnership (RPP) since the Fall of 2017 (Coburn & Penuel, 2016; Coburn et al., 2013). This partnership examines mutual problems of practice related to teacher PD and designing equitable instruction in CS education. In 2018–2019, Code Savvy and LT Media Lab engaged in continuous improvement evaluation and research activities for the MN Coding in the Classroom Leadership Cohort using a "plan, do, study, and act" model (Bryk et al., 2016). The pre-and post-year survey findings from these activities help inform this chapter's description of the cohort. Names have been anonymized to protect cohort members' identities.

Guiding Frameworks of MN Coding in the Classroom Leadership Cohort

Code Savvy's in-service educator cohort is anchored in the K–12 CS Framework (K–12 Computer Science Framework Steering Committee, 2016) and is guided by commitments to supporting gender and racial equity within computing (National Center for Women & Information Technology) and creating effective teacher PD experiences (Darling-Hammond et al., 2017; Menekse, 2015).

K–12 Computer Science Framework

This framework's development was co-led by the Association for Computing Machinery, Code.org, Computer Science Teachers Association, Cyber Innovation Center, and National Math and Science Initiative in partnership with states and districts. The result of this collaboration was the identification of five core CS concepts: computing systems, networks and the internet, data and analysis, algorithms and programming, and impacts of computing. In addition, there are seven core CS practices supported by the framework: fostering an inclusive computing culture, creating computational artifacts, collaborating around computing, recognizing and defining computational problems, testing and refining computational artifacts, developing and using abstractions, and communicating about computing. The intention for this framework is to provide building blocks for state and local-level contexts to build their own standards and curricula. These concepts and practices serve as a roadmap for the design of the MN Coding in the Classroom Leadership Cohort.

Broadening Participation in CS Education

One of Code Savvy's values is a focus on fostering inclusive practices that interrupt and counteract gender, racial, and economic bias. Importantly, it is not just through more access to CS experiences but the ways in which those experiences are designed and facilitated pedagogically. Margolis et al. (2015) argue that persistent structural inequalities within CS education, a widespread biased belief system, and policies that implicate access to CS learning experiences contribute to the underrepresentation of marginalized people in CS education. The issue of underrepresentation in computing is complex and needs a multi-faceted approach to help educators understand ways that they can address it. In the cohort, teachers are encouraged to consider their own bias, how their bias impacts their instruction, and the larger systems-level policies and procedures in their school that impacts who engages in computing.

Design of Effective Professional Development

The MN Coding in the Classroom Leadership Cohort is an exemplary model for teacher PD because of a combination of its thoughtfully planned content and its effective, research-based approach to teacher learning. Darling-Hammond et al. (2017) conducted a meta-analysis of studies on successful teacher PD and outlined seven characteristics of effective PD. Best practices in teacher PD take time to implement and support, and none of the included studies in Darling-Hammond et al. (2017) happened in a solitary, one-off workshop. On average, the studies included experiences that lasted 49 hours over the course of a year. Oftentimes these experiences included longer (4–8 hour) workshops with shorter opportunities for teachers to reflect and connect in between workshops, sometimes virtually. The MN Coding in the Classroom Leadership Cohort model directly aligns with these research-based characteristics. This alignment is illustrated in Table 13.1 and the remainder of this chapter.

TABLE 13.1   The Alignment of the Seven Characteristics of Effective Teacher Professional Development and the Design of the MN Coding in the Classroom Leadership Cohort

Characteristics of Effective Teacher PD (Darling-Hammond et al., 2017)	MN Coding in the Classroom Leadership Cohort Elements
Focused content Model activities for teachers to experience as students themselves	• Focus on CT across content areas • Visit institutions & experience how they approach CS education • Cohort members lead CS/CT activities for cohort peers to experience as students
Active learning and adult learning theory Incorporate teachers' prior experience, choice in learning experiences, & reflection	• Cohort workshops include: – Hands-on unplugged activities – Thematic stations w/CT physical computing and robotic tools (cohort members have autonomy in station selection)
Collaboration Discuss barriers, share resources, seek advice, and build relationships	• All activities are designed for and model collaboration • Google group and Twitter discussions by members between workshops • Small group discussion & sharing
Model effective practice Observe others' lessons, review lesson plans, or analyze student work	• Modeling of equitable CS/CT unplugged and digital activities • Community grounding activities begin each workshop • Cohort members lead activities they hope to do w/ students during workshops • Small group peer coaching and lesson plan reflection
Coaching and expert support 1:1 coaching	• 1.5 hour small group coaching (3x) • Full day workshops (6) led by experts • Cohort alumni volunteers lead activities at workshops • Visit & learn from/with industry experts
Opportunities for *feedback and reflection*	• Sharing activity and lessons w/cohort for peer and expert feedback • Reflection is built in throughout year • Organization of & presentation at summit
Sustained *duration*	• 58 hours total of synchronous workshops & coaching • Virtual support via Google group, email, and Twitter between workshops • Year-long cohort with opportunities to engage as alumni in next year • Lending Library supports educators to continue their learning beyond workshops

Similar Models

The Code Savvy cohort model has similarities with other programs such as the Disciplinary Commons for Computing Educators (DCCE; Morrison et al., 2012) and Exploring Computer Science (ECS; http://www.exploringcs.org; Goode et al., 2012) whose goals are not simply to prepare educators to teach CS, but also create a community of professionals who often work in isolation. All three programs meet many times over the course of a year rejecting the "one and done" workshop philosophy. The Code Savvy cohort diverges from DCCE and ECS in that it includes educators from elementary to high school settings. Further, participating educators teach different content courses as opposed to only CS classes.

EXEMPLAR: CODE SAVVY'S IN-SERVICE EDUCATOR COHORT MODEL

Overview

The MN Coding in the Classroom Leadership Cohort annually brings together a new group of 35 K–12 educators from across Minnesota who represent all grade levels and content areas, with varying exposure to and experience in teaching CS/CT, for a year-long, hybrid PD experience (see Table 13.2). The cohort is facilitated by two instructors: the founder of Code Savvy's MNCodes Educator Training initiative and cohort program, who is a makerspace, CS, and ESL educator at an alternative high school; and an elementary content coach and former makerspace and 5th grade teacher at an elementary school. Cohort participants have the option to earn three graduate credits for their efforts in the cohort through the College of St. Scholastica.

Educator Recruitment

Applications for cohort participation open annually in early May to K–12 educators from formal and informal learning spaces. There are no prerequisites for CS/CT knowledge or experience and the application encourages all experience levels. The questions on the application focus on participants' school/organization demographics and location information, the role(s) and grade level taught(s), a gauge of experience with CS (as both a learner and an educator), and open-ended questions on how they view their participation impacting sustainability and equity of CS education. Each applicant must also document administrator approval to confirm that they can be absent for one school day to participate in the annual summit and that they will have support in using new skills/knowledge with students and teachers at their school.

Cohort applications are reviewed by Code Savvy's executive director, program director, and cohort facilitators as well as representatives from its advisory board who aim to balance several factors when selecting cohort members, including: (a) diversity of location (urban, rural, suburban) with no more than two educators at a time coming from one district, and a focus on including schools with over 50% of students of color and those qualifying for free and reduced lunch; (b) a range of experience with CS education; (c) equal representation from elementary, middle, and high school grades; and (d) a strong interest and commitment to becoming a champion for equitable CS education in their district or organization. Each year participation varies slightly; however, as a sample demographic, in the 2018–2019 cohort ($n = 27$) teachers self-identified as 67% female, 29% male, 4% nonbinary/third gender, and racially as White (89%), Asian/Asian American (7%), and American Indian (4%).

Cohort leaders have struggled to recruit teachers of color to participate in the cohort, which is representative of an ongoing mismatch between the racial makeup of Minnesota K–12 teachers and the racial makeup of its students (Shockman, 2019; Wilder Research, 2019). In 2018–2019, over 81% of the cohort members worked at public schools, 11% worked at charter schools, and 7% worked at private schools. Of these schools, 37% were elementary schools, 19% were middle schools, 30% were high schools, and 4% were online. Seven percent (7%) of members worked across K–12, and 4% worked in higher education. The majority of the cohort members (59%) had roles that worked directly with students (e.g., grade-level classroom teachers, math teachers, science teachers, or library media specialists). A smaller contingent (19%) indicated they had roles that mainly supported teachers with technology integration, and 23% indicated their full-time job was split between an indirect and direct position with students.

Participant Incentives

The MN Coding in the Classroom Leadership Cohort offers educators a stipend to participate. Cohort participants receive $500 upon completion of program requirements at the end of the cohort in May. Participants who live outside of the Twin Cities metro area are also given a travel stipend to reduce costs and barriers of participation. In addition, every in-person workshop includes breakfast, lunch, and free parking.

TABLE 13.2 Sample MN Coding in the Classroom Leadership Cohort Calendar and Alignment With CS Core Practices

Workshop Date/Location	Topic	CS K–12 Core Practices From the K–12 Computer Science Framework (https://K12cs.org/)
August Unisys Corp (global IT company)	Computational thinking and creative computing	Intro to all Core Practices
September Online	Curriculum integration and equity	1: Fostering an Inclusive Computing Culture 4: Developing and Using Abstractions
October Target Headquarters	Hackathon: Design thinking + computing	2: Collaborating Around Computing 3: Recognizing and Defining Computational Problems 5: Creating Computational Artifacts
November Clockwork (software company)	Robotics: Intro to PD	6: Testing and Refining Computational Artifacts 7: Communicating About Computing
December Online	Individual check-ins on unit planning Initial summit planning	1: Fostering an Inclusive Computing Culture 2: Collaborating Around Computing
January Minneapolis Community & Technical College	Physical computing, anti-bias approaches and CoderDojo volunteering	4: Developing and Using Abstractions 7: Communicating About Computing
February Middle school's STEM FabLab	Maker ed and computational thinking	3: Recognizing and Defining Computational Problems 5: Creating Computational Artifacts
March Online	Differentiation	1: Fostering an Inclusive Computing Culture 5: Creating Computational Artifacts
April Science Museum of Minnesota	Equity and social justice in STE(A)M	1: Fostering an Inclusive Computing Culture 2: Collaborating Around Computing
May University of Minnesota	#MNCodes Summit (www.mncodessummit.org)	

The Components of Code Savvy's In-Service Educator Cohort

Throughout the cohort, members (a) develop their skills and understanding of CS and CT through participation in hands-on activities; (b) explore and integrate concepts and practices with each content area and MN academic standards; (c) create and share CS curricular resources that align with MN academic standards; (d) engage in a community of practice; (e) learn, apply, and reflect on equitable and inclusive teaching practices; and (f) facilitate training for other educators (see Table 13.2). While these components often intersect and impact each other, we have broken them down to provide structure and specific details to better highlight what makes this program an exemplar in CS PD.

Develop Skills and Understanding of CS and CT

Hands-on workshops provide cohort participants opportunities to experience CT and CS as learners, which aligns with two of the characteristics of effective PD identified by Darling-Hammond et al. (2017; focused content and active learning; see Table 13.1). One participant shared that "testing out and playing with technology has been very valuable . . . This continued exposure has helped me gain confidence that even though I haven't had many undergrad CS classes that programming is something I can learn along with my students" (post-program survey response, 2018–2019). Unplugged activities (i.e., activities done away from a computer), thematic station choices, guest speakers, and conversations with others in education contribute to participants' understanding of and skills related to CS and CT (see Figure 13.1). For instance, when workshops are held at corporate locations, teachers are able to hear from industry professionals, see where computer scientists work, how they approach their jobs, and discuss the connections between K–12 CS education and the economy. In addition to the industry perspectives, cohort participants also explore other educational institutions' approaches to CT and CS, including a STEM fabrication lab at a school district in the southern metro area. Further, the cohort receives hands-on experience using a variety of technologies, but cohort participants also learn about CT across content areas, new course offerings, student recruitment, and strategies to obtain funding for computing equipment. One participant explained how these different activities informed their own knowledge:

> Being a member of the cohort was very impactful for me overall, but I would say the mere understanding of the difference between CS, coding, and computational thinking was key in helping me to frame my thoughts about what I am doing, why I am teaching it, how I am teaching it, and why I am teaching it the way I am, was a profound example of the significance of the cohort. Additionally, any activity we did involving integration was helpful, such as unplugged coding/logic/computational thinking activities. (post-program survey response, 2018–2019)

In the evaluation study (2018–2019) completed in partnership with the University of Minnesota, there was an overall positive increase in participants' confidence in integrating CT into their lessons/activities for

Figure 13.1   Cohort participants compare Scratch blocks to Python code.

students. Learning is extended beyond the workshop times, too, as the tools used during workshops comprise Code Savvy's Technology Lending Library, which makes equipment such as robots, programmable microcontrollers, tablets, books and other materials available to cohort members to borrow for use in their classrooms free of charge. This lending library allows teachers and schools the chance to explore and implement CS-related resources and tools they may not otherwise have access to and provides a "try before you buy" opportunity.

Explore and Integrate CT Concepts and Practices With Content Areas

The cohort facilitators model content integration during the workshops and provide opportunities for educators to explore translations into different content areas (model effective practice). Specifically, each of the stations that the educators explore during the workshops model the intersection of a targeted computer science core practice (see Table 13.2), pedagogical approaches, and the use of the tool to teach content. There is always a variety of stations to choose from to accommodate the range of grade levels and experience. For instance, when the topic is creative computing, stations include ScratchJr, Scratch 3.0 + extensions, Edison Robots, Digital Making with Raspberry Pi, and Raspberry Pi: Hack a Python Game. A participant from the 2018–2019 cohort shared that an outcome of deeper exploration of CT integration is that "I hope to get my department on board to incorporate more in our mainstream classes. I feel strongly that exposure to all students will be how we get more students interested in computer science" (post-program survey).

As part of the cohort, educators sign up during the monthly workshops to lead an activity they have done or hope to do with their students (feedback and reflection). The other cohort members are then able to experience activities as students would (see Figure 13.2). After the activity, they discuss how the activity could be adapted for different age groups and content areas. These experiences, conversations, and reflections often lead to educators creating their own curriculum. For example, a 2017–2018 cohort alumni created a unit that positions students to make positive community impacts using CT within a science unit. Inspired by the book, *Launch: Using Design Thinking to Boost Creativity and Bring Out the Maker in Every Student*, by Spencer and Juliani (2016), and the three devastating hurricanes of 2017 (Harvey, Irma, and Maria), the participant created a unit that has students research hurricanes while prototyping and building vehicles that can be used in disaster zones (https://z.umn.edu/hurricane_unit).

Create and Share CS Curricular Resources

Throughout the cohort experience participants must also develop and teach a CS curriculum unit that integrates with another content area and

Figure 13.2 Cohort participants develop an algorithm through the maze to avoid the "hot lava."

meets Minnesota and CSTA academic standards (collaboration and feedback and reflection). Educators' final unit write-ups are uploaded to an online database and shared freely with the general public. Code Savvy has been collecting resources created by cohort members since 2015. Having access to open-source materials that showcase CS/CT in non-CS disciplines is key to systematic change within education (Barr & Stephenson, 2011). Open public access to these resources is currently available through the Code Savvy's MNCodes Educator Training Program website (www.mncodes. org/resources) and includes lessons for primary, middle, and high school levels and over 14 content areas.

Engage in a Community of Practice

Collaboration is a critical component of the cohort and a characteristic of effective teacher PD (collaboration, coaching, and feedback and reflection). The positive relationships and peer support built through the cohort experience was a recurrent theme in the post-program survey: "The most impactful information from the cohort was building a network of teachers to go to and ask help...having people to go to for ideas and support is so valuable" (post-program survey response, 2018–2019). The cohort structure intentionally emphasizes community building by grounding each workshop in a community-building activity, incorporating small group conversations and reflection, and providing an online, asynchronous space for connection between workshops. Throughout the course of the year, participants are teaching lessons, identifying barriers to teaching/integrating CT and CS, brainstorming solutions, reflecting on learning, and both modeling and sharing pedagogical strategies (see Figure 13.3). One cohort member shared, "I've really liked all the learning resources, but I think the most impactful element for me is being able to be part of a group working on this, and being motivated by all the tremendous activity that other remarkable educators are performing!" (post-program survey response, 2018–2019). This community of practice is not confined to the duration of the program as many educators leave having formed lasting relationships: "I have also appreciated the collaborative nature of each meetup. I have gained valuable contacts through the program" (post-program survey response, 2018–2019).

Learn, Apply, and Reflect on Equitable and Inclusive Teaching Practices

Another core component of many of the workshops is equity anchored in computer science Core Practice 1: Fostering an Inclusive Computing Culture. The content for this component of the cohort moves from a broad to more practical approach as the year progresses, and is curated from a variety of sources, including the National Center for Women & Information Technology (NCWIT) and excerpts from the book, *Stuck in the Shallow End*

Figure 13.3 Cohort alumna teaches 2018–2019 participants about using Micro. bits in the classroom.

(Margolis et al., 2017). The cohort year begins by sharing data and stories about the diversity gaps within computing and introducing participants to strategies outlined by NCWIT that can engage marginalized groups who experience bias and barriers in accessing and belonging within computing (model effective practice and feedback and reflection). The cohort digs into resources, organizations, and campaigns whose missions are to broaden participation and considers how these approaches could address equity issues in their own education contexts. Facilitators also bring in local computing professionals who work at organizations committed to disrupting inequity in computing to cohort meetings. For instance, in one meeting, two staff members from Software for Good (https://softwareforgood. com), a local software development firm, comprised of women of color working in technology, came in to discuss their personal and professional journeys in CS with cohort members.

In the second half of the year, cohort members start to consider their own (un)conscious biases and how these implicate their CS instruction. The cohort members use MIT Teaching Systems Lab's "Unconscious Bias in Teaching" (https://mit-teaching-systems-lab.github.io/unconscious-bias/behaviors.html) and Harvey Mudd's CS Teaching Tips (http://csteachingtips.org/tips-for-reducing-bias) resources to understand and prepare to respond to bias and inequities in their classrooms/schools/districts. Cohort members are also introduced to a STEM justice framework used by the Kitty Andersen Youth Science at the Science Museum of Minnesota, and cohort members apply its ideas for direct classroom implementation. These experiences and focus on equity often lead to an increased awareness of CS equity and access issues as educators reflect on areas to improve—pedagogy, curriculum, and/or structures of their school systems. For example, one participant shared that she had not considered "student voice within computational thinking" prior to the cohort, and another shared that he is revising his Introduction to Computer Science content to have "a greater and more visible emphasis on equity issues" (post-program surveys, 2018–2019).

Facilitate Training for Other Educators

To build sustainability of CS/CT beyond their own classrooms or learning contexts, cohort participants commit to designing and leading a PD session related to CS education to at least 10 other educators in their geographic region (collaboration and feedback and reflection). These PD session outlines are also housed within the online database hosted on Code Savvy's MNCodes website. The 2018–2019 evaluation survey documented an overall positive increase in participants' confidence in teaching other teachers and administration about CT. Participation in the year-long cohort has also resulted in many cohort alumni becoming change agents in their schools, districts, and communities to support and expand continuous and consistent CS learning opportunities. For example, the only high school CS teacher from Rochester, MN went on to start his own nonprofit, the Rochester Area Youth Tech Foundation or RAYTF (http://www.raytc.org/).

The MN Coding in the Classroom Summit, a 1-day conference hosted by Code Savvy each spring (http://www.mncodessummit.org), concludes the year for cohort participants as they organize, attend, and present their learning alongside cohort alumni and other Minnesota educators. The summit is the only K–12 educator conference in the state dedicated solely to CS education, and primarily draws educators who teach or would like to teach CS education in their classrooms. At the 2019 summit, there were over 30 teacher-led sessions that drew over 215 attendees. This culmination of the cohort experience consists of hands-on learning, exploration, and collaboration, all of which plant the seeds for new ideas and approaches for the next school year. Practically, the money raised by the summit serves as one of the primary sources of funding for the following year's educator cohort.

NEXT STEPS

The MN Coding in the Classroom Leadership Cohort is an exemplar of CS/CT in-service teacher PD. Key design elements that are hallmarks of this PD experience include (a) the modeling of active learning that positions cohort members as students within CS/CT experiences, (b) the role of community that incorporates opportunities for teachers to collaborate and reflect with each other, (c) the duration of the program, and (d) the affordances for cohort members to apply and design new learning in their own contexts. As Code Savvy looks to the future and continues to improve upon their model, we will be working to further strengthen our equity content, scale up our model to reach more teachers through grants, and explore more formal partnerships with other organizations like school districts and higher education institutions. In the meantime, we acknowledge that this model might not be replicable in every context, but encourage the adaptation of the following research-supported key design elements in CS/CT PD practice and policy for K–12 in-service teachers: community, expertise and space, and equity.

Community

Many cohort members feel isolated within their schools and districts as they are often one of few teachers interested in or experienced in CS education. One of the strongest themes from the post-program survey data was the positive impact of networking and community. While the cohort members came from different grade bands, teaching roles, and experience levels, their shared workshop experience and creation of CS/CT units became a uniting thread. The development of these relationships was purposefully designed by cohort leaders and was just as important as the CS/CT pedagogical content within each workshop. Intentionally creating a professional learning community and a sense of belonging supports educators in their evolution as a CT/CS practitioner (Ryoo et al., 2016).

Expertise and Space

While research and policy have called for the integration of CS/CT into compulsory education, there is still a lot to be learned about what that actually looks like (Rich et al., 2020; Voogt et al., 2015). Educators may be new to CS content, but they still bring in their expertise on students, standards, and instructional practices. It is useful for educators to first experience CS as a learner before they are provided the space (time and environment) to configure and design what CS/CT could look like in their own classrooms (Rich et al., 2019). This space includes opportunities to try lessons and activities with peers or students, as well as reflection and feedback loops. The MN Coding in the Classroom Leadership Cohort's curriculum unit development requirement provides a structure for cohort members to make something useful to their personal practice.

Equity

Computing education has a long history of excluding female, Black, Hispanic, Indigenous, disabled and English language learners through access, instructional practices, bias, and curriculum (Margolis et al., 2017). The CSforALL movement is grounded in the belief that students should have equitable CS educational opportunities, and in order to enact this movement "policies, practices, and belief systems" must change (Goode, Skorodinsky, et al., 2020). Teachers need to both identify bias and the beliefs they hold about who belongs in CS and develop rigorous and inclusive pedagogical practices in order to be change agents for CS education (Goode, Skorodinsky, et al., 2020; Goode et al., 2021). Code Savvy's PD design and content presents content and inclusive pedagogies in a cohesive manner that both brings awareness to (in)equity within computing and allows for cohort members to identify, collaborate, and reflect on what actionable steps they can take to address inequities within their contexts (personal, curriculum, and schools). Cohort members leave with a deeper understanding of CS/CT content and equitable strategies to bring that content into their classrooms.

Recommendations

The purpose of the MN Coding in the Classroom Leadership Cohort is to empower educators with skills and knowledge to teach CS and CT as well as to connect educators with a network of support. Establishing a long-term cohort model has provided Minnesota educators with resources and connections to overcome some of the barriers in teaching CS, as well as training to improve their own skills and practices. This model of year-long PD and networking can be valuable to others hoping to engage in or improve CS education PD for in-service teachers. We conclude by sharing a list of considerations and recommendations for practitioners that may be helpful when designing a cohort-based PD program (Table 13.3).

TABLE 13.3 Recommendations and Considerations for CS/CT PD	
Recommendations	**Considerations**
Use research-informed frameworks to guide your design and practice	• What professional development frameworks can be used to intentionally anchor and guide your PD program? • What CS education frameworks can be used to intentionally anchor and guide your PD program? • What content area frameworks or concepts can be used to intentionally anchor and guide your PD program?
Understand the landscape of CS education in your state or geographic region, including a focus on gap areas and opportunities for increased access to equitable and engaging CS education	• What is already happening? • How could a cohort model support and extend those efforts?
Coordinate with local, state, and national CS education efforts	• What efforts can be utilized as foundations for your program? • What partnerships can support work toward broadening participation?
Align cohort content to best match the needs of local educators and students	• Is integration into core academic subjects the best approach for your area, given the availability of CS standards or licensure credentials? • How will you differentiate cohort content to best match participants' grade levels, content areas, experience levels with CS, and student populations? • How will content be delivered to accommodate for differentiation and hands-on experiences—in-person and/or online?
Seek opportunities to partner with others	• What organizations, districts, schools, departments, or institutions are possible partners? • What type of partnerships are possible? • How can these partners increase reach to educators? • How can these partners extend or strengthen emphasis on content or equity?
Strengthen equity content	• What resources will you use within your program? • How will you cohesively and comprehensively support educators in embedding equitable and inclusive teaching practices within CS instruction?
Identify sustainable funding sources	• Are there local grants, educational organizations, or industry companies that would support efforts around CS education PD? • Are there any conferences or events that could assist in raising money and/or that could be woven into the design of the PD?

REFERENCES

Barr, V., & Stephenson, C. (2011). Bringing computational thinking to K–12: What is involved and what is the role of the computer science education community? *ACM Inroads, 2*(1), 48–54. https://doi.org/10.1145/1929887.1929905

Bernier, D., & Margolis, J. (2014). *The revolving door: Computer science for all and the challenge of teacher retention* [Working Paper 3]. Exploring Computer Science Working Paper. http://www.exploringcs.org/wp-content/uploads/2014/04/The-Revolving-Door-CS-for-All-and-the-Challenge-of-Teacher-Retention-Final.pdf

Bocconi, S., Chioccariello, A., Dettori, G., Ferrari, A., & Engelhardt, K. (2016). *Developing computational thinking in compulsory education – Implications for policy and practice*. Publications Office of the European Union. https://ec.europa.eu/jrc/en/computational-thinking

Bryk, A. S., Gomez, L. M., Grunow, A., & LeMahieu, P. G. (2016). *Learning to improve: How America's schools can get better at getting better*. Harvard Education Press.

Bureau of Labor Statistics, U.S. Department of Labor. (2020). *Labor force statistics from the current population survey*. https://www.bls.gov/cps/cpsaat11.htm

Coburn, C., & Penuel, W. (2016). Research-practice partnerships in education: Outcomes, dynamics, and open questions. *Educational Researcher, 45*(1), 48–54. https://doi.org/10.3102/0013189X16631750

Coburn, C. E., Penuel, W. R., & Geil, K. (2013). Research-practice partnerships at the district level: A strategy for leveraging research for educational improvement. *William T. Grant Foundation*. https://wtgrantfoundation.org/library/uploads/2015/10/Research-Practice-Partnerships-at-the-District-Level.pdf

Code.org, CSTA, & ECEP Alliance. (2020). *2020 State of computer science education: Illuminating disparities*. https://advocacy.code.org/stateofcs

College Board. (2019). *AP program participation and performance data 2019*. https://research.collegeboard.org/programs/ap/data/archived/ap-2019

Corbett, C., & Hill, C. (2015). *Solving the equation: The variables for women's success in engineering and computing*. AAUW.

CSforAllMN. (2018, December). *#CSforAllMN: State of computer science education in Minnesota*. https://csforallmn.files.wordpress.com/2019/11/csforallmn-1.23.19.pdf

Darling-Hammond, L., Hyler, M. E., & Gardner, M. (2017). *Effective teacher professional development*. Learning Policy Institute.

Delyser, L. A., Goode, J., Guzdial, M., Kafai, Y., & Yadav, A. (2018). *Priming the computer science teacher pump: Integrating computer science education into schools of education*. http://computingteacher.org/

Goode, J., Chapman, G., & Margolis, J. (2012). Beyond curriculum: The exploring computer science program. *ACM Inroads, 3*(2), 47–53. https://doi.org/10.1145/2189835.2189851

Goode, J., Chapman, G., & Margolis, J. (2014). *Curriculum is not enough: The educational theory and research foundation of the exploring computer science professional development model* [Conference session]. In *Proceedings of the 45th ACM technical symposium on computer science education* (pp. 493–498). Association for Computing Machinery. https://dl.acm.org/doi/10.1145/2538862.2538948

Goode, J., Ivey, A., RunningHawk Johnson, S., Ryoo, J. J., & Ong, C. (2021). Rac(e)ing to computer science for all: How teachers talk and learn about equity in professional development. *Computer Science Education, 31*(3), 374–399. https://doi.org/10.1080/08993408.2020.1804772

Goode, J., Peterson, K., Malyn-Smith, J., & Chapman, G. (2020). Online professional development for high school computer science teachers: Features that support an equity-based professional learning community. *Computing in Science & Engineering, 22*(5), 51–59. https://doi.org/10.1109/MCSE.2020.2989622

Goode, J., Skorodinsky, M., Hubbard, J., & Hook, J. (2020). *Computer science for equity: Teacher education, agency, and statewide reform.* Frontiers in Education.

Google Inc., & Gallup Inc. (2016). *Diversity gaps in computer science: Exploring the underrepresentation of girls, Blacks and Hispanics.* http://goo.gl/PG34aH

Google Inc., & Gallup Inc. (2020). *Current perspectives and continuing challenges in computer science education in U.S. K–12 schools.* https://csedu.gallup.com/home.aspx

K–12 Computer Science Framework Steering Committee. (2016). *K–12 computer science framework.* http://www.k12cs.org.

Mannila, L., Dagiene, V., Demo, B., Grgurina, N., Mirolo, C., Rolandsson, L., & Settle, A. (2014). *Computational thinking in K–9 education* [Conference Session]. In *Proceedings of the Working Group Reports of the 2014 on Innovation & Technology in Computer Science Education Conference* (pp. 1–29). Association for Computing Machinery. https://doi.org/10.1145/2713609.2713610

Margolis, J., Estrella, R., Goode, J., Jellison-Holme, J., & Nao, K. (2017). *Stuck in the shallow end: Education, race, & computing* (2nd ed.). MIT Press.

Margolis, J., Goode, J., & Chapman, G. (2015). An equity lens for scaling: A critical juncture for exploring computer science. *ACM Inroads, 6*(3), 58–66. https://doi.org/10.1145/2794294

Menekse, M. (2015). Computer science teacher professional development in the United States: A review of studies published between 2004 and 2014. *Computer Science Education, 25*(4), 325–350. https://doi.org/10.1080/08993408.2015.1111645

Morrison, B. B., Ni, L., & Guzdial, M. (2012, September). Adapting the disciplinary commons model for high school teachers: improving recruitment, creating community [Conference Session]. In *Ninth Annual International Conference on International Computing Education Research* (pp. 47–54). Association for Computing Machinery. https://doi.org/10.1145/2361276.2361287

Office of the Legislative Auditor. (2016). *Evaluation report: Minnesota teacher licensure.* State of Minnesota. https://www.auditor.leg.state.mn.us/ped/pedrep/teachers.pdf

Pew Research Center. (2018, January). *Women and men in STEM often at odds over workplace equity.* https://www.pewsocialtrends.org/2018/01/09/diversity-in-the-stem-workforce-varies-widely-across-jobs/

Rich, K. M., Yadav, A., & Larimore, R. A. (2020). Teacher implementation profiles for integrating computational thinking into elementary mathematics and science instruction. *Education and Information Technologies, 25*, 1–28.

Rich, K. M., Yadav, A., & Schwarz, C. (2019). Computational thinking, mathematics, and science: Elementary teachers' perspectives on integration. *Journal of Technology and Teacher Education, 27*(2), 165–205.

Ryoo, J., Goode, J., & Margolis, J. (2016). It takes a village: Supporting inquiry-and equity-oriented computer science pedagogy through a professional learning community. *Computer Science Education, 25*(4), 351–370.

Sadler, P. M., Sonnert, G., Hazari, Z., & Tai, R. (2012). Stability and volatility of STEM career interest in high school: A gender study. *Science Education, 96*(3), 411–427. https://doi.org/10.1002/sce.21007

Shockman, E. (2019, February 12). *Bill aims to get more teachers of color in Minnesota classrooms.* Minnesota Public Radio. https://www.mprnews.org/story/2019/02/12/bill-aims-to-get-more-teachers-of-color-in-minnesota-classrooms

Voogt, J., Fisser, P., Good, J., Mishra, P., & Yadav, A. (2015). Computational thinking in compulsory education: Towards an agenda for research and practice. *Education and Information Technologies, 20*(4), 715–728.

Wilder Research. (2019, January). *2019 biennial Minnesota teacher supply and demand.* https://mn.gov/pelsb/assets/2019%20Supply%20and%20Demand%20Report_tcm1113-370206.pdf

Yadav, A., Hong, H., & Stephenson, C. (2016). Computational thinking for all: Pedagogical approaches to embedding 21st century problem solving in K–12 classrooms. *TechTrends, 60,* 565–568. https://doi.org/10.1007/s11528-016-0087-7

PART IV

ALTERNATIVE PROFESSIONAL DEVELOPMENT
APPROACHES: UNIVERSITY COURSES
AND MICRO-CREDENTIALS

CHAPTER 14

SUPPORTING IN-SERVICE TEACHERS IN UNDERSTANDING THE POTENTIAL OF DATA AND ARTIFICIAL INTELLIGENCE TO INFLUENCE AND IMPACT LEARNING

Justin Olmanson
University of Nebraska Lincoln

Jennifer Davis
Pender Public Schools, Nebraska

Matthew Kilbride
Montgomery County Community College, Pennsylvania

Professional Development for In-Service Teachers, pages 319–340
Copyright © 2022 by Information Age Publishing
www.infoagepub.com

ABSTRACT

The importance of computer science (CS) in today's digital world only continues to grow in prominence. In this paper we share our findings regarding the experiences of K–12 teachers in a design-based graduate course aimed at developing an understanding of CS principles via a focus on the potential of artificial intelligence (AI) and data in educational contexts. In the course, teachers survey a range of AI tools and application programming interface (API) accessible datasets and apply this understanding to the design of a web-based application for use in their classroom. Our findings suggest that the constructionist, open-ended nature of the course and the use of a culminating student-selected design project served as an engaging framing device and a gateway toward developing understanding and interest in programming and other CS principles. Even for participants with little to no CS background, the process of exploring AI tools and data sets and designing a web application for use in their content area raised their level of interaction with programming and increased awareness about the presence and potential for AI in their classroom. A description of the course, more detailed unpacking of the findings, and an outlining of the implications will be the focus of the chapter.

The prominence and centrality of computer science (CS) in today's technology-centric world continues to grow. As a field, CS has enabled the design and development of technologies that have altered our society in profound ways (Wing, 2006). For more than 40 years, how humans communicate, earn a living, identify partners, arrange travel, consume entertainment, and learn new things has been continually digitally re/mediated. While CS has made these societal remediations and reinventions possible, the prevalence of such systems has increased the importance of CS education and highlighted the rising need to offer more CS-related courses and train educators to teach them (Ozturk et al., 2018; Wang, 2017; Yadav et al., 2016).

Organizing a K–12 CS curriculum and integrating CS into existing K–12 content areas has commonly been accomplished via a focus on elements of problem identification and resolution known as *computational thinking* (CT; Wing, 2006). CT forms the foundation of CS learning and is also useful as a 21st century mode of understanding the world (Yadav et al., 2016; Wing, 2014).

A large and growing part of life in the 21st century involves the application of CT in the automation of tasks that had previously required human understanding and reasoning abilities—namely, artificial intelligence (AI). The rising profile of AI in society as well as in schools can be understood as the continued application and integration of CS across all disciplines and spheres of life, including educational contexts (DeNisco, 2019).

The school-based application and integration of CS via AI is multifaceted. It supports teacher decision-making based on multidimensional student data, new and augmented approaches to learning (e.g., intelligent tutoring), and the diversification of domain exploration via AI-tools and data (known in the early 2010s as *big data*). While STEM-related initiatives within school contexts are seen as especially aligned with CS principles and CT, this type of thinking is applicable across K–12 disciplines (Yadav et al., 2017). Furthermore, although programming is often considered the central and culminating instantiation of CS and computational understanding, it is also possible to maintain a focus on teachers' disciplinary contexts while integrating programming in a supportive, less central role (Yadav et al., 2017). This potential to integrate programming, CS principles, and CT into the existing curriculum without overtly or exclusively teaching programming stands as an alternative strategy in introducing these concepts despite the dearth of K–12 teachers who are familiar with CS and programming in the classroom, the lack of funding for dedicated CS teachers in K–12 settings, and the dynamics that exclude CS courses from the curriculum due to pressure to teach the disciplines subject to high stakes testing (Google & Gallup, 2016).

Herein, we explore the experiences of five K–12 educators who took a design-based graduate course meant to raise awareness about AI in education. Specifically, the course was developed to expose students to a range of existing AI-supported learning software, support their learning via a technology design project, and enable their participation in conversations at the intersection of data, privacy, policy, AI, learning, and schools. Our inquiry in this chapter focuses on the potential for a 15-week graduate-level course on AI and data to support understanding gains in and attitudinal shifts regarding the larger field of CS and CS principles—including programming but without an overt course focus on it.

This study took place within a course that is primarily offered to certified classroom teachers with minimal prior familiarity with AI, data science, and CS. The aim of the course is to afford non-experts in AI and data science the opportunity to better understand, via wide reading, prototyping, and design, how both have historically impacted K–12 classrooms and what that impact might mean in their current and future teaching. The collaborative, constructionist, design-focused, open-ended nature of the course supports participant engagement with multiple dimensions of CS and CT, including principles of software engineering and programming (Bulger, 2016; Van Gog, 2006). In the following section, we unpack the broad foundation that guided the content, design, and implementation of the course.

BACKGROUND

Defining Terms and Situating Constructs

Computer Science

CS includes both the theoretical study of what is mathematically computable as well as the design of computer hardware and software (Newell et al., 1967). Within education, CS has been used as a way to teach mathematics, science, linguistics, and, increasingly at the K–12 level, as a stand-alone subject (Falkner et al., 2018; Feurzeig et al., 1969; Kale et al., 2018; Yadav et al., 2018).

Challenges abound for teachers and administrators who aim to build programs that integrate CS into schools and into the content areas. While the number of courses offered in CS has grown along with parent and student interest overall, normalizing the presence of CS in the K–12 curriculum and in in-service and preservice teacher education must overcome several hurdles (Falkner et al., 2018; Wang, 2017). Teacher education programs specializing in CS education are rare, and preservice teacher education programs in the content areas are seldom able to add additional credit requirements without a major overhaul of their programs. On the K–12 side, districts and schools face a lack of funding as well as a lack of qualified teachers interested in and adequately trained to integrate CS into the content areas—much less trained to teach a CS or CT course (Wang, 2017).

CT describes the creative and procedural CS processes humans have developed to guide and inform problem solving, problem understanding, and problem formulation that can be applied to any domain (Yadav et al., 2017). While CT is often expressed via programming, it is the conceptual approaches to problems that best define it (Wing, 2006). These approaches involve the CS tools and techniques of abstraction, generalization, decomposition, algorithms, data representation, automation, modeling, and error detection and correction (Angeli et al., 2016; ISTE, 2011; Kalelioglu et al., 2016).

Within education, CT has been advocated for across the K–12 curriculum. Since the 1980s, educators such as Papert (1980) asserted that affording learners opportunities to use CT to program sprites on computer screens and robots in the physical world, improved their capacity to understand their own thinking. It is listed explicitly in the Next Generation Science Standards as one of the eight science and engineering practices to be embedded throughout the K–12 experience (NGSS Lead States, 2013). In terms of content area teachers and CT, the literature reflects the potential for mathematics, science, language learning, and other subjects to benefit from the integration of a wide variety of approaches that embed CT across disciplines. To this end, while increasing access to programming and other CS professional development opportunities will no doubt aid teacher growth, enabling educators to experience the value of integrating

CT concepts into their content is essential in creating successful integration and lasting interest in its implementation (Google & Gallup, 2016).

Towards this end, Bell and Lodi (2019) explored CS Unplugged, a constructivist pedagogical toolkit designed to expose students to CT concepts without explicitly using computers, and found that both students and educators alike reveled in their conceptual exploration. Through this toolkit, without requiring a prerequisite of programming skills, students acquired an appreciation for CT and CS concepts and were able to apply their discoveries to the learning of their disciplines.

Similarly, Kale et al. (2018) present a multitude of content area CT-focused modules where educators are able to modify their existing content to integrate these concepts and emphasize problem solving. Some revisions include the use of open source programming software such as Scratch to build interactive games that create more active learning environments. Other successful integration approaches include helping educators shift towards problematizing their content (Barr & Stephenson, 2011) and allowing students to "solve" CT-challenges via a series of interactions. Additionally, injecting aforementioned CT-focused processes, such as algorithms, automation, and pattern recognition, into curricula boosted familiarization. Even in primary school environments efforts to incorporate CT have dramatically increased both content-area knowledge and student problem-solving skills (Calao et al., 2015).

Synthesizing the Opportunities

Within highly digital 21st century learning spaces and amidst a rise in curriculum initiatives for CS, it is increasingly important for K–12 teachers to be comfortable with CT and CS principles. Constructionism provides a unique pathway by which learners can create meaningful experiences that have been shown to hold the capacity to cultivate understanding and sustained engagement (Ackermann, 2001; Papert & Harel, 1991; Przbylla, 2014; Wilkerson-Jerde, 2014). While the use of design-centered, project-based learning has a long history, its potential for engaging in-service teachers in complex technical fields such as AI and data science—and the potential for this engagement to provoke learning gains in CS—is largely unknown. In this study, we seek to better understand the potential of constructionist design methods in combination with AI tools as points of entry in developing an understanding of programming among in-service teachers.

Artificial Intelligence

AI is a concept and field with complex technical, social, and philosophical facets. Philosophically and practically, AI is about the design of systems which approximate rational or human reasoning or automate rational or human actions (Russell & Norvig, 2016). Technically, the field of AI spans hundreds of approaches and boasts thousands of applications—advancing at a rate that outpaces academic journal publication cycles (Hawley, 2019). Societally, what constitutes AI is an ever-changing target whose wow-factor technologies are gradually taken for granted as they become accepted and integrated into daily life.

Within education, AI has been used as a tutor, a teachable agent, an adaptive evaluator, and to promote a range of specialized services (DeNisco, 2019; Pierce & Hathaway, 2018; Sora & Sora, 2012). Much of the current literature advocates the implementation of AI as a dynamic classroom assistant that provides a service to students. Examples of such agents can be seen along a spectrum of functionality, from learning management systems that incorporate choice as part of the learning process, to adaptive or intelligent agents that respond to student input (Bulger, 2016).

Even when specific educational outcomes are not at the forefront, AI is used in campus and district security systems, as well as for data analysis and task automation. Institutions are leveraging data and AI to calculate dropout intentions, course recommendations, student disposition, and final grades for student, educator, and administrative use (Rovira et al., 2017; Lykourentzou et al., 2009). Pierce and Hathaway (2018), for instance, employed AI and machine learning techniques to evaluate websites for institution-level appropriateness filtering and blacklisting, allowing their systems to go beyond simple keyword filtering or specific site blocking.

METHODS AND DATA COLLECTION

Research Design and Procedure

In this chapter we focus our inquiry on the use of AI as a gateway to learning about CS concepts and through that learning conceiving a role for AI in the classroom. Specifically we ask, "To what extent can a graduate course on AI support content-area teachers in better understanding the role of AI in their teaching and how does this affect their relationship with computer science?" This inquiry is the continuation of a research line that explores the role of design, problem based learning, and social constructionist interactions play in supporting preservice and in-service teachers in making new types of learning possible via technology and human centered design.

Description of the Course

In the Fall of 2015, the first author began designing a course on the use of AI, application programming interfaces (API), and data in the design of learning experiences. Since then, he has taught three sections of the course (i.e., during the Spring of 2016, 2018, and 2019). Given the growing ubiquity of AI in our society, the course was designed out of a perceived need to support educators in joining conversations and debates about the role of AI and data in education as well as using the course as a way for teachers to leverage their existing pedagogical and disciplinary knowledge to design new types of AI and data-supported learning experiences.

In TEAC 882D—Data Science and Artificial Intelligence in the Design of Learning, students survey the field of AI—from computational linguistics to machine learning and from the blockchain to APIs and cloud-based services. In most cases, students in the course are educators who have deep disciplinary and pedagogical expertise but have limited experience considering the role of AI, data, and CS in education. Weekly course modules consisted of three to seven readings, two to five videos, two to four simulations or interactive experiences, and an expectation that students engage with a subset of the offered materials that most aligned with their interests. By the next class, each student was expected to represent their experiences interacting with the week's content via the design of a multimodal slide in that week's Google slide deck. Student slides included key quotes, memes, links to additional articles, videos, simulations, and as the semester went on, data visualizations, AI platform experiments, and, eventually, code snippets and design mockups.

By the ninth week of the semester, readings and interactive content changed from instructor-curated to student-selected materials related to their self-selected design projects. These projects served as authentic gateways toward deepened engagement with the relevant data repositories and AI tools. In most cases, multiple platforms, tools, and repositories offer overlapping services—allowing students to experiment with more than one to identify which platform's graphical user interface, code tutorials, or which API's code examples were the most accessible to them.

Although students are not required to have any previous knowledge of CS concepts and their final project need not be something they fully develop, in the process of interacting with weekly course modules and designing their final project they regularly conduct proof-of-concept testing that often requires that they interact with existing code via reading, editing, or rewriting/programming it with the support of tutorials or code sandboxes.

Final projects, formed at the intersection of teacher technological, pedagogical, and content knowledge (TPACK; Mishra & Koehler, 2006) and available data repositories and artificial intelligence tools, have taken many forms. Student designs from TEAC 882D have been implemented in classrooms in Nebraska and have formed the basis for internal and external funding proposals, student research, and collaborative learning experiences.

Participants

We reached out via email to former TEAC 882D students who were in-service or certified teachers at the time they took the course and inquired as to their willingness to participate in a study focused on their experiences in

TABLE 14.1 Participant Demographics

Pseudonyms	Gender Identity	Ethnicity	Subject Taught	Years Teaching
Jane	Woman	White	English	15
Rachael	Woman	White	English & History	23
Patrick	Man	White	Sixth Grade Self Contained	11
Jasmine	Woman	White	Science	16
Marcus	Man	White	Social Studies	1

TEAC 882D and how those experiences influenced their past and present use of and attitudes toward AI and CS in their lives and in the classroom. Content area teachers enrolled in graduate programs at the university where TEAC 882D is taught have a great deal of latitude regarding which courses they take at both the masters and doctoral levels. Most stated their interest in technology and intrigue regarding AI as their rationale for taking the course. Available resources and participant interest allowed us the opportunity to work with five teachers (see Table 14.1).

Data Collection and Analysis

The study draws on qualitative, ethnographic methodologies to inquire into the extent to which a graduate course supported students in learning about CS concepts as a latent benefit of working to complete weekly course assignments and a final design project in AI and K–12 learning. We use grounded theory to analyze the semi-structured interviews we conducted with five in-service and certified teachers (Strauss & Corbin, 1998; Weiss, 1995).

Data collection took place in the Summer of 2019 in Eastern Nebraska. In order to understand the extent to which participation in a graduate course on AI impacted their relationship with CS, members of our research team conducted semi-structured interviews with in-service and certified teachers who were students in one of three sections of the UNL course on AI, data, and learning [TEAC 882D]. We employed an iterative analytical approach (Anfara et al., 2002; Olmanson et al., 2016) wherein we conducted unit-coding of interview transcripts and artifacts in a qualitative research application called HyperRESEARCH. In all, a total of 398 unit level base codes were generated and assigned to portions of participant interview data and participant artifacts. For example, the interview transcript snippet of, "I was always interested in learning programming but thought it was just for math people" might be coded both as "participant interest in learning to program" *and* "participant self-assessment of math knowledge too low to learn programming." The work of unit coding was carried out by the group as a whole, with the first author taking the lead—overseeing the generation of each code as well as the assignation of each code to each portion of transcript and artifact data. Due to the involvement of the first author in each generated code and its assignment, inter-rater reliability was not measured.

Codes were then resized based on frequency and organized by topic on a 5760 pixel-wide 1060 pixel-high code mapping space within the research application. Once the unit codes were grouped by theme in the mapping space, we arranged them around key codes and moved them into proximity to other themes and subthemes. Within and between these organized groupings we identified and cultivated our findings.

DATA, RESULTS, AND DISCUSSION

We organize this section around the temporal themes of (a) participants' relationships to CS and AI prior to the course, (b) participants experiences with AI and CS learning during the course, and (c) participants' attitudes about and experiences with AI and CS since they completed the course. Our findings offer models for instruction and professional development for in-service teachers beginning the process of infusing computing ideas in their content areas. We particularly focus on findings related to CS; namely, the background and prior experiences of the participants, the dynamics between participants and the course curriculum and pedagogical approach, the role of programming in participant approaches to learning, and participant post-course perspectives and experiences with programming, CS, and AI.

AI-Curious but With CS Trepidations: Pre-Course Participant Relationships to CS and AI

In this study we interviewed content area teachers who took a course in AI in education. The participants were not former CS majors or CS teachers. Most of them were concerned that their lack of a CS background would hold them back in the course and single them out as less capable than their peers. While the majority of participants mentioned a willingness to explore and try things out as part of their approach to learning, they nonetheless held trepidations about taking a course they viewed as technically complex.

Three of the five participants reported an affinity for technology and for figuring things out on their own. Jasmine, a high school biology teacher, when asked about her disposition toward technology said, "I think maybe I'm just a little more comfortable in those areas, I'm just ready to go out and learn stuff, technical stuff." Along those same lines, Marcus, a former social studies teacher said, "With computers, I'm not afraid to touch, tinker, and try and fix something or try and understand what I'm seeing in front of me."

Two of the five participants had taken a prior CS course but, in both cases, they were several decades removed from those experiences. "I took a semester of Basic programming when I was in HS [high school] . . . it was my junior year of HS, so probably 1979 or 1980," said Patrick, a sixth grade self-contained and middle school history teacher who came to teaching after a career in the U.S. military. In Jasmine's case she said the Java course she took in 1997 didn't make her feel connected or excited about the field, saying, "To me [the Java course] was 'make a red circle on your screen and get it checked off by the TA' and it just didn't really speak to me." Additionally, Jane, a middle school English teacher mentioned that she learned HTML in a high school physics class in the 1990s.

Alternatively, Marcus had no CS coursework in his background saying, "I mean programming was always something that I thought was interesting, but not something that I ever thought I would get into." When we asked Rachael, a middle school English and social studies teacher, about the extent of her familiarity with technology prior to the course she said that she and her students only did "basic" things and that "there was no interaction on the computer except for writing papers and turning them in." In terms of Rachael having any interest in CS before the course she said, "No, not at all, I wouldn't even know where to start, as you remember, in the very first class I tried to quit, but that's a different story."

Participants reported feeling excited to learn about AI and data but most were simultaneously concerned that they would be the student with the least amount of CS knowledge and, consequently, the least equipped to participate in, and benefit from, course activities. Given that most of these participants were also technology leaders in their schools and districts, more exposure to CT and CS in their teacher education programs and continuing education credit hours may have allayed their concerns and increased their confidence to participate. Nonetheless, it appears that mere exposure to CS in any format, may not always be sufficient in building teacher knowledge and confidence given the way several participants characterized their prior experiences with CS as impersonal, disconnected, and tangential.

In-Course Participant Experiences With CS and AI

Student Agency via Peer-Sharing

Once the course got underway and students realized they were not the only non-programmer they tended to feel less anxious about their lack of programming background. Marcus pointed to how sharing the experience with non-programmer peers was helpful, saying, "[It] didn't really feel like anyone came in knowing what they were doing. So each week we all kind of tackled these readings and these big questions together . . . what definitely helped me was having a group of people that were trying to do the same thing."

Meaningful interaction with AI platforms and APIs was delayed based on not knowing where to start. Participants identified this as the primary psychological obstacle that needed to be overcome before they could "dive in" and interact with the more CS and technical aspects of course content. A dearth of previous exposure to programming and data science seemed to influence otherwise exploration-oriented learners to hold back.

Jasmine was one of the first students in her class to share the results and process of her exploration efforts in her weekly slide. While she started with services on platforms that offered menu-driven graphical user interfaces like Dialogflow, IBM Watson, and Microsoft Azure, she said she soon found that she "would probably need to know code to" accomplish her design goals. Attempts to gain literacy or familiarity in a programming language which Jasmine called "knowing code" was a common practice among participants that was undertaken at varying levels of effort and at different times during the course. In describing her process of using tutorials and API documentation Jasmine said, "I almost always would try to find the code out there and model it or edit it to make it my own."

By the end of the semester, Jasmine designed a chatbot to support middle school students in refining their initial science fair ideas. She said she used "trial and error. I signed up for Google [Cloud] first, [then] Dialog Flow and started playing around. As I learned, I started hitting walls and jumped to other tools. I ended up diving into Microsoft's tools and LUIS with language understanding . . . [And then,] with Watson, I just kind of dove in and started making things from scratch."

For Marcus, both knowing that his classmates were novices and seeing examples of their attempts to interact with course content impacted his willingness to engage with AI platforms, APIs, and code. In reference to seeing the results of peer explorations in the weekly shared slide deck, he said, "They found something that they thought was interesting and wanted to share it with everyone else, it was empowering. I would definitely say, seeing other people dive in headfirst made it a little bit easier for me to start trying to figure out things."

Overall, participants pointed to the level of agency they were given within the course, specifically, the open-endedness of the weekly and final assignments and the collaborative organization of class time. The open-ended, distributed constructionist pedagogical approach of the course was seen as a boon for meaningful learning. Multiple optional readings per week and encouragement that students read and explore in the direction of their interests, sharing their exploration in the weekly slide deck, final projects, and guest speakers were pointed to as gateways to exploring affinities and ideas at the intersection of AI, CS, and their content areas.

"The autonomy and self-directed learning [in the course was] huge, I really thrive on those," Jasmine said.

Accustomed to more structured learning experiences, Rachael described the course as a perfect storm for learning, saying, "We would start something and I would have an impression of what it was going to look like or where we were going with it. But then it would change and it would be okay and there were possibilities rather than so much structure. The possibility that it would morph into something else was okay and so that was part of the [perfect] storm."

Yet, autonomy and enthusiasm on their own were not enough to overcome feelings of being overwhelmed by novelty and complexity. To use an analogy, trying a routine on an AI cloud service or editing and running an API code snippet for the first time seemed to be a lot like working up the nerve to jump off of a high diving board for the first time. In other words, there was often prolonged hesitation overcome by a combination of in-class demonstrations and, interestingly, peer sharing. While in-class activities supported initial exploration, participants pointed to the weekly shared Google slides experience as a key contributor to the growth of feelings of adequacy and empowerment. Each report of a peer's successful tinkering or discovery encouraged their classmates to tinker and discover for themselves. Over the semester, the slides became a platform for showcasing their experimentation and brainstorming next steps. Across participants, the slides did not act as a missing blueprint for how to do something but rather as permission to try things in spite of not knowing exactly what they were doing.

Code-Construct Connections

One of the primary ways, Marcus relates, that he learned once he dove in and started experimenting was via his early interaction with the Wolfram Alpha API. This API affords computational knowledge query answering via a few lines of code. "In the beginning when we first started working with Wolfram Alpha I was able to create a little Python script that [asked] it a question and it would reach out to the website and give a response," Marcus said,

> So the wheels started turning there, where you have this API that someone could potentially type a question in and you get a response back. What was great was that if you wanted to edit it or adjust it for your own means you'd change a couple of lines or add a word or two and hope it worked. [What] I started noticing is that, as a social studies teacher, a lot of websites like CNN and *The New York Times* or *New York Post* or things like that, they all have these APIs that were able to grab information.

Jane, who designed a portal to connect student Genius Hour questions (e.g., "How does screen time effect mood?"; "Does air quality affect happiness?"; "What are the best ways to stop the spread of viruses?") with individuals with the relevant expertise via her LinkedIn network, said,

> [Designing the final project] stretched me a lot. It started to make me think about how different platforms and things integrate with each other and education, it just really started getting me to think about different ways to use technology, AI, and APIs in the classroom.

While participants used a variety of approaches to build and apply their CT skills toward learning CS and using AI, editing existing code was one of the primary avenues reported as a gateway to understanding the potential of data and AI tools in education. Patrick described editing code during the third week of the course, saying, "It was very exciting. It was one of those self actualization moments—look what I've done, look, what I'm capable of learning and doing." Reading and editing example code might be seen as an example of scaffolded learning, Vygotsky's zone of proximal development (Wood & Wood, 1996), legitimate peripheral participation (Lave & Wenger, 1991), tinkering (Bevan et al., 2015), and as building technology knowledge within the TPACK framework (Mishra & Koehler, 2006). Although participants did not see code editing as legitimate CS, it was a gateway to increased engagement with programming and CS principles.

Participant data suggests a code-construct connection. In other words, there was a reciprocally beneficial relationship between students exploring and learning about specific AI tools and APIs and learning about and using the programming elements that enabled the exploration. Moreover, understanding how the API worked required interacting with it—in turn this prompted interaction with the underlying code. Learning how to interact with the code not only brought a better understanding of programming, but also a better understanding of how APIs worked.

Design > Development

Describing the focus of his efforts to create a bibliography-building chatbot for history students, Marcus said,

> Eventually participant projects that centered on development instead of design hit a wall: I got so bogged down that I wanted XYZ to work. It took me a long time to get over that and just think of what possibilities are available [and] what's able to be created…I felt like it was something that was inaccessible, I don't have a CS degree. I'm just a history teacher with a little bit of computer experience.

Similarly, Patrick, who designed an attendance application for schools based on computer vision said,

I think it was two weekends before the course ended. I was working on that final project and I had returned to Azure, and I was trying to learn how to do or repeat what I had done [previously]. I know I put probably 12 hours in over a weekend trying to relearn that with the tutorials that Azure offers and I just wasn't able to connect those dots at that point. It was frustrating.

He went on to connect some of his frustrations to his lack of formal CS training and his perceived skills in comparison to his peers, saying, "I felt that everybody in the [class] could code but me. So I felt like I was trying to make up for things that I didn't know." Jasmine also felt that the time required to gain familiarity with the tools and the underlying computing principles in order to develop a working application was more than she could do, saying, "The idea of using API's and pulling in real data is powerful, but it's still a step away from being accessible to a busy teacher."

Participant Post-Course Reflections on CS, AI, and TEAC 882D

Frustrations and challenges on their final projects due to limited participant CS background knowledge and understanding when working with AI tools and APIs—and the CS principles that enable them—however did not lead to an aversion to engaging with CS in the future. All five participants said they felt taking TEAC 882D brought them closer to CS concepts including programming. Patrick said, "I've gone back to Azure and downloaded their 'you can learn this in a month of lunches' booklet. That's one of the things on my shortlist to get done over the summer." Jasmine said, "As nerdy as it sounds, I think I would also do it for fun in my spare time, I want to learn more about the computer science concepts."

Participants have gone on to apply the AI, API, and CS concepts learned in TEAC 882D in their classrooms and schools. Rachael used APIs with her students as they completed a cross-disciplinary unit on natural disasters. Jane supported Genius Hour students when they needed to learn programming skills to accomplish their projects. Jasmine reviewed several district vendors and recommended her district purchase learning software that leverages data and intelligent tutoring in support of student literacy development. Additionally, Jasmine, Patrick, and Marcus all stated an interest in designing learning experiences that use data and AI tools in support of learning. Jasmine, in fact, wondered if only that Java course she took 20 years ago had been more personally meaningful and constructionist she might have majored in CS, saying, "[The TEAC 882D experience] unfortunately makes me feel wistful, like I would have done really well in computer science. So, you know, it feels a little tragic."

Rachael, whose interactive, API-populated, history timeline is still used by her district 3 years after she designed it as her final course project, reported that despite her lack of experience or interest in CS concepts prior to the course, she approached administrators regarding teaching CS, saying, "After taking [TEAC 882D], there are coding [initiatives] happening in [my district] that were just starting up and I requested my principal allow me to go into coding rather than stay in social studies."

DISCUSSION

In this study we found that student-selected, distributed constructionist approaches to learning about data and AI offered latent benefits to students (i.e., in-service teachers) in the form of a more positive outlook on CS, an interest in engaging with CS principles, and an ability to understand how those principles enable the development of new learning technologies. Specifically, participants stated that effective elements of the course included the fore-fronting of student exploration, sharing, and the open-ended final project. Moreover, in-service teachers who participated in the study were also able to apply CS principles directly and indirectly in their classrooms, campuses, and districts.

These findings have implications in that they suggest additional ways *in* to the field of CS, particularly for classroom teachers. First, design-centric, affinity-based, constructionist pedagogical approaches to learning were well received and seen as non-alienating pathways toward CS learning among participating educators. Such pathways, in positioning CS as an enabling element within a larger course that is contextualized by student interests and expertise, offer generative reasons for engaging with CS.

Second, participant trepidation to engage with code due to a lack of CS understanding was, for several participants, overcome when they witnessed peer experiences with content and code via the weekly shared Google slide deck. Consistent peer sharing diminished feelings of not being ready to engage with code and content due to a lack of experience and supported risk taking.

Third, in the course of their design work, generative engagement with AI-related tools put them in contact with the underlying code (e.g., APIs). This appeared to have a bi-directionally beneficial impact. Understanding the potential of APIs for science, math, or social studies learning is a complex, synthetic endeavor that most students did not fully appreciate until they edited the code that made up the API query and viewed the returned results. The need to edit the code and view results led to conceptual understanding gains that had little to do with the syntax of the code itself. Likewise, the need to engage with an API required the participants to interact with code and take note of programming features and conventions.

Fourth, the balance between participants gaining insights into the design of their idea via developing it, while recognizing when they reached a point of diminishing returns in their attempts at development proved difficult to maintain. Once students engaged with the data, platforms, tools, and ideas of their project—and the accompanying underlying code they often spent hours attempting to get one facet to work at the expense of more robustly designing their application/project.

Fifth, the holistic experience of the course led to participants seeking out further opportunities to learn and interact with CS tools and principles despite identifying no or little such interest in doing so prior to the course.

Overall, this study suggests that in-service teachers with a strong background in content and pedagogy as well as a lived understanding of the nature/culture of schooling and the classroom can indeed design and prototype learning technologies based on complex CS-driven technologies. Moreover, teacher educators can leverage such practices in offering alternative, perhaps less alienating, pathways for learning CS. Table 14.2

TABLE 14.2   Study Recommendations Based on Participant Dynamics and Pre-Study Course Instructional Practices

Participant Dynamic	Existing Instructional Approach	Course Changes Based on Study Recommendations
Student concerned they don't know enough, or concerned they know less than others	Weekly paired peer discussion	Keep and expand to 2–3 pair discussions per class
	Multimodal slide sharing	Keep and ensure slides are forefronted each class
		Assign this book chapter as Week 1 reading
Student unsure where to start and hesitant to begin	Pre-class explorations	Keep and align demos and explorations with student domain expertise
	In-class modeling/demos	
	Multimodal slide sharing	Keep and ensure slides are forefronted each class
Nonexistent or negative prior experiences with CS	CS positioned as not a prerequisite to the course	Further position CS as enabling but not primary
	Student-identified problem used as a gateway to CS	Keep and add student tech/CS office/lab hours to ensure ample student support
Conceptually complex elements (e.g., APIs) difficult to fully understand	Course readings & videos	Keep and ensure alignment across readings, videos, tutorials, demos, and student tinkering
	In-class tutorials & demos	
	Student tinkering	Implement the use of an IDE for python
		Add computational thinking focus and extend demos with scaffolded challenges
Lack of balance between design and development	Encourage code tinkering	Keep and add discussion regarding the benefits of tinkering with a design focus

outlines and connects participant dynamics with pedagogical and curricular elements of the course.

NEXT STEPS

This study has been a catalyst for course redesign recommendations on a curricular and instructional scale. Based on the findings and discussion section above, next steps involve redesigning the course in order to integrate the recommended instructional strategies and modifications (see Table 14.2). While the course changes listed above form a part of the instructional redesign, engagement with the research literature on the integration of CS principles and CT in K–12 spaces and with K–12 teachers as well as participant data informed curricular shifts in the course. Previously, beginning with Week 2, course content and class activities were both focused on a weekly tour of AI subdomains and the tools and data that supported each subdomain (e.g., Machine Learning, TensorFlow, and compatible datasets; Natural Language Processing, Natural Language Toolkit, project Gutenberg dataset). Based on participant reports of leveraging their domain knowledge and pedagogical expertise as a gateway to design ideas and AI, data, and CS learning we have identified an organizing focus in alignment with that (see Figure 14.1).

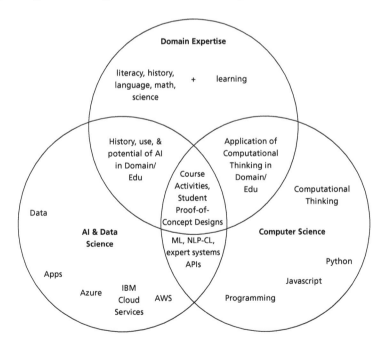

Figure 14.1 Venn diagram of redesigned course organization.

Our findings demonstrate that students enter AI and data science as well as CS through the lens of education, learning, and their specific domain, as represented by the top circle in Figure 14.1. By emphasizing entry through points of familiarity, some of the noted discomfort and uncertainty hurdles may be overcome for course participants, allowing for an even greater possibility that they will venture beyond their domains in the future.

Moving forward, in Week 1 of the course students will read this current book chapter as a way to better understand the experiences of their peers who took the course before them and the course's curricular evolution. In Week 2, readings and videos on AI, data, and CS will be more tightly coupled with learning and education. Previously, students watched some videos on the history of AI and then jumped into learning about APIs and Natural Language Processing and the tools and data of that subfield. In future iterations, students will watch three 10 minute videos that introduce AI, CS, and CT. They will read Luckin et al.'s (2016) *Intelligence Unleashed: An argument for AI in Education* as well as Liu et al.'s (2008) article on APIs in education. These two articles connect AI and data with education and learning contexts that are familiar to students.

Additionally, students will read Grover & Pea's (2013) article on CT in K–12—thus bridging education and CS. While they read, they will be tasked with asking, "In what ways does computational thinking apply to my domain? And, what is the data of my domain?" They will also spend 10 minutes or more exploring a browser-based python interpreter that comes preloaded with a program they can edit and execute. Penultimately, students will make a multimodal slide that captures their thoughts and experiences with the content. We anticipate that by further connecting the student learning experiences with their domain expertise, students may move more naturally into interacting with code. Finally, the next steps on the programming side of the course include the use of a professional integrated development environment (IDE) for python (e.g., PyCharm) as a way to more robustly scaffold student growth and experimentation with python libraries and API packages.

In terms of next steps, while five in-service teacher-participants may be a modest number, the noted bidirectional benefit of (a) learning to code as a way to understand data science concepts; and (b) exploring data science concepts as a way to better understand programming, merits further investigation. Moreover, in-service content area teachers, within a supportive environment can indeed successfully participate in a CS-focused course as they design learning experiences at the intersection of data science, AI, and their content areas. Thus, increasing support for earlier student engagement with programming within the course via the above-mentioned strategies may deepen student understanding and encourage experimentation and risk-taking. Better understanding and enhancing the latent benefits and further ameliorating the challenges participant identified are the focus of our next round of scholarship of teaching and learning related to TEAC 882D.

REFERENCES

Ackermann, E. (2001). Piaget's constructivism, Papert's constructionism: What's the difference? *Future of Learning Group.* http://www.sylviastipich.com/wp-content/uploads/2015/04/Coursera-Piaget-_-Papert.pdf

Anfara, V. A., Jr., Brown, K. M., & Mangione, T. L. (2002). Qualitative analysis on stage: Making the research process more public. *Educational Researcher, 31*(7), 28–38.

Angeli, C., Voogt, J., Fluck, A., Webb, M., Cox, M., Malyn-Smith, J., & Zagami, J. (2016). A K–6 computational thinking curriculum framework: Implications for teacher knowledge. *Journal of Educational Technology & Society, 19*(3), 47–57.

Barr, V., & Stephenson, C. (2011). Bringing computational thinking to K–12: What is involved and what is the role of the computer science education community? *ACM Inroads, 2*(1), 48–54.

Bell, T., & Lodi, M. (2019). Constructing computational thinking without using computers. *Constructivist Foundations, 14*(3), 342–351.

Bevan, B., Gutwill, J. P., Petrich, M., & Wilkinson, K. (2015). Learning through STEM-rich tinkering: Findings from a jointly negotiated research project taken up in practice. *Science Education, 99*(1), 98–120.

Bulger, M. (2016). Personalized learning: The conversations we're not having. *Data and Society, 22*(1), 1–29.

Calao, L. A., Moreno-León, J., Correa, H. E., & Robles, G. (2015). Developing mathematical thinking with scratch. In G. Conole, T. Klobučar, C. Rensing, J. Konert, & E. Lavoué (Eds.), *Design for teaching and learning in a networked world* (pp. 17–27). Springer International Publishing.

DeNisco, A. (2019). Adding AI instruction readies students for the future. *District Administration, 55*(4), 12–12.

Falkner, K., Vivian, R., & Williams, S. A. (2018). An ecosystem approach to teacher professional development within computer science. *Computer Science Education, 28*(4), 303–344. https://doi.org/10.1080/08993408.2018.1522858

Feurzeig, W., Papert, S., Bloom, M., Grant, R., & Solomon, C. (1969). Programming-languages as a conceptual framework for teaching mathematics (NSF-C 558 No. 13, p. 5). National Science Foundation.

Google, & Gallup. (2016). *Trends in the state of computer science in U.S. K–12 schools.*

Grover, S., & Pea, R. (2013). Computational thinking in K–12: A review of the state of the field. *Educational Researcher, 42*(1), 38–43.

Hawley, S. H. (2019). Challenges for an ontology of artificial intelligence. *Perspectives on Science, 71*(2), 83–93.

ISTE. (2011). *Computational thinking in K–12 education: Leadership toolkit.* https://cdn.iste.org/www-root/2020-10/ISTE_CT_Leadership_Toolkit_booklet.pdf

Kale, U., Akcaoglu, M., Cullen, T., Goh, D., Devine, L., Calvert, N., & Grise, K. (2018). Computational what? Relating computational thinking to teaching.

TechTrends: Linking research & practice to improve learning, 62(6), 574–584. https://doi.org/10.1007/s11528-018-0290-9

Kalelioglu, F., Gülbahar, Y., & Kukul, V. (2016). A framework for computational thinking based on a systematic research review. *Baltic Journal of Modern Computing, 4*(3), 583.

Lave, J., & Wenger, E. (1991). *Situated learning: Legitimate peripheral participation.* Cambridge University Press.

Liu, M., Horton, L., Olmanson, J., & Wang, P. Y. (2008). An exploration of mashups and their potential educational uses. *Computers in the Schools, 25*(3/4), 243–258.

Luckin, R., Holmes, W., Griffiths, M., & Corcier, L. B. (2016). *Intelligence unleashed: An argument for AI in education.* Pearson.

Lykourentzou, I., Giannoukos, I., Mpardis, G., Nikolopoulos, V., & Loumos, V. (2009). Early and dynamic student achievement prediction in e-learning courses using neural networks. *Journal of the American Society for Information Science & Technology, 60*(2), 372–380.

Mishra, P., & Koehler, M. J. (2006). Technological pedagogical content knowledge: A framework for teacher knowledge. *Teachers College Record, 108*(6), 1017–1054.

Newell, A., Perlis, A. J., & Simon, H. A. (1967). Computer science. *Science, 157*(3795), 1373–1374.

NGSS Lead States. (2013). *Next Generation Science Standards: For states, by states.* http://www.nextgenscience.org

Olmanson, J., Kennett, K., Magnifico, A., McCarthey, S., Searsmith, D., Cope, B., & Kalantzis, M. (2016). Visualizing revision: Leveraging student-generated between-draft diagramming data in support of academic writing development. *Technology, Knowledge and Learning, 21*(1), 99–123.

Ozturk, Z., Dooley, C. M., & Welch, M. (2018). Finding the hook: Computer science education in elementary contexts. *Journal of Research on Technology in Education, 50*(2), 149–163.

Papert, S. (1980). *Mindstorms: Children, computers, and powerful ideas.* Basic Books.

Papert, S., & Harel, I. (1991). Situating constructionism. In I. Harel & S. Papert (Eds.), *Constructionism: Research reports and essays, 1985–1990* (p. 13). Ablex Publishing.

Pierce, D., & Hathaway, A. (2018). The promise (and pitfalls) of AI for education: Artificial intelligence could have a profound impact on learning, but it also raises key questions. *THE Journal, 45*(3), 21–22.

Przybylla, M., & Romeike, R. (2014). Physical computing and its scope—Towards a constructionist computer science curriculum with physical computing. *Informatics in Education, 13*(2), 241–254.

Rovira, S., Puertas, E., & Igual, L. (2017). Data-driven system to predict academic grades and dropout. *PLOS ONE, 12*(2), e0171207.

Russell, S., & Norvig, P. (2016). *Artificial intelligence: A modern approach.* Pearson.

Sora, J. C., & Sora, S. A. (2012). *Artificial education: Expert systems used to assist and support 21st century education: (525192013-002)* [Data set]. American Psychological Association.

Strauss, A., & Corbin, J. (1998). *Basics of qualitative research techniques.* SAGE Publications.

van Gog, T. (2006). *Uncovering the problem-solving process to design effective worked examples* [Unpublished doctoral dissertation]. Open University of the Netherlands.

Wang, J. (2017). Is the U.S. education system ready for CS for all? Insights from a recent Google-Gallup national research study seeking to better understand the context of K–12 CS education. *Communications of the ACM, 60*(8), 26–28.

Weiss, R. S. (1995). *Learning from strangers: The art and method of qualitative interview studies.* Simon and Schuster.

Wilkerson-Jerde, M. H. (2014). Construction, categorization, and consensus: Student generated computational artifacts as a context for disciplinary reflection. *Educational Technology Research and Development, 62*(1), 99–121.

Wing, J. M. (2006). Computational thinking. *Communications of the ACM, 49*(3), 33–35.

Wing, J. M. (2014). *Computational thinking benefits society.* 40th anniversary blog of social issues in computing, 2014, 26.

Wood, D., & Wood, H. (1996). Vygotsky, tutoring and learning. *Oxford Review of Education, 22*(1), 5–16.

Yadav, A., Gretter, S., Good, J., & McLean, T. (2017). Computational thinking in teacher education. In P. J. Rich & C. B. Hodges (Eds.), *Emerging research, practice, and policy on computational thinking* (pp. 205–220). Springer Nature.

Yadav, A., Gretter, S., Hambrusch, S., & Sands, P. (2016). Expanding computer science education in schools: Understanding teacher experiences and challenges. *Computer Science Education, 26*(4), 235–254.

Yadav, A., Krist, C., Good, J., & Caeli, E. N. (2018). Computational thinking in elementary classrooms: Measuring teacher understanding of computational ideas for teaching science. *Computer Science Education, 28*(4), 371–400.

CHAPTER 15

CREDENTIALING COMPUTATION

Empowering Teachers in Computational Thinking Through Educator Microcredentials

Quinn Burke
Digital Promise Global

Colin Angevine
Digital Promise

Chris Proctor
University at Buffalo

Josh Weisgrau
Digital Promise

Kerri Ann O'Donnell
Swampscott School District

Professional Development for In-Service Teachers, pages 341–360
Copyright © 2022 by Information Age Publishing
www.infoagepub.com
All rights of reproduction in any form reserved.

ABSTRACT

This chapter details Digital Promise's development and implementation of educator micro-credentials (MCs) in computational thinking (CT). The chapter is divided into three sections. The first section details Digital Promise's development of educator MCs in CT both in terms of relevant concepts (e.g., students' understanding & creating algorithms) and best pedagogical practices (e.g., effectively assessing CT). The development process detailed in Part I is framed by the wider backdrop on competency-based education in the United States. The second part, details the implementation of the MC model and highlights select MC submissions from participating educators. The third and final part looks ahead to the future of CT MCs as an increasingly viable means for educators to demonstrate instructional mastery in the area of CT. Given the remarkable national demand for CS/CT instruction, there is an imperative for alternative models and pathways for CS/CT teacher preparation. The chapter closes examining the future potential of MCs as a means to teacher professional learning and as an alternative pathway for for statewide teacher endorsement and certification in CS/CT education.

Demand for K–12 CS Constrained by Teacher Shortage

According to the national non-profit Code.org, to date, a total of 33 states have enacted computer science (CS) standards for their K–12 public schools, and 44 states have implemented at least one policy related to CS education in K–12 schools. Nine more states are in the process of developing statewide CS standards. In addition, 35 states have established teacher certification and/or endorsements in CS for teachers (Code.org, 2019a). While states are certainly moving at different paces, there is a national trend among state departments of education to mobilize CS and CT efforts. As highlighted in a report commissioned by Google (Proctor & Blikstein, 2018), K–12 CS education has gained tremendous ground just over the past 5 years. What was once considered an erudite, even arcane, technical skill is now promoted as a fundamental 21st century literacy.

The same Google report, however, also points to a series of systemic obstacles for future growth. Perhaps the most prominent of these obstacles—and an obstacle directly mentioned by all fourteen interviewees in the Google report—is scaling effective teacher development. The national teacher shortage (Economic Policy Institute, 2019) has only exacerbated the lack of qualified teachers who can teach or integrate CS and CT into their classroom instruction. Remarkably, despite the pressing economic need and states' growing efforts, less than two-thirds of K–12 schools still offer any CS based curricula, and fewer than 10% of school districts nationally have developed meaningful pathways incorporating computational thinking (CT) across the K–8 grade levels (ECS, 2017; Sahami, 2016). While there is an assortment of coding and CT related tools available to schools, teachers are not prepared to systematically implement CT-integrated curricula and assessment within classrooms. This is especially problematic on the K–8 level, where CT can potentially offer rich possibilities for integrating computing into existing disciplines (e.g., Burke, 2016; Proctor & Blikstein, 2018), ranging from math to science to English language arts. According to the 2018 National Survey of Science and Mathematics Education, while thousands of teachers with existing licensure in other disciplines have undertaken teaching CS coursework, little more than half (56%) have any credentials specific to teaching CS.

Preparing More CS Teachers Is Difficult

The gap between high demand for K–12 CS coursework and the dearth of qualified teachers suggests that we ought to be training more instructors and developing formal processes for endorsing and certifying such instructors. This point has been reiterated by recent studies (Proctor & Blikstein, 2018; Yadav et al., 2016), though the ongoing challenge for recruiting such teachers stems back to Gal-Ezer and Stephenson's (2010) identification of two primary barriers to increased K–12 CS teacher preparation: "A lack of clarity, understanding, and consistency with regard to current certification requirements, and a lack of connection between existing certification requirements and the actual content of the discipline" (p. 62). As an emerging field without a clear and consistent definition, CS is frequently shoehorned into different parts of the existing K–12 disciplinary taxonomy. Often, this is in terms of mathematics, where CS is conceived as "grounded math" applying algorithms and algebraic principles such as Boolean Logic to functional programs; more often however, the connection between CS and other disciplines is far more tenuous—as multiple school districts and state departments of education have incorrectly considered graphic design and even keyboarding as veritable CS offerings (Burke, 2016). When no subject-specific credential for CS exists, it is difficult to marshal the necessary resources to prepare teachers for the specific challenges of teaching. But without full-time CS teacher job openings, there is perceived little demand for CS teacher preparation coursework. The result is a persistent "chicken vs. egg" dilemma facing states, in which teacher certification standards, teacher preparation programs, definition and requirement of CS coursework, and teacher job openings are unable to advance without coordinated efforts across the entire system (Code.org, 2017; Guzdial, 2015).

The Potential to Train Existing Teachers?

The United States has over 1,200 schools, colleges and departments of education, and teacher education programs exist in 78% of all universities and colleges (Levine, 2007; Worrel et al., 2014). The educational technology course is required by approximately 80% of initial teacher licensure programs across the United States (Ottenbreit-Leftwich et al., 2012). And while this course could be particularly well-suited as a potential integration point for incorporating CS and CT into pre-service education coursework (e.g., Mouza et al., 2018; Yadav et al., 2014), still only very few programs (Michigan State University, Saint Scholastica, and Indiana University, among others) have done so. While these early models give reason to be optimistic that U.S. teacher preparation infrastructure will eventually be able to prepare a growing numbers of K–12 CS teachers, there is more immediately the challenge of providing professional development (PD) to train existing teachers to teach CS. This goal has gained in popularity over the last decade, with PD generally aimed at high school teachers and delivered as summer courses or in-service workshops (Menekse, 2015). However, Meneske's (2015) review of K–12 CS teacher PD also found substantial variation in the goals of PD (interdisciplinary CT, CS content knowledge, and increasing diversity and accessibility of CS). What most had in common was their ineffectiveness at changing teacher practice—a measure, in fact, often left entirely unincorporated with numerous PD models. Meneske's analysis of teacher PD in the area of computing makes it clear that even though teachers may receive quality training, whether or not such training translates into improved classroom practice is not only *not* guaranteed but frequently entirely not assessed. This is highly problematic; for while it may be unsurprising that learning to effectively teach CS is multi-faceted and altogether difficult based on minimal PD (Yadav et al., 2016), such PD programs should nonetheless develop measures to assess whether their training leads to classroom implementation in the first place.

Micro-Credentials as Supportive of Training Teachers Already on the Job

This chapter posits educator micro-credentials (MCs) as a necessary next step for school districts to ensure qualified educators follow through on their efforts to integrate CS and CT into their classrooms, particularly on the K–8 level where CT offers the integrative potential to heighten existing coursework and activities in mathematics, science, music, ELA, and social studies. MCs are a timely solution as the U.S. K–12 schools clearly have a demonstrated need for more CS and CT instructors, as well as a more coherent means to endorse and certify instructors in these areas. MCs are a flexible solution with the capacity to fit into current teachers' (and schools') existing schedules, and they likewise address the isolation that instructors already teaching computing often face, working within a nontraditional academic discipline that colleagues often know little about. Moreover, MCs offer the opportunity to effectively measure and improve teacher practice by closely reviewing the content and quality of student projects and artifaces submitted by teachers as evidence of competency in the discipline. Once labeled as a decidedly "alternative" form of certification and endorsement, we, in fact, see educator MCs as a crucial solution to an identified problem of practice, and a solution that is both personalized and sustainable.

BACKGROUND

Brief Overview of CT

Before proceeding, it is worthwhile to first address the distinction between coding, CS, and CT. In its report "Computational Thinking for a Computational World," Digital Promise (2017) made the distinction between these concepts, using three co-centric circles to highlight where they overlap and stand uniquely apart (Figure 15.1).

While Digital Promise considers coding as a discrete technical skill and CS represents an academic discipline, CT is more challenging for K–12 schools to grasp and incorporate. Wing's 2006 formulation of CT as an essential skill represented an important call to action—yet, the persistent lack of clarity (and wider debate, see Grover's [2018] "A Tale of Two CTs") around

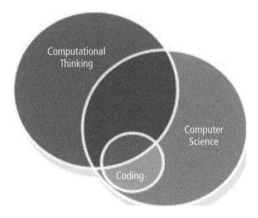

Figure 15.1 Distinguishing between CS as a discipline, coding as a skill, and CT as a process.

what exactly constitutes CT has left districts largely bereft of a meaningful definition. In practice, the oft-given (and largely off-hand) definitions of CT as "problem solving" and "thinking like a computer" are far too nebulous to predicate meaningful curricular and pedagogical action on the part of schools. On the other hand, treating CT simply as more end-user minded programming neglects to understand it in terms of logic and modeling and its integrative potential within other disciplines (Burke, 2016; Grover & Pea, 2018; Tedre & Denning, 2016). Altogether these competing points of view, while meaningful, can often make it challenging for states and school districts to set the goals and metrics needed to assess student learning. In response, some have argued that schools and districts will need to construct local understandings of CT embedded in their existing practices (Proctor et al., 2019) or that, like earlier debates over how to define literacy, there should be dialogue between multiple definitions of CT reflecting different pedagogical and even political priorities (Kafai et al., 2019; Vakil & Higgs, 2019). Faced with this challenge of a definition, Digital Promise based its own operational definition of CT in a series of competencies.

As evident from Figure 15.2, Digital Promise breaks its competency-driven definition of CT into the two categories of "Foundations" and "Practices." While Foundations focuses on the cognitive processes necessary to write computer programs, Practices combine the foundations with additional skills and knowledge to solve an applied problem, whether that

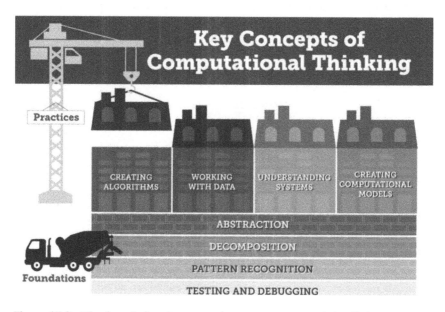

Figure 15.2 The foundational cross-cutting components and the distinct practices that result.

end result is a computer program, a better comprehension of a biological ecosystem, or an increased appreciation of how human migration patterns relate to geographical landscapes.

Brief Overview of Competency-Based Education

While Digital Promise's (2017) report "Computational Thinking for a Computational World" identifies key foundations and practices for integrating CT into existing curricula, its focus on discrete competencies also very much connects to the wider nature of competency-based education. Also referred to as "personalized learning," competency-based education (CBE) began to gain momentum in the United States in the late 1980s and early 1990s with K–12 schools and post-secondary programs beginning to focus on students demonstrating mastery in a particular set of skills and/ or knowledge (Hodge, 2007). Considered more learner-focused (and often learner-directed), CBE does not associate learning gains as necessarily correlative with time spent in a classroom (i.e., "time in a seat"), but rather through the effective demonstration of such mastery through the submission of sample work and/or demonstration (Johnstone & Soares, 2014). While CBE was originally conceived largely with students in mind, its underlying principles were recognized as also a means to certify and endorse teachers (see Serdenciuc, 2013) with programs such as the National Board for Professional Teaching Standards (NBPTS) issuing "National Board Certification" to educators who had demonstrated teaching proficiency through an extended portfolio of lessons and sample student projects. As a manifestation of CBE, educator MCs too rely on the demonstration of a specific competency and continue to grow as an alternative means for teachers to distinguish themselves for compensation, career advancement, and licensing (DeMonte, 2017).

THE DIGITAL PROMISE MODEL

Developing MCs for Computational Thinking

Since 2014, Digital Promise and its 40 content partners have developed over 300 MCs that address a variety of educator skills and competencies. These range from highly specific aspects of pedagogy (e.g., an MC in teacher "Wait Time" to help foster better instructional questioning) to more ambitious areas of instruction, such as "Creative Thinking and Innovation" and "Working With Data" (Kohl et al., 2018). There are a total of ten CT

MCs—five of which focus on CT practices and five of which focus on CT Pedagogies (Figure 15.3).

These ten CT MCs developed by Digital Promise are organized around the technological pedagogical content knowledge (TPACK) framework (Mishra & Koehler, 2006). This framework is an extension of pedagogical content knowledge (Shulman, 1987), the idea that knowledge of how discipline-specific learning can be effectively supported is a distinct domain from the content knowledge itself. Learning happens differently in different disciplines and being a domain expert does not imply that one is also an expert in helping others to learn in that domain. The TPACK framework extends this with the additional dimension of knowing how to effectively use technology to support discipline-specific pedagogy. Organizing these MCs around the three dimensions of TPACK allows them to support teachers of other disciplines in learning what CT is, how it can be effectively taught, and how technology can be effectively used to support teaching and learning CT within their disciplines.

The definition of CT adopted by these MCs relies on two recent National Research Council reports on the scope and nature of CT (NRC, 2010), as well as the pedagogical aspects of CT (NRC, 2011). It also incorporates Weintrop et al.'s (2017) synthesis of what CT means for secondary mathematics and science. Weintrop and his co-authors identified four primary domains of CT: data practices, modeling and simulation practices, computational problem-solving practices, and systems thinking practices. These align with four of the five MCs devoted to content knowledge. The fifth content-focused MC, on computational literacy, does not correspond to one of Weintrop et al.'s domains of CT in mathematics and science. The content of this MC is more closely aligned with the core concerns of the humanities and social sciences; namely, fostering students' capacity to approach computing as a means for communication and not just computation. To earn each of the first five MCs, teachers are required to demonstrate competency to show that their students are learning CT content. Successful student learning of CT content also suggests the presence of effective CT pedagogical strategies, as there are consistently mutual processes co-occurring at different levels in any learning environment. The assessments for content-focused MCs ask teachers to examine what the students are learning conceptually rather than highlight their own pedagogical strategies supporting the learning. When feasible, teachers are encouraged to pursue several MCs simultaneously. For example, a teacher might plan a sequence of lessons in which students design and test algorithms, while also mutually focusing on her assessment practices. This would enable the teacher to demonstrate competency for both the "Creating Algorithms" MC and the "Assessing Computational Thinking" MC.

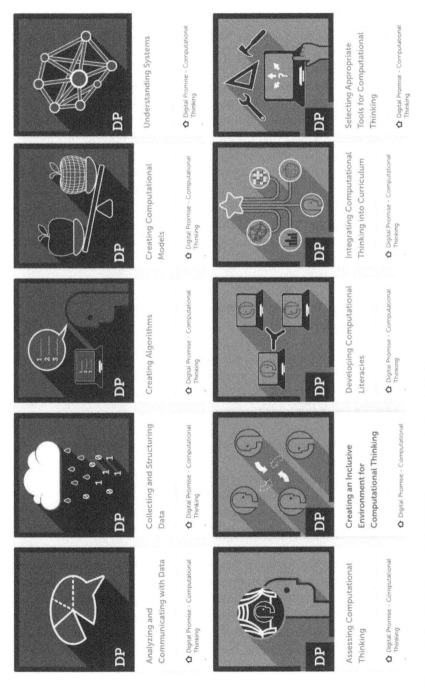

Figure 15.3 Digital promise's 10 MCs in computational thinking.

Three MCs specifically address pedagogical strategies particularly well-suited for supporting the learning of CT. These three MCs address creating equitable learning environments, using CT to explore the essential questions of a discipline, and assessing CT. Each of these pedagogical practices raises specific issues when applied to CT. Finally, TPACK is a particularly salient concern for CT, considering the close relationship between CT and computers. Digital Promise takes the stance (discussed further below) that programming and computers are excellent practices and tools for developing and using CT, but that they are not the only context in which CT can be used. As evident with Tim Bell's acclaimed CS Unplugged curricula (https://csunplugged.org/en/), screens are not mandatory to develop CT practices, especially at the earlier grade levels of elementary school. Therefore, the last two MCs address how computers can be powerful tools for learning, and engage teachers in the process of designing, or at the very least selecting, the computational tools that will optimally support their pedagogical practices.

The Process for Teachers' Demonstration of CT Competencies MCs

With its focus on foundations and practices, Digital Promise approaches CT comprehension by targeting single competencies with demonstrable evidence from classroom implementation. Participating instructors are asked to submit the following sources of evidence:

- a project or lesson plan, including evaluation guides or scoring rubrics;
- two to three student work samples (depending on the MC); and
- a page-long reflection from the instructor, reflecting on the challenges faced and lessons learned while planning and teaching; reflections should be supported by direct classroom observations.

These three sources of evidence are then evaluated by a minimum of two reviewers (external to Digital Promise) with specific content knowledge in CT. These reviewers individually analyze the three part submission, subsequently confer with each other with their independent reviews, and arrive at a final decision. Finally, one reviewer responds to the submitter with either a "Pass" or "No Pass" outcome. The reviewers also communicate specific feedback (within 300–500 words per Source of Evidence) as to where the individual submitter addressed (or fell short) of the respective criterion.

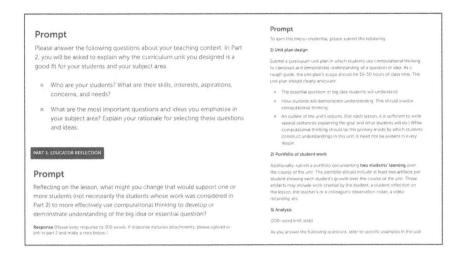

Figure 15.4   Three different prompts associated with an MC submission.

Sample MC Submissions

Perhaps most crucial to advancing MCs as a potential resource for credentialing teachers is seeing examples of teachers' MC submissions from a range of grade levels and content areas. This section highlights three such submissions.

The first is a submission from a ninth grade biology teacher who successfully earned the MC of "Analyzing and Communicating With Data." This MC asks teachers to demonstrate their competence in guiding students through computational approaches to analyzing and communicating with data to more richly investigate an identified question or problem. In this particular educator's submission, the instructor describes a project in which students conducted a science experiment of their choosing. The experiment itself was open game, though each student needed to submit a (a) topic question, (b) hypothesis, (c) procedure statement prior to approval, followed by (d) data reporting via a table and/ or graph, and finally (e) a conclusion discussing the results and hypothesis as well as next steps/ limitations. Throughout the lesson, the ninth grade biology instructor supported the students in using Google Docs and Google Sheets to analyze and present the findings from the experiment.

Artifacts of student work from this submission came by the way of spreadsheets from student submissions (see Figures 15.5 and 15.6). In Figure 15.5, students used computational tools to investigate questions related to what degree hours of sleep per night correlated to successful completion of a designated performance task the following day (in this case, answering 50

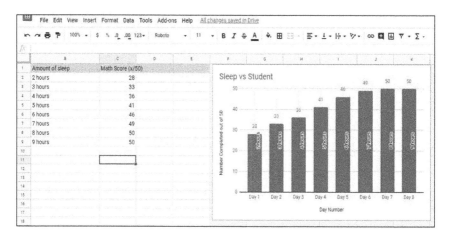

Figure 15.5 Do hours of sleep per night correlate to performance in math?

unique algebra questions). Using oneself as the "test subject," the student collected data on both hours of sleep and math questions answered correctly, stored it in a spreadsheet, and presented it to the instructor and class, with preliminary results pointing towards a strong correlation (<6 hours) between sleep and success on such questions.

The ninth grade biology instructor submitted a second example of student work. Another student in the same class hypothesized there would be a correlation between the growth rates of plants based upon varying amounts of caffeine introduced into their soil (below).

As evident from Figure 15.6, plants are not coffee drinkers but nonetheless grow (if at an apparently reduced rate) even with caffeine mixed into the soil. In both cases though, the submitted artifacts demonstrate students using computational tools to analyze and communicate with data. In the educator's reflection on the project, the individual describes how it was heartening to help students "create a self-contained experiment which challenges them to inquire about a natural phenomenon, make a prediction through a hypothesis, record data, analyze their findings, and summarize them into a conclusion." The activity supports the curricular goals of the ninth grade biology class, yet also effectively highlights the educator's ability to identify how the CT practice of analyzing and communicating with data intersects with the subject area.

Interestingly, as of the Fall of 2019, 64% of Digital Promise's MC submissions in CT have either been around Data (28% for "Analyzing and Communicating With Data"; 38% for "Collecting and Structuring Data"). Working with data appears to be more readily identified by educators as a CT practice with direct application within their own content areas and/or more readily

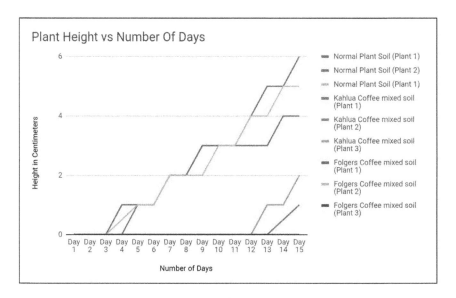

Figure 15.6 Caffeine and plant growth?

integrated into their instruction and student work. Other examples of data integration via these two MCs include:

- Experimental studies in physical sciences
  - Middle school physics: "Students were testing gravity, potential and kinetic energy by changing the height of a ramp and releasing hot wheels cars down the track."
  - Grade 4 grade geology unit: "The essential question was to analyze past high magnitude earthquakes along the San Andreas fault, and to then use a trend line to predict potential future earthquakes along the fault."
- Elementary school math
  - Grade 3 math teacher collecting and analyzing data about the books in their classroom library. "Students built an argument using data by clearly identifying trends in their peers' reading."

Another elementary math MC in Analyzing and Communicating with Data submission warrants further detail. Here, a second grade math teacher had students investigate a question of their choice by way of surveying their classmates. Students then communicated their results to a real-world audience, their peers, by way of Microsoft Excel spreadsheets or Google Sheets. In the reflection component of the submission, the educator explained that this example:

really let them [the students] take ownership of this data. They were also answering questions in Google forms on their specific data graphs that they created so they had an opportunity to analyze their own question. Many students enjoyed this part of the lesson because it went beyond just making a graph but pushed them to think deeper about their topic and why bar graphs and spreadsheets are useful.

As shown in Figure 15.7, these second graders showed limited spelling capabilities, yet clearly demonstrated the range of flavor preferences of their peers and ably demonstrated how to illustrate such a breakdown by the way of basic bar graphs, which many students do not encounter well into their middle school years (Bell et al., 1987).

Third and last, in another submission, a high school statistics teacher earned an MC for "Assessing Computational Thinking." The submitted activity involved data collection and analysis on a topic of the students' choosing. The educator identified three content area standards addressed by the activity while keeping the focus of students' submissions on their capacity to demonstrate CT. As outlined by the method components of the MC, this requires the educator to assess situated learning and the potential to support future learning.

Student artifacts and teacher reflections demonstrated evidence of these principles of assessing CT. One student analyzed academic performance data, and two others analyzed athletic performance data. While the instructor submitted student-generated graphs and tables charting academic and athletic performance over time, what made this submission unique was the student testimonials the instructor likewise included:

> The unit projects in statistics help in the application of [CT?] vocabulary and concepts being taught.... <Teacher's>[1] feedback always helps me understand any potential areas of misunderstanding and where I can go back and spend

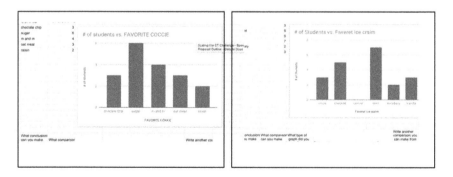

Figure 15.7 Favorite "cokkie" & "ice craim" [*sic*] flavors in a particular second grade classroom.

more time digging into the content. After receiving feedback, I was able to go back and make corrections to my work to demonstrate my new understanding. (Student 1)

I've really enjoyed the unit projects that we've done. . . . I also like that we can share our presentations for English credit. For the linear regression unit, <Teacher's> feedback made me recognize the importance of knowing what different statistical values mean. Not only do I need to calculate them, but I have to know how to interpret them so they help me understand the analysis of the data. (Student 2)

The information is more meaningful and retainable when I connect the curriculum with real data or newspaper articles/journals. I did, however, remember the importance of collecting more data to further support my conclusions. In the future, I will make sure I choose a topic in which there is enough available data or where I can select more individuals/teams/et cetera to be in my study. (Student 3)

In the Reflection section, the high school teacher stated, "This process (i.e., submitting the CT MC) made me focus on analyzing each of my student's strengths and weaknesses and how to help them on their continuum of understanding." These comments reflect the instructor's own progress helping her students articulate their own experience with situated learning and connecting statistics and probabilities with the capacity to think computationally.

NEXT STEPS

Moving forward, there are a number of factors that will certainly and immediately affect the future use of CT MCs (and MCs in general) among K–12 teachers. Here, we have highlighted three challenges, in particular: emphasizing best review practices, continuing advocacy, and ramping up internal research.

Emphasizing Best Review Practices

MCs do not succeed based upon their conceptual novelty. Ultimately, MCs succeed due to the timely and informed feedback from our reviewers and the capacity of such feedback to meaningfully inform the practice of numerous dedicated K–12 teachers across the country. Going forward, Digital Promise is particularly interested in explicitly gauging the effectiveness of their MC program in CT by measuring the rate of re-submission from educators who were not awarded the respective MC the first time. Feedback that is meaningful points to distinct areas for improvement and is ultimately rooted in encouragement. Certainly, there needs to be further research examining the connection between teachers' participation in MCs and student learning outcomes (Berry, 2016).

However, as highlighted in a 2014 report from the Bill and Melinda Gates Foundation, teachers ought to have greater say in the PD their schools and districts offer. As the report indicated, focusing teacher PD specifically on actual classroom practices and competency-driven learning has been enthusiastically received from many classroom teachers, who point out that too often school and district PD sits far from actual classroom practice and has little to do with their daily classroom routines and realities. This of course ties directly back to research cited earlier (Meneske, 2015) that points to the often wide gap between teacher PD and what actually subsequently gets enacted in the classroom (if enacted at all).

Continuing Advocacy Through Teacher Profiles and Growing Library Submissions

Digital Promise has profiled a range of teachers who have used MCs (see https://digitalpromise.org/micro-credentials-personal-stories-real-teachers/), sharing their own personal stories using MCs and how it has informed their teaching and students' learning. Given the growing need for computing teachers nationally, and in particular the need for K–8 educators to integrate CT into existing subject matter, profiling teachers integrating CT and the MCs they have submitted is a priority for Digital Promise. It is likewise a growing interest to states and school districts committed to CT and competency-driven PD.

In their recent 2019 report "Micro-Credentials: A Pathway for Certification and Professional Learning," Code.org points out that multiple states (including Arizona, Kentucky, Minnesota, Rhode Island, and Virginia) are exploring the use of MCs for computing teacher certification and endorsement. As a provider of CT MCs, Digital Promise is one component in a wider system needed to support teacher MCs and make them count directly toward teacher PD. As outlined in the white paper report "Micro-Credentials and Education Policy in the United States," Berry and Byrd (2019) note that organizations such as Digital Promise and the individual MC submitting teachers only represent half the equation as the platform (i.e., online provider) and earner, respectively. The other two components are the issuer, namely the certified university and/ or professional learning provider who can award the degree, and then the wider recognizer (i.e., the state and/ or local education agencies) that gives the MC recognition for advancement, compensation (salary lane change), and/or endorsement.

Ramping Up Internal Research

As mentioned earlier in the chapter, the majority (68%) of CT MCs that Digital Promise has received so far have been in manipulating and representing data. This warrants further investigation and to what degree data represents a "best first step" for teachers as a means to introduce CT within their own classrooms. In other words, if manipulating and presenting data is the first, most achievable CT step, is there a best next step in terms of teachers demonstrating specific CT competencies? These are two of the more immediate questions Digital Promise is interested in pursuing around CT and MCs, but there are many others, including, "What is the relationship between teacher PD and the successful completion of MCs?" and, for that matter, "What is the relationship between teacher PD and simply the successful submission of MCs?" At the very least, MCs—even before questions of teacher certification and teacher endorsement enter the equation—represent the opportunity to assess fidelity of implementation of PD. Namely, is such PD leading to changes in practice and delivery of content? Too often teachers get PD with absolutely no follow-up and no sense of clarity as to whether such PD informed/changed practice. Therefore, these questions matter not simply to Digital Promise as a provider of MCs but to the states and local education agencies tasked with incorporating CT into their classrooms and more widely, tasked with the continuing job to provide meaningful PD to the 50+ million K–12 public school teachers in this country.

To conclude, as noted at the outset of this chapter, too often educator MCs are tacitly dismissed as the "alternative" approach for developing teachers. Here, we argue in the mix of computing, competency driven education, and a national shortage of instructors, educator MCs in CT represent a promising model to endorse and certify teachers.

NOTE

1. The teacher's name has been redacted here and thereafter.

REFERENCES

Bell, A., Brekke, G., & Swan, M. (1987). Misconceptions, conflict and discussion in the teaching of graphical interpretation. In J. D. Novak (Eds.), *Proceedings of the second international seminar: Misconceptions and educational strategies in science and mathematics* (Vol. 1; pp. 46–58). Cornell University.

Berry, B. (2016). *Transforming professional learning: Why teachers' learning must be individualized—and how.* Center for Teaching Quality. https://www.teachingquality.org/transforming-professional-learning

Berry, B., & Byrd, A. P. (2019, June). *Micro-credentials and education policy in the United States: Recognizing learning and leadership for our nation's teachers.* http://digitalpromise.org/wp-content/uploads/2019/06/mcs-educationpolicy.pdf

Bill & Melinda Gates Foundation. (2014). *Teachers know best: Teachers views on professional development.* http://k12education.gatesfoundation.org/wp-content/uploads/2015/04/Gates-PDMarketResearch-Dec5.pdf

Burke, Q. (2016). Mind the metaphor: Charting the rhetoric about introductory programming in K–12 schools. *On the Horizon, 24*(3), 210–220.

Code.org. (2017, September 2). *Universities aren't preparing enough computer science teachers.* Medium. https://medium.com/@codeorg/universities-arent-preparing-enough-computer-science-teachers-dd5bc34a79aa

DeMonte, J. (2017). Micro-credentials for teachers: What three early adopter states have learned so far. *American Institutes for Research.* https://www.air.org/sites/default/files/downloads/report/Micro-Creditials-for-TeachersSeptember-2017.pdf

Digital Promise. (2017). *Computational thinking for a computational world.* http://digitalpromise.org/wp-content/uploads/2017/12/dp-comp-thinking-v1r5.pdf

Economic Policy Institute. (2019, March 26). *The teacher shortage is real, large and growing, and worse than we thought.* https://www.epi.org/files/pdf/163651.pdf

Gal-Ezer, J., & Stephenson, C. (2010). Computer science teacher preparation is critical. *ACM Inroads, 1*(1), 61–66.

Grover, S. (2018, November). *A tale of two CTs* (and a revised timeline for computational thinking). Communications of the ACM. https://cacm.acm.org/blogs/blog-cacm/232488-a-tale-of-two-cts-and-a-revised-timeline-for-computational-thinking/fulltext

Grover, S., & Pea, R. (2018). Computational thinking: A competency whose time has come. In S. Sentance, E. Barendsen, & S. Carsten, S. (Eds.), *Computer science education: Perspectives on teaching & learning* (pp. 20–34). Bloomsbury.

Guzdial, M. (2015, April. 15). *The danger of requiring computer science in K–12 schools.* Communications of the ACM. https://cacm.acm.org/blogs/blog-cacm/173870-the-danger-of-requiring-computer-science-in-k-12-schools/fulltext

Hodge S. (2007). The origins of competency-based training. *Australian Journal of Adult Learning, 47*(2), 179–209.

Johnstone, S. M., & Soares, L. (2014). Principles for developing competency based education programs. *Change: The Magazine of Higher Learning, 46*(2), 12–19. https://doi.org/10.1080/00091383.2014.896705

Kafai, Y. B., Proctor, C., & Lui, D. A. (2019). *Framing computational thinking for computational literacies in K–12 education* [Conference session]. The Weizenbaum Conference 2019 "Challenges of Digital Inequality–Digital Education, Digital Work, Digital Life," Berlin. https://doi.org/10.34669/wi.cp/2.21

Kohl, K., Berry, B., & Eckert, J. (2018, April). Micro-credentials and the transformation of professional learning in California schools. *Center for Teaching Quality.* https://www.teachingquality.org/wp-content/uploads/2018/04/Microcredentials_and_the_transformation_of_CA_schools.pdf

Levine, A. (2007). *Educating researchers.* Education Schools Project.

Menekse, M. (2015). Computer science teacher professional development in the United States: A review of studies published between 2004 and 2014. *Computer*

Science Education, 25(4), 325–350. https://doi.org/10.1080/08993408.2015.11
11645

Mishra, P., & Koehler, M.J. (2006). Technological pedagogical content knowledge:
A framework for integrating technology in teacher knowledge. *Teachers College
Record, 108*(6), 1017–1054.

Mouza, C., Basu, S., Yang, H., & Pan, Y. C. (2018). New content for new times:
Pre-service teachers' exploration of computer programming in educational
technology coursework. In E. Langran & J. Borup (Eds.), *Society for information technology & Teacher Education International Conference* (pp. 1635–1642).
Association for the Advancement of Computing in Education. https://www
.learntechlib.org/primary/p/182747/

National Research Council. (2010). *Report of a workshop on the scope and nature of
computational thinking.* The National Academies Press. https://doi.org/10
.17226/12840

National Research Council. (2011). *Report of a workshop on the pedagogical aspects of
computational thinking.* The National Academies Press. https://doi.org/10
.17226/13170

Ottenbreit-Leftwich, A., Brush, T., Strycker, J., Gronseth, S., Roman, T., Abaci, S.,
van Leusen, P., Shin, S., Easterling, W., & Plucker, J. (2012). Preparation versus practice: How do teacher education programs and practicing teachers
align in their use of technology to support teaching and learning? *Computers
and Education, 59*(2), 399–411.

Proctor, C., Bigman, M., & Blikstein, P. (2019). *Defining and designing computer science education in a K–12 public school district* [Conference session]. In *Proceedings of the 2017 ACM SIGCSE Technical Symposium on Computer Science Education*
(pp. 314–320). ACM.

Proctor, C., & Blikstein, P. (2018, June 23–27). *How broad is computational thinking?
A longitudinal study of practices shaping learning in computer science* [Conference
session]. In J. Kay & R. Luckin (Eds.), *Rethinking learning in the digital age:
Making the learning sciences count, 13th International Conference of the Learning
Sciences* (pp. 544–551). International Society of the Learning Sciences.

Sahami, M. (2016). Why computer science education in K–12 settings is becoming increasingly essential. *Huffington Post.* https://www.huffingtonpost.com/
acm-the-association-for-computing-machinery/why-computer-science
-educ_b_12010476.html

Serdenciuc, N. (2013). Competency-based education: Implications on teachers'
training. *Procedia: Social and Behavioral Sciences, 76,* 754–758.

Shulman, L. S. (1987). Knowledge and teaching: Foundations of the new reform.
Harvard Educational Review, 57(1), 1–22.

Tedre, M., & Denning, P. J. (2016, November 24–27). *The long quest for computational
thinking* [Conference session]. In *Proceedings of the 16th Koli Calling conference
on computing education research* (pp. 120–129). ACM.

Vakil, S., & Higgs, J. (2019, March). It's about power. *Communications of the ACM, 62*(3),
31–33. https://www.scholars.northwestern.edu/en/publications/education
-its-about-power

Weintrop, D., Beheshti, E., Horn, M., Orton, K., Jona, K., Trouille, L., & Wilensjy, U. (2017). Defining computational thinking for mathematics and science classrooms. *Journal of Science Education and Technology, 25*(1), 127–147.

Wing, J. M. (2006). Computational thinking. *Communications of the ACM, 49*(3), 33–35.

Worrell, F., Brabeck, M., Dwyer, C., Geisinger, K., Marx, R., Noell, G., & Pianta, R. (2014). *Assessing and evaluating teacher preparation programs.* American Psychological Association.

Yadav, A., Mayfield, C., Zhou, N., Hambrusch, S., & Korb, J. T. (2014, March). Computational thinking in elementary and secondary teacher education. *ACM Transactions on Computing, 14*(1), 1–16. https://doi.org/10.1145/2576872

Yadav, A., Gretter, S., Hambrusch, S., & Sands, P. (2016). Expanding computer science education in schools: Understanding teacher experiences and challenges. *Computer Science Education, 26*(4), 235–254.

CHAPTER 16

FROM CLOCK-BASED TO COMPETENCY-BASED

How Micro-Credentials Can Transform Professional Development

Melissa A. Rasberry
American Institutes for Research

Gretchen Weber
American Institutes for Research

Joseph P. Wilson
American Institutes for Research

ABSTRACT

As the Computer Science (CS) for All initiative transitions from vision to reality, it is becoming increasingly important to prepare and support high-quality CS teachers. Pathways into CS are as diverse as the teachers who teach it. Some enter the classroom with formal degrees in CS, whereas others are recruited from other subjects (such as mathematics and science) to teach stand-

Professional Development for In-Service Teachers, pages 361–383
Copyright © 2022 by Information Age Publishing
www.infoagepub.com
All rights of reproduction in any form reserved.

alone CS courses. At the elementary and middle school levels, teachers often venture into CS as a way to integrate computational thinking with more traditional content areas. The rise in popularity for CS education comes at the same time that personalized learning for students is growing in popularity. But what about teachers? Micro-credentials present one option for shifting from clock-based to competency-based professional development, allowing teachers to more easily prepare to teach CS based on their unique needs and interests. In this chapter, we describe how micro-credentials can serve as a professional development model, which values teacher practice, focuses on active learning, and ensures continuous improvement, while also exploring the local and state policy implications for implementing them.

As the Computer Science (CS) for All initiative transitions from vision to reality, it is becoming increasingly important to prepare and support high-quality CS teachers (Menekse, 2015; The White House: Office of the Press Secretary, 2016). Pathways into CS are as diverse as the teachers who teach it. Few enter the classroom with formal CS degrees; most are recruited from other subjects (such as mathematics and science but not exclusively) to teach stand-alone CS courses (Code.org, 2019). At the elementary and middle school levels, teachers often venture into CS as a way to integrate computational thinking (CT) with more traditional content areas (Rich et al., 2019). The rise in popularity for CS education comes as interest in personalized learning for students is growing (Pane et al., 2017). But what about teachers?

A growing need exists for teachers to have personalized professional development (PD). Traditional PD activities, such as those that require teachers to simply "clock hours" are proving to be ineffective in changing teaching practice. In addition, teachers no longer want these kinds of PD activities. A clock-hours model represents a requirement for teachers to log their hours of PD activities and submit that log for review to earn continuing education units within their district and licensure renewal or additional license endorsements in their state. This model does not require a demonstration of practice or an assessment of competency in that practice. In CS PD, evidence of knowledge and skills is particularly important because most CS teachers have little to no background or training in the subject (Menekse, 2015).

Micro-credentials (MCs) present one option for shifting from clock-based to competency-based PD, allowing teachers to customize their learning, based on their unique needs and interests. In this chapter, we describe a PD model based on MCs that values teacher practice, focuses on active learning, ensures continuous improvement, and explores the policy implications for implementation.

BACKGROUND

Characteristics of Effective PD

For continuous improvement of their practice, teachers need ongoing professional learning (Barber & Mourshed, 2007). Nearly 20 years of research has synthesized common characteristics of what effective teacher PD and learning look like. Based on a literature review, high-quality PD exhibits the following six characteristics (Archibald et al., 2011; Darling-Hammond et al., 2017):

- alignment with school goals; state and district standards and assessments; and other professional learning activities, including formative teacher evaluation;
- a focus on core content and modeling of teaching strategies for the content;
- inclusion of opportunities for active learning of new teaching strategies;
- provision of opportunities for collaboration among teachers;
- inclusion of embedded follow-up and continuous feedback, especially coaching and expert support; and
- sustained duration that goes beyond one-time or intermittently occurring events.

These characteristics are consistent with those identified by many other studies (e.g., Desimone et al., 2002; Garet et al., 2001) and statements put forth by organizations focused on educator learning, such as Learning Forward (Wei et al., 2009), the Council of Chief State School Officers (Blank & de las Alas, 2009), and the Center for Public Education (Gulamhussein, 2013). The characteristics serve as guiding principles for how to design and implement ongoing professional learning for teachers. In fact, multiple studies have shown that intensive, content-focused PD with these characteristics helped improve teachers' knowledge and some aspects of their practices (Garet et al., 2008, 2010, 2016). Furthermore, the Elementary and Secondary Education Act, as amended by the Every Student Succeeds Act (ESSA), reinforces the characteristics of high-quality PD identified by the body of research as sustained, collaborative, data driven, job embedded, and an integral part of the overall strategy for ensuring that students receive a well-rounded education. The ESSA states that PD activities

- (a) "are an integral part of school and local educational agency strategies for providing educators (including teachers, principals, other school leaders, specialized instructional support personnel, paraprofessionals, and, as applicable, early childhood educators) with the knowledge and skills necessary to enable students to succeed in a well-rounded education and to meet the challenging State academic standards" (para. 42); and

- (b) "are sustained (not stand-alone, 1-day, or short term workshops), intensive, collaborative, job-embedded, data-driven, and classroom-focused." (Every Student Succeeds Act, 2015, 20 USC § 7801[42], para. 42)

Research, policy, and what teachers want for PD now coalesce and strongly intersect. In 2014, the Bill & Melinda Gates Foundation contracted with the Boston Consulting Group to conduct a research study on PD for teachers to help identify needs and opportunities for improvement. After surveying thousands of stakeholders, the results were published in the Teachers Know Best study (Bill & Melinda Gates Foundation, 2014). A key finding was that teachers and administrators largely agree on five characteristics of what good professional learning looks like, as follows:

- *Relevant.* Learning can look different in every context, but it must speak to practical needs.
- *Interactive.* The PD involves hands-on strategies and/or opportunities to practice, collaborate, and demonstrate competence.
- *Delivered by someone who understands the teaching experience.* Preferably, the PD should be practical and facilitated by someone with classroom experience in one-on-one or small-group coaching environments.
- *Respectful of teachers as professionals.* The professional learning empowers teachers to take control of their own professional growth.
- *Sustained.* Growth is an iterative process, and learning by doing, such as through an ongoing approach, is essential.

Evidence from multiple research studies, shifts in policy through the ESSA (2015), and the clarity of what we hear from teachers themselves all point to an evolution in teacher PD.

If we take what we know about the characteristics of high-quality PD and what educators want in their PD, it is clear that traditional professional learning structures—"sit and get" learning, "one and done" experiences, and "one-size-fits-all" events—are no longer viable for advancing and supporting teacher practice (Menekse, 2015). In an ever-changing world where student demographics are changing and community contexts matter more than ever, we must think about how we build teacher capacity, especially for a content area such as CS education, which draws teachers from different backgrounds and preparation routes. We also must think about how to make the learning experiences of teachers more grounded in their classroom practices and steeped in inquiry and reflection.

Micro-Credentials as Competency-Based Education

One innovative solution to address some of the issues with current PD structures is competency-based education (CBE) for teachers. CBE is growing in popularity for students because its focus is on the mastery of learning goals (Surr & Redding, 2017). Students advance based on their ability to master a skill or competency at their own pace, rather than focusing on "seat time" in courses as the metric to determine progress and credits (Haynes et al., 2016; Surr et al., 2017). This same concept could be used for teacher PD where teachers are (a) focusing on a set of skills or competencies aligned to goals and standards; (b) learning about and honing core teaching strategies, especially in their content areas; (c) receiving feedback and support in that cycle of inquiry and improvement from their peers across time; and (d) demonstrating mastery of those competencies within the context of their current teaching practice as an active learning experience.

Engaging teachers in a CBE experience is a big culture shift from traditional PD models, which often are one size fits all in their approach. One emerging structure to make this shift more appealing is the use of MCs. A typical teaching credential covers all the skills and competencies required to teach students of a particular grade range and/or subject area; it is essentially the baseline credential earned from an accredited teacher preparation program and certified by the state based on its licensure policy. Compared with a full teaching credential, MCs focus on discrete skills or competencies. One reason that MCs are appealing to teachers, districts, and states is that they break down complex instructional skills into fundamental parts. Teachers can develop and demonstrate competence in each bite-sized element of instruction and then weave these skills together to demonstrate mastery in complex skills. MCs are a digital form of a micro-certification indicating proven competence and mastery of one skill at a time and built through a portfolio of evidence. Teachers earn a MC after completing and being assessed on the requirements to demonstrate mastery of that specific skill. As each bite-sized element of instruction builds, MCs become a form of active, portfolio-based (evidence-based) professional learning (Figure 16.1).

According to various studies, developing a portfolio is a powerful learning experience for teachers as they reflect on their teaching practice in light of standards (Chung, 2008; Gearhart & Osmundson, 2009; Sato et al., 2008). As part of earning a MC on platforms such as Bloomboard and Digital Promise, educators must create a portfolio of their learning as they

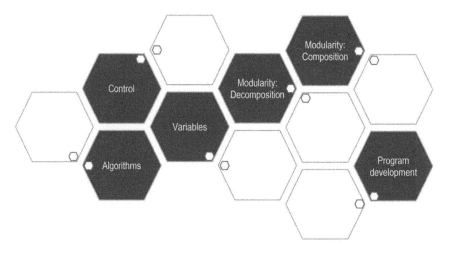

Figure 16.1 Example of a set of micro-credentials that could demonstrate competency in algorithms and programming.

demonstrate it in their practice, often consisting of short videos of teaching practice, student progress or learning data, classroom photographs, examples of student work, student interviews, planning or instructional materials, and other forms of evidence (DeMonte, 2017). This evidence is then submitted to a trained third-party expert reviewer as part of the micro-credential application and assessment process.

While collecting and submitting evidence for assessment, teachers also engage in an inquiry cycle of analyzing and evaluating their practice on that particular skill or competency. Rowland et al. (2018) describes cycles of inquiry as follows:

> In general, a cycle of inquiry (a) establishes current thinking; (b) identifies needs and questions; (c) requires some investigation of information, ideas, and data; (d) sorts the information and makes meaning out of it; and (e) applies the learnings. The analysis yields new action, which in turn suggests new inquiry into the results, so the cycle begins again. (p. 2)

The process of conducting cycles of inquiry is similar to implementing Plan-Do-Study-Act (PDSA) cycles (Figure 16.2), in which teachers test changes to practice, document results, and revise how to achieve their aim (Regional Educational Laboratory West, 2017). Rather than participate in an 8-hour off-site workshop, a 2-hour professional learning community meeting after school, or a 6-hour online course on a set of general teaching practices—all away from and with limited relevance to the classroom context and potentially misaligned to specific goals or standards—teachers

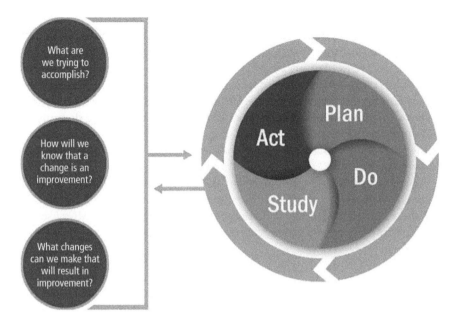

Figure 16.2   Diagram of a PDSA cycle. *Note:* See https://www.air.org/resource/ using-networked-improvement-communities-improve-educational-practice for more details on PDSA cycles.

can shift from a clock-hours approach to a competency-based approach to PD through MCs.

Micro-Credentials in CS Education

Some states across the country, from Arizona to Rhode Island, are exploring the use of MCs for CS education (Code.org, 2019). The rapidly growing need for qualified CS teachers, combined with the dearth of teacher preparation programs in CS, has created conditions for exploring innovative practices for teacher learning to meet the demand (Rasberry & Wilson, 2019). Some CS teachers have been pulled from different content areas, as far reaching as history and physical education, to participate in summer CS training workshops (Vaidyanathan, 2018). Still others, particularly at the elementary and middle school grades, are simply self-taught using online resources and video tutorials to enhance their learning. MCs would allow for districts and states to recognize these diverse paths into teaching CS and for teachers to demonstrate their learning and proficiency of particular CS standards.

Because MCs are a relatively new model of professional learning, very little research or evidence points to them as a positive intervention to change teacher practice or impact student achievement (Ross, 2016). Limited research to date describes the individual components brought together in the micro-credentialing process, not combined under a set of research questions (e.g., cycles of inquiry have not been researched in combination with portfolio-based assessments of practice). Furthermore, no research has been conducted on whether one MC and the feedback provided changes teacher practice or whether a stack of MCs is necessary to see demonstrated, impactful change. Also, little existing state or district policy or language in teacher bargaining agreements codifies implementation (National Education Association, 2018).

We now outline one pilot program and the feedback of district and state leaders on their use of MCs. This example is not meant to fully address all of the research questions; it demonstrates one approach to MCs use and the preliminary results on their effectiveness for teacher learning in CS.

EXEMPLAR

Developing an Elementary CS Micro-Credential

In late 2017, a state education agency in the western half of the United States sent out a request for proposals related to developing educator MCs, including those for elementary CS, as a potential alternative for traditional teacher PD. In early 2018, we worked with this state agency and a virtual platform provider to develop and pilot a MC focused on integrating key pillars of CT, including decomposition, pattern matching, abstraction, and algorithms, into elementary mathematics and science instruction. This approach to integrating CT within elementary mathematics and science instruction was intentional; it recognized that elementary teachers already had numerous instructional requirements and situated CS and CT as tools to support teachers' existing instructional practice. As part of their portfolio of evidence, educators were asked to do the following four integrated primary tasks:

- *Task 1.* Reflect on existing teaching practices and identify (through specific examples) where educators thought they had already implemented aspects of that CT pillar in their mathematics and science lessons.
- *Task 2.* Create a mathematics or science lesson that more intentionally integrates one of these CT pillars, including their best attempt at formative measures to assess to what extent their students learned the mathematics/science content and the CT pillar.

- *Task 3.* Gather evidence of learning from the lesson articulated in Task 2 and upload it to the platform.
- *Task 4.* Analyze to what extent students learned the mathematics/science and CT content and reflect on how the educator might change the lesson in the future.

Piloting the Elementary CS Micro-Credential

In Spring 2018, a small pilot cohort of four educators from a single district within the state participated in the MC process. This pilot was meant to gather initial reactions, feedback, and time estimates for completion. In Summer 2018, the prototyped MC was revised based on feedback from the Spring 2018 cohort. The state coordinator worked with regional educational units to recruit districts and teachers to participate in an expanded cohort in Fall 2018 using the revised MC. In Fall 2018, 116 teachers enrolled in the MC from September 2018 to December 2018 and agreed to submit the full portfolio of evidence to earn the MC. During this time, all elementary teachers enrolled received a small stipend and had access to a virtual platform to ask questions, get feedback, and collaborate with other teachers enrolled across the state. Because of an existing collaboration with a CS education coach across several districts, a subset of these teachers ($n = 53$) also were part of a multidistrict consortium that provided regular, in-person coaching related to the micro-credential.

Assessing Portfolios of Educators

Portfolios were evaluated by three assessors (individuals who assess or evaluate the portfolios of educators) who engaged in virtual training led by the MC platform provider and developer for interrater reliability and quality control processes to ensure that all ratings were consistent and feedback was given within several days. Through this training, assessors scored an initial batch of MC submissions using a written proprietary rubric, which was developed by the MC platform based on the Computer Science Teachers Association's K–12 CS Framework. After submitting their scores, assessors attended a webinar where the lead assessor (who also developed this pilot) examined each submission to ensure the calibration of scores and the provision of thorough feedback to the educators. To ensure quality control, each MC assessment was submitted for approval to the lead assessor, who provided a final checkpoint to ensure that the assessment matched the rubric guidelines and specific feedback was worded constructively. Once approved, educators received notification indicating whether their MC was awarded or if their portfolio needed to be reworked and resubmitted based on feedback from the assessor.

METHODS AND DATA COLLECTION

Several goals guided the evaluation of the MC pilot: (a) the desire to understand the intentions of state and district leaders in implementing a MC program for CS educators; (b) participant submission status from the MC platform; (c) the manner in which educators viewed the implementation of the MC program; and (d) the extent in which the implementation of the MC program matched its intent.

Perspectives of Intent and Implementation From State and District Leaders

We wanted to supplement participant data with feedback from those responsible for developing and implementing MC programs. Through semistructured interviews, we interviewed three individuals (one district leader and two state leaders) about their intent with MC, and, for those who had implemented a MC program, how their intent matched the reality of implementation. Specifically, the following three primary questions guided the interviews:

1. "What is the purpose of CS MCs for educators in your district or state?"
2. "What do you see as similarities and differences between traditional PD and MC PD?"
3. For those who implemented the MC program, "How did the implementation of the CS MC process compare with your expectations?"

Participant Submission Status From the Micro-Credential Platform

Through the MC submission platform, we had access to the status of MC submission (initially enrolled; submitted at least once; submitted at least once and not earned; submitted at least once and earned) for each participant in the pilot. Through the coordination of a four-district consortium, we also segmented the results of the consortium participants from the state's overall participants.

Perspectives From Elementary CS Micro-Credential Participants

The multidistrict consortium, described earlier, developed an 11-question virtual survey to understand the implementation of the elementary CS MC. Specifically, the survey had constructs related to teacher motivation (for those who did and did not complete the micro-credential), teacher use of resources provided in the platform for each part of the portfolio, teacher perceptions of MC support and utility, and feedback to improve the MC process. We employed thematic analysis, a qualitative analytic method, to uncover high-level constructs in open-ended responses from the survey participants (Braun & Clarke, 2006).

RESULTS AND DISCUSSION

Intent of Micro-Credentials From State and District Leaders

Before jumping into the specific elementary CS MC pilot implemented across the four-district consortium and the state, we want to understand the intent of state and district leaders in implementing MCs. Through interviews with administrators, several high-level themes emerged from their responses to the first two questions: (a) flexibility for educators, (b) connection to specific classroom practice, and (c) currency for professional advancement. Table 16.1 describes some of the phrases used by state and district leaders related to each theme.

Flexibility for educators was one of the strongest themes that emerged from the three interviews about the potential of CS MCs. Interviewees viewed MCs as a way for educators to receive PD at times that made sense for them, compared with traditional PD with a specific time and place for the learning to occur. Specifically, the interviewees believed that MCs seemed to solve the inherent challenge of educators being asked to do too much without having the time to do it. Closely related, all three interviewees viewed CS MCs as a way for educators to demonstrate competencies that were rooted in specific classroom practice. Specifically, they liked the idea of rooting the CS MCs in developing a lesson, implementing it, analyzing to what extent students learned the CS concepts, and reflecting on how their practice could change to improve student learning (i.e., a cycle of inquiry). Last, all interviewees viewed MCs as potential currency for professional advancement. Because many states are still developing and rolling out CS standards and licensure protocols, few options exist to recognize educators who are already implementing CS in their classrooms. In the elementary

TABLE 16.1 Emergent Themes From Semi-Structured Interviews of State and District Leaders Related to Micro-credentials in CS Education

Theme	Response Examples
Flexibility for Educators	DL1: "At the classroom level, we are aiming toward student voice…so similarly, how do we craft learning experiences with teachers in a similar fashion?…We don't have release time for teachers for PD, [we] have a sub shortage. This is another way to have deep professional learning (potentially—depending on how it is structured). This could be a way to offer agency and choice for teachers."
	SL1: "Teachers can do one micro-credential faster than a full semester's class. It [a micro-credential] is flexible in timing…."
	SL2: "[Micro-credentials] allow teachers in their busy schedules to [attend] this training, inform their instruction, and do it when necessary."
Connection to specific classroom practice	DL1: "Micro-credentials are closely connected…to classroom practice—[they are] different than a 'sit and soak' [PD] workshop."
	SL1: "Teachers get overwhelmed by what we ask of [them]….Stuff keeps getting added to the plate and not much is taken off. For the current teacher workforce, it [micro-credentials] gives them something bite size that isn't a college-level course….I like that [the micro-credential focus] is [on] smaller chunks [of competencies]."
	SL2: "[Micro-credentials are]…convenient and applicable to what they [teachers] are doing. They [teachers in a micro-credential] are actually applying…and getting feedback right away….Feedback is really from experts from the field, and it [the micro-credential process] isn't 'sit and get.' They [teachers in the micro-credential program] actually have to create lesson plans, work with students, [and] evaluate [their practice]."
Currency for professional advancement	DL1: "As a teacher, this [micro-credential] can count toward licensure and certificate renewal. If it can run congruent to state-level requirements, it is a good thing…will the micro-credential mean anything if there is no currency at the state level?"
	SL1: "The biggest picture is about teacher growth. We need solutions for teacher licensure. We need teachers who have the skills necessary to teach it [CS] in the classroom….We have districts that have started to look at micro-credentials as ways to incentivize teacher pay."
	SL2: "The goal is to use this [micro-credential] as a 'stackable' type credential. In renewing their state license, they [teachers in the state] have to have…[a certain number of] hours of professional development. What better way [to count toward those hours] than stackable micro-credentials?…It is 'comprehensive PD' for me…it feels like a real consistent, solid PD over time."

Note: SL = state leader; DL = district leader.

CS MC pilot described in this chapter, elementary educators received partial credit toward their state recertification that would have otherwise been achieved by sitting in a clock-hours model of PD.

Elementary CS Micro-Credential Implementation in the State and the Four-District Consortium

All 116 teachers initially enrolled in the elementary CS MC pilot had access to the virtual platform that included digital resources intended to support educators in the submission process (creating and uploading artifacts of learning) and a virtual messaging system to get feedback from both a dedicated facilitator and other teachers enrolled. Teachers in the four-district consortium also had access to a local coordinator who scheduled in-person meetings and provided ongoing support.

Table 16.2 shows the status of teachers enrolled in the pilot elementary CS MC program for those in the four-district consortium and across the entire state (including the consortium):

- *Initially enrolled* means educators expressed interest in the program and signed up for the MC on the virtual platform.
- *Submitted at least once* means educators were initially enrolled and attempted submission of an evidence portfolio at least once, regardless of whether they received credit for the MC.
- *Submitted at least once and not earned* means educators were initially enrolled, attempted submission at least once, and did not earn the MC by the end of December 2018.
- *Submitted at least once and earned* means educators were initially enrolled, attempted submission at least once, and earned the elementary CS MC.

All educators could submit and resubmit as many times as needed during the submission window.

Across the state, 116 elementary educators initially enrolled in the MC, with 53 educators in the four-district consortium. Almost half of those enrolled in the four-district consortium (25 of 53) submitted evidence for the MC at least once compared with one third of those not in the four-district consortium (38 of 116). Of those educators across the state who submitted at least once, a large majority (34 of 38) earned the MC. Two thirds (25 of 38) of those teachers who submitted at least once were in the four-district

TABLE 16.2 Elementary CS Micro-Credential Status

Micro-Credential Status	Four-District Consortium	State Total
Initially enrolled	53	116
Submitted at least once	25	38
Submitted at least once and not earned	3	4
Submitted at least once and earned	22	34

consortium. The educators initially enrolled in the four-district consortium had a dedicated, local coordinator who provided in-person support on top of the virtual support offered to all participants. Unsurprisingly, a higher percentage of teachers who submitted a portfolio of evidence at least once in the elementary CS MC pilot were in the four-district consortium rather than in other parts of the state. After submitting their evidence for the MC, educators received rubric scores and feedback for each task (described in the Exemplar section). If an educator did not receive a passing score for a specific task, the educator was asked to rework and resubmit that portion of the MC.

Perspectives of Educators in the Four-District Consortium

Of the 53 participants initially enrolled in the MC in the four-district consortium, 19 (36%) responded to a supplemental survey sent by the four-district consortium MC coordinator. Specifically, the survey included constructs related to teacher motivation (for those who did and did not complete the MC), teacher use of resources provided in the platform for each part of the portfolio, teacher perceptions of MC support and utility, and feedback to improve the MC process. Figures 16.3–16.6 showcase the perspectives of educators in the four-district consortium initially enrolled in the statewide elementary CS MC.

From this pilot in the four-district consortium (Figure 16.3), only 47% ($N = 9$) would recommend the MC to colleagues. In addition, only 63% ($N = 12$) of the survey respondents felt that the MC process was an effective form of PD. However, this does not explain what could be affecting these ratings or how respondents view other types of PD comparatively.

In Figure 16.5, we can see that 79% ($N = 15$) of survey respondents read, used, and learned from less than 50% of the materials and resources provided through the virtual platform for the MC. In addition, in Figure 16.6,

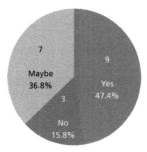

Figure 16.3 Responses to the question—"Would you recommend this micro-credential to a colleague?"—for participants in the four-district consortium ($N = 19$).

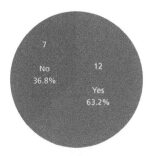

Figure 16.4 Responses to the question—"Did you find the CS micro-credential process an effective form of professional development?"—for participants in the four-district consortium ($N = 19$).

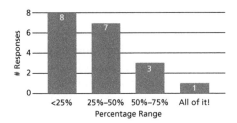

Figure 16.5 Responses to the question—"How much of the materials and resources in the [micro-credential]…did you read, use, and learn from?"—for participants in the four-district consortium ($N = 19$).

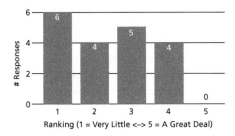

Figure 16.6 Responses to the question—"How well did the…materials and resources [in the micro-credential]…help you with lesson planning and classroom implementation?"—for participants in the four-district consortium ($N = 19$).

we can see that 79% ($N = 15$) of survey respondents rated the materials and resources provided in the virtual platform as 1, 2, or 3 (on a scale from 1 [*very little*] to 5 [*a great deal*]). These two figures indicate that respondents in this four-district consortium did not use most of the resources provided and did not find them useful to their classroom implementation. This result

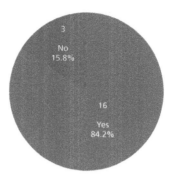

Figure 16.7 Responses to the question—"Did you find the updates from the co-ordinator helpful, timely, and containing information you needed?"—for participants in the four-district consortium (*N* = 19).

likely speaks to both the quality and quantity of resources provided to teachers in the MC program; providing high-quality, relevant resources is a key area of improvement for future iterations of this MC program. These sentiments likely drove many of the responses in Figure 16.3 regarding the MC as an effective form of PD. However, educators in the four-district consortium also had access to a local coordinator for supplemental support in this pilot. Figure 16.7 shows that 84% of the survey respondents (*N* = 16) found the updates and support from the local coordinator helpful, timely, and containing information that they needed. This seems consistent with reflections (discussed later in this section) from the district leader in charge of implementation that being able to supplement the virtual platform with a local contact was important for educators to feel supported throughout the MC process.

In addition, the four-district consortium was interested in understanding what kept educators going throughout the process if they started and submitted evidence for the MC. Table 16.3 highlights several emergent themes from educators who responded to the open-ended question, "If you started and submitted the CS micro-credential, what kept you going throughout the process?": (a) determination; (b) reminders, guidelines, and feedback; (c) professional advancement and incentives; or (d) peer support.

Educators in the four-district consortium who persisted felt determined to complete the CS MC; they wanted to "finish what they started." These educators also were supported by reminders, guidelines, and feedback through the virtual platform and local coordinator. They were motivated by professional advancement and incentives, specifically getting professional credit and receiving a stipend. Last, educators valued the support of other peers in the MC process.

For the educators who did not work through the CS MC, they noted that the biggest barrier to completing the process centered on a mismatch in

TABLE 16.3 Emergent Themes From Four-District Consortium Survey Respondents (N = 14) to the Question: "If you started and submitted the CS micro-credential, what kept you going throughout the process?"

Theme	Response Examples
Determination	• "Determination and perseverance to complete." • "Once I received feedback for areas that I did not pass, I felt determined to improve in those areas, for my own personal growth. I wanted to understand them better." • "The desire to not fail." • "Wanting to finish what I had started." • "I wanted to learn more and wanted to finish what I started." • "Wanting to earn my credential and continue learning about CS."
Reminders, guidelines, and feedback	• "Following the guidelines and timetables provided in [the virtual platform." • "Check-ins and reminders were helpful. I also wanted to receive the clock hours so that was incentive to finish." • "Midpoint deadlines along the way. Motivation and check-in from our key district leader." • "It was a very interesting way to view my math instructions through the lens of computational thinking. I also received positive feedback after my first submission."
Professional advancement and incentives	• "Knowing I wouldn't get paid until I passed and that I wanted the micro-credential for this." • "Knowing I would not get the clock hours unless I submitted, and I would not get paid unless I earned it. Also, I really want the micro-credential on my résumé." • "I also wanted to receive the clock hours so that was incentive to finish.
Peer support	• "Talking with the other teachers in my district who were also working on this program." • "There were a lot of colleagues supporting me. I pushed myself because of that."

expectations and reality between how much time and effort the MC process took. In addition, when educators in the four-district consortium were asked about additional tools and resources that would be helpful to stay connected and informed, the following items were in the top three:

- In-person meet-ups ($N = 13$, 68%)
- Optional periodic video conferences ($N = 8$, 42%)
- In-person visits to my school ($N = 7$, 37%)

These responses indicate that educators would prefer a hybrid approach to MCs, supplementing the virtual experience with in-person support.

Perspectives of Implementation From State and District Leaders

Through semi-structured interviews, the chapter authors interviewed two individuals (one district leader and one state leader) about the third guiding question: "How did the implementation of the CS MC process compare with your expectations?" Several themes emerged that seemed consistent with those identified previously in Figure 16.5, Figure 16.6, and Table 16.3:

- *A cohort model with dedicated coordinators is key.* The cohort model helped provide an additional level of support for educators pursuing the MC. "That was kind of a surprise, how important that was. It also brings in another level of a community of learners." Dedicated coordinators—ideally in-person but also virtual—were necessary to ensure successful implementation. "It is critical to have leadership, and they understand and guide the process [for educators in the MC] ..." Ideally, future implementation of this MC would have someone dedicated to providing a mixture of outreach and support to teachers (e.g., regular email updates cohort wide and individually, regular community of practice meetings [whether virtual or in person], and just-in-time support [ideally in person but also through the platform]).
- *High-quality resources are necessary.* Participants in the four-district consortium did not widely use the materials and resources on the MC platform, and those that were used did not receive high ratings in terms of usefulness. In the development of future versions of MCs, more attention to curating and disseminating high-quality resources, including recordings of integrating CS and CT into classroom instruction, are necessary for stronger wraparound support of educators.

NEXT STEPS

As the data from participants and administrators indicated, designing and launching a successful CS MC program is a complex process. At a systems level, managing change creates challenges for even the best leaders to effectively implement all the necessary elements. Numerous stakeholders must work together to ensure continuous improvement for that implementation. In the exemplar study, materials could not simply be created for teacher use; the teachers in the program needed a local coordinator to support them through the micro-credentialing process. Further, the virtual platform left many participants desiring in-person connectivity, whether through meet-ups or peer/mentor observations. Expectations regarding time and commitment also were unclear, causing many teachers to not submit their MC materials.

On the other hand, the potential for teacher learning through a cycle of inquiry was a strongly held belief in the program. Several district and state leaders noted the "bite size" nature of the PD model, making it easier for busy teachers to tackle. They also appreciated its direct connection and relevance to classroom instruction. Further, MCs offered teachers' agency over their own learning, a principle that many educators were providing to their students yet rarely received for themselves.

Although the exemplar study raises as many questions as it does lessons, we still believe MCs deserve more practice and study. Their promise for revolutionizing teacher learning and PD is too great to ignore. To more effectively implement MCs, we recommend the American Institutes for Research's continuous improvement model (Figure 16.8). In the first phase of Reflect and Prepare, time would be taken to understand the history of past and present PD initiatives in CS in a state or district and then gather feedback from key stakeholders, particularly CS teachers. A district might convene educator forums and parent meetings to engage with stakeholders, while also creating a broad-based communication strategy for all interested parties.

During the Plan phase, goals would be set; a target audience (e.g., a pilot group) would be identified for the CS MC pilot; and a timeline for planning and implementation, through the leadership of a representative steering committee, would be developed. Data would be gathered and analyzed for a gap analysis, which would then feed into a rigorous implementation plan. Content for the CS MCs also would be developed. The Launch phase would encapsulate the execution of all plan components, including communication and validation of the MCs. CS teachers would be trained on the platform to be used for entering MC evidence to minimize any technology issues.

During the Implement, Monitor, and Support phase, a continuous improvement cycle would be fostered, allowing for ongoing improvements to the CS MC process. Teachers would be supported (whether in person, online, or a preferred hybrid model) in how to approach the tasks assigned. Quality assurance processes would be implemented with course corrections made, as needed. Finally, during Sustain and Innovate, resources and best practices would be adopted based on initial lessons learned, and the CS MC would be scaled up. Knowledge would be curated, and the infrastructure redesigned, to ensure long-term success.

With implementation comes policy implications. Districts and states must consider how the use of CS MCs impacts other areas in the talent management pipeline. For example,

- If CS teachers have earned MCs in one district, do they transfer to another? Is this important to note in the recruitment or hiring pro-

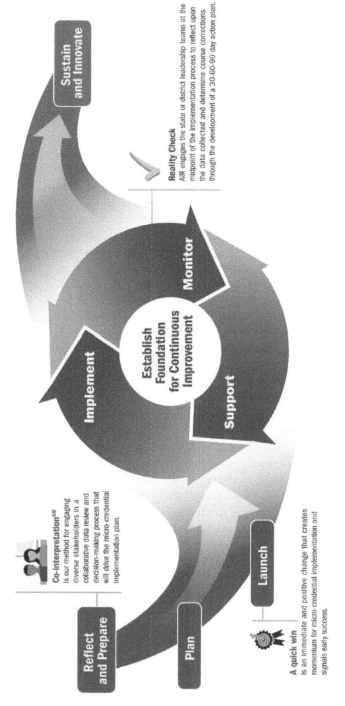

Figure 16.8 American Institutes for Research continuous improvement model.

cess, especially if districts are looking for highly skilled CS teachers? Does this require a change in district policy for acceptance (or not) of MCs earned elsewhere? Are CS candidates with earned MCs more desirable than other candidates?

- Will MCs start to outweigh degrees or graduate-level coursework for CS, which may not require demonstration of competency?
- What compensation or other incentives are available to CS teachers who earn MCs? What level of compensation or incentives is appropriate? Can CS teachers earn salary lane-change credits for MC and, if so, how many are equivalent to the typical +15 increments of graduate-level PD? Is the digital badge earned enough recognition as an incentive or, is more required?

Traditional PD activities for teachers are proving to be ineffective in changing teaching practice. MCs present one personalized option for shifting from clock-based to competency-based PD, allowing teachers to customize their learning based on their unique needs and interests. However, the work required to implement and support MCs is complex. As the CS for All initiative grows in size and scope, these changes can reap huge benefits for both teachers and the students they serve, particularly in CS.

REFERENCES

Archibald, S., Coggshall, J., Croft, A., & Goe, L. (2011). *High-quality professional development for all teachers: Effectively allocating resources.* National Comprehensive Center for Teacher Quality. https://gtlcenter.org/sites/default/files/docs/HighQualityProfessionalDevelopment.pdf

Barber, M., & Mourshed, M. (2007). *How the world's best-performing school systems come out on top.* McKinsey & Company. https://www.mckinsey.com/industries/public-and-social-sector/our-insights/how-the-worlds-best-performing-school-systems-come-out-on-top

Bill & Melinda Gates Foundation. (2014). *Teachers know best: Teachers' views on professional development.* http://k12education.gatesfoundation.org/resource/teachers-know-best-teachers-views-on-professional-development/

Blank, R. K., & de las Alas, N. (2009). *Effects of teacher professional development on gains in student achievement: How meta-analysis provides scientific evidence useful to education leaders.* Council of Chief State School Officers. https://files.eric.ed.gov/fulltext/ED544700.pdf

Braun, V., & Clarke, V. (2006). Using thematic analysis in psychology. *Qualitative Research in Psychology, 3*(2), 77–101.

Chung, R. R. (2008). Beyond assessment: Performance assessments in teacher education. *Teacher Education Quarterly, 35*(1), 7–28.

Code.org. (2019). *Micro-credentials: A pathway for certification and professional learning.* http://advocacy.code.org/

Darling-Hammond, L., Hyler, M. E., & Gardner, M. (2017). *Effective teacher professional development.* Learning Policy Institute.

DeMonte, J. (2017). *Micro-credentials for teachers: What three early adopter states have learned so far.* American Institutes for Research. https://www.air.org/sites/default/files/downloads/report/Micro-Creditials-for-Teachers-September-2017.pdf

Desimone, L. M., Porter, A. C., Garet, M. S., Yoon, K. S., & Birman, B. F. (2002). Effects of professional development on teachers' instruction: Results from a three-year longitudinal study. *Educational Evaluation and Policy Analysis, 24*(2), 81–112.

ESSA. (2015). *Every Student Succeeds Act of 2015*, Pub. L. No. 114-95 § 114 Stat. 1177 (2015–2016).

Garet, M. S., Cronen, S., Eaton, M., Kurki, A., Ludwig, M., Jones, W., Uekawa, K., Falk, A., Bloom, H., Doolittle, F., Zhu, P., & Sztejnberg, L. (2008). *The impact of two professional development interventions on early reading instruction and achievement* (NCEE 2008-4030). U. S. Department of Education, Institute of Education Sciences, National Center for Education Evaluation and Regional Assistance. https://ies.ed.gov/ncee/pdf/20084030.pdf

Garet, M. S., Heppen, J. B., Walters, K., Parkinson, J., Smith, T. M., Song, M., Garrett, R., Yang, R., & Borman, G. D. (2016). *Focusing on mathematical knowledge: The impact of content-intensive teacher professional development* (NCEE 2016-4010). U. S. Department of Education, Institute of Education Sciences, National Center for Education Evaluation and Regional Assistance. https://ies.ed.gov/ncee/pubs/20164010/pdf/20164010.pdf

Garet, M. S., Porter, A. C., Desimone, L., Birman, B. F., & Yoon, K. S. (2001). What makes professional development effective? Results from a national sample of teachers. *American Educational Research Journal, 38*(4), 915–945.

Garet, M. S., Wayne, A., Stancavage, F., Taylor, J., Walters, K., Song, M., Brown, S., Hurlburt, S., Zhu, P., Sepanik, S., & Doolittle, F. (2010). *Middle school mathematics professional development impact study: Findings after the first year of implementation* (NCEE 2010-4009). U.S. Department of Education, Institute of Education Sciences, National Center for Education Evaluation and Regional Assistance. https://ies.ed.gov/ncee/pubs/20104009/pdf/20104009.pdf

Gearhart, M., & Osmundson, E. (2009). Assessment portfolios as opportunities for teacher learning. *Educational Assessment, 14*(1), 1–24. https://doi.org/10.1080/10627190902816108

Gulamhussein, A. (2013). *Teaching the teachers: Effective professional development in an era of high stakes accountability.* Center for Public Education. http://conference.ohioschoolboards.org/2017/wp-content/uploads/sites/17/2016/07/1pm111317A114Job-embedPD.pdf

Haynes, E., Zeiser, K., Surr, W., Hauser, A., Clymer, L., Walston, J., Bitter, C., & Yang, R. (2016). *Looking under the hood of competency-based education: The relationship between competency-based education practices and students' learning skills, behaviors, and dispositions.* American Institutes for Research. https://www.air.org/resource/looking-under-hood-competency-based-education-relationship-between-competency-based

Menekse, M. (2015). Computer science teacher professional development in the United States: A review of studies published between 2004 and 2014. *Computer*

Science Education, 25(4), 325–350. https://doi.org/10.1080/08993408.2015 .1111645

National Education Association. (2018). *Micro-credential guidance.* https://www.nea .org/sites/default/files/2021-01/Micro-credential%20for%20Certified%20 Educators.pdf

Pane, J. F., Steiner, E. D., Baird, M. D., Hamilton, L. S., & Pane, J. D. (2017). *Informing progress: Insights on personalized learning implementation and effects.* RAND Corporation.

Rasberry, M., & Wilson, J. P. (2019). *Three strategies for preparing teachers of computer science.* American Institutes for Research. https://www.air.org/resource/three -strategies-preparing-teachers-computer-science

Regional Educational Laboratory West. (2017, December). Introduction to improvement science. *Institute of Education Sciences.* https://ies.ed.gov/ncee/ edlabs/regions/west/Blogs/Details/2

Rich, K. M., Yadav, A., & Schwarz, C. V. (2019). Computational thinking, mathematics, and science: Elementary teachers' perspectives on integration. *Journal of Technology and Teacher Education, 27*(2), 165–205. https://www.learntechlib .org/primary/p/207487/

Rowland, C., Feygin, A., Lee, F., Gomez, S., & Rasmussen, C. (2018). *Improving the use of information to support teaching and learning through continuous improvement cycles.* American Institutes for Research.

Ross, J. (2016). *Findings and considerations from a review of literature on micro-credentialing.* Appalachia Regional Comprehensive Center.

Sato, M., Wei, R. C., & Darling-Hammond, L. (2008). Improving teachers' assessment practices through professional development: The case of National Board Certification. *American Educational Research Journal, 45*(3), 669–700. https://doi.org/10.3102%2F0002831208316955

Surr, W., Bitter, C., Zeiser, K., Clymer, L., & Briggs, O. (2017). *CBE 360 survey toolkit: A guide to using the Student Experiences and Teacher Practices Competency-Based Education Surveys.* American Institutes for Research. https://www.air.org/ resource/cbe-360-survey-toolkit

Surr, W., & Redding, S. (2017). *Competency-based education: Staying shallow or going deep? A deeper, more personal look at what it means to be competent.* American Institutes for Research. https://www.air.org/sites/default/files/CBE_Going Deep.pdf

The White House: Office of the Press Secretary. (2016). *Fact sheet: A year of action supporting Computer Science for All.* https://obamawhitehouse.archives.gov/the-press-office/ 2016/12/05/fact-sheet-year-action-supporting-computer-science-all

Vaidyanathan, S. (2018, November 26). *What does computer science professional development look like?* EdSurge. https://www.edsurge.com/news/2018-11-26-what -does-computer-science-professional-development-look-like

Wei, R. C., Darling-Hammond, L., Andree, A., Richardson, N., & Orphanos, S. (2009). *Professional learning in the learning profession: A status report on teacher development in the United States and abroad* [Technical Report]. National Staff Development Council. https://edpolicy.stanford.edu/sites/default/files/ publications/professional-learning-learning-profession-status-report-teacher- development-us-and-abroad.pdf

ABOUT THE EDITORS

Chrystalla Mouza, EdD, is distinguished professor and director of the School of Education at the University of Delaware. Her research focuses on teacher learning and professional development, applications of emerging technologies in K–12 classrooms, and computer science education. She directed several projects aimed at improving teaching and learning with technology in high-need schools, preparing in-service and preservice teachers in computer science, and broadening participation in computing. Dr. Mouza's work has been published in key outlets including the *Journal of Research on Technology in Education* and *Teachers College Record*. She is the recipient of the 2010 Distinguished Research in Teacher Education Award from the Association of Teacher Educators and current editor-in-chief of the journal of *Contemporary Issues in Technology and Teacher Education*.

Anne Ottenbreit-Leftwich, PhD, is the Barbara B. Jacobs chair in education and technology and professor of instructional systems technology within the School of Education and an adjunct professor of computer science at Indiana University—Bloomington. Dr. Leftwich's expertise lies in the areas of the design of curriculum resources, the use of technology to support preservice teacher training, and development/implementation of professional development for teachers and teacher educators. Dr. Leftwich investigates ways to teach computer science and expand these offerings at the preservice and in-service levels. She is Indiana's co-lead for the Expanding Computing Education Pathways (ECEP) alliance and working with CSforIN to increase computer science access opportunities for all K–12 Indiana students. Her

Professional Development for In-Service Teachers, pages 385–386
Copyright © 2022 by Information Age Publishing
www.infoagepub.com
385

research focuses on teachers' value beliefs related to technology and computer science, as well as how those beliefs influence teachers' adoption and implementation.

Aman Yadav, PhD, is a professor of educational psychology and educational technology at Michigan State University with extensive experience in research, evaluation, and teacher professional development. His research and teaching focuses on improving student experiences and outcomes in computer science and engineering classrooms at the K–16 level. Within this line of inquiry, he studies: (a) how to prepare pre-service and in-service teachers to teach computer science and integrate computational thinking ideas within subject areas; and (b) how to implement active learning approaches to improve student outcomes in undergraduate computer science and engineering. His work has been published in a number of leading journals, including *ACM Transactions on Computing Education, Journal of Research in Science Teaching, Journal of Engineering Education,* and *Communications of the ACM.*

ABOUT THE CONTRIBUTORS

W. Richards (Rick) Adrion is a professor emeritus of computer science in the University of Massachusetts Amherst, College of Information and Computer Sciences. Following a long career in software engineering research and education, Adrion helped develop and has led a number of initiatives that focused on broadening participation in computer science. These included the Commonwealth Information Technology Initiative (CITI), the NSF BPC Commonwealth Alliance for Information Technology Education (CAITE), and the NSF BPC Expanding Computing Education Pathways (ECEP) Alliance. Currently he leads an NSF-funded research practice partnership of UMass Amherst; Five Colleges, Inc.; SageFox Consulting Group; and the Springfield Massachusetts Public Schools that is introducing integrated, equitable, and standards-based computational thinking curricula across 33 K–5 elementary schools. Adrion is a fellow of the ACM and AAAS.

Emma Anderson is a research scientist at the Scheller Teacher Education Program at the Massachusetts Institute of Technology. Her research centers around science, art, making, and play with a focus on teacher professional development and interdisciplinary curriculum design for technology integrated learning environments. Emma is a former environmental educator at Baltimore Woods Nature Center where she brought science lessons into urban kindergarten through sixth grade classrooms and led summer campers around the woods.

Professional Development for In-Service Teachers, pages 387–401
Copyright © 2022 by Information Age Publishing
www.infoagepub.com

Colin Angevine is an educator, researcher, and facilitator focused on themes of equity, design, organizational change, and collaboration. He is a fellow at the Joan Ganz Cooney Center at Sesame Workshop and a designer at Onward. Colin's perspective draws from previous work experiences as an educator (in middle and high schools), a technologist (in edtech and legal tech startups), and as a researcher (in researcher–practitioner partnerships). Most recently, Colin was the project director for Challenge Collaboratives at Digital Promise, where he developed and facilitated new models for equity-driven R&D in education. Colin holds an MSEd from the University of Pennsylvania in learning sciences and technologies. He lives in the Pacific Northwest.

Sarah Barksdale is a doctoral candidate in the learning technologies program within the University of Minnesota's Department of Curriculum and Instruction. A former secondary English and theater teacher, her research interests center on teacher education and professional development, equitable K–12 computer science education, and the integration of technology and computational thinking into content areas.

Quentin Biddy is an assistant research professor at the University of Colorado Boulder in the Institute of Cognitive Science. He is currently working with the Schoolwide Labs, STEM Career Connections, the NSF National AI Institute for Student-AI Teaming, and Inquiry Hub projects researching and developing open-source resources to support high school and middle school science teachers transitioning to phenomena-driven, three-dimensional learning and assessment aligned to the NGSS while integrating computational thinking using a programable Data Sensor Hub (DaSH). Through this work, he is focusing on supporting middle school science teachers intentionally integrating computational thinking practices into students' learning experiences through co-designed CT integrated NGSS aligned storylines. His research/work experience and interests focus on effective science learning and teaching, phenomena-driven learning, NGSS aligned 3D learning and formative assessment, CT integration, pedagogical content knowledge, teacher professional learning, and the nature of science and history of science in science education.

Quinn Burke is director of computational thinking research at the national education non-profit Digital Promise. Quinn's research at Digital Promise examines the effectiveness of different activities by which to introduce students to programing and how computational thinking (CT) can be integrated into schools to support core curricula coursework. Prior to his time at Digital Promise, Quinn taught on the high school and college levels. His research has been supported by a number of state and federal grants. He has written numerous articles around integrating computing into the school day, as well as co-authored two books on K–12 coding and digital gaming through MIT Press.

Alexandra Gendreau Chakarov is an assistant professor of computer science and science education at San José State University. She received her PhD in computer science and cognitive science from the University of Colorado Boulder where she explored how to integrate computational thinking into middle school science curriculum using programable sensor technologies as part of the SchoolWide Labs project. Her research interests revolve around increasing representation of women and underrepresented groups in computer science at all levels through the use of coherent, personally relevant instruction guided by student interest.

S. Megan Che is an associate professor of mathematics education in the Department of Teaching and Learning in the College of Education at Clemson University. In collaboration with co-PIs and graduate students, her most recent NSF-funded research project, CRōCS (Culturally Responsive Computer Science), prepares teachers to teach introductory high school computer science courses from a culturally responsive perspective, while investigating the nature of pedagogical content knowledge in computer science.

Tom Cozzolino has been teaching in the Twin Cities, Minnesota area for 12 years. He has taught in a variety of positions from elementary grade level classroom, facilitating a school wide makerspace, and teaching middle school computer science. Tom also works with Code Savvy (www.codesavvy. org) where he helps with educator professional development opportunities focused on improving equitable and engaging computer science education opportunities for all students.

Jennifer Davis is the technology director and a science educator at Pender High School in Pender, Nebraska, where she is dedicated to implementing meaningful technologies and promoting equity throughout the district. She is an adjunct instructor in the Department of Educational Foundations and Leadership at Wayne State College in Wayne, Nebraska and a doctoral candidate in the innovative learning technologies program at the University of Nebraska Lincoln. Her research focus lies at the intersection of artificial intelligence and science education.

Leigh Ann DeLyser has spent her career building the K–12 computer science (CS) field. As an executive director of CSforALL (csforall.org), she oversees programs and strategic planning and supervises research to build support for high quality CS education at all levels. A former high school and university CS educator, Leigh Ann understands challenges faced by teachers, administrators, and students developing their competency in the field and accessing high-quality learning opportunities and resources. Her influential "Running on Empty" report guides policies and research that support high-quality program implementation. Previously, Leigh Ann was director of Research and Education at CSNYC, which built a foundation for CS in New York City public schools. She received a PhD in computer science and cognitive psychology, with a focus on CS education, from Carnegie Mellon University.

Barbara Ericson is an assistant professor in the School of Information at the University of Michigan. Her research is focused on improving computing education through interactive ebooks, adaptive learning, active learning, and mentoring programs for students from groups who are underrepresented in computing. She and her husband, Dr. Mark Guzdial, received the 2010 Karl V. Karlstrom Outstanding Computing Educator Award for their work on media computation.

Una Fleming is a computer science education researcher and has recently conducted research to investigate the rollout of coding and computer science into Ireland's post-primary schools as part of her master's research. This research was funded by Science Foundation Ireland and was a collaboration between LERO (the Irish software research center) and EPI*STEM (the national center for STEM education). As a qualified teacher, Una has taught in a diverse range of schools in the Irish context.

Carol Fletcher is director of EPIC (Expanding Pathways in Computing) at UT Austin's Texas Advanced Computing Center (TACC) where she oversees research and professional development projects in STEM and CS education such as the nationally recognized WeTeach_CS program. She is PI for two NSF projects focused on broadening participation in computing (BPC), the Expanding Computing Education Pathways (ECEP) Alliance and Accelerating Women's Success and Mastery in CS (AWSM in CS). Carol is a former middle school teacher and an elected Pflugerville ISD School Board Trustee from 2001 to 2019. Her experiences as a teacher, policymaker, and researcher bridge the gap between education, workforce, and policy. Additional leadership roles include chair of the Texas Computer Science Task Force, CS4TX Steering Committee, the TEA's STEM Educator Standards & IT Industry Advisory Committees, and numerous NSF funded STEM education grant advisory boards.

Dave Frye is director of Program Development and Operations at Code.org, leading development and execution of national-level education programs in support of teachers, students, facilitators and our regional partner network. Dr. Frye has over 20 years' experience developing strategic, broadscale initiatives and next-generation education systems that will prepare students for the rapidly changing world in which they will live. Over the past 5 years, Dave has worked at the intersection of policy, research, and practice to expand opportunities and broaden participation in computer science in North Carolina and nationally. He was a member of the committee that developed the CSTA Standards for CS Teachers (2020), provides leadership for NC in the 23-state Expanding Computing Education Pathways (ECEP) Alliance, and chairs the board of csedreserch.org.

Merrilyn Goos is professor of education at the University of the Sunshine Coast, Australia. Previously, she was professor of STEM education and director of EPI•STEM, the National Centre for STEM Education, at the University of Limerick. Her research has investigated students' mathematical thinking, the impact of digital technologies on mathematics learning and teaching, numeracy across the curriculum and the lifespan, the professional learning of mathematics teachers and mathematics teacher educators, curriculum and assessment reform, and gender equity in STEM education. She is currently vice-president of the International Commission on Mathematical Instruction and co-editor-in-chief of *Research in Integrated STEM Education*, a new journal to be published by Brill in March 2023.

Brian Gravel is an assistant professor of education in the School of Arts and Sciences at Tufts University. He studies how people of all ages use representations to work and learn in STEM. Brian's work is grounded in community partnerships, using co-design practices to build humanizing approaches to STEM. His research focuses on learning with representations, materials, and processes in making spaces and with expressive computational technologies. Major threads include makerspaces in schools, designing culturally sustaining learning ecologies, and the study of transdisciplinary practices in STEM and computation.

Mark Guzdial is a professor in computer science & engineering and engineering education research at the University of Michigan. He studies how people learn computing and how to improve that process, with a particular focus on students using programing for purposes other than software development. He was one of the founders of the International Computing Education Research conference. He was a lead on the NSF alliance, Expanding Computing Education Pathways, which helped U.S. states improve and broaden their computing education. With his wife and colleague, Barbara Ericson, he received the 2010 ACM Karl V. Karlstrom Outstanding Educator award for the development and assessment of the Media Computation curriculum. He is an ACM Distinguished Educator and a Fellow of the ACM. His most recent book is *Learner-Centered Design of Computing Education: Research on Computing for Everyone* (Morgan & Claypool Publishers, 2015). He was the recipient of the 2019 ACM SIGCSE Outstanding Contributions to Education award.

Ling Hsiao is a research scientist at Scheller Teacher Education Program at Massachusetts Institute of Technology. Her research interests include teacher development and how the affordances of innovative technologies advance both student and teacher learning in science classrooms. Ling is a former science teacher at Boston Public Schools and a medical simulation training specialist at Boston Children's Hospital.

Jennifer Jacobs is an associate research professor at the University of Colorado Boulder in the Institute of Cognitive Science. Dr. Jacobs' research focuses on classroom teaching and learning of mathematics and science, and models of professional development to support teachers and their students. Currently Dr. Jacobs is a co-principal investigator on research studies related to SchoolWide Labs (integrating computational thinking into middle school STEM classes) and the TalkBack application (automating feedback for teachers on their classroom discourse). She has co-authored numerous articles, book chapters, and monographs on professional development, including *Learning and Teaching Geometry: Video Cases for Mathematics Professional Development* (WestEd) and *Mathematics Professional Development: Improving Teaching Using the Problem-Solving Cycle and Leadership Preparation Models* (Teachers College Press, 2015).

Keith Johnston is an assistant professor in the area of ICTs in education and director of postgraduate teaching and learning at the School of Education, Trinity College Dublin. He has worked as a teacher educator for almost 20 years teaching courses mainly in the area of ICTs in education. His main research interests are the development and implementation of ICT policy in primary and post-primary education, the use of ICTs to support teaching and learning at these levels, and in teacher professional development particularly in the context of educational reform. His work has been published in a number of international journals and is a frequent contributor to international conferences.

Matthew Kilbride is the instructional technology simulation specialist for Montgomery County Community College in Blue Bell, PA. He currently fixates on advocating and implementing simulation-based learning tools both in and out of the higher education classroom. His research focuses on, but is not limited to, virtual reality, augmented reality, mixed reality, physical simulations, and how educational leaders can leverage these tools to extend new and unique learning opportunities. Favoring the constructivist platform, he integrates technologies that preserve student expression and allow ample space for collaboration, communication, and play during learning.

Eileen Kraemer is a professor in the School of Computing at Clemson University and the coordinator of the PhD program in human-centered computing. She served as the C. Tycho Howle director of the school from 2014–2018. With collaborators Megan Che and Murali Sitaraman she is a Co-PI on the

NSF-funded research project, CRōCS (Culturally Responsive Computer Science), which prepares teachers to teach introductory high school computer science courses from a culturally responsive perspective and investigates the nature of pedagogical content knowledge in computer science. She currently divides her time between academic administration, teaching, and research in computer science education and human aspects of software development.

Rachel A. Larimore is the chief visionary of Samara Early Learning. Her work focuses on the intentional integration of nature to support young children's holistic development, including science learning, by learning with nature to expand their worlds and live rich, full lives. She has written three books including *Establishing a Nature-Based Preschool* (National Association for Interpretation, 2011) and *Preschool Beyond Walls: Blending Early Childhood Education and Nature-Based Learning* (Gryphon House, Inc., 2019). As an educator, speaker, consultant, and author she helps early childhood educators start nature-based schools or add nature-based approaches into their existing program. Prior to founding Samara, she spent more than 20 years in environmental education including directing one of the first nature-based preschools in the United States.

Y. Rhoda Latimer is a PhD candidate at Clemson University, where she plans to graduate with her degree in curriculum and instruction with an emphasis in mathematics education. She is currently a coordinator of mathematics instruction for middle and secondary. Her research background includes project-based learning, culturally responsive computing, and the experiences of Black and Hispanic learners. Her passion is to provide positive educational experiences in mathematics for all students, particularly those from minoritized populations.

Irene Lee is a research scientist at Massachusetts Institute of Technology and a distinguished scientist at EDC. She is the founder and program director of Project GUTS: Growing Up Thinking Scientifically. Currently, Irene leads three NSF STEM+C projects focused on understanding how students' engagement in using, decoding, and modifying computer models impacts their scientific understanding of the phenomenon being modeled, and two ITEST projects focused on developing AI literacy of K–12 teachers and students. Irene served as the chair of the Computer Science Teachers Association (CSTA) Computational Thinking Task Force and was a member of the CSTA K–12 Computer Science Standards and the K–12 CS Framework writing teams. She is currently an advisor to the AI4K12 initiative and numerous K–12 computational thinking focused research projects.

Victor R. Lee, associate professor in the Graduate School of Education at Stanford University in Learning Sciences and Technology Design. His research examines and designs new technologies and experiences for teaching and learning of STEM. Major focuses include studying learning with data across contexts, maker education, and elementary computer science education with an emphasis on unplugged and screen-free entry points into computing. He served as a co-author of the National Academies of Science, Engineering, and Medicine consensus report on *Cultivating Interests and Competences in Computing* (2021).

Oliver McGarr is an associate professor at the School of Education, in the University of Limerick, Ireland. His research and teaching interests are in the areas of educational technology, reflective practice in teacher education, and STEM education. He is the former head of the School of Education and a former course director of the master's in ICT in education and the postgraduate diploma in education (technology). He is also a former recipient of the university's Excellence in Teaching award and has published a number of studies in relation to his teaching work. His other research work has mainly focused on STEM education in schools, the adoption of ICT in schools, and reflective practice in teacher education.

Clare McInerney is the education and public engagement manager with Lero, the Science Foundation Ireland Research Centre for Software based at the University of Limerick. She has developed a number of initiatives to engage primary and post-primary level students and teachers in computing, including the development of resources (scratch.ie) and the design and delivery of professional development for teachers in computing. She conducts research on the introduction of new computer science curricula at post-primary level schools in Ireland.

Ha Nguyen is a PhD candidate in teacher education and learning sciences at North Carolina State University (North Carolina), Vietnam-based college lecturer, classroom teacher, instructional designer, professional learning specialist, and educational leader. Ha was granted the Fulbright scholarship to complete dual Master of Arts degrees in TESOL and teacher leadership at Southern Illinois University in Carbondale (Illinois). She was invited to attend a UN Agency of Refugees' meeting on online learning strategies for refugees in Copenhagen (Denmark) in 2019. Her research interests include EFL teacher professional development, intercultural competence, Massive Open Online Courses, and project management and implementation.

Kerri-Ann O'Donnell is the digital learning integration specialist for the Swampscott Public School District and the co-founder of ODLA consultants. Her recent work centers around the integration of technology into the content areas and designing and implementing equitable professional development pathways for K–12 educators. Kerri-Ann has over 20 years of experience in public education. She is a former secondary English teacher, district administrator, and technology director. Kerri-Ann holds an MSEd from the University of Pennsylvania in teaching, learning, and leadership and an MS from the University of Massachusetts, Lowell in Information Technology.

Maria C. Olivares is a poet, artist, and research assistant professor at the Earl Center for Learning and Innovation at Boston University. In collaboration with youth, teachers, community artists, and other researchers, Dr. Olivares designs learning experiences, environments, and community engagement initiatives aimed at exploring and promoting expansive understandings of STEM, STEM education, and justice-oriented leadership and research practice. Dr. Olivares' orientation to educational, social, and artistic design centers sustainability and capacity building as necessary components for transformative and far-reaching impact. As such, Dr. Olivares also designs sustainable social systems and organizational structures aimed at connecting people along lines of intergenerationality and transdisciplinarity to enable creative and collective living, learning, thriving, and social transformation. Originally from South Central Los Angeles, Dr. Olivares is the proud daughter of Mexican immigrants and the first in her family to gain access to higher education.

Justin Olmanson is an associate professor of learning technologies at the University of Nebraska Lincoln. His work focuses on the design, integration, and use of technologies such as natural language processing, learning analytics, data science, and qualitative inquiry to make new forms of meaning-making and expression possible, to overcome barriers to understanding and expression, and to reduce the alienation and oppression often associated with learning in academic contexts. He collaboratively designs, builds, and studies emerging technologies that support people as they learn difficult practices including (a) developing literacy in logosyllabic or abjad writing systems, (b) writing in unfamiliar academic genres, and (c) learning new academic constructs.

Emrah Pektas is a doctoral student in the Department of Teacher Education and Curriculum Studies at the University of Massachusetts, Amherst. His research interest is in computational thinking (CT) and CT integration into subject areas such as science and ELA with elementary school students, specifically in student learning at the intersection of CT and subject areas. He is also interested in how public elementary school teachers who are not specialized in computer science adopt CT integrated curricula and teach them to elementary students.

William (Bill) Penuel is a professor of learning sciences and human development in the Institute of Cognitive Science and School of Education at the University of Colorado Boulder. He designs and studies curriculum materials, assessments, and professional learning experiences for teachers in science. He works in partnership with school districts and state departments of education, and the research he conducts is in support of educational equity in three dimensions: (a) equitable implementation of new science standards; (b) creating inclusive classroom cultures that attend to students' affective experiences and where all students have authority for constructing knowledge together; and (c) connecting teaching to the interests, experiences, and identities of learners. His research employs a wide range of qualitative and quantitative research methods, including an approach his colleagues and he have developed called design-based implementation research. Dr. Penuel is an elected member of the National Academy of Education, a fellow of the International Society of the Learning Sciences, the International Society for Design and Development in Education, and the American Educational Research Association.

Lana Peterson is the director of Community Engagement for the Learning + Technologies Collaborative at the University of Minnesota. She is a community engaged scholar with one foot in academia and another in K–12 teaching and learning spaces. Through several Research–Practice Partnerships with Minnesota school districts and organizations, Lana studies technology integration, online learning, equitable computer science education, and teacher development.

Dr. Chris Proctor is an assistant professor of learning sciences at the University at Buffalo (SUNY), where he is leading the development of one of New York's first K–12 computer science teacher preparation programs. Chris studies K–12 computer science education through the disciplinary lenses of learning sciences and new literacies. He is interested in the ways computational interfaces (educational technologies as well as games and social media) can support youth in critical identity authorship, resulting in more equitable learning opportunities and critical transformation of computer science as a discipline. Much of Chris's work is participatory design-based research, working with middle- and high-school students and teachers to design new technologies and then using mixed methods to study the emergent practices they support. Chris is the lead developer and researcher of Unfold Studio (https://unfold.studio), a web application for reading and writing interactive stories which weave together text and code. As a former secondary teacher of English/language arts and computer science, Chris has over a decade of experience working toward inclusive and equitable institutional change.

Melissa Rasberry is an accomplished education professional with proven visionary leadership and strategic communication skills, honed through 22 years of experience in public K–16 classrooms and education nonprofits. Before joining the Friday Institute for Educational Innovation at North Carolina State University, Rasberry served as principal technical assistance consultant for education at the American Institutes for Research (AIR). Dr. Rasberry led a portfolio of computer science and STEM projects, including the CS for All Teachers virtual community, the Teachers Assessing Learning in Exploring CS (TALECS) project with SRI International, the Advancing Methods and Synthesizing Research in STEM Education project, and the collaborative Hindsight 2020 project with a consortium of CS researchers, all funded by NSF. She has developed elementary micro-credentials and regularly presents about CS and other STEM issues on national calls and meetings.

Mimi Recker is a professor in the Department of Instructional Technology at Utah State University, in the beautiful mountains of Northern Utah. She received her PhD from the University of California, Berkeley, and has held academic positions at the Georgia Institute of Technology and Victoria University of Wellington, New Zealand. She studies the role that prior experiences and understanding play in shaping how teachers and learners make sense of new computing concepts.

Kathryn M. Rich is a senior researcher at the American Institutes for Research. Her research and expertise lie at the intersection of mathematics education, computer science education, and educational technology. She is particularly interested in ways that technology can support quality mathematics teaching and learning in elementary school, including via integration of computational thinking and programing activities into mathematics lessons. She has extensive experience developing instructional materials, providing professional development to teachers, and employing qualitative research methods to understand how teachers and students make sense of and use various instructional resources. She led the development of the literature-based learning trajectories for computational thinking concepts as part of the Learning Trajectories for Everyday Computing project at the University of Chicago.

Aubrey Rogowski is a doctoral candidate in the Department of Instructional Technology and Learning Sciences at Utah State University. She is a former elementary school teacher. Her research activities revolve around STEM-rich making and maker education, computational thinking in K–6 contexts, and teacher professional development.

Mark Samberg is the director of IT Strategy and Transformation at the North Carolina Department of Public Instruction and an assistant teaching professor of learning design and technology at NC State University. His work focuses on leadership in digital learning environments, K–12 IT infrastructure and policy, digital/open education resources, and hybrid learning environments. Mark has worked in North Carolina Public Schools for over 15 years as a high school computer science teacher and media coordinator, instructional technology facilitator, school district chief technology officer, and most recently as director of Technology Programs at NC State's Friday Institute for Educational Innovation.

Cassandra Scharber is an associate professor of learning technologies and the director of the Learning + Technologies Collaborative at the University of Minnesota. She is committed to community-engaged projects and scholarship, and serves as a lead for CSforAll-MN, Minnesota's chapter of the Expanding Computing Education Pathways (ECEP) alliance that supports K–12 computer science education. Her research spans the areas of K–12 technology integration, digital literacies, online teaching and learning, and computer science education.

Christina Schwarz is a professor of science education in the Teacher Education Department at Michigan State University. Schwarz's research focuses on engaging PK–16 learners in scientific practices, particularly scientific modeling and computational thinking. She is also an elementary science teacher educator who works with her own teacher candidates and other teacher educators around the country towards enabling all elementary teachers to find joy in teaching science and engage their students in equitable scientific sense-making. She co-edited and was an author of the NSTA book entitled *Helping Students Make Sense of the World Using Next Generation Science and Engineering Practices* (2016).

Murali Sitaraman is a professor in the School of Computing at Clemson University. He is a principal investigator of the multi-institutional RESOLVE software engineering research and education effort that has been continuously funded by the U.S. National Science Foundation for 30 years. Broadening participation in computing and helping students to learn how to reason correctly and soundly about the behavior of the code they write are among the goals of his group's CS education research. To date, the results have reached over 30,000 students and over 200 educators. Dr. Sitaraman is a co-editor of a Cambridge University Press book *Foundations of Component-Based Systems* (2011). His publications have appeared in *ACM Transactions on Computing Education, Computer Science Education,* and ACM SIGCSE and ACM ITiCSE conference proceedings.

Florence R. Sullivan is a professor of learning technology in the Department of Teacher Education and Curriculum Studies at the University of Massachusetts, Amherst. Her research interests include K–8 student computational thinking; equity-based CS professional development; and equitable assessment in CS. Dr. Sullivan is the author of *Creativity, Technology, and Learning: Theory for Classroom Practice,* published in 2017 by Routledge. Dr. Sullivan has directed several federally funded research projects related to student learning with computational media. The results of these research projects have been published in leading educational research journals including the *Journal of Research in Science Teaching, Journal of the Learning Sciences, British Journal of Educational Technology,* and *Educational Technology Research and Development.* Dr. Sullivan coordinates the master's program in learning, media, and technology and the Digital Media Design and Making certificate at UMass, Amherst. Her teaching includes courses on computational thinking, theories of learning, and socio-cultural approaches to educational research.

Tamara Sumner is the director of the institute of cognitive science and a professor in computer and cognitive science at the University of Colorado. She leads an interdisciplinary R&D lab that studies how computational tools—combining cognitive science, machine intelligence, and interactive media—can improve teaching practice, learning outcomes, and learner engagement in STEM.

Eli Tucker-Raymond is a research associate professor of education with the Earl Center for Learning and Innovation at Boston University. His work focuses on creating and understanding humanizing learning environments at the intersections of STEM, literacy, and the media/arts for people who have been marginalized in schools. With Dr. Brian E. Gravel, he is author of the book *STEM Literacies in Makerspaces: Implications for Teaching, Learning, and Research* (2019).

Catherine Tulungen is a PhD candidate in teacher education and school improvement at the University of Massachusetts Amherst, and a master instructor in and chair of the Department of International Student Achievement at Culver Academies in Indiana. Prior to Culver Academies, Cathy worked for almost 20 years in Indonesia in English teacher education. Her research interests are in the mapping of salient meanings in texts and the teaching of academic language and disciplinary literacies.

Andrea Wilson Vazquez is the director of educator training and school partnerships with Code Savvy, a Minnesota nonprofit that empowers youth and educators with knowledge, skills, and support to create new things with technology, all while working to interrupt and counteract gender, racial, and economic gaps in computing. Andrea is also a teacher and innovative instructional coach at an alternative high school, where she specializes in engaging students with a variety of unique learning needs through creative problem solving with technology.

Heidee Vincent is the instructional lab supervisor for the math department at the University of North Texas. Her research focuses on STEM, making, computational thinking, teacher professional development, and remedial math education.

Jayce R. Warner leads the research team for the Expanding Pathways in Computing (EPIC) division of the Texas Advanced Computing Center at the University of Texas at Austin. He conducts research across a variety of areas in education, managing multiple projects aimed at improving educational outcomes for students and teachers. His current work focuses on developing robust methods to quantify equity issues in computer science education, using multilevel modeling to better understand educational outcomes, and identifying and measuring psychosocial factors that underlie student and teacher behavior. His other research interests include teacher professional development, psycholinguistics, and early childhood.

Gretchen Weber is a senior managing director at WestEd where she leads a portfolio of work focused on taking a systems approach to ensuring every student has access to and education from effective teachers and leaders in their schools. Prior to joining WestEd, Weber was a vice president at the American Institutes for Research where she led federal, state, and district level projects aimed at attracting, supporting, and retaining effective educators, including projects with an emphasis on CS teachers. Part of many research studies on teacher effectiveness and teacher professional development, Weber has supported decision makers using findings to set policy or create new practices. She has served on boards or in advisory roles for nonprofits such as Boundless Readers, the Morton Arboretum, and Chicago's Adler Planetarium and Astronomy Museum, and has served on statewide committees including the Illinois New Teacher Induction Policy team. Weber is a national board-certified teacher in early adolescent English language arts and her expertise and experience as a public school teacher continue to inform and enhance her current work.

Josh Weisgrau is the senior director of learning experience design at Digital Promise, leading initiatives that seek to transform learning experiences to empower the next generation of creators and change makers. Josh is an experienced educator with over 10 years' experience teaching computer science, digital media, and design in middle and high school. As the lead for Digital Promise's learning experience programs, he has supported the development of empowering and engaging student and professional learning experiences in the areas of maker learning, computational thinking, next generation science, and challenge-based learning.

Joseph ("Joey") P. Wilson is a principal consultant at the American Institutes for Research (AIR), where he leads the organization's first computer science education practice hub (CS@AIR), which houses nearly twenty projects and partnerships funded through state and federal sources. He is a current principal investigator, co-principal investigator, and project director for seven National Science Foundation and Department of Defense-funded research and evaluation projects, ranging in topics from CS educator micro-credentials to virtual communities of practice for CS teachers to integrating computer science into elementary instruction in culturally relevant ways. Previously, Joey has held a variety of roles, including high school science teacher, managing director of Teach for America's national STEM education initiative, and head of Tata Consultancy Services' GoIT computer science education outreach program across the United States and Canada.

Stephanie Wortel-London leads the Policy Research and Evaluation division at CSforALL. She has worked for more than a decade to reinforce the sharing of knowledge and strengthen connections between K–12 STEM education and higher ed STEM research. Prior to joining CSforALL, she developed and led enrichment and mentoring programs serving under-represented youth through in-person and virtual programing at the New York Academy of Sciences. She has taught in Germany, Malaysia, China, and across the United States, and her career in science education began as an Earth Science teacher in a South Bronx public school. She was also a curriculum writer and educator at the American Museum of Natural History. She earned her PhD in science education at Stony Brook University's Institute for STEM Education by studying the development of science identity in groups historically underrepresented in STEM through informal learning experiences, and has served as an adjunct professor for the Space Systems course in the AMNH Master of Arts in teaching residency graduate program.

Lauren Wright is a doctoral student in the interdisciplinary studies in human development program at the University of Pennsylvania's Graduate School of Education, where she studies cognitive development and learning in early childhood, with specializations in the impacts of stress and trauma on development and ecological factors that promote optimal growth and learning. Lauren has extensive experience working in equity-oriented, systems-change interventions, as a former senior project manager for the Strategic CSforALL Resource & Implementation Planning Tool (SCRIPT) program, as well as a research coordinator for the Consortium for Mental Health and Optimal Development at Penn's Graduate School of Education. Lauren is also a former visual arts educator.

Milton Keynes UK
Ingram Content Group UK Ltd.
UKHW021516021224
3319UKWH00042B/1146